"The field has been waiting far too long for a book like this! Harris, an international authority on grief in the context of non-death losses, has distilled her vast clinical experience and theoretical knowledge into a highly readable and practical text. Bringing together leading international scholars and clinicians, the volume eloquently explores this vital subject in a deeply considered and ultimately practical way. Its exploration of individual, social, cultural, and political perspectives leaves the reader with a deep understanding of the impact of a wide range of non-death losses. I cannot recommend this ground-breaking book highly enough."
—*Christopher Hall, MA, BEd, GradDipAdol&ChildPsych, director, Australian Centre for Grief and Bereavement; past chair, International Work Group on Death, Dying and Bereavement; past president, Association for Death Education and Counseling*

"Too often the array of non-death losses which arise in many of life's settings are not credited as requiring support as well as therapeutic interventions. This collection of the impressive writings of specialists in this field provides understanding as well as useful methods for providing direct care."
—*J. Shep Jeffreys, EdD, FT, assistant professor, Psychiatry, Johns Hopkins School of Medicine*

"Harris offers an unprecedented and very welcome collection representing a rich diversity of non-death-related losses. Along with the sorrows and brokenness these losses bring into grievers' lives are the challenges in relearning how to live with hope and meaning, and this volume provides guidance for those who offer them compassionate support."
—*Thomas Attig, PhD, author of* How We Grieve: Relearning the World

Non-Death Loss and Grief

Non-Death Loss and Grief offers an inclusive perspective on loss and grief, exploring recent research, clinical applications, and current thinking on non-death losses and the unique features of the grieving process that accompany them.

The book places an overarching focus on the losses that we encounter in everyday life, and the role of these loss experiences in shaping us as we continue living. A main emphasis is the importance of having words to accurately express these "living losses," such as loss of communication with a loved one due to disease or trauma, which are often not acknowledged for the depth of their impact. Chapters showcase a wide range of contributions from international leaders in the field and explore individual perspectives on loss as well as experiences that are more interpersonal and sociopolitical in nature.

Illustrated by case studies and clinical examples throughout, this is a highly relevant text for clinicians looking to enhance their support of those living with ongoing loss and grief.

Darcy L. Harris, PhD, RN, RSW, FT, is an associate professor in the Department of Interdisciplinary Programs and the coordinator of the Thanatology Program at King's University College at Western University in London, Ontario, Canada. She also maintains a private clinical practice and does consulting and presentation work specializing in issues related to change, loss, transition, and grief.

The Series in Death, Dying, and Bereavement

Series Editors: Robert A. Neimeyer, PhD, *University of Memphis, Tennessee, USA* and Darcy L. Harris, PhD, *Western University Canada, Ontario, Canada*

Volumes published in the Series in Death, Dying, and Bereavement are representative of the multidisciplinary nature of the intersecting fields of death studies, suicidology, end-of-life care, and grief counseling. The series meets the needs of clinicians, researchers, paraprofessionals, pastoral counselors, and educators by providing cutting edge research, theory, and best practices on the most important topics in these fields—for today and for tomorrow.

Attachment-Informed Grief Therapy: The Clinician's Guide to Foundations and Applications
Phyllis S. Kosminsky and John R. Jordan

The Crafting of Grief: Constructing Aesthetic Responses to Loss
Lorraine Hedtke and John Winslade

Sibling Loss Across the Lifespan: Research, Practice, and Personal Stories
Edited by Brenda J. Marshall and Howard R. Winokuer

Understanding Child and Adolescent Grief: Supporting Loss and Facilitating Growth
Edited by Carrie Arnold

Chronic Sorrow: A Living Loss, 2nd Edition
Susan Roos

Continuing Bonds in Bereavement: New Directions for Research and Practice
Edited by Dennis Klass and Edith Steffen

Prescriptive Memories in Grief and Loss: The Art of Dreamscaping
Edited by Nancy Gershman and Barbara E. Thompson

Loss, Grief, and Attachment in Life Transitions: A Clinician's Guide to Secure Base Counseling
Jakob van Wielink, Leo Wilhelm, and Denise van Geelen-Merks

Non-Death Loss and Grief: Context and Clinical Implications
Edited by Darcy L. Harris

For more information about this series, please visit www.routledge.com/Series-in-Death-Dying-and-Bereavement/book-series/SE0620.

Non-Death Loss and Grief

Context and Clinical Implications

Edited by
Darcy L. Harris

First published 2020
by Routledge
52 Vanderbilt Avenue, New York, NY 10017

and by Routledge
2 Park Square, Milton Park, Abingdon, Oxon, OX14 4RN

Routledge is an imprint of the Taylor & Francis Group, an informa business

© 2020 selection and editorial matter, Darcy L. Harris; individual chapters, the contributors

The right of Darcy L. Harris to be identified as the author of the editorial material, and of the authors for their individual chapters, has been asserted in accordance with sections 77 and 78 of the Copyright, Designs and Patents Act 1988.

All rights reserved. No part of this book may be reprinted or reproduced or utilised in any form or by any electronic, mechanical, or other means, now known or hereafter invented, including photocopying and recording, or in any information storage or retrieval system, without permission in writing from the publishers.

Trademark notice: Product or corporate names may be trademarks or registered trademarks, and are used only for identification and explanation without intent to infringe.

Library of Congress Cataloging-in-Publication Data
A catalog record for this book has been requested

ISBN: 978-1-138-32081-9 (hbk)
ISBN: 978-1-138-32082-6 (pbk)
ISBN: 978-0-429-44605-4 (ebk)

Typeset in Minion
by Apex CoVantage, LLC

To my Dad, Roy Harris:
Thank you for your fierce love and unwavering belief in me.
I love you.

Contents

Series Foreword		xii
Robert A. Neimeyer		
Acknowledgments		xiv
About the Contributors		xv
Introduction		1
Darcy L. Harris		
1	**Non-Death Loss and Grief: Laying the Foundation**	7
	Darcy L. Harris	
Part I The Social Context of Loss and Grief		17
Neil Thompson		
2	**Disenfranchised Grief and Non-Death Losses**	25
	Kenneth J. Doka	
3	**Social Death**	36
	Michael Brennan	
4	**Discrimination, Oppression, and Loss**	50
	Neil Thompson	
5	**Mourning in Trump's America: An Existential Account of Political Grief**	61
	Sheldon Solomon	

Part II Understanding and Treating the Unresolved Grief of Ambiguous Loss: A Research-Based Theory to Guide Therapists and Counselors   73
    Pauline Boss

6   **Losses of Birth Mothers in the Adoption Triad**   81
    Darcy L. Harris

7   **Living in a Liminal Space: The Experience of Caring for a Spouse with Alzheimer's Disease**   91
    Dan Festa and Darcy L. Harris

8   **Grief and Loss in Addictions**   101
    Thomas Dwyer

9   **Ambiguous Loss in Coming Out and Trans*itioning**   112
    Mae-Lynn Germany, Anna C. Pederson, and Sara K. Bridges

10 **Supporting the Families of Missing People: More Than an Investigation**   128
    Elizabeth Davies, Emmanuel Kassiotis, and Keesha Quinn

Part III Nonfinite Loss: Living with Ongoing Loss and Grief   139
    Darcy L. Harris

11 **Nonfinite and Cumulative Loss in Foster Care**   147
    Monique B. Mitchell

12 **The Loss of Loneliness in Emerging Adults**   157
    Lara Schultz and Ann Laverty

13 **Families' and Children's Experiences of Loss in the Family Justice System**   170
    Rachel Birnbaum

14 **Midlife Children Caring for Their Aging Parents**   180
    Darcy L. Harris

Part IV Chronic Sorrow   193
    Susan Ross

15 **Parenting a Child With a Serious Disability**   205
    Annie Cantwell-Bartl

16 **Environmental Grief**   216
    Kriss A. Kevorkian

17 **Grief and Mental Illness**   227
    Lauren J. Breen and Maria E. Fernandez

	Part V Tangible and Intangible Losses Darcy L. Harris	237
18	**The Threshold of Shattered Dreams** Ted Bowman	243
19	**Sexual Assault, Loss, and the Journey to Justice** Tashel C. Bordere and Laura Danforth	256
20	**Loss and Forced Displacement** Athir N. Jisrawi and Carrie Arnold	270
21	**Loss of Love: When the Relationship Is What Dies** Darcy L. Harris	279
	Part VI Pulling It All Together—Change, Loss, and Transition Darcy L. Harris	291
22	**Where's the Grief in Non-Death Loss Research?** Mae-Lynn Germany	297
23	**Supporting People Through Living Losses** Darcy L. Harris	311
24	**Meaning-Making After Non-Death Losses** Robert A. Neimeyer and Lara Krawchuk	324
	Conclusion: Impermanence, Change, and the Dynamic Experience of Living Darcy L. Harris	339
	Index	341

Series Foreword

Readers of this volume will recognize a well-kept secret, one that has been hidden in plain view for most of the history of thanatology as a profession. That secret is this: That in a field focused on the rupture in attachment bonds and associated grief in the aftermath of the death of a significant person, the far vaster domain of non-death losses has receded into relative invisibility, though the grief that attends them often may be equally substantial. In fact, as editor Darcy L. Harris and her hand-picked team of scholars, activists, and clinicians emphasize, losses of health, relationship, career, country, sobriety, social status, and dreams can fracture or erode our sense of security fully as much as many losses through bereavement, as the forces of trauma, injustice, mental illness, addiction, and more can undermine our sense of connection to self and society. Moreover, by placing such losses in the overarching social, political, and natural worlds that surround us like an atmosphere, contributors to this volume take a long step toward conceptualizing such nonfinite losses in contextual terms, mitigating the narrower focus on intrapsychic and intimately interpersonal factors that characterizes most bereavement care and research.

So, what beyond advocacy to attend to these losses will readers encounter in these pages? A great deal. First, they can expect to be immersed in a treatment of the topic that is as broad as it is deep, widening the horizon of their vision about what constitutes sociologically and psychologically complicated losses that compel closer consideration by both researchers and practitioners. Second, they can anticipate a nuanced consideration of what makes non-death losses especially unsettling, including their ambiguity, pervasiveness, marginalization, chronicity, disenfranchisement, and often privacy. Third, they will be assured of the relevance of many familiar models of mourning to this broader context, as several chapters address the application of grief theory and therapy beyond literal bereavement, in a way that suggests principles and practices for those of us who work and walk alongside those persons, families, and communities challenged by living losses.

In sum, the collection of inquiries, insights, and interventions that inform *Non-Death Loss and Grief: Context and Clinical Implications* make it a compelling read for those who seek greater orientation in confronting the pervasive presence of loss in human life. I encourage you to sit back, take out your highlighter, and prepare to push back the overshadowing focus on bereavement to reveal a wider range of losses no less deserving of thoughtful and compassionate attention.

Robert A. Neimeyer, PhD, Co-Editor
Routledge Series on Death, Dying and Bereavement

Acknowledgments

Putting together a volume like this is like putting together a quilt of many different colors and patterns to make something that has overall beauty as well as usefulness. I am incredibly grateful to the contributors to this book for their passion, dedication, and willingness to participate in this project. The many conversations, dialogues about different aspects of grief in various contexts, and the sense of being entrusted by many with their life's work has been deeply humbling. Truly, to say thank you to each contributor just doesn't seem like enough. A special note of gratitude goes to Dr. Bob Neimeyer for his ongoing support of my passion and belief in the need to validate the grief that occurs after non-death loss experiences, which has carried me through times when I've grappled with pieces that didn't initially seem to fit with the whole.

Much gratitude is also extended to Mark Shelvock for his unwavering assistance (and persistence) with so many of the details that needed to be completed to bring the project to completion. I also wish to thank many of my students and clients who have openly shared their hopes and dreams with me, and I wish to especially thank those who have granted permission for me to share their experiences as case studies in this book.

I wish to express my deepest appreciation for my partner, Brad Hunter, and his tireless support which provided me with ready access to someone who would dialogue about different aspects of the concepts, encourage my thinking in unconventional ways, and most of all, who just loved me and believed in me. Finally, I am deeply grateful to my daughter, Lauren, and her ability to make me laugh and to challenge me to see things in ways that would not have been possible before her entrance into my life.

About the Contributors

Carrie Arnold, PhD, MEd, RSW, CCC, FT, is Assistant Professor of thanatology at King's University College, Western University, and has been teaching since 2005. She has provided psychotherapy and counseling to children, adolescents, and adults since 1999, specializing in grief, loss, trauma, and attachment. Research interests have included bereaved university students and the use of creative responses in bereavement.

Rachel Birnbaum, PhD, RSW, LL.M, is Professor at King's University College at Western University in London, Ontario. Her primary areas of teaching focus on children and families post separation and divorce, ethics and the law, and research methods. Dr. Birnbaum has extensive clinical practice and research experience in working with children and families of separation and divorce. She has presented and published both nationally and internationally on parenting assessments, child legal representation, children's participation in family disputes, and on the intersection between law and social work. Dr. Birnbaum is Member of The Royal Society of Canada, College of New Scholars, Artists, and Scientists. She is the recipient of the Hugh Mellon Distinguished Research Award, the Stanley Cohen Distinguished Research Award, and the Association of Family and Conciliation Courts-Ontario Excellence in Family Justice. She was the President of the Ontario College of Social Workers and Social Service Workers (OCSWSSW) from 2005 to 2009; the President of the Canadian Council of Social Work Regulators (CCSWR) from 2012 to 2014; the President of the Association of Family and Conciliation Courts-Ontario (AFCC-O) from 2014 to 2015; and a former board member of the Canadian Research Institute for Law & The Family, in Calgary, Alberta, from 2017 to 2018.

Tashel C. Bordere, PhD, CT, is Assistant Professor of Human Development and Family Sciences and State Extension Specialist at the University of Missouri-Columbia. She teaches Death, Loss, and Bereavement, Black Families, and Adolescent Development. Dr. Bordere developed S.H.E.D. Loss and Grief Tools. Dr. Bordere is a Forward Promise Fellow through the Robert Wood Johnson Foundation. She is past editor of The ADEC

Forum, past ADEC Board Member, and past Chair of the Multicultural Committee. Dr. Bordere is a speaker, researcher, and author focusing on diversity and social justice issues around trauma and loss. She conducts workshops across the country. Dr. Bordere's research focuses on African American youth and family grief.

Pauline Boss, PhD, is Professor Emeritus at the University of Minnesota; a Fellow in the American Psychological Association and American Association for Marriage and Family Therapy; a former President of the National Council on Family Relations; and a family therapist in private practice. With her groundbreaking work as a scientist-practitioner, Dr. Boss is the principal theorist in the study of ambiguous loss, a term she coined in the 1970s. Since then, she has researched various types of ambiguous loss, summarizing her work in the widely acclaimed book, *Ambiguous Loss: Learning to Live with Unresolved Grief* (Harvard University Press, 2000). For professionals and for treatment, she wrote *Loss, Trauma, and Resilience: Therapeutic Work with Ambiguous Loss* (W. W. Norton, 2006). Dr. Boss's most recent book, written for families, is *Loving Someone Who Has Dementia: How to Find Hope While Coping with Stress and Grief* (Jossey-Bass, 2011). For more information, see www.ambiguousloss.com.

Ted Bowman is an educator who specializes in change and transition, whether it occurs in families, an organization, or the community. He is an Adjunct Professor teaching grief and loss courses at the University of Saint Thomas School of Social Work. For over 35 years, he has led workshops throughout the United States, and for the past 20 years he has worked annually in England, Scotland, and Ireland. Ted Bowman is the author of more than 100 articles, chapters, booklets, and poems. His booklets, *Loss of Dreams: A Special Kind of Grief* and *Finding Hope When Dreams Have Shattered*, are well-known resources about grief and loss. A volume of poetry, *The Wind Blows, The Ice Breaks*, all by Minnesota poets addressing themes of loss and renewal, co-edited by Ted, was released in 2010. *It Starts with Hope*, which he also co-edited, was released in 2016, a book in honor of the 30th anniversary of the Center for Victims of Torture.

Lauren J. Breen, PhD, FT, is Associate Professor in the School of Psychology at Curtin University, Perth, Australia, where she researches and teaches grief and loss.

Michael Brennan is Senior Lecturer in Sociology at Liverpool Hope University, UK. He has written widely on public mourning following disasters and deaths of high-profile public figures. Recent work has explored the materiality of mourning; the theoretical contribution of sociology's founding thinkers to thanatology; the productive uses of creativity triggered by bereavement and loss; and, as a corollary of public mourning, the recent tendency toward the public sharing of narratives of terminal illness ("pathographies") by the dying and bereaved. He is the author of *Mourning and Disaster* (2008) and editor of *The A–Z of Death and Dying* (2014).

Sara K. Bridges, PhD, is Associate Professor at the University of Memphis, former President of the Society for Humanistic Psychology (Division 32 of the American Psychological Association), coeditor of the five-volume series *Studies in Meaning*, and co-director of the Coherence Psychology Institute. She has a distinguished record of awards for academic and community service, including the 2012 Distinguished Teaching Award of the University of Memphis, and maintains a small private practice.

Annie Cantwell-Bartl, PhD, is a psychodynamic psychologist in private practice in inner Melbourne, Australia. She and some colleagues formed the Loss and Grief Practitioners' Association, a peak body for loss, grief, and bereavement practitioners. She runs groups for parents of children with disabilities and long-term psychotherapy groups. She has had a long history in loss, grief, and bereavement: from the time she was a nurse in palliative care; then into research where she interviewed close to seven hundred patients with a terminal illness and their family members about their experiences; and subsequently doctoral research, publication, and private practice. She is passionate about non-death losses and in teaching professionals about this, as well as its intersection with social justice. She has worked in many different areas where people's lives are on the margins and where there is profound loss, from working with people in prisons, to homeless people, to those with addictions. She served on the Accreditation Committee and the Committee of Management for the National Association for Loss and Grief. She has taught for the Australian Centre for Grief and Bereavement. She has also written widely on issues of loss, on traumatic loss and its family impact including in international peer-reviewed journal articles, in the media and has presented widely throughout Australia and internationally.

Laura Danforth, PhD, LCSW, MSW, is an assistant professor in the Department of Social Work at the University of Arkansas at Little Rock. She currently teaches graduate-level courses, including Social Welfare Policies, Management and Community Practice Methods, and Research Methods for Social Workers, all of which prepare future master's-level social workers to engage in policy practice and to work efficiently with communities and organizations. She is currently the Chair of the Management and Community Practice (MCP) track of the Master of Social Work program and helps students develop skills that will allow them to initiate and guide macro-level change efforts in order to further social justice. As a critical race scholar, her research interests revolve around resiliency practices for racially marginalized communities, women, and communities experiencing a traumatic event or disaster. She is also interested in feminist research frameworks and methodologies.

Elizabeth (Liz) Davies completed her social work degree at the University of New South Wales, Sydney, Australia, and is an accredited mental health social worker. From 2010 to 2018, Liz worked in the missing persons sector, coordinating a one-of-its-kind service providing policy advice, clinical and group support to those impacted by the loss of a missing person. Liz has more than 30 years of experience working in the public and private sectors, as a manager, clinician, clinical supervisor, and now researcher and counselor in private practice. Liz is currently completing PhD research, studying the psychosocial experience of young people, their parents, and carers impacted by the loss of a missing family member. Liz has worked with people of all ages who have experienced a range of losses—death- and non-death-related—and associated trauma, including a loved one going missing and death as a result of suicide. She has worked with those who have experienced the trauma of physical, sexual, and domestic violence.

Dr. Kenneth J. Doka is Professor of Gerontology at the Graduate School of the College of New Rochelle and Senior Consultant to the Hospice Foundation of America. A prolific author, Dr. Doka has authored or edited over 30 books and over 100 articles and book chapters. Dr. Doka is editor of both *Omega: The Journal of Death and Dying* and *Journeys: A Newsletter to Help in Bereavement*. Dr. Doka was elected President of the Association for Death Education and Counseling in 1993. In 1995, he was elected to the Board of Directors of the International Work Group on Dying, Death and Bereavement and served as chair from 1997 to 1999. ADEC presented him with an Award for Outstanding Contributions in the Field of Death Education in 1998. In 2000 Scott and White presented him an award for Outstanding Contributions to Thanatology and Hospice. His alma mater, Concordia College, presented him with their first Distinguished Alumnus Award. He is a recipient of the Caring Hands Award as well as the Dr. Robert Fulton CDEB Founder's Award. In 2006, Dr. Doka was grandfathered in as a Mental Health Counselor under New York State's first licensure of counselors.

Thomas Dwyer received his bachelor's in finance from Susquehanna University in 1978. He worked in the large corporate financial industry for over 25 years. During this time, he volunteered facilitating addiction family support groups. Tom left the banking world to pursue his passion of addiction counseling. In 2009, he received his master's in counseling psychology from Fairleigh Dickinson University. After completing his clinical hours at different addiction rehabilitation facilities, he became a Licensed Professional Counselor and a Licensed Clinical Alcohol and Drug Counselor in 2014. Later that year, he started his own practice, called the Gateway Center for Counseling and Recovery. In 2015, Tom became Certified in Thanatology (CT) through the Association for Death Education and Counseling. Tom specializes in mental health, addiction, and grief counseling. In service to the community, he offers a biweekly, pro bono addiction bereavement support group. He also provides sponsored lectures and accredited workshops to professional counselors on the subject of addiction grief.

Maria E. Fernandez, MPsych, is a clinical psychologist at the Department for Communities, Child Protection and Family Support in Geraldton, Australia, where she provides psychological interventions for Aboriginal children in foster care.

Rev. Dr. Dan Festa was recently granted the status of honorably retired as Pastor at Covenant Presbyterian Church in Marshall, Missouri. Dan has had a rich career punctuated by teaching and educational opportunities. He received biomedical ethics training at the Kennedy Institute at Georgetown University in the District of Columbia. He served as Chaplain and Coordinator of Bereavement Services on the Medical Campus of Virginia Commonwealth University. Throughout the last 30 years of his career, Dan has done work with several organ procurement agencies and has taught internationally on death, grief, and bereavement. Dan has been a regular attendee and presenter at the International Death, Grief, and Bereavement Conference and has published several research studies, contributed chapters to several books, and had a book published entitled *Through the Eyes of the Heart: Stories of Love and Loss*.

Mae-Lynn Germany, MS, is a doctoral candidate in counseling psychology at the University of Memphis. Over the course of her training, she has co-authored several articles and co-instructed courses focused on training undergraduate and graduate students in topics such as multicultural counseling, the psychology of grief and loss, as well as constructivist psychotherapies. She has over 10 years of research experience in disparate areas including: educational psychology, linguistic analysis, personal constructions of gender and sexuality, as well as grief related to nondeath losses. Currently, her work focuses on LGBT coming out and transitioning, social justice practices in research, and disenfranchised grief as well as nondeath and ambiguous losses.

Athir N. Jisrawi holds Bachelor of Medical Sciences from Western University and a Graduate Diploma in international relations from the University of London. She is currently pursuing a master's degree in counseling psychology at Yorkville University and is a teaching assistant at King's University College in London, Ontario.

Emmanuel Kassiotis completed his social work degree at the University of New South Wales in 2001 and has experience working in the social work field within mental health, disability, child protection, grief and loss, and with young people who have experienced trauma and abuse both in Australia and in Scotland. In 2010 Emmanuel began working in the missing persons sector, providing clinical and group work support to those impacted by the loss of a missing person. In 2018 Emmanuel enrolled in a post-graduate diploma program in bereavement counseling (working with bereaved children).

Kriss A. Kevorkian, PhD, MSW, holds a doctoral degree in thanatology, the study/science of death, dying and bereavement. She combined her passion for thanatology with her love of whales and the environment through her research on environmental grief and ecological grief. She is a Contributing Faculty Member in the MSW program at Walden

University, where she teaches classes on trauma, crisis, and disasters, to name a few. She hosts/facilitates a Death Café monthly at the Gig Harbor Library, is a trained Climate Leader through the Climate Reality Project, a member of the Steering Committee of the Meaningful Movies Gig Harbor and is a member of the Gig Harbor Sustainability Coalition. She is founder of the Legal Rights for the Salish Sea, an organization educating communities and stakeholders about getting the rights of nature to save the Southern Resident Killer Whales and the Salish Sea herself.

Lara Krawchuk, MSW, LCSW, MPH, is Owner of Healing Concepts, LLC, offering counseling, continuing education, and consulting in West Chester, Pennsylvania. She teaches Advanced Clinical Practice and End of Life and Loss Across a Lifecycle classes for the University of Pennsylvania School of Social Policy and Practice. She is a national lecturer on issues of grief and loss, caregiving, physical illness, end of life, and compassion fatigue. She has written four chapters for two editions of the *Techniques of Grief Therapy* series, edited by Robert A. Neimeyer, PhD. Lara created the popular professional healing retreat When Helping Hurts: Self-Care for Helping Professionals. This program has been featured in the award-winning documentary *Professional Caregivers: Their Passion, Their Pain.*

Ann Laverty, PhD, is a psychologist at the University of Calgary, SU Wellness Centre in Canada. Her primary focus is providing individual and group counseling to students and supervision of graduate practicum students and interns. Her doctoral research explored adult sibling bereavement and she continues to pursue research and resource development related to grief/bereavement and post-secondary mental health concerns.

Monique B. Mitchell, PhD, FT, is Director of Translational Research & Curriculum Development at the Dougy Center: The National Center for Grieving Children and Families and the Executive Director of Life Transitions International. Her areas of expertise include life transitions, trauma, grief and loss, ambiguity, and youth empowerment. Dr. Mitchell regularly provides consultation and training on the lived experience of children in foster care. Her child-centered research has informed child welfare policy and practice throughout the United States. She is the author of *The Neglected Transition: Building a Relational Home for Children Entering Foster Care* (Oxford University Press, 2016), and *Living in an Inspired World: Voices and Visions of Youth in Foster Care* (Child Welfare League of America Press, 2017).

Robert A. Neimeyer, PhD, is Professor of Psychology, University of Memphis, where he maintains an active clinical practice. He also directs the Portland Institute for Loss and Transition, which provides training internationally in grief therapy. Since completing his doctoral training at the University of Nebraska in 1982, he has published 30 books, including *Techniques of Grief Therapy: Creative Practices for Counseling the Bereaved and Grief* and the *Expressive Arts: Practices for Creating Meaning*, the latter with Barbara Thompson, and serves as Editor of the journal *Death Studies*. The author of nearly 500 articles and book chapters, he is currently working to advance a more adequate theory of grieving as a meaning-making process, both in his published work and through his frequent professional workshops for national and international audiences. Dr. Neimeyer served as President of the Association for Death Education and Counseling (ADEC), and Chair of the International Work Group for Death, Dying, and Bereavement. In recognition of his scholarly contributions, he has been granted the Eminent Faculty Award by the University of Memphis, made a Fellow of the Clinical Psychology Division of the American Psychological Association, and given Lifetime Achievement Awards by both the Association for Death Education and Counseling and the International Network on Personal Meaning.

Anna C. Pederson, MS, is a doctoral student in the University of Wisconsin–Madison's Counseling Psychology program. Previously, she received a master's in clinical mental health counseling from the University of Memphis. Her research interests include improving counselor competency when working with populations that have been historically stigmatized or pathologized, intersectionality, and non-death loss.

Keesha Quinn completed her social work degree at the University of New South Wales in 2011 and has experience working in the social work field within acute mental health, child protection and with young people who have experienced trauma. From 2016 to 2018, Keesha worked in the missing persons sector, providing clinical support to those impacted by the loss of a missing person. In 2017 Keesha completed a Graduate Certificate in Loss, Grief and Trauma Counselling.

Susan Roos, PhD, ACSW, has maintained a psychotherapy practice with an emphasis on grief and loss. She completed a one-year training program with Jim Norwood, M. Div., Midwest Institute for Gestalt Therapy, and 30 hours with Erving and Miriam Polster (Gestalt Training Center, San Diego) in Dallas. She is past President of the Dallas Society for Psychoanalytic Psychology and currently serves on the arts committee. She is a consultant to Trauma Support Services of North Texas and is a Fellow in Thanatology, Association for Death Education and Counseling. She is the author of *Chronic Sorrow: A Living Loss*, with the second edition released in 2018.

Lara Schultz, PhD, is a registered psychologist in a regional grief program in Canada. Her primary focus is providing individual and group counseling to bereaved adults. Her areas of research and clinical specialization are grief and bereavement, with particular experience related to loss for emerging adults. Lara's graduate research explored the influence of maternal bereavement on young women's identity development, and her doctoral research focused on the lived experience of parental suicide bereavement for emerging adults.

Sheldon Solomon is Professor of Psychology at Skidmore College. His studies of the effects of the uniquely human awareness of death on behavior have been supported by the National Science Foundation and Ernest Becker Foundation, and were featured in the award-winning documentary film *Flight from Death: The Quest for Immortality*. He is co-author of *In the Wake of 9/11: The Psychology of Terror* and *The Worm at the Core: On the Role of Death in Life*. Sheldon is an American Psychological Society Fellow, and a recipient of an American Psychological Association Presidential Citation (2007), a Lifetime Career Award by the International Society for Self and Identity (2009), and the Association of Graduate Liberal Studies Programs Annual Faculty Award (2011).

Neil Thompson, PhD, D. Litt., is an independent writer, educator, and adviser based in Wales. His recent books include *Applied Sociology* (Routledge, 2018), *Effective Communication* (3rd ed, Palgrave, 2018) and *Mental Health and Well-being: Alternatives to the Medical Model* (Routledge, 2019). His website and blog are at www.NeilThompson.info.

Introduction
Darcy L. Harris

This book is an exploration of how loss and grief shape our everyday lives. At times, we might accommodate the losses we experience readily, without a great deal of upheaval. At other times, the losses we encounter may be overwhelming, and grief may completely consume us. While it may be quite straightforward to acknowledge the grief that results from the death of a loved one, it can be harder to recognize the grief that occurs from a loss experience where nobody has physically died. Sometimes, what dies might be an individual's hopes or dreams, a relationship, or perhaps an ability that is no longer readily accessible as it was before.

I teach in a university-based Thanatology program. In one of our courses that explores personal experiences with grief and loss, students are asked to create a timeline using tick marks on a line drawn from one side of the paper to the other, indicating specific losses that they experienced at various ages. It's common for some of the younger students to struggle with this exercise, feeling unable to complete the assignment because they may not have experienced a death-related loss. When we talk a bit more, I will ask them if they ever moved from a place where they felt was home, experienced the loss of friendships through various means, knew the disappointment of not being accepted into programs or picked for teams they wanted to join, if there are injuries that now prevent them from engaging in sports they previously enjoyed, or about breakups of intimate relationships. As we discuss these types of experiences, the students begin to realize that while they may not be familiar with death-related losses, they are well acquainted with many non-death loss experiences and the grief that accompanied them. It's not unusual for these same students to then complete their loss lines with many tick marks and experiences noted. The importance of this exercise is not to put forward the idea that we live in a chronic state of grief throughout life; rather, it is to recognize how loss and grief have shaped our lives, our choices, and how we now see ourselves and the world.

An important aspect of the loss line exercise, and in everyday experiences, is to recognize that how a loss is perceived and defined is dependent upon the subjective appraisal of each person. While professional training and work in the field may provide professionals with language to describe experiences and the ability to adeptly discuss the grieving process, only the individual affected can truly determine whether a loss has indeed occurred—and the significance of that loss. *A loss can be defined as an experience where there is a change in circumstance, perception, or experience where it would be impossible to return to the way things were before.* An image that I often use to define a loss experience is that of a shattered pane of glass. While it might be possible to use glue to put the broken pieces of glass back into place, the glass that once existed as a whole, single pane will never exist in that form again. So it is with a significant loss experience. There are times when you will not be able to un-do what has happened, un-know what you now know, un-see what you have seen, and you will no longer be naïve to an experience that you have now endured.

There is often an unstated understanding between people who have experienced similar losses and know the unique grief that accompanies them. Many veterans who return from active duty where they were engaged in combat find re-entry into the everyday, mundane life they once knew to be very difficult. The home they left now feels foreign as the experiences in their tour of duty have deeply altered their views of the world, of others, and of themselves. When groups of veterans who served together reunite after returning from deployment, there is often an unspoken bond of shared experience that many of them feel with each other. We find solace in knowing that others have also survived the shattering of their world in the same way as we might have.

While the losses we have experienced and the grieving process that accompanies them may be painful and disorienting, there is also the potential for transformation and growth to occur during this time. Viorst (1986) states that the losses we experience are necessary for us to grow and adapt as part of our normal development. Maas (2008) suggests that experiences of loss and transition may present opportunities that did not exist before. However, the recognition of these opportunities is often overshadowed by having to let go of what was familiar, comfortable, or even safe. In her discussion of adaptation to lifestyle changes, Maas describes our tendency towards dichotomous thinking (i.e., good versus bad, or positive versus negative) rather than approaching loss and change in a way that recognizes the multifaceted and multidimensional effects of choices and events. It is common for individuals who have lived through incredibly difficult events to later emerge feeling stronger and wiser. Much has been written about the phenomenon of 'doing well' or post-traumatic growth (PTG) and resilience after enduring traumatic experiences (Bonanno, 2004; Gorman, 2011; Tedeschi & Calhoun, 2004). Other terms that refer to the ability to thrive after a traumatic event include rebounding, self-righting, and ordinary magic (Madsen, 2007). Thus, change, loss, and transition can challenge us in ways that may be initially overwhelming; however, these same experiences can provide the catalyst for growth and a deeper appreciation for life.

In his book, *When Everything Changes, Change Everything*, Walsh (2009) talks about the importance of change and transition in everyday life. He identifies three central areas where change and loss are most likely to assault our deeply held views of the world and ourselves:

- *Relationships*—losses may involve a loss of contact and meaningful connection with others and those we once loved, loss of connection with ourselves or a sense of knowing ourselves, and/or loss of connection with the universe and what is transcendent.
- *Finances*—the ability to feel secure; financial independence and stability underscore our ability to determine how we live, the choices we are able to make, and how we are perceived socially.
- *Health*—physical and mental health determine our ability to do what is needed and/or desired in life; loss of health is equated with loss of a sense of agency and uncertainty about the future.

Sofka (2008) developed the Loss History Checklist (Figure 0.1). This list may be helpful in identifying different loss experiences and pondering their potential impact. Of interest is that this checklist includes both death-related and non-death loss experiences.

Overview of the Book

We begin with an initial chapter that lays the foundation for the theoretical underpinning of grief in the context of non-death losses. The first major section of the book explores the social context of different types of loss experiences, including experiences that occur as a result of social policies, pressures, and conflict with established social norms within given locations. While grief is described as an individual's unique response to loss, the grieving process is shaped and molded to a great extent by the social, cultural, and political milieu in which the grieving individual identifies and resides. This section starts with a discussion about how these contextual factors influence the perception of individual experiences, including expectations about how grief should be expressed and experienced, and also the supports and resources that may or may not be available to grieving individuals. While losses that are due to the death of a loved one may engender offers of support and sympathy, loss experiences that are not as obvious or that do not involve a death may be *disenfranchised* (Doka, 2002), resulting in the additional loss of the very supports that we need during a time when we are hurting and vulnerable. We then move to a discussion of the concept of *social death*, which is a unique form of non-death loss that is socially defined and determined. The next chapter in this section explores how social justice issues, such as *racism, marginalization, and oppression* create their own form of unique grief for specific members and groups. This section concludes with a discussion of the concept of *political grief*, exploring the current political climate in the United States, where deep divisions and polarization have been created by the ideology and practices of the current populist governmental movement.

Loss History Checklist Revised		
A. Losses through death of:		
Biological mother	Biological father	Child(ren)
Adopted mother	Adopted father	Grandchild(ren)
Foster mother(s)	Foster father(s)	Grandparent(s)
Brother(s)	Sister(s)	Other relative(s)
Husband/wife	Companion/lover	Friend(s)
Pet(s)	Counselor/therapist	Support person(s)
Other(s)? Describe:		
B. Relationship losses that did not involve death:		
My own divorce	My own separation	Loss of boyfriend/girlfriend
Divorce of parents	Separation of parents	Loss of neighbor(s)
Loss of friendship(s)	Loss of co-worker(s)	Loss of doctor(s)
Loss of support person(s)	Loss of counselor/ therapist	Loss of contact with parent(s) (biological/adopted/foster)
Loss of contact with child(ren)	Inability to have children (infertility or other reason)	Loss of contact with brother(s)/sister(s)
Loss of contact with friend(s)	Temporary separation due to employment, military deployment, or another reason:	
Other? Describe:		
C. Other losses (non-death/abstract losses) such as:		
Loss of home/residence	Loss of support services	Loss of possessions
Being homeless	Loss of identity	Abuse (all forms)
Loss of job	Loss of a career	Loss of ability to work
Loss of independence	Loss of potential	Loss of freedom
Loss of control	Loss of time/years	Loss of dreams
Loss of physical health	Loss of mental health	Loss of a goal or opportunity
Loss of vision	Loss of hearing	Loss of physical functioning
Loss of a limb	Loss of life as it was	Loss of hope
Loss of sexuality	Loss of personhood	Loss of spirituality/faith
Loss of trust	Loss of neighborhood	Frequent moves
Loss of safety	Loss of security	Loss of comfort
Loss of childhood/ innocence	Loss of country/homeland (refugee/resettlement)	Loss of confidence
Loss of self-esteem	Bad accident or fire	Loss of respect
Loss of privacy	Loss of future as desired or imagined	
Other? Describe:		
D. Significant impact of historical events (impact on self or significant others):		
War or conflict (specify):		
Holocaust	September 11, 2001	Act(s) of terrorism
Other? Describe:		

Figure 0.1 Loss History Checklist
Source: Adapted from Sofka (2008).

The next four sections of the book each address specific types of non-death loss, including ambiguous loss, nonfinite loss, chronic sorrow, and tangible/intangible non-death losses. Each of these sections opens with an overarching descriptive chapter, followed by several short chapters that "flesh out" examples of the specific types of losses, along with clinical implications and suggestions. These sections are housed under a capstone chapter that is meant to draw connections and overlaps between various types of losses. Once the various concepts, descriptions, and examples of the different types of non-death loss experiences are explored, a review of current and relevant research in these areas will be offered.

The thread of meaning, both lost and found, fractured and deepened, is woven throughout the book, and a chapter that explores meaning-making after our view of the world and ourselves has been shattered will help to tie these strands together. We then proceed with a chapter that explores the unique clinical considerations involved in supporting individuals as they begin the process of rebuilding their world after significant non-death loss experiences. Finally, the concluding chapter is an overview and reiteration of the recognition of the reality of impermanence and our need to adapt, integrate, and accommodate losses of all types into everyday life.

Words can be empowering. This book is designed to provide vocabulary and descriptions to help individuals articulate their losses, both in the identification of what has actually been lost and in the depth of their loss experience. Loss, change, and transition are universal experiences, but the personal responses and appraisals of these experiences are highly individual and unique. The ability to name and describe an experience fully helps us to find our voice when we have been stunned and silenced. Grappling with difficult and painful experiences and trying to understand them (even if they initially seem beyond our comprehension) is a key part of our human need to understand ourselves and to make sense of our world. It is my hope that this book will provide a greater understanding of non-death loss experiences, offer suggestions for how to best accompany those who are in the throes of grief as they live through their losses, and hopefully foster further discussion of the *living losses* that create such painful potential in our lives.

References

Bonanno, G. A. (2004). Loss, trauma, and human resilience: Have we underestimated the human capacity to thrive after extremely aversive events? *American Psychologist, 59,* 20–28.

Doka, K. J. (Ed.) (2002). *Disenfranchised grief: New directions, challenges, and strategies for practice.* Champaign, IL: Research Press.

Gorman, E. (2011). Adaptation, resilience, and growth after loss. In D. L. Harris (Ed.), *Counting our losses: Reflecting on change, loss, and transition in everyday life* (pp. 225–237). New York: Routledge.

Maas, V. S. (2008). *Lifestyle changes: A clinician's guide to common events, challenges, and options.* New York: Routledge.

Madsen, W. C. (2007). *Collaborative treatment with multi-stressed families* (2nd ed.). New York: Guilford Press.

Sofka, C. (2008). For the butterflies I never chased, I grieve: Incorporating grief and loss issues in treatment with survivors of childhood sexual abuse. *Journal of Personal and Interpersonal Loss, 4*(2), 125–148.

Tedeschi, R. G., & Calhoun, L. G. (2004). Post-traumatic growth: Conceptual foundations and empirical evidence. *Psychological Inquiry, 15*(1), 1–18.

Viorst, J. (1986). *Necessary losses*. New York: Simon and Schuster.

Walsh, N. (2009). *When everything changes, change everything*. Ashland, OR: EmNin Books.

CHAPTER 1

Non-Death Loss and Grief: Laying the Foundation

Darcy L. Harris

Introduction

While most of the theorizing about grief has been associated with death-related losses, several aspects of bereavement theory are readily applicable to non-death losses as well. We begin this chapter with a discussion of attachment theory, which has provided an important foundation from which to understand the grieving process. We then explore the assumptive world construct as a partner with the attachment system, providing a perspective for viewing grief more inclusively as a response to all types of losses, not just those that occur as the result of death. We then briefly touch upon a few relevant theories that describe aspects of the experience of grief, applying each to the context of non-death losses. At the end of this chapter are the theoretical understandings that will inform the content of this book.

Attachment Theory

As research began to inform the understandings of grief, Bowlby's theory of attachment (1969, 1973) proved to be especially relevant. Bowlby observed young children who were separated from their parents and described regular patterns of behavior that occurred in response to the separation. He ultimately applied his observations and theories about attachment and separation to bereavement, comparing grief after the death of a loved one to the separation distress that children demonstrated when removed from their parents. He proposed that when a primary attachment figure dies, the "affectional bond" is broken, resulting in grief (1970). Thus, grief was described as the response to a broken attachment bond.

Bowlby's view of attachment was influenced considerably by primate research conducted by Harlow (1963), whose descriptions of infant monkeys' responses to separation from the mother paralleled Bowlby's descriptions of the separated children in his studies. These same responses were also seen in other animal species, such as birds and other mammals. Bowlby concluded that the attachment behavioral system had developed through natural selection to discourage the prolonged separation of an infant from the primary attachment figure(s) in order to increase the chances of survival. This inclusion of the ethological (biological) origins of attachment was unique during a time when the psychoanalytic school was the primary approach of those who were trained in psychiatry. The implication for the biological underpinning of this model was the conclusion that the grief response (a form of separation distress) was an extension of the attachment system, and thus had also evolved as a process to ensure safety and survival. However, the assumption that grief was the response to a broken attachment bond was challenged when later bereavement research demonstrated that the majority of bereaved individuals actively seek out and maintain an intangible relationship (referred to as a *continuing bond*) with their deceased loved ones (Field, Gao, & Paderna, 2005; Klass, Silverman, & Nickman, 2014). The implication of this research was that the attachment bond is not necessarily broken when a loved one dies. Thus, there needed to be further exploration of what actually triggers the grief response.

Bowlby (1969) posited that early-life attachment experiences lead individuals to form "working models" of the self and of the world; for example, a normal working model based upon secure attachment represents the world as capable of meeting one's needs and provides a sense of safety and security. Bowlby also suggested that loss can threaten these working models, leading to efforts to rebuild or restructure one's working models to fit the post-loss world. Building upon Bowlby's work, Parkes (1975) extended the concept of the "internal working model" to that of the "assumptive world," which he stated was a "strongly held set of assumptions about the world and the self, which is confidently maintained and used as a means of recognizing, planning, and acting" (p. 132), and that it is "the only world we know, and it includes everything we know or think we know. It includes our interpretation of the past and our expectations of the future, our plans, and our prejudices" (Parkes, 1971, p. 103).

The Assumptive World

Parkes (1971) stated that the assumptions individuals form about how the world works are based upon their early life experiences and attachments. He also emphasized that experiencing a significant loss can threaten one's assumptive world. In her extensive work that examined the construct of the assumptive world in the context of traumatic experiences, Janoff-Bulman (1992) stated that expectations about how the world should work are established earlier than language in children, and that assumptions about the world are a result of the generalization and application of early childhood experiences into adulthood. The assumptive world is an organized schema reflecting all that a person assumes to be true about the world and the self; it refers to the assumptions, or beliefs, that create a sense of security, predictability, and meaning/purpose to life. This description resonates with Bowlby's descriptions of the development of the attachment system to ensure a sense of safety in the individual and would suggest that the attachment system and the assumptive world construct are formed through similar mechanisms and are probably interrelated. The assumptive world is most likely informed and shaped as part of the attachment system, and the assumptions that are formed are deeply ingrained into the fabric of how individuals live their lives and interpret life events.

Janoff-Bulman (1989, 1992) suggested that there are three primary categories within the assumptive world, each of which of which is comprised of several assumptions. The three main categories are:

1. *Benevolence of the world*—in general, this category consists of how an individual perceives the world in an overarching sense, and also the expectations of benevolence of others.
2. *Meaningfulness of the world*—this category involves people's beliefs about the distribution of outcomes, including expectations of fairness and justice, perceived control over events, and the degree to which randomness is explainable in the course of events.
3. *Worthiness of the self*—the view of how an individual perceives the ability to respond to events, and to act in ways that ensure self-protection and control over life events.

In further exploration of the assumptive world construct in various scenarios, we might suggest that there indeed may be three overarching/main assumptions, but these assumptions will be predicated upon how an individual has come to view the world, self, and others through formative experiences. Thus, the view of others may not incorporate a primary sense of benevolence. The view of the world may not be one that has a sense of justice or predictability. Finally, the view of self may not include an assumption that the self is worthy or capable of controlling or responding to adverse events. Thus, the revised working model of the assumptive world may involve assumptions that are not generalized for everyone in the same way; however, the basic assumptions may center around the same concepts. So, our assumptive world may be composed of:

1. How we tend to view others and their intentions.
2. How we believe the world should work.
3. How we tend to view ourselves.

In this version of the construct, there is allowance for individuals who have grown up in a world where they have not known safety, or where foundational individuals in a person's life have not been well-intentioned, or the view of self has been mirrored in a way that does not affirm the individual's worth, capacity, or value.

Janoff-Bulman (1992) stated that our basic assumptions about how the world should work can be shattered by life experiences that do not fit into our view of ourselves and the world around us. Neimeyer, Laurie, Mehta, Hardison, and Currier (2008) discuss events that "disrupt the significance of the coherence of one's life narrative" (p. 30) and the potential for erosion of the individual's life story and sense of self that may occur after such events. What is apparent is that the experience of a significant life event that does not fit into our beliefs can throw us into a state of disequilibrium. Coping, healing, and accommodation after such experiences are part of a greater process that individuals undertake in an effort to "relearn" their assumptions about the world in light of confrontation with a reality that does not match their existing expectations or assumptions (Attig, 1996). It is important to note that the assumptive world is more than a cognitive construct; these assumptions exist at the very core of what in life provides us with a sense of meaning, purpose, and security. Each category of assumption will have cognitive aspects, but will also incorporate social, spiritual, emotional, and psychological components as well.

In the aftermath of significant loss experiences, the core beliefs that comprise our assumptive world are challenged, and the entire structure that we have built our lives upon begins to crumble. The hopes, expectations, and predictions we had in place are now rendered irrelevant and useless in light of the reality that now presents itself to us. Those assumptions, which have kept us steady and have given coherence to our lives, now seem like naïve illusions. The realization of how little control we have over what happens to us becomes blaringly evident. The glass shatters. There is no going back; the way the world made sense before and the expectations and beliefs that we deeply held about ourselves and others are no longer salient. Losing one's assumptions about the world means the loss of safety, logic, clarity, power, and control (Beder, 2005). There is an overwhelming sense of disequilibrium and disorientation that occurs while we flounder, trying to navigate in a new, unfamiliar reality. In essence, we are grieving the loss of our assumptive world, and our grief (although painful and disorienting) provides us with the process by which we will grapple with the assault on our most deeply held assumptions and beliefs to eventually rebuild a new assumptive world that will be able to take into account the lived experience that catapulted us into this uncharted territory. *A central theme of this book is that grief is a process that is both adaptive and necessary in order to rebuild the assumptive world after its destruction from significant loss experiences.*

The Dual Process Model

Through their research with bereaved individuals, Stroebe, Schut, and Stroebe (2005) proposed the Dual Process Model of grief. In this model, the grieving process is described as an oscillation between immersion in the loss experience (loss orientation) alternated with the focus upon the aspects of daily life, adjustment, and functioning (restoration orientation), with both processes encompassing the totality of grief (see Figure 1.1). Interestingly, in her descriptions of responses to traumatic events, Janoff-Bulman (1992) also posited oscillation between numbness (often described as avoidance of the event) with confrontation (and re-traumatization) as part of the attempt to reconcile a seemingly senseless event that has happened with a belief system that hinges upon benevolence and meaning. This description is very similar to the Dual Process Model of coping with grief, suggesting the need to oscillate between avoidance of the loss and focusing on everyday functioning alternated with confronting the loss and its effects. While the Dual Process Model was based upon research with individuals whose loss involved the death of a loved one, the model is readily applicable to grief in non-death loss experiences (see Figure 1.2).

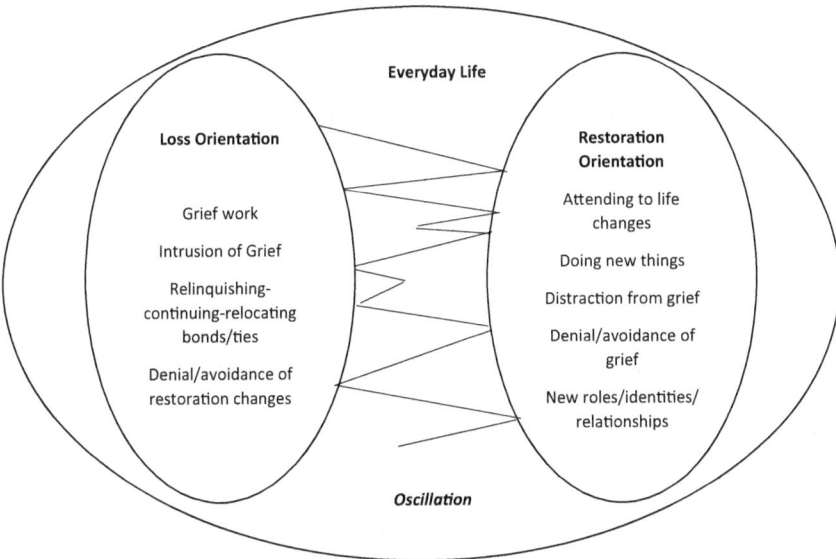

Figure 1.1 The Dual Process Model of Coping with Bereavement
Source: Stroebe and Schut (1999).

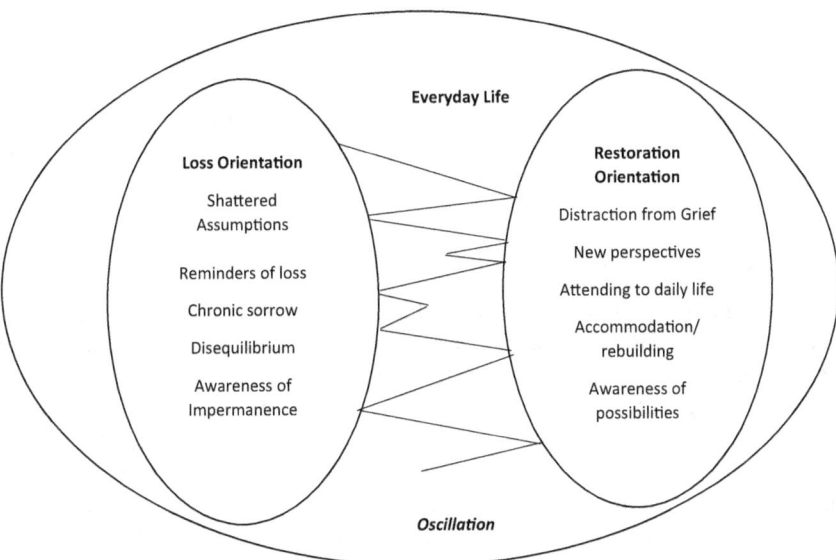

Figure 1.2 The Dual Process Model for Non-Death Loss and Grief
Source: Adapted from Stroebe, Schut, and Stroebe (2005) by Harris.

In a review of empirical literature, Stroebe et al. (2005) discussed the relationship between attachment style and how individuals may oscillate between loss orientation and restoration orientation. According to Bowlby (1973, 1980), individuals with a secure attachment style have positive mental models of being valued and worthy of others' concern, support, and affection. The case could be made that individuals with a secure attachment style may indeed be aligned with Janoff-Bulman's original description of the three assumptions in the assumptive world construct; it would make sense that people whose attachment pattern is mostly secure will tend to see others as generally benevolent, to see the world as meaningful, and to view themselves as competent, worthy, and valued. Those whose attachment style is not secure will have assumptive worldviews that reflect views of others, the world, and themselves in ways that may not be as positive, and their ways of coping with significant losses would be consistent with specific aspects of insecure/anxious attachment. For example, individuals whose attachment style is primarily anxious/ambivalent may tend to ruminate about their loss experiences, have difficulties adjusting to change, experience higher levels of distress when losses are encountered, and are more prone to depression (Bowlby, 1980; Wayment & Vierthaler, 2002). In the Dual Process Model, these individuals are more likely to spend more of their time and energy in the loss orientation, with much less time venturing into the restoration orientation aspects of grief (Collins & Feeney, 2000). Individuals whose attachment style is primarily anxious/avoidant often see significant others as being unreliable, or desiring too much intimacy, and they tend to disengage from their attachment systems and may not experience emotional distress. The consequence of actively avoiding affective reactions is the possibility of increased levels of somatic symptoms. Thus, those with a predominantly anxious/avoidant attachment style may report little emotional distress when a significant loss occurs, and they may predominantly gravitate towards the restoration orientation aspects of grief, with a tendency to have more bodily symptoms in the process (Pennebaker & Beall, 1986).

The Social Context of Loss

The fact that our attachment system and assumptive world form our core beliefs, views, and expectations about life is a strong indicator of our social nature and the importance of social interactions to us, beginning when we are born and continuing throughout our lives. The underlying foundation of attachment theory is that we are shaped and influenced by the people that surround us. We are not isolated and separate from our interactions with others, and we possess a strong innate need to belong, to be loved, and to exist within a community. It is impossible to separate out our individuality from the social context that shapes us in so many different ways. Indeed, there is even neuroscience research that underscores the importance of being accepted and feeling a sense of belonging to our selected community of individuals (MacDonald & Leary, 2005). Thus, while we can examine individual responses to specific loss events, it would be simplistic and unrealistic to consider individual responses to loss outside of the social context in which they occur. Many non-death loss experiences are *disenfranchised* because they are ambiguous or intangible in nature, or because they don't involve the death of a loved one (Doka, 1989). When the individual's subjective appraisal of a loss falls outside general social norms and expectations, the experience of grief is compounded by isolation and pressure to deny the subjective account, creating a disparity between how a loss *should* be experienced (as determined by the dominant social narrative) versus how a loss is *actually* experienced by that individual. The importance of the social context and social factors in loss experiences will be expanded upon further in the next section.

Meaning-Making After Loss Experiences

Originally described in Constructivist Psychology, the concept of making meaning extends from the idea that human beings construct life narratives, and part of this construction is also the assignment of meaning or attaching significance to events that occur. It might also be suggested that meaning-making is one of the primary processes in which individuals engage when there is dissonance between their life experiences and their existing assumptive world. Pre-existing assumptions that are no longer viable in describing the world, and one's inner working models or schemata, must somehow be re-worked in order for the person to feel safe in the world again, and this process can be very difficult. Searching for meaning after significant loss appears to be an almost universal phenomenon and an important part of the grieving process (Davis, 2001; Neimeyer, 2001; Neimeyer & Sands, 2011). The trauma, shock, and anguish of significant losses challenge our fundamental assumptions about the world. Meaning-making can occur with a re-interpretation of negative events as opportunities to learn new lessons about one's self or life in general, as a means of helping others, or contributing to society in some way that is related to the experience that occurred (such as the formation of an advocacy group or efforts to help others in similar situations).

Neimeyer (2001; Neimeyer et al., 2002) discusses the social constructivist view of meaning-making through the use of narrative re-framing in individuals who have experienced significant losses. His description of the "master narrative," which is an "understanding of one's life and experiences, along with meanings attached to these" (p. 263) is very similar to the descriptions of the assumptive world described in the earlier section of this chapter. He states that significant losses disrupt taken-for-granted narratives and strain the assumptions that once sustained them. Individuals must find ways to make meaning of the life events that have been disruptive through a "reweaving" process that incorporates the new experiences into the existing life narrative so that it is once again coherent and sustaining.

Searching for meaning in what seems to be a meaningless event is how human beings attempt to re-establish a sense of order and security in their world and to minimize the high degree of vulnerability that occurs after basic assumptions are shattered. Thus, it can be said that *meaning-making is the primary task involved in rebuilding the assumptive world after it has been shattered by significant loss experiences; the process of meaning-making and the grief response are intricately entwined.* An exploration of meaning-making after non-death loss experiences will be discussed more fully in Chapter 24.

Summary

In this chapter, the theoretical foundations of bereavement have been extrapolated to various aspects of grief after non-death losses. These foundational perspectives form the basic understandings for the contents of this volume:

1. Grief is the instinctually programmed response to the loss of significant, core aspects of our assumptive world.
2. While grief may no longer be viewed as the result of a broken attachment bond, early experiences and attachment style will, to a large degree, determine how grief is experienced and expressed.
3. An individual is inseparable from the surrounding social context. An individual's perception, appraisal, and response to experiences are filtered through the social norms and structures in which that individual identifies and/or resides.

Key Terms

Assumptive World: Fundamental beliefs that individuals hold regarding how the world works and how others and one's self are viewed. The assumptive world is thought to provide individuals with a sense of safety and security in everyday life situations.

Attachment Theory: The formation of significant and stable connections with significant people in an individual's life. This process begins in early infancy, as the child bonds with one or more primary caregivers, and later extends to other significant relationships through the lifespan. Attachment is thought to be an instinctual construct with the purpose of ensuring safety and survival.

Continuing Bonds Theory: Bereaved individuals may be well served to find ways to reconnect to their deceased loved one in ways that are meaningful; often summed up in the statement that death ends a life, but not a relationship.

Dual Process Model: A model of grief that posits that bereaved individuals will "oscillate" regularly between restoration orientation (e.g., activities of daily living, distractions, and focusing on life) and loss orientation (e.g., focusing on the loss, reminiscing about life before the loss, and feeling the pangs of grief).

Meaning-Making: A social constructivist model that utilizes a "master narrative," which can be described as a coherent overarching story and understanding of one's life and experiences, along with the meanings that are attached to these experiences. This narrative construction is facilitated by the grieving process.

Questions for Reflection

1. What influenced your first conceptions or assumptions about grief? Did you have realistic expectations or ideas surrounding non-death loss and grief?
2. While attachment is innately within human nature, do you believe that your attachment style is a "life sentence"? For instance, is it possible for adult individuals to work towards changing an insecure attachment style obtained in childhood? Explore reasons for how an attachment style could be changed, or how this is a "life sentence."
3. Think of a situation in your life when you or someone you know experienced a non-death loss, and the personal narrative surrounding it. What are some of the assumptions that were challenged by this loss? Did this loss experience change how you viewed yourself, others, or the world?

References

Attig, T. A. (1996). *How we grieve: Relearning the world.* New York: Oxford University Press.

Beder, J. (2005). Loss of the assumptive world—How we deal with death and loss. *Omega: The Journal of Death and Dying, 50*(4), 255–265.

Bowlby, J. (1969). *Attachment and loss: Attachment (Vol 1).* London: Hogarth.

Bowlby, J. (1970). Disruption of affectional bonds and its effects on behavior. *Journal of Contemporary Psychotherapy, 2*(2), 75–86.

Bowlby, J. (1973). *Attachment and loss, Vol. 2: Separation.* New York: Basic Books.

Bowlby, J. (1980). *Attachment and loss, Vol. 3: Loss, sadness, and depression.* New York: Basic Books.

Collins, N. L., & Feeney, B. C. (2000). A safe haven: An attachment theory perspective on support-seeking and caregiving processes in intimate relationships. *Journal of Personality and Social Psychology, 78,* 1053–1073.

Davis, C. G. (2001). The tormented and the transformed: Understanding responses to loss and trauma. In R. A. Neimeyer (Ed.), *Meaning reconstruction and the experience of loss* (pp. 137–155). Washington, DC: APA.

Doka, K. J. (Ed.). (1989). *Disenfranchised grief: Recognizing hidden sorrow.* Lexington, MA: Lexington.

Field, N. P., Gao, B., & Paderna, L. (2005). Continuing bonds in bereavement: An attachment theory based perspective. *Death Studies, 29*(4), 277–299.

Harlow, H. F. (1963). The maternal affectional system. In B. M. Foss (Ed.), *Determinants of infant behavior II* (pp. 3–33). London: Methuen.

Janoff-Bulman, R. (1989). Assumptive worlds and the stress of traumatic events: Applications of the schema construct. *Social Cognition, 7*(2), 113–136.

Janoff-Bulman, R. (1992). *Shattered assumptions: Towards a new psychology of trauma.* New York: Free Press.

Klass, D., Silverman, P. R., & Nickman, S. (Eds.). (2014). *Continuing bonds: New understandings of grief.* Abingdon: Taylor & Francis.

MacDonald, G., & Leary, M. R. (2005). Why does social exclusion hurt? The relationship between social and physical pain. *Psychological Bulletin, 131*(2), 202.

Neimeyer, R. A. (2001). The language of loss: Grief therapy as a process of meaning reconstruction. In R. A. Neimeyer (Ed.), *Meaning reconstruction & the experience of loss* (pp. 261–292). Washington, DC: APA.

Neimeyer, R. A., Botella, L., Herrero, O., Pecheco, M., Figueras, S., & Werner-Wilder, L. A. (2002). The meaning of your absence. In J. Kauffman (Ed.), *Loss of the assumptive world: A theory of traumatic loss* (pp. 31–47). New York: Brunner-Routledge.

Neimeyer, R. A., Laurie, A., Mehta, T., Hardison, H., & Currier, J. M. (2008). Lessons of loss: Meaning-making in bereaved college students. *New Directions for Student Services, 121*, 27–39.

Neimeyer, R. A., & Sands, D. (2011). Meaning reconstruction in bereavement: From principles to practice. In R. Neimeyer, D. L. Harris, H. Winokuer, & G. Thornton (Eds.), *Grief and bereavement in contemporary society: Bridging research and practice* (pp. 9–22). New York: Routledge.

Pennebaker, J. W., & Beall, S. K. (1986). Confronting a traumatic event: Toward an understanding of inhibition and disease. *Journal of Abnormal Psychology, 95*, 274–281.

Parkes, C. M. (1971). Psycho-social transitions: A field for study. *Social Science & Medicine, 5*, 101–115.

Parkes, C. M. (1975). What becomes of redundant world models? A contribution to the study of adaptation to change. *British Journal of Medical Psychology, 48*, 131–137.

Stroebe, M., & Schut, H. (1999). The Dual Process Model of coping with bereavement: Rationale and description. *Death studies, 23*(3), 197–224.

Stroebe, M., Schut, H., & Stroebe, W. (2005). Attachment in coping with bereavement: A theoretical integration. *Review of General Psychology, 9*(1), 48–66.

Wayment, H. A., & Vierthaler, J. (2002). Attachment style and bereavement reactions. *Journal of Loss &Trauma, 7*(2), 129–149.

PART I

The Social Context of Loss and Grief
Neil Thompson

Introduction

The idea that our understanding of loss and grief issues can benefit from being viewed through a sociological lens is certainly not new (see, for example, Howarth & Jupp, 1996; Thompson, 2012; Thompson & Cox, 2017). However, it remains the case that the dominant approaches to making sense of loss and grief remain largely individualistic and therefore psychological in their focus, with sociological perspectives playing a relatively minor secondary role, if at all, for the most part. This chapter, therefore, explores the significance of the social context and highlights some of the problems that can arise if it is not given sufficient attention.

What Do We Mean by the Social Context?

One of the basic premises of sociology is that whatever is done is done within a social context (Thompson, 2018a). That is, there will be a range of social forces that will be playing a part—large or small—in shaping what is happening and how it is being understood. As we shall see, this applies particularly to issues of loss and grief. This reflects the well-established idea that no [wo]man is an island. Every one of us is a unique individual, but a unique individual within a social context—and a social context that will have played a major part in shaping that uniqueness (and the uniqueness of each of the people we encounter; Thompson, 2016). To focus on what makes us unique as individuals without also considering the wider social context is to tell only half the story, to rely on a distorted and one-sided picture. In supporting people who are grieving, such a distortion can be highly problematic.

The social context comprises a number of different aspects. These include social structure (comprising the "social divisions" of class, ethnicity, gender, and so on); culture (shared meanings, and "unwritten rules" that are passed from one generation to the next); and power relations (hierarchies of dominance and subordination that operate through various channels). These are just some of the important factors that can play such a significant role in shaping individual experience, but they should be enough to make the point that there is a complex, multidimensional context that merits careful consideration.

Why Consider the Social Context?

The traditional "common sense" view of the social context is that it is simply the passive backdrop for the important psychological processes and issues that are going on in the foreground. It reflects a view of the individual person being "in" society but takes no account of society being "in" the individual—that is, the way social issues will have shaped that person's identity, experiences and circumstances, their opportunities, constraints and understanding of the world. This has at times been referred to as the "soup and bowl" model of the relationship between the individual and society—the individual (soup) rests within society (bowl), but they remain separate entities. However, a more sociologically sophisticated approach can be characterized as "coffee and cream"—the individual (cream) is integrated within society (coffee)—they become a single, bi-dimensional entity, fully integrated, rather than two separate entities (Thompson et al., 2016). If we think carefully about this, we should be able to see that this latter model more fully reflects the nature of social reality in the sense that there could be no society without individuals, and no individuals without society. To look at the individual in isolation is an abstraction, a distortion, and oversimplification of the complex reality of human existence. "Atomism" is the technical term for such a problematic approach (as opposed to "holism," which seeks to understand human experiences in light of the full picture of the individual *and* their social context).

Atomism is problematic in general terms because of its distorting effects—it is giving us only one part of the picture. More specifically, there will be more particular problems associated with this approach. For example, an atomistic approach to people grieving may pay no attention to significant differences in cultural understandings of grief and expectations in relation to patterns of mourning. The result may well be culturally inappropriate responses that do more harm than good (Rosenblatt, 2016). Similarly, an atomistic approach may fail to appreciate the significance of gender in shaping patterns of grief reaction and may thereby create additional problems and tensions (Doka & Martin, 2010).

Social class is also a key sociological factor that can play a significant part. For example, access to financial resources will be very significant in relation to access to potential sources of support (health care, counseling, legal services, and so on) when difficulties and life challenges are encountered. In addition, class factors will be significant in terms of the nature, extent, impact, severity, and frequency of such life challenges. Seeing someone as "just an individual" like every other individual involves making the mistake of disregarding a range of factors that can very often make a crucial difference.

A Case in Point

Tami's husband had left her and their three children after he became involved with a colleague at work. Tami was really struggling with the complex range of feelings this situation generated in her. She was angry and bitter at his betrayal, but she also felt a huge sense of loss and yearning because, for all his faults, she loved him dearly and desperately wanted him back. Part of her wanted to punish him by stopping him from seeing the children, but she also knew what a good father he had been and how hurtful it would be for the children if they did not see him. She was facing a maelstrom of complex, conflicting emotions that left her feeling not only very vulnerable, but also exhausted.

She was able to access confidential counseling support via her workplace and this proved helpful to begin with, as she was relieved to have someone to talk to about her feelings. However, she discontinued the counseling after a while as she felt the counselor did not appreciate her particular circumstances. In her culture it was considered shameful for a woman to bring up children without a husband at her side. Consequently, she felt very guilty and ashamed that she was now a single parent. But, when she spoke to the counselor about her feelings of guilt, about how she should have been a better wife and then perhaps he wouldn't have left, she was simply given reassurances that feeling guilty is a "normal part of grieving" and she was advised to simply ignore these feelings as they would subside over time. Tami felt that the counselor just did not understand her circumstances, and the fact that he was a man just added to her sense of guilt and shame. She started to become depressed and would often withdraw into a world of her own. Although she loved her children very much and would not dream of harming them, she was beginning to neglect them because she was so cut off from their needs. The more aware she became of this, the more guilty and ashamed she felt and the more depressed she became. She had entered a vicious circle. The counselor's lack of awareness of Tami's cultural background and its profound effects on how she viewed and managed her current situation had contributed significantly to her difficulties, rather than helped to relieve them.

This scenario, and potentially so many more examples that are not too difficult to find, highlight the importance of taking account of the social context and not relying on an atomistic view that rests upon isolating the individual from their social reality.

Making Sense of the Social Context

A common misunderstanding of the sociological emphasis on the social context is that it is so often misperceived as a deterministic approach—that is, one that denies human agency and presents individuals as simply powerless puppets, with their strings being pulled by social forces. This is a fundamental misunderstanding of sociological thinking. The idea that individuals are simply passive recipients of social influences does not reflect the complexity of social thought. A more accurate portrayal would involve appreciating that there is a complex interplay between individual actions and wider social forces (a "dialectic," to use the technical term)—the two sets of factors interact and influence one another.

An important concept here is "reductionism." This refers to the unhelpful tendency to reduce complex, multi-level phenomena to simple, single-level phenomena (Sibeon, 2004). Reducing complex psychosocial matters to simple psychological ones without accounting for the wider social picture is, as we have already noted, known as atomism. However, going to the other extreme of recognizing social influences, but denying or neglecting human agency, is also a significant methodological mistake. Neither version of reductionism is helpful or theoretically sound. A theoretical framework that I have introduced in my earlier work (Thompson, 2016, 2018a, 2018b) that can help to clarify the complex interrelationships is that of PCS analysis (with PCS standing for personal, cultural and structural). It is based on the idea that individual persons (P) are part of wider frameworks of meaning or cultures (C) that have a profound and far-reaching effect on us as individuals—for example, in relation to identity development, our sense of belonging, and, in a number of ways, our sense of spiritual connectedness. If we try to understand individuals without considering their cultural context, then once again we are not seeing the full picture. But, cultural contexts do not operate in a vacuum, either. These are embedded within a wider framework of social structures (S) built around such social divisions as class, race/ethnicity, gender, age, and so on.

Consider the following:

- As an individual (P), much of my life experience has been shaped by the cultural context I was brought up in and the cultural context I now live in (C) in terms of shared meanings, taken-for-granted assumptions, unwritten rules and worldviews. For example, my views about gender will no doubt reflect the patriarchal culture I was brought up in.
- That cultural context (C) will reflect the wider structures of society. Consequently, the patriarchal culture I was brought up in does not exist by coincidence; it is a reflection of the patriarchal relations of dominance and subordination at the structural level (S).

I have used gender as an example here, but the same logic can apply to ethnicity, age, language group, sexuality and so on (social divisions).

PCS analysis helps us to understand that there are powerful social forces that act upon us. However, PCS analysis is not deterministic; it is dialectical—that is, it recognizes that the flow of influence is two way. The structural level of power relations shapes the cultural level of shared meanings, which in turn influence each of us as individuals. However, it works the other way, too. What we do (individually and/or collectively) contributes to the cultural level (which is why cultures, although largely stable, do change over time). Cultures do not exist in their own right in any absolute sense—they have to be constantly recreated through our actions and interactions. They are both an influence on our actions and the culmination of those actions. Similarly, structural power relations do not exist in their own right in an absolute way; they are constantly being recreated by cultural formations that support them. For example, it would be difficult for a patriarchal set of structures to be sustained if there were no cultural forces maintaining and reinforcing them.

What we have, then, is a complex set of interactions in both directions that PCS analysis: (1) enables us to understand; and (2) act upon. That is, by being aware of the complex dynamics PCS analysis highlights, we are in a better position to influence those dynamics in a positive direction.

PCS Analysis and Grief

A key message of this book is that we need to move away from the stereotype of grief as a reaction to death and understand it more fully and holistically as a reaction to any major loss. That stereotype, of course, exists at the cultural level—it is part of the shared meanings that are passed from one generation to the next through socialization and disseminated through society by the mass media, the education system and other such social institutions. This is just one example of how PCS analysis can offer a basis for understanding grief in its wider context—by seeing its narrow conceptualization as a reaction to death as a *stereotype*, a feature of the cultural context. For example, the portrayal of grief in response to a death often features strongly in cinema, television dramas, novels, plays, newspaper reporting and so on, whereas grief as a reaction to other significant losses will generally feature far less prominently, and—importantly—where it does feature, it is far less likely to be acknowledged explicitly as *grief* (rather than as just general sadness, disappointment or whatever).

Disenfranchised Grief and Non-Death Losses

The concept of disenfranchised grief is an important one in general terms, as a grief that is not acknowledged or socially sanctioned is likely to be more difficult to bear, as the important work of Doka and his colleagues has demonstrated (Doka, 2002). However, what has received far less attention is the recognition that non-death-related losses in particular can be understood as disenfranchised—the strong tendency to equate loss with bereavement and thereby artificially restrict grief to situations involving death serves to distract attention from the often major role of grief in our lives in relation to losses that have no connection with death (Thompson & Doka, 2017).

One of the implications of this is that people grieving losses that are not associated with death may not realize that they are grieving. They will no doubt be aware that they are distressed and in other ways operating outside of their comfort zone, but they may not appreciate why they feel that way—thereby adding to the confusion and the sense of vulnerability and insecurity. It could also mean that they do not seek support, unlike situations involving death-related losses where there will be cultural expectations that dictate not only that it is acceptable to seek emotional and practical support, but also that it is likely to be offered as a matter of course. The disenfranchisement of losses that are not death related will mean that it is far less likely that support will be offered and, significantly, less likely that it will be sought. It should also be noted, from a sociological point of view, that the very notion of disenfranchised grief is social in origin. While it will clearly have psychological consequences for the individual(s) concerned, its roots are in cultural expectations and social processes—clearly sociological phenomena, thereby providing a further illustration of the need to incorporate sociological as well as psychological factors. Further in-depth discussion of disenfranchised grief and non-death losses will be offered by Kenneth J. Doka in this section.

Conclusion

Grief is our response to death.
   It is an individual matter rooted in human psychology.
   These two statements are widely accepted, at least implicitly. However, their wide acceptance does not mean that they are true. In fact, as we have seen, both of these statements are not only untrue, but also dangerously misleading. Let us, by way of conclusion, consider each of these statements in turn. In terms of the first statement, a more accurate and less misleading statement would be that grief is our response to any major loss in our lives. That will, of course, involve significant deaths, but if we limit our understanding of grief primarily or exclusively to death-related losses, we are contributing to disenfranchising some highly significant losses in people's lives. We are also, in the process, contributing at a philosophical level to an understanding of human experience that does not do justice to the highly significant role of loss, change, transition, crisis, growth and resilience in our lives.

In terms of the second statement, the psychological factors are no doubt important, often of crucial importance. But again, we are engaging in distortion and oversimplification if we limit our understanding of grief to a psychological phenomenon, rather than see it in more holistic terms as a phenomenon with psychological, biological, sociological and spiritual dimensions (Thompson, 2012). In addition, a narrow individualistic perspective contributes, at a philosophical level, to a far-from-adequate understanding of human experience by failing to recognize the other dimensions of human existence and the complex ways in which they interact. It is therefore essential to recognize that grief is a much broader concept than is generally realized and there are more dimensions to it than the psychological, important though those psychological factors generally are.

Key Terms

Atomistic View: Assumes that each individual in a society operates as an independent, self-sufficient unit. The individual is described as the "atom" of society and is therefore the only object of concern for analysis. This view is in direct opposition to the holistic view.

Holistic View: Assumes that each individual is a complex member of a societal system, incorporating the individual into social contexts and their environmental surroundings. The individual is considered a component of society who has complex integrations with the world in which the individual exists within. This view is in direct opposition to the atomistic view.

PCS Analysis: A framework that examines the personal, cultural, and structural (PCS) factors of human experience. This analysis identifies how individual persons exist within meaningful and specific social cultural frameworks, and how these frameworks are further embedded within a social structure consisting of other human beings and differing factors of social class.

Reductionism: The attempt of simplifying and/or minimizing phenomena. This is a flawed methodology and ideology when attempting to explore the complex and multidimensional nature of human beings.

Questions for Reflection

1. How does understanding the social context and social reality of individuals increase comprehension surrounding the grieving process?
2. Reflect upon the case study of Tami in this chapter. What other social factors could be explored to better understand Tami's grief? What strategies would you utilize to identify Tami's social context, and to provide social validation?
3. The author posits that understanding the psychological experience of grief for the individual is essential for grief support, and that it is crucial to understand grief in more "holistic terms." What do you think the author means by these two statements? What does a holistic perspective of non-death loss mean for you, and how can this have value in providing grief support?

References

Doka, K. J. (Ed.). (2002). *Disenfranchised grief: New directions, challenges, and strategies for practice*. Champaign, IL: Research Press.
Doka, K. J., & Martin, T. L. (2010). *Grieving beyond gender: Understanding the ways men and women mourn*. New York: Routledge.
Howarth, G., & Jupp, P. (Eds.). (1996). *Contemporary issues in the sociology of death, dying and disposal*. Basingstoke, UK: Palgrave Macmillan.
Rosenblatt, P. C. (2016). Cultural competence and humility. In D. L. Harris & T. C. Bordere (Eds.), *Handbook of social justice in loss and grief: Exploring equity, diversity and inclusion* (pp. 67–74). New York: Routledge.
Sibeon, R. (2004). *Rethinking social theory*. Thousand Oaks: Sage.
Thompson, N. (2012). *Grief and its challenges*. Basingstoke, UK: Palgrave Macmillan.
Thompson, N. (2016). *Anti-discriminatory practice: Equality, diversity and social justice* (6th ed.). London: Palgrave Macmillan.
Thompson, N. (2018a). *Applied sociology*. New York: Routledge.
Thompson, N. (2018b). *Promoting equality: Working with diversity and difference* (4th ed.). London: Palgrave Macmillan.
Thompson, N., Allan, J., Carverhill, P. A., Cox, G. R., Davies, B., Doka, K., . . . Wittkowski, J. (2016). The case for a sociology of dying, death, and bereavement. *Death Studies, 40*(3), 172–181.
Thompson, N., & Cox, G. (Eds.). (2017). *Handbook of the sociology of death, grief, and bereavement*. New York: Routledge.
Thompson, N., & Doka, K. J. (2017). Disenfranchised grief. In N Thompson & G. Cox (Eds.), *Handbook of the sociology of death, grief, and bereavement* (pp. 177–190). New York: Routledge.

CHAPTER 2

Disenfranchised Grief and Non-Death Losses[1]

Kenneth J. Doka

Introduction: The Biography of a Concept

It was slightly over a century ago that Freud (1917) published his seminal essay on *Mourning and Melancholia* that may very well be considered one of the very beginnings of the scientific study of grief. Interestingly, Freud's case that began this essay was not a bereaved parent, a grieving child, or a widowed spouse. Rather, it was a bride abandoned at the altar. Perhaps the point was to reaffirm that grief is about loss—however it is experienced—rather than simply a response to death.

Every concept has a biography or a history of how that concept was born, developed, and matured. The concept of *disenfranchised grief* began in a graduate seminar on aging that I was teaching early in the 1980s. As we were exploring widowhood in later life, one of my students, a middle-aged woman, remarked: "If you think widows have it rough, you ought to see what happens when your ex-spouse dies." I was intrigued by her comment and I asked her if she would share her experiences. She did. She had been divorced. Two years after her divorce, her ex-spouse died of cancer. The divorce had been angry and painful. She had caught him having an affair with a neighbor whom she viewed as a friend. She spoke of the awkward experiences in visiting her ex-husband at the hospital or attending his subsequent funeral. The student found little support as she struggled with her ambivalence and grief in the aftermath of that death. They had been divorced, they surmised; why would she feel grief? Some friends even ventured that it was a sweet revenge. She noted that she had to take vacation days to attend the funeral. Her workplace bereavement policies offered leave for present spouses—not past ones.

Beyond the compelling nature of the student's story, her narrative resonated for another reason. I had been asked to present a paper at a Foundation of Thanatology Conference in New York on "Unsanctioned and Unrecognized Grief." This seemed like an interesting and appropriate topic. As I researched the loss of an ex-spouse, one thing surprised me. Most of the ex-spouses I interviewed compared the grief of the death of their ex-spouse with their grief over the divorce. Yet in the days before Google Scholar, if a researcher cross-listed "divorce" and "grief" in an academic index, nothing would emerge. At best one might be redirected to the "Psychological Sequelae of Grief."

I became intrigued by the notion that individuals often experienced losses that are not recognized or acknowledged by others. As I presented on the topic, I realized there that I had touched on, in these very different situations of loss, a common chord. Subsequently in 1985, I presented a conceptual paper on what I now called *disenfranchised grief*. In that paper (Doka, 1985a), I defined *disenfranchised grief* as the grief that results when a person experiences a significant loss where the resultant grief is not openly acknowledged, socially validated, or publicly mourned. In short, though the individual is experiencing a grief reaction, there is no social recognition that the person has a right to grieve or a claim for social sympathy or support. These losses included certain sorts of deaths, such as the death of a lover or an ex-spouse, but they also encompassed multiple types of non-death losses.

The Disenfranchisement of Grief

The concept of disenfranchised grief integrates psychological, biological, and sociological perspectives on grief and loss. Since the middle of the 20th century, there has been considerable research about the psychological and biological or physiological responses to loss (see, i.e., Bowlby, 1980; Lindemann, 1944; Parkes & Weiss, 1983). This research has demonstrated the myriad affective, physical, cognitive, behavioral, and spiritual ways grief is manifested. Yet, the social aspect of grief often is neglected. Though the individual grieves, others do not acknowledge that the individual has a right to grieve. Such persons are not offered the "rights" or the "grieving role" such as a claim to social sympathy and support, or such compensations as time off from work or diminishment of social responsibilities.

In order to understand the social aspect of grief, it is important to remember that every society has norms that govern not only behavior, but also affect and cognition as well. Hochschild (1979), for example, speaks of "feeling rules" or norms that govern what individuals are supposed to feel in a given situation. Statements such as "I know I should not feel guilty" or "I have every right to feel angry" bear testimony to the reality of these feeling rules. These statements justify feelings on the basis of shared understandings or what feelings are to be expected in a given social context. Similarly, there are "thinking rules" as well, that govern how one is supposed to think in a given situation. Again, statements such as "how can you think like that?" imply that an individual's cognitions are outside a social range of acceptability or understanding of logic and reason. In addition, there are "spiritual rules." These rules tell us what to believe. For example, in some religions one might be expected to believe that expressions of grief are inappropriate, as the deceased has entered a wonderful afterlife. Perhaps it is better to think of these as "internal rules" that govern all internal processes such as cognition, belief, and affect just as external rules or norms regulate behavior.

As part of these rules, every society has norms that frame grieving. These internal norms govern what losses one grieves, how one grieves them, who legitimately can grieve the loss, and how and to whom others respond with sympathy and support. These norms exist not only as folkways, or informally expected behaviors, but also as "laws," meaning that these norms may carry sanctions. For example, these norms are evidenced in company policies that extend bereavement leave to certain individuals as well as regulations and laws that define what family member or other person has control of the deceased's body or funeral rituals. In the United States and many other Western societies, these grieving rules emphasize that family members have a right to grieve the deaths of other family members. When a family member dies, one is allowed and expected to grieve, often in a specified way. Family members then are accorded rights such as time off from work, diminished social responsibilities, and social support.

Yet individuals experience a range of losses that are not death related. Divorce or the relinquishment of a child in adoption or foster care are examples of non-death related loss that can arouse grief. Even possessions can take on great significance and meaning in our lives. One of the most profound cases of grief I ever encountered was a woman who lost 400 years of Christmas ornaments, a family heirloom, in the Red River Floods in the mid-1990s. In such situations, the personal experience of grief is discordant with the society's grieving rules. The person experiences a loss, but others do not recognize that grief. Their losses may fall outside of a society's grieving rules and may be disenfranchised to a degree. Yet, the central question remains—why is grief disenfranchised? Why are only deaths of family members accorded social recognition and support? There are probably a number of reasons for that. First and foremost, in most Western societies, the family is the primary unit of social organization. Hence, kin ties have clear acknowledgment in norms and laws. While most individuals actually live their lives in "intimate networks," or associations that include both kin and non-kin, only kin have legal standing.

Another principle of contemporary Western societies has been rationality. That means that beyond the family, organizations such as businesses attempt to organize work policies in fair, functional, and rational ways. The grieving rules reflect that. As Kamerman (1993) observes, to extend grieving roles to non-death situations or to non-kin, would create organizational burdens. Organizations would be forced to define "levels of friendship" or "types of loss." They might be required to broaden the concept of bereavement leave, at considerable cost. Acknowledging the death of kin alone makes organizational sense. It recognizes the grief of kin when a family member dies, at least symbolically. Limiting the acknowledgment of loss to family members avoids confusion and potential abuse, affirming a single rational standard. This keeps organizations from having to assess on an individual standpoint, whether this loss or relationship is entitled to recognition. These policies then serve to reflect and project societal recognition and support, again reaffirming and sanctioning the familial relationships. They also point to another significant factor—the relationship of grieving rules to ritual. As an inter-psychic process, mourning refers to the ways that grief is socially acknowledged; for example, the accepted behaviors such as mourning dress that signify that an individual has experienced a loss. Rituals that connote loss are critical to mourning. These rituals allow structure and support to the expression of grief. For example, Durkheim claims that:

> Mourning is not a natural movement of private feelings; it is a duty imposed by the group. One weeps, not simply because he is sad, but because he is forced to weep.
>
> (1915, p. 443)

Durkheim, in justifying the critical importance of social norms, exaggerates. Yet, he does contribute a central point—social expectations frame the experience of grief.

Pine (1989) stresses the critical role that rituals have in enfranchising grief. The funeral becomes the vehicle by which grief is acknowledged and sanctioned, and where support is extended. For example, the primacy of a family at the funeral reaffirms that these survivors have experienced a loss, and that their subsequent grief needs sanction, acknowledgment, and support. The rite of the funeral publicly testifies to and affirms the right to grieve.

The discussion so far has emphasized the sociological aspects of disenfranchised grief. Yet, as Kauffman (2002) stresses, there is an intrapsychic dimension to disenfranchised grief as well. These societal grieving rules are internalized. The rules become standards by which we assess and judge the legitimacy of our own grief reactions. Thus, disenfranchisement is not only imposed by the society. It can be self-initiated. Here, shame and guilt over one's own attachments and subsequent grief may define a particular grief reaction as inappropriate or unworthy. As a result, the griever disenfranchises his or her own reactions to the loss.

Neimeyer and Jordan (2002) contribute a term that integrates the societal and intrapsychic dimensions of disenfranchised grief while offering a clinically important concept for assessing and treating this grief. To Neimeyer and Jordan (2002), the essential issue in disenfranchised grief is *empathic failure*. Empathic failure is defined as "the failure of one part of the system to understand the meaning and experience of another" (Neimeyer & Jordan, 2002, p. 96). Here, there is a failure to understand any given individual's personal experience or meaning construct of a particular loss and therefore to render sufficient sympathy and support. This failure can take place at a very basic level—the very interface between self-experience and self-interpretation. This would refer to Kauffman's (2002) intrapsychic dimension of disenfranchised grief. Neimeyer and Jordan (2002) offer here the example of a mother of a child with significant disabilities that struggles with the intense ambivalent emotions that frame her grief reaction to her son's death. Empathic failure can occur at the level of family and intimate network as those in the immediate surroundings fail to acknowledge and support another's grief. It can take place within the larger community where there is little recognition or validation of support. It can even involve a sense of transcendent reality where an individual mourner feels alienated from one's own sense of spirituality or divinity as the mourner copes with loss. The role of counselors, then, is to analyze and counter this empathic failure.

The sources and reasons for disenfranchised grief then are diverse and multifaceted. Yet, the results are the same—an individual experiences a loss that is not socially sanctioned, publicly acknowledged, or openly mourned. This particularly becomes an issue in mourning non-death losses. Here, there is often little validation of ensuing grief.

Typologies of Disenfranchised Grief

In earlier works on disenfranchised grief (Doka, 1989, 2002a), I proposed five categories of disenfranchised grief. Two are particularly relevant in understanding non-death losses.

The Relationship Is Not Recognized

As stated earlier, in our society most attention is placed on kin-based relationships and roles. Grief may be disenfranchised in those situations in which the relationship between the bereaved and deceased is not based on recognizable kin ties. Here, the closeness of other non-kin relationships may simply not be understood or appreciated. The attachments to lovers, friends, neighbors, foster parents, colleagues, in-laws, stepparents and stepchildren, caregivers, counselors, co-workers, and roommates (for example, in nursing homes) may be long-lasting and intensely interactive, but even though these relationships are recognized, mourners may not have full opportunity to publicly grieve a loss. At most, they might be expected to support and assist family members an almost familial way. Yet, despite such strong metaphors of family, the grief of staff members when a resident died was often disenfranchised. Even relationships that existed primarily in the past may experience grief. Ex-spouses, past lovers, or former friends may have limited contact, or they may even engage in interaction in the present. Yet the death of that significant other can still cause a grief reaction because it brings finality to that earlier loss, ending any remaining contact or fantasy of reconciliation or re-involvement.

The Loss Is Not Acknowledged

Then there are cases in which the loss itself is not socially validated. Here is where non-death losses can predominate. Thanatologists have long recognized that significant losses can occur even when the object of the loss remains physically alive. Sudnow (1967) for example, discusses "social death," in which the person is alive but is treated as if dead. Examples may include those who are institutionalized or comatose. Similarly, "psychological death" has been defined as conditions in which the person lacks a consciousness of existence (Kalish, 1966), such as someone who is "brain dead." One can also speak of "psychosocial death," in which the persona of someone has changed so significantly, through mental illness, organic brain syndromes, or even significant personal transformation (such as through addiction, conversion, Alzheimer's disease and related dementias, and so forth), that significant others perceive the person as s/he previously existed as dead (Doka,

1985b). In all of these cases, spouses and others may experience a profound sense of loss, but that loss cannot be publicly acknowledged for the person is still biologically alive.

Rando (2000), in her exemplary work on anticipatory mourning, explores the range of losses that persons experience and mourn in life-threatening illness. Rando's point is that individuals do not simply mourn the fact that they, or someone they love, have a terminal disease and will one day die. While that is part of their grief, they mourn as well, all the secondary losses experienced along the way, such as changes in lifestyle of other relationships, may also be mourned.

In the years since this concept of disenfranchised grief was proffered, this category seems to have generated the most research. Studies have applied the concept of disenfranchised grief to the reactions of the loss of romantic relationships in adolescence (Kaczmarek & Backlund, 1991) and young adults (Robak & Weitzman, 1995); grief responses to reproductive inabilities (Gray & Lassance, 2003) and perinatal losses (Hazen, 2003); and reactions to the experiences of incest (Dwyer & Miller, 1996), disability (Doka, 2002a), job loss (Leana & Feldman, 1992), or growing up in a dysfunctional family (Zupanick, 1994). In addition, the concept has been applied to the grief process of cultural re-entry (Lester, 2001). It has even been utilized to understand the effects of the Great Irish Hunger (1846–1852) as a cultural grief reaction experienced by the descendants of that Irish Diaspora (Peck, 2000). Berra et al. (1993) documented that the loss of a religious identity, due to changes in belief, created a sense of grief in many respondents.

Harris (2011), in an earlier edition, widely expanded this work, noting the very significant losses experienced in life. These can include a sense of loss of safety and security, loss of an assumptive world, and relational losses due to factors other than death, such as divorce, alienation, or relinquishing a child to foster care or adoption. Moreover, Harris also explored losses of identity including factors such as migration, functionality, employment, or infertility. In addition, one could also note development losses that are experienced as individuals age. For example, at each stage of life, persons may have to give up important roles, significant activities, dreams, ideals, or self-images associated with earlier phases in the life cycle.

The Griever Is Excluded

There are situations in which the characteristics of the bereaved in effect disenfranchise their grief. Here, the person is not socially defined as capable of grief; therefore, there is little or no social recognition of his or her sense of loss or need to mourn. Despite evidence to the contrary, others typically perceive persons with dementia, persons with intellectual disabilities, and very young children as having little comprehension of, or reaction to the death of a significant other. These groups are often then excluded from discussions and rituals (Raphael, 1983). Naturally, their experience of both death and non-death related losses are both likely to be disenfranchised.

Circumstances of the Death/Loss

In the 1989 volume, it was suggested that certain circumstances surrounding the death might disenfranchise grief. The nature of the death may constrain the solicitation of the bereaved for support as well as limit the support extended by others. For example, many survivors of a suicide loss often feel a sense of stigma, believing that others may negatively judge the family because of the suicide. Similarly, the stigma of AIDS may lead survivors of an AIDS-related loss to be circumspect in sharing the loss with other (see Doka, 1993). Here, survivors may fear the responses of others, including isolation, judgment, or a morbid curiosity.

Rando (1993) has further developed this idea, asserting that deaths that provoke anxiety (such as suicide, mutilating loss, the death of a child, etc.) or embarrassment (i.e., death from autoerotic asphyxiation, homicides, especially those that incur media notoriety or involve other family members, etc.) are likely to be disenfranchised. Other circumstances that minimize support may be where support is withheld punitively (for example, when an individual is executed) or where the deceased is otherwise devalued (i.e., the death of an alcoholic, etc.).

The Ways an Individual Grieves

The way an individual grieves both death and non-death losses also can contribute to disenfranchisement. Martin and Doka (1999) suggested that there are different styles of grieving. Some individuals grieve in a more intuitive way—experiencing and expressing grief as deep feeling. Those who are more instrumental experience and express grief reactions in a way that is more physical, cognitive, or behavioral. The counseling community tends to disenfranchise instrumental grievers since counselors often place high value on affective response (see Martin & Doka, 1999; Sue & Sue, 1999). Yet, the larger community disenfranchises instrumental grievers early in the grieving process when affective displays are expected, and intuitive grievers later in the grieving process where affective responses are considered less appropriate (Martin & Doka, 1999). Certain cultural modes of expressing grief such as stoicism or wailing may fall beyond the grieving rules of a given society, and thus be disenfranchising (Doka & Davidson, 1998).

Disenfranchised Grief as a Complicating Factor

Disenfranchised grief has been identified as a complicating factor in bereavement (see Rando, 1993). The problem of disenfranchised grief can be expressed in a paradox. The very nature of disenfranchised grief creates additional problems for grief, while removing or minimizing sources of support. The disenfranchisement of grief may exacerbate the problem of bereavement in a number of ways, especially in non-death losses. Here, despite the insights of Freud, non-death losses are generally discounted as unlikely to engender a grief response. Often there is no recognized role or ritual in which mourners can assert the right to mourn and thus receive support. Grief may have to remain private. Though they may have experienced an intense loss, they may not be given time off from work, have the opportunity to verbalize the loss, or receive the expressions of sympathy and support characteristic in a death. Even traditional sources of solace, such as religion, are unavailable to those where certain losses such as divorce may be sanctioned or condemned within that faith tradition.

Counseling Disenfranchised Grievers

These complications often experienced by the person disenfranchised in his or her grief reinforce Neimeyer and Jordan's (2002) concept of empathic failure. Their approach to counseling persons experiencing disenfranchised grief is to begin by assessing this empathic failure. Among the questions they suggest therapists consider are queries that attempt to assess where empathic disconnection occurs. How much does an individual contribute to his or her own disenfranchisement? Does an individual isolate him- or herself or shroud a loss in secrecy or deception, thereby minimizing support? Do the norms and values of their family or community censure certain behaviors or relationships limiting support? Does an individual's spirituality create a sense of spiritual alienation? Does disenfranchisement seem to occur at any particular time in the mourning process? Is there a sense of support early in the grieving process that dissipates over time? Neimeyer and Jordan (2002) emphasize that at least clinically disenfranchised grief should be viewed as a lens that helps interpret the individual's experience that the loss is not validated by others, rather than a rigid typology of loss.

Once an assessment is made, empathic failure can be countered. Sometimes the very naming of the grief as disenfranchised has power—breaking the silence around the loss and offering a sense of legitimacy (Kuhn, 2002). As Neimeyer and Jordan (2002) stress that disenfranchised grief is grief—the techniques that one would use in counseling persons who are grieving can be applied here. There is evidence that support groups are a useful strategy (Pesek, 2002). Since rituals are often unavailable or limited in meaning to persons experiencing disenfranchised grief, Doka (2002b) has suggested the value of employing therapeutic rituals within the counseling process. The very act of counseling is valued since it offers support and validation that might not be provided elsewhere.

Implications and Conclusion

It is likely that bereavement counselors will have increased exposure to cases of disenfranchised grief—especially in non-death losses. In fact, the very nature of non-death losses, disenfranchised grief, and the unavailability of informal support make it likely that those who experience such losses will seek formal supports. Death education also needs to consider the many kinds of relationships and subsequent losses that people can experience.

Many years ago, I spoke at a conference about disenfranchised grief. After the presentation, I met an old childhood friend, now a clinician. He had moved in his early adolescence and we had no contact since that point. He jokingly reminded me of an incident in which his baseball glove had been stolen. He remembered that I had stayed and sympathized with him over his loss. "I was," he claimed, "your first case of disenfranchised grief."

As the myriad circumstances of loss become more recognized, there is a pressing need for research that really describes the particular and unique responses to different types of losses; compares reactions, outcomes, and problems associated with these losses; assesses possible interventions; and describes the critical variables affecting each loss. Yet one clear benefit of the concept of disenfranchised grief is that it offers a conceptual framework that allows for both acknowledging and treating the wide range of non-death losses that generate grief.

Key Terms

Disenfranchised Grief: Refers to situations in which the loss is not recognized as valid, the griever is not recognized as a valid person to mourn a loss, the grief response of the individual falls outside of social norms, or in which the loss itself has a social stigma attached to it.

Empathic Failure: The failure to comprehend, acknowledge, support, or provide empathy to another individual's meaning construct or personal loss experience.

Rituals: Rituals that incorporate loss are integral to both the personal and social aspects of the grieving process and can allow for acknowledgment, structure, and support for an individual's expression of grief. Rituals can involve an action that is initiated on the part of the bereaved individual to give a symbolic expression to certain feelings or thoughts.

Social Norms: Rules and expectations about how members of a certain society should behave, think, and believe, and identification of what is considered acceptable behavior within a social group.

Questions for Reflection

1. Non-death loss and grief is unique to the individual, and yet there is a clear social context that influences grief. Provide specific examples of social influences that could hinder an individual's grief experience. Additionally, provide examples of how grief might be "enfranchised."
2. Does your family, culture, or religious/spiritual background suggest rituals to facilitate the grieving process? Discuss how these rituals might help or hinder the grieving process. What recommendations would you have for those who have experienced disenfranchised grief, and wish to construct their own rituals?
3. Have you ever disenfranchised your own experience of loss? Explore the personal and societal dimensions of why and/or how this happened.
4. One of the few certainties in life appears to be loss. Why do you think grief is so marginalized on both the personal and societal levels? How can individuals

learn to acknowledge loss, cultivate acceptance towards grief, and support others who are grieving to minimize disenfranchisement?

Note

1. This paper draws from the author's earlier work on disenfranchised grief (see Doka 1985a, 1985b, 1986, 1987, 1989, 2002a).

References

Berra, D. M., Carlson, E., Maize, M., Murphy, W., O'Neal, B., Sarver, R., & Zinner, E. S. (1993). The dark night of the spirit: Grief following a loss in religious identity. In K. J. Doka & J. Morgan (Eds.), *Death and spirituality*. Amityville, NY: Baywood Publishing Co.

Bowlby, J. (1980). *Attachment and loss: Sadness and depression*, Vol. 3. New York: Basic Books.

Doka, K. J. (1985a, April 25). *Disenfranchised grief*. Paper presented to a Symposium on Death Education of the Foundation of Thanatology, New York.

Doka, K. J. (1985b, March). *Crypto-death and real grief*. Paper presented to a symposium of the Foundation of Thanatology, New York.

Doka, K. J. (1986). Loss upon loss: Death after divorce. *Death Studies, 10*, 441–449.

Doka, K. J. (1987). Silent sorrow: Grief and the loss of significant others. *Death Studies, 11*, 455–469.

Doka, K. J. (Ed.) (1989). *Disenfranchised grief: Recognizing hidden sorrow*. Lexington, MA: Lexington Press.

Doka, K. J. (1993). The spiritual needs of the dying. In J. D. Morgan and K. Doka (Eds.), *Death and spirituality* (143–150). New York: Baywood.

Doka, K. J. (Ed.) (2002a). *Disenfranchised grief: New directions, challenges and strategies for practice*. Champaign, IL: Research Press.

Doka, K. J. (2002b). The role of ritual in the treatment of disenfranchised grief. In K. J. Doka (Ed.), *Disenfranchised grief: New directions, challenges and strategies for practice*. Champaign, IL: Research Press.

Doka, K. J., & Davidson, J. (1998). *Living with grief: Who we are, and how we grieve*. Washington, DC: The Hospice Foundation of America.

Durkheim, E. (1915). *The elementary forms of religious life*. New York: Free Press.

Dwyer, J., & Miller, R. (1996). Disenfranchised grief after incest: The experience of victims/daughters/mothers/wives. *Australian and New Zealand Journal of Family Therapy, 17*, 137–146.

Freud, S. (1917). Mourning and melancholia. In J. Stacey (Ed. & Trans.). *The standard edition of the complete psychological works of Sigmund Freud* (Vol. 14, 1957). London: Hogarth.

Gray, K., & Lassance, A. (2003). *Grieving reproductive loss: The healing process*. Amityville, NY: Baywood Publishing Co.

Harris, D. L. (Ed.). (2011). *Counting our losses: Reflecting on change, loss, and transition in everyday life*. New York: Routledge.

Hazen, M. (2003). Societal and workplace responses to perinatal loss: Disenfranchised grief or healing connections. *Human Relations, 56*, 147–168.

Hochschild, A. R. (1979). Emotion work, feeling rules and social support. *American Journal of Sociology, 85*, 551–573.

Kaczmarek, M., & Backlund, B. (1991). Disenfranchised grief: The loss of an adolescent romantic relationship. *Adolescence, 26*, 253–259.

Kalish, R. (1966). A continuum of subjectively perceived death. *The Gerontologist, 6*, 73–76.

Kamerman, J. (1993). Latent function of enfranchising the disenfranchised griever. *Death Studies, 17*, 281–287.

Kauffman, J. (2002). The psychology of disenfranchised grief: Liberation, shame and self-disenfranchisement. In K. J. Doka (Ed.), *Disenfranchised grief: New directions, challenges and strategies for practice*. Champaign, IL: Research Press.

Kuhn, D. (2002). A pastoral counselor look at silence as a factor in disenfranchised grief. In K. J. Doka (Ed.), *Disenfranchised grief: New directions, challenges and strategies for practice*. Champaign, IL: Research Press.

Leana, C., & Feldman, D. (1992). *Coping with job loss: How individuals, organizations and communities respond to layoffs*. Lexington, MA: Lexington Press.

Lester, J. (2001). Strangers in their own land: Culture loss, disenfranchised grief, and re-entry adjustment. *Dissertation Abstracts International: Section B: The Sciences and Engineering, 61*(9-B), 4992.

Lindemann, E. (1944). Symptomatology and management of acute grief. *American Journal of Psychiatry, 101*, 141–149.

Martin, T., & Doka, K. (1999). *Men don't cry, women do: Transcending gender stereotypes of grief*. Philadelphia: Brunner Mazel.

Neimeyer, R., & Jordan, J. (2002). Disenfranchisement as empathic failure: Grief therapy and the co-construction of meaning. In K. J. Doka (Ed.), *Disenfranchised grief: New directions, challenges and strategies for practice*. Champaign, IL: Research Press.

Parkes, C. M., & Weiss, R. (1983). *Recovery from bereavement*. New York: Basic Books.

Peck, D. (2000). Silent hunger: The psychological impact of the great Irish hunger: An Gorta Mor (1845–1852). *Dissertation Abstracts International: Section B: The Sciences and Engineering, 61*(5-B), 2819.

Pesek, E. (2002). The role of support groups in disenfranchised grief. In K. J. Doka (Ed.), *Disenfranchised grief: New directions, challenges and strategies for practice*. Champaign, IL: Research Press.

Pine, V. (1989). Death, loss and disenfranchised grief. In K. J. Doka (Ed.), *Disenfranchised grief: Recognizing hidden sorrow*. Lexington, MA: Lexington Books.

Rando, T. A. (1993). *Treatment of complicated mourning*. Champaign IL: Research Press.

Rando, T. A. (2000). *Clinical dimensions of anticipatory mourning*. Campaign, IL: Research Press.

Raphael, B. (1983). *The anatomy of bereavement*. New York: Basic Books.

Robak, R., & Weitzman, S. (1995). Grieving the loss of romantic relationships in young adults: An empirical study of disenfranchised grief. *Omega: The Journal of Death and Dying, 30*, 269–281.

Sudnow, D. (1967). *Passing on: The social organization of dying*. Englewood Cliffs, NJ: Prentice-Hall.

Sue, D. W., & Sue, D. (1999). *Counseling the culturally different* (3rd ed.). New York: Wiley.

Zupanick, C. (1994). Adult children of dysfunctional families: Treatment from a disenfranchised grief perspective. *Death Studies, 18*, 183–195.

CHAPTER 3

Social Death
Michael Brennan

Introduction

Is it possible to be dead while still alive? Conversely, is it possible to be alive while being dead? So asks David Canter (2017) in the foreword to Jana Králová and Tony Walter's recent examination of the concept of social death. The answers to these questions, while affirmative in both instances, depends not only upon the social context within which human interaction takes place, but also—as Neil Thompson has illustrated in the opening to this section of the book—upon culture and the "social divisions" that serve to structure human life. In what follows, therefore, I examine the social context and bases by which social death operates, the application of the concept to a variety of non-death losses across a number of disciplines, and conclude by providing some practical suggestions for limiting the possibility that someone may be perceived as socially dead even before biological death has occurred. I begin first, however, by unpacking the very notion of social death.

What Is Social Death?

Simply put, social death refers to the social isolation, exclusion, and abandonment of particular individuals by the rest of society. So much so that while still functioning physiologically, the individual may be completely overlooked and treated as a "non-person" (Goffman, 1959, 1961, 1963); in effect, *as if they were already dead*. Much of the discussion surrounding social death in modern Western societies has been largely confined to the medical-thanatological sphere (Leoman, 2001; Sweeting & Gilhooly, 1997), where it has been used to describe the treatment by medical staff of often aged and "hopelessly comatose" (Glaser & Strauss, 1965, p. 108) hospital patients as "merely a body" (Small, 1997, p. 217). In this sense, it is clear to see how it is possible to be dead while still alive. Thus, as Clive Seale (1998) explains:

> The material end of the body is only roughly congruent with the end of the social self. In extreme old age, or in disease where mind and personality disintegrate, social death may precede biological death.
>
> (p. 34)

Again, to echo the importance of social context highlighted in "The Social Context" introductory section by Thompson in this volume, and as we shall see from my discussion here, the likelihood of being regarded as socially dead by wider society depends much less upon individual characteristics than it does upon social variables (of class, gender, race/ethnicity, sexuality, age, etc.). To this extent, social death can be understood quite clearly as socially patterned; influenced by social forces that help determine who, and in what context, an individual may be deemed to be socially dead.

Away from the social deaths first described in the hospital ethnographies of the 1960s in which the term originated (e.g., Glaser & Strauss, 1965, 1968; Sudnow, 1967), anthropological studies of non-Western societies have revealed too how social death may precede the cessation of biological functioning of the human body. Jack Goody's (1962) observations of the LoDagaa of West Africa, for example, reveal how the elderly and infirm, by virtue of their de facto exclusion from society, were buried alive or left to die, as they were regarded as having exhausted their social usefulness and contribution to society; they were thus, in effect, already socially dead.

In contrast, the observations of 19th-century anthropologist Robert Hertz (a member of Emile Durkheim's "Annee Sociologique" school), revealed how, contrary to attitudes prevalent in Western societies, death in many non-Western societies was not viewed as instantaneous but understood as only complete following the natural disintegration of the body (Hertz, 1960, cited in Sweeting & Gilhooly, 1997). In the interim between death and decomposition of the body, the dead were treated as if they were still alive, requiring nourishment through food and the company of others; and were thus considered still alive while being dead. Only following a final ceremony marking the departure of the dead to the realm of the ancestors were the deceased regarded as fully dead, and mourners permitted re-entry into the society of the living—for they too, during this period, were regarded as socially dead, set apart temporarily from participation in community life as "people of death" (ibid.).

Two further illustrations will suffice, for the time being, to highlight the second of Canter's two questions with which I began this chapter; namely, that of being socially alive while physically dead—a notion that, to many (like being dead while still alive) will appear counter-intuitive. The first is provided by cross-cultural comparison with societies that practice ancestor worship, such as some cultures in Japan, in which the dead continue to have a social presence in the lives of the living for many years—sometimes interminably—following death (Goss & Klass, 1999). A second, and further testimony of the continuing bonds theory (Klass, Silverman, & Nickman, 1996), in which the living may be said to have an ongoing relationship with the deceased, are social practices by which the deceased are granted a social existence; for example, talking to the dead using social media (Walter, Hourizi, Moncur, & Pitsillides, 2011), during visits to their grave (Clegg, 1988; Woodthorpe, 2010), or conversing with the deceased's cremated remains (Heessels, 2012; Kellaher, Prendergast, & Hockey, 2005; Prendergast, Hockey, & Kellaher, 2006). The dead may also be seen to be granted a social existence in the memories invoked by the material objects they leave behind (Hallam & Hockey, 2001) and in the material markers left by others at the place of death, interment and/or commemoration (Bleyen, 2010; Brennan, 2018). Material objects, however, even—or especially—those of the deceased, may themselves undergo a social death, discarded, abandoned, or put into storage (Hallam & Hockey, 2001), while the routine familiarity that comes of regularly passing by a makeshift memorial may render it socially invisible.

Let us now return, however, to the social context in which the concept of social death first originated: that of institutional health care.

The Institutionalization of Death and Dying

In contrast to the beginning of the 20th century, when most people died at home, by the end of the century, the vast majority of deaths in modern Western societies occurred in hospitals, hospices, or residential care facilities—a trend that has continued largely unabated in the 21st century. Though the exact location in which people are most likely to spend their final days differs across the developed world (in the UK, for example, it is the hospital, while in Norway, it is the nursing home), some three quarters of the population will draw their last breath in an institution (Walter, 2019). This is the result of two main factors: (1) extended life expectancy; and (2) the medicalization of society. The combined effect of these factors is an increased likelihood of social death. Let me explain.

Improvements in both public health (including better sanitation, nutrition, and personal hygiene) and medical technology (such as the development of antibiotics and life-extending procedures), allied to changes occurring at the wider social, cultural, and environmental levels (for example, declining rates of tobacco use, reductions in air pollution, and a fall in the number of hazardous heavy industrial jobs), have all combined to extend longevity well beyond what our ancestors could have expected only a generation or two previously. In the most economically developed nations of the world, people can now routinely expect to reach their 80s—a far cry from the mid-19th century, when life expectancy at birth was around 40 years (Taylor, 2007).

That people are living longer is a cause for celebration. It nevertheless means that people are dying of different causes, often of non-communicable diseases that extend the process of dying over the course of weeks, months, or even years. This is in contrast with the past, when people died relatively quickly, and not necessarily in old age, from infectious diseases. Living longer thus allows cells to die (resulting in Alzheimer's) or to grow abnormally (resulting in cancer), each of which present particular challenges for society, for the individuals experiencing these diseases, and for those charged with caring for people who, as a result of these conditions, are likely to experience lingering deaths, or what we might call extended "dying trajectories."

To those who care for people, often well into the 9th and 10th decades of their lives, the challenges are especially acute. Such people are likely not only to experience multiple morbidities, including impaired cognitive functioning, serious bodily decline, and general levels of frailty amounting to a "prolonged dwindling," but to have also outlived their peers. For health care professionals, residential caregivers, and families of persons in such parlous states, these people may be perceived, and treated, as if they are *already dead*, and may come to be classified as socially dead precisely because they have *not* died (Kastenbaum, 1969, cited in Sweeting & Gilhooly, 1991, p. 263). Those in such circumstances, who have outlived their social context, can be counted among the "living dead," whose experience amounts, no less, to that of "death-in-life" (Kastenbaum, 1988, p. 12).

This experience of living longer, though often living with radically diminished lives, is shaped by the social context in which it occurs. In modern Western societies, this experience, as we have seen, has been largely institutionalized, subject to the impersonal procedures that govern bureaucratic systems, of which health care is a part. Allied to modern biomedicine and its tendency to objectify patients as a disease category, the experience for the moribund may be a bitter one (Elias, 1985), robbed of any meaningful sense of personhood. It is precisely this experience that is so richly described in the "atrocity stories" (Seale, 1998) documented in the hospital ethnographies in which the concept of "social death" first emerged (e.g., Glaser & Strauss, 1965, 1968; Sudnow, 1967).

What Does Social Death Entail?

The ethnographies of Barney Glaser and Anselm Strauss (1965, 1968), and in particular of David Sudnow (1967), are important for a number of reasons. First, such ethnographies—literally understood as "writing about people" (Fulcher & Scott, 2011, p. 80)—provide rich, observational accounts of life inside hospitals based on first-hand experience. Accounts providing "thick descriptions" (Geertz, 1973) of life within such institutions are thus derived from researchers coming into close personal contact with the everyday lives of the people they are studying (Brewer, 2000). Detailed case studies of this sort reveal the particular dynamics governing how individuals and groups behave within an institutional setting.

For our purposes, such ethnographies are significant in helping reveal how "death" and "dying" are not simply biological facts but also *social processes* that are constructed during interaction. Glaser & Strauss's (1965) influential development of "awareness contexts," for example, illustrated how the non-disclosure of information to patients by medical staff about their impending death was crucial in shaping the experiences of patients, their families, and medical staff alike. Sudnow himself writes in this respect that:

> [T]he categories of hospital life, e.g., "life," "illness," "patient," "dying," "death" ... are to be seen as *constituted by the practices of hospital personnel* as they engage in their daily routinized interactions within an organizational milieu.
> (Sudnow, 1967, p. 8; emphasis in original)

The experience of social death, which for Sudnow (1967, p. 74) is marked by the point "at which socially relevant attributes of the patient begin permanently to cease to be operative as conditions for treating him [sic]," involves treating the person as essentially a corpse even before clinical (the appearance of "death signs" upon physical examination) or biological death (the cessation of cellular activity) has occurred. Three such examples described by Sudnow serve as cases in point. The first involves an attempt by a nurse to close the eyelids of a woman who the nurse explained was "dying." This, as Sudnow observed, was routinely performed before death, when it was easier to manipulate the body before the muscles have begun to tighten, so that the deceased will resemble a sleeping person. It was justified on the grounds both of efficiency (allowing ward personnel to wrap the body quickly following death) and consideration for others (especially of hospital personnel who preferred to handle corpses as little as possible).

A second involves the allocation of patients to beds. Here, Sudnow describes how patients admitted to hospital in a near-death state were frequently left on the stretcher on which they were admitted or placed in a laboratory room so as not to "mess a bed up," as the patient would soon die anyway. Again, the goal of efficiency governing the operation of bureaucratic organizations appears to serve as a guide to action, for upon death, as Sudnow (1967, p. 83) notes, "the complete bedding must be stripped, the room thoroughly cleansed, disinfected, etc."

A third example involves medical staff speaking openly in the presence of a dying patient as if the patient was already dead—the kind of "non-person" treatment first identified by Goffman (1959, 1961, 1963), which Sudnow acknowledges provided the impetus for his own investigations into social death. Sudnow thus reports an instance of two resident physicians who discussed a patient's forthcoming autopsy while the terminally ill patient in front of them—in the early stages of a coma from uremic poisoning—was still alive:

A: Do you think, really that both kidneys are as bad?
B: I know they're both bad because the output is so damned low. Let's put it this way, neither one is good.
A: Well, we'll find out for sure at autopsy.
B: Right (Sudnow, 1967: pp. 73–74).

Sudnow also cites the practice of completing autopsy permits for patients prior to their death but is careful to limit his usage of the term social death to instances warranting the literal sense of "death" rather than simply as a metaphor for the radically asocial treatment of a person. This is also the aim of Jana Králová (2015), who cautions against the loose conceptual usage of "social death" and argues instead for a more restricted application to only the most severe instances by which personhood is compromised or lost; namely, loss of social identity, loss of social connectedness, and losses associated with disintegration of the body. The first of these, the loss of social identity, is a key feature identified by Goffman in the experience of inmates of total institutions—places such as prisons, the military, and asylums, in which all aspects of inmates' lives are heavily regulated and proscribed, cut off from the outside world of everyday life, where individual decision-making, autonomy, and choice contribute to our sense of personhood. Goffman coins a term analogous to social death, "mortification of the self," by which a person is stripped of their defining characteristics, and given, for example, a number or uniform, the net effect of which is dehumanization, by which a person is divested of their "human capacities and functions" until that person "becomes less than a man [sic]" (Veil, 1964, p. 599). In hospitals and residential care facilities, the institutional walls are metaphorical rather than literal. Nevertheless, the segregation of the dying from the elderly, decrepit, and long-term sick, the gradual phasing of attention given to the dying, and their "non-person" treatment by medical staff, all contribute to a feeling for those on the receiving end of such ministrations of being already dead while still physically alive (Glaser & Strauss, 1965, p. 108).

Who Is a Candidate for Social Death?

A major contribution of sociology (and other allied disciplines) is the attention it has drawn to the social patterning of various phenomena, including illness, disease, and death. The probability of a person's candidacy for social death, like various other "life chances" (such as education and income) are not random but are related to a host of social variables linked to wider "social divisions" in society. A person's candidacy for social death can thus be linked to a range of social characteristics, including social class, race/ethnicity, gender, age, and so on.

Within the hospital setting described by Sudnow, it was social factors outside of it, such as a person's age, socioeconomic status, and their perceived moral character, that served as reliable predictors of whether one's life was deemed by others as "socially viable" (Timmermans, 1998) and thus, in the context of resuscitative efforts, worth saving. Social death in this sense functions as a self-fulfilling prophecy, determining both the likelihood of a person being pronounced "Dead on Arrival" (DOA) at the Emergency Room, as well as the lengths medical staff are prepared to go to in resuscitating someone close to death. In regard of a person's condition upon arrival at ER, Sudnow writes:

> [I]t could be remarked that determinations of "dying" and being "dead" were partially a function of social class, and not simply in the usual sense of the wealthy getting better care. If one anticipates having a critical heart attack, it is best that he keeps himself well-dressed and his breath clean if there is any likelihood of his being brought in the County Emergency Unit as a possible "Dead on Arrival." For the old, the poor, and the alcoholic bum, the inattention is such that the possibility could become an actuality without intervention.
>
> (Sudnow, 1982, p. 199)

Within the specific context of emergency medicine just described, some social groups are thus more likely to be perceived by medical staff as more socially dead than others. As a predictor of biological death during resuscitative efforts, social death guides the actions of medical staff so that action is rationed on the basis of a patient's social characteristics and position within the moral hierarchy

(Timmermans, 1998). Age is perhaps the most salient characteristic of a person's social viability during such efforts, followed closely by implicit moral judgments about those at the bottom of the social hierarchy (drug addicts, alcoholics, the homeless), for whom death may be perceived as a "blessing" or "just reward" for self-inflicted injury and an "immoral lifestyle." Some characteristics, such as age and medical history, may even assume the status of "master traits" (Hughes, 1971) that come to override all others during resuscitative efforts. Epidemiological studies (Timmermans, 1998) indicate similarly that race, gender, and socioeconomic status play a statistically significant role in determining survival rates during sudden cardiac arrest in ways that can be linked to notions of "social death."

The loss of moral entitlement to care, then, as we have just seen, is not guided according to purely clinical criteria but by a person's perceived "social viability," often in ways that influence the clinicians' decisions to resuscitate, regardless of a person's chances of surviving the intervention (Borgstrom, 2017, p. 6) and the biomedical protocols and legal guidelines aimed at preventing the implicit social rationing of care (Timmermans, 1998). The solutions to tackling this kind of social rationing, like the social death that anticipates and predicts it, lie outside of the hospital in addressing the wider societal foundations that produce the social inequality on which it is based.

Outside the context of emergency medicine, in residential care, it is the elderly "very worn out geriatric" and "terribly deteriorated patients" (Glaser & Strauss, 1965, p. 85) who are the most likely candidates for social death, not least because longevity increases the risk of Alzheimer's disease (where onset is most typical in those aged over 65), but also because the elderly may have outlived their social network of family and friends. In the case of Alzheimer's, significant memory loss and disorientation in the sense of self may prevent the sufferer from being seen as "an active agent in the lives of others" (Mulkay, 1993, p. 33), itself a defining feature of social death. In such instances, the person who was once known to family and friends has already been lost, often long before physical death occurs, thereby cruelly smearing bereavement across the years (Sutcliffe, 2007), leaving relatives "grieved out" (Glaser & Strauss, 1968, p. 154) by the time of actual death. Such "pulling away" from the person rendered unrecognizable to loved ones by Alzheimer's disease may well accompany the "anticipatory grief" (Fulton & Fulton, 1971; Fulton & Gottesman, 1980) experienced by relatives and is emblematic of Alzheimer's as a form of "living death" epitomized by the dislocation of the body from the self. In such circumstances, the individual may come to be seen as "an uncollected corpse" that "the undertaker has cruelly forgotten to collect" (Howarth, 2007, p. 182; Miller, 1990).

The social segregation of the elderly from the ongoing social world (Komaromy, 2010; Mulkay, 1993, p. 36), the end result of which is social death, reflects not only their disengagement (Cumming & Henry, 1961) from society following retirement from paid employment and relinquishing of roles previously fulfilled earlier in the course of life (such as that of parent or guardian), but also a general disregard for the elderly reflective of the low social esteem in which they are held in modern Western societies. The most egregious segregation is the "warehousing" described by Miller and Gwynne (1973), in which the elderly, because they are perceived as socially dead, are left simply to "rot," without proper care, attention, and stimulation. Allied to circumstances in which the mind is severely compromised, such mental frailty can put a person on "an undignified journey towards non-existence" (Gilleard & Higgs, 2017, p. 34) and is rightly feared by Westerners (Walter, 1999) as the archetypal "bad death" characteristic of the "fourth age" in which the body outlives and exceeds the functionality of mind, exposing the mentally frail to the potential for mistreatment and abuse.

Outside of the medical domain and social care setting, certain people may experience social death via proxy because of their associations with the deaths of others. In the Victorian era, for example, widows were bound by social conventions of the time to observe a three-year period of mourning, the first year of which in particular involved the severe curtailment of social activities (Morley, 1971); widows were thus expected to enter a social death sequence out of respect for their husbands, and on their husbands' behalf, thereby experiencing a kind of surrogate death of their own (Mulkay, 1993). More recently, persons bereaved by stigmatizing deaths (such as suicide), or by losses that are disenfranchised (Doka, 1989; such as perinatal deaths), may encounter the social withdrawal of others in ways analogous to social death. In such circumstances, including the death of a child, which in contemporary society subverts the "natural order" of how life is expected to proceed (and where children are, axiomatically, expected to survive their parents), friends, family, neighbors and co-workers may passively withdraw for fear of not knowing what to say or of saying the "wrong thing."

Finally, for now, we can also extend our discussion of who may be regarded as socially dead to groups "othered" by society, whose existence is rendered abject by structural inequalities, "social divisions," and the deep-seated prejudices underpinning them. Refugees, slaves, and Jews during the Holocaust are all examples of groups whose experience involves not only non-death losses of various kinds (e.g., loss of nation/homeland; loss of capital—social, cultural, and economic; loss of citizenship and rights accrued to it), but whose social death predisposes them to actual death. The loss of rights associated with citizenship, including the indefinite withdrawal of social, cultural, and legal protection, leaves such persons vulnerable to being killed at any time, by anyone—including a sovereign power—without the perpetrator facing charge (Králová, 2015). We see this most clearly in the work of Giorgio Agamben (1998), who invokes the archaic notion of *homo sacer*, from Roman law, to illustrate how the reduction of the outcast's experience to that of "bare life" renders them susceptible to extermination. We see it too in Orlando Patterson's (1982) work on slavery, where the slave's "natal alienation" from ancestral ties (both future and past), and non-existence outside of that of his or her master, renders them socially dead. The attempted erasure of the memory of an ethnic or racial group—as yet another form of social death—is, for Claudia Card (2010, p. 237), "the central evil of genocide"; reason enough, in her view, for the inclusion of deliberate social death by a sovereign power in the UN definition of genocide (Králová, 2015). Let us return now, however, to the impact of social death within a clinical and social care setting, especially how to guard against it.

Countering Social Death

The approach taken by health care professionals and social care providers, including treating people *as if* they are dead while still alive, has significant implications, both for the type of interaction that takes place between the carer and the cared-for (Borgstrom, 2017, p. 7), as well as for the outcomes achieved through care (Brannelly, 2011, p. 667). The inherent dangers of objectifying patients in biomedicine, together with the dehumanizing effects of institutional care and the impersonal routines that result from its bureaucratic organization—as we have seen from the preceding discussion—have been well documented in the medical-thanatological literature. A goal of the modern hospice movement was to make social and biological death coincide, pushing back social death as far as possible through the promotion of life-affirming activities and creative therapies until biological death occurs (Seale, 1998). Active euthanasia, it should also be noted, pursues the same goal, albeit by different means, hastening physical death so that social death can be avoided (Seale, 1998; Walter, 1999).

The task of delivering care that does not diminish but enhances the personhood of the individual being cared for is considerable, especially in a context in which hospice itself has faced the pressures of institutionalization that it was first set up to challenge. There are, nevertheless, a number of practical, sometimes small, steps that people working with or caring for elderly, frail, the long-term sick, and persons with Alzheimer's can implement in order to minimize treating people as if they are already dead. These include:

- Striving toward *better understanding of the biography of the person being cared for* as a means of enriching social interactions (Bouchard Ryan, Bannister, & Anas, 2009; Clare, 2010). Taking interest in the lives of those we care for may seem minor but is crucial, for as Brannelly (2011, p. 670) suggests: "Each interaction has the potential for transformative citizenship or for disempowerment."
- *Changing the language* employed when referring to people with Alzheimer's disease away from terms like "victims," which disempower, and toward terms like "mentor," which acknowledge the contribution people with Alzheimer's can make in enriching the lives of others (George, 2010). Such a simple change in the language we use, though we may not think it, may yield dramatic results, transforming exclusion into inclusion (Hayes et al., 2014).
- *De-emphasizing the body in disease management* (Borgstrom, 2015; Sampson, Finlay, Byrne, Snow, & Nelson, 2014) through the use of complementary and alternative medicine (CAM). This can be delivered as part of a package of holistic, whole-person care in order to help re-establish the sense of personhood undermined or diminished by impersonal institutional care and aggressive biomedical therapies, such as chemotherapy, that carry powerful side effects (nausea, alopecia, fatigue) and leave the person feeling wretched (Roques, 2014) and robbed of self-esteem.
- *Enhancing the agency of people being cared for* by involving them in conversations about end-of-life planning, advance directives, etc., in order to help restore

a sense of control and decision-making in circumstances in which a person may feel as if they have lost autonomy and control in a life dominated by pain and institutional routine.
- *Being reflexive and attentive to the impact we may have in the interactions with those we care for.* This requires strategic interventions by care teams so that practitioners learn the habits of reflecting regularly, and critically, upon how we may inadvertently influence care outcomes in ways we had not intended (Brookfield, 1995, p. 1). A critical approach to reflective practice of this sort is one that "takes into account the wider social picture—in relation to, for example, racism, sexism, ageism, and other forms of discrimination" (Thompson & Thompson, 2008, p. 29).

Being alert to the dangers of social death—the analogue of "ill-being" and opposite of "well-being" (Králová, 2016)—means being sensitive to how we treat people in various care contexts, as well as recognizing that interactions within these contexts (and any other, for that matter) are shaped by wider social forces. Because people, including those who work within care settings, do not live outside of society (the "soup and bowl" analogy used by Thompson, as stated earlier) but carry around the prevailing ideas of society in their heads and in their actions (the "coffee and cream" approach favored by Thompson et al., 2016), desisting from treating certain people as socially dead involves tackling the broader structural foundations that lead us to perceive some groups as more or less socially dead than others, placing "their moral entitlement to treatment and care at risk" (Borgstrom, 2017, p. 6). Thus, as Timmermans (1998, p. 467) puts it: "the disabled and seriously ill are not socially dead only in the Emergency Department but also in the outside world."

Conclusion

Social death, as we have seen, represents a particular type of non-death loss, even though it often resides in close proximity to, and may even be a reliable predictor of, actual physical death. In the medical-thanatological context in which it has had the greatest traction, it has been used to refer to the cessation of the individual as an active agent in the lives of others (Mulkay, 1993; Mulkay & Ernst, 1991), but it has also been used in reference to the attempted destruction of an entire people or ethnic group, where a group's social exclusion and invisibility function as a precondition for genocide. The prejudices of wider society may themselves be carried over into the social rationing and disbarment of care administered to individuals deemed to be socially dead by virtue of their membership of particular social groups.

Let me finish with a couple of caveats. First, is it possible that a person may be socially dead in one context but not another? Second, is it possible that a person may actively choose social death? In the first instance, it may well be the case that a person is socially dead to some but not others, where, for example, the elderly may be perceived as alive to their peers but socially dead to wider society, especially its younger and more economically active members. A conceptual "solution" to this problem is provided if we understand social death less in binary terms and more as a continuum: of the individual as more or less socially dead (Králová, 2015). In the second, there is evidence to suggest that some people may voluntarily withdraw from day-to-day interaction in ways homologous to social death (Caswell & O'Connor, 2015). The elderly and terminally ill may also choose social withdrawal in ways that reflect their disengagement from social life, especially if frustrated by the lack of opportunities afforded to them for participation in it, sometimes to the point that they no longer have much interest in living (Charmaz, 1994), and are thus socially dead.

Even if we accept, as some have argued, that voluntary withdrawal from life should not be mistaken for social death (Králová, 2015), it is possible, using a sociological lens, to explain how the perception of others may contribute to a person's retreat from social life, and thus to the influence of others in the symbiosis between self-perceived and other-perceived social death (Kalish, 1985).

What matters most, however, in social death is the sense in which the individual is stripped of their personhood and the rights associated with it. The challenge and responsibility that confronts all of us is how we safeguard and restore the dignity and agency of individuals and groups so as to prevent them from being treated as socially dead.

Key Terms

Ethnography: The systematic study of people and cultures. This research methodology can provide an observational and first-hand experience to better comprehend people's experiences.

Extended Dying Trajectories: Dying trajectories symbolize a person's health over time as one approaches death. In contemporary society, dying trajectories have become extended ("lingering deaths") due to advances in public health, medical technology, societal development, cultural reform, and other environmental reasons.

Social Characteristics: The characteristics of a person or group of people that contribute to a perceived social identity. Some examples are: age, socioeconomic status, gender, ethnicity, culture, sexual orientation, disability, or religious beliefs.

Social Death: The exclusion, abandonment, and isolation of distinct individuals from other members of society; treating individuals who are biologically alive as if they were already dead.

Questions for Reflection

1. Find an article or news story that illustrates the concept of social death. How is social death portrayed? Consider the positive and/or negative aspects of the article or story, and identify the potential biases, credibility, and methodologies that are present.

2. What suggestions do you have for preventing social death, and for restoring the dignity of those who are currently experiencing social death? What strategies can be utilized for accomplishing positive social change?
3. Consider the critique and suggestions for change regarding the medical institution that is provided in this chapter. What are your thoughts regarding the emphasis on science and technology versus the "patient" in Western medicine? What suggestions do you have for acknowledging personhood in the environment of medical institutions?

References

Agamben, G. (1998). *Homo sacer: Sovereign power and bare life*. Stanford, CA: Stanford University Press.
Bleyen, J. (2010). The materialities of absence after stillbirth: Historical perspectives. In J. Hockey, C. Komaromy, & K. Woodthorpe (Eds.), *The matter of death: Space, place and materiality* (pp. 69–84). Basingstoke: Palgrave Macmillan.
Borgstrom, E. (2015). Social death in end-of-life care policy. *Contemporary Social Science*, 10(3), 272–283.
Borgstrom, E. (2017). Social death. *QJM: An International Journal of Medicine*, 110(1), 5–7.
Bouchard Ryan, E., Bannister, K. A., & Anas, A. P. (2009). The dementia narrative: Writing to reclaim social identity. *Journal of Aging Studies*, 23(3), 145–157.
Brannelly, T. (2011). Sustaining citizenship: People with dementia and the phenomenon of social death. *Nursing Ethics*, 18(5), 662–671.
Brennan, M. (2018). Why materiality in mourning matters. In Z. Newby & R. Toulson (Eds.), *Materiality in mourning: Cross-disciplinary perspectives*. London & New York: Routledge.
Brewer, J. D. (2000). *Ethnography*. Buckingham: Open University Press.
Brookfield, S. (1995). *Becoming a critically reflective teacher*. San Francisco: Jossey-Bass Books.
Canter, D. (2017). Foreword. In J. Králová & T. Walter (Eds.), *Social death: Questioning the life-death boundary* (pp. xi–xii). Abingdon: Routledge.
Card, C. (2010). *Confronting evils: Terrorism, torture, genocide*. Cambridge: Cambridge University Press.
Caswell, G., & O'Connor (2015). Agency in the context of social death: Dying alone at home. *Contemporary Social Science*, 10(3), 249–261.
Charmaz, K. (1994). Conceptual approaches to the study of death. In R. Fulton & R. Bendikson (Eds.), *Death and identity* (pp. 28–79). Philadelphia: Charles Press.
Clare, L. (2010). Awareness in people with severe dementia: Review and integration. *Aging & Mental Health*, 14(1), 20–32.
Clegg, F. (1988). *Decisions at a time of grief*. University of Hull, unpublished.
Cumming, E., & Henry, W. (1961). *Growing old*. New York: Basic Books.
Doka, K. J. (Ed.). (1989). *Disenfranchised grief: Recognizing hidden sorrow*. Lexington, MA: Lexington Books.
Elias, N. (1985). *The loneliness of the dying*. Oxford: Blackwell.
Fulcher, J., & Scott, J. (2011). *Sociology* (4th ed.). Oxford & New York: Oxford University Press.
Fulton, R., & Fulton, J. (1971). A psychological aspect of terminal care: Anticipatory grief. *Omega: The Journal of Death and Dying*, 2(2), 91–100.
Fulton, R., & Gottesman, D. J. (1980). Anticipatory grief: A psychosocial concept reconsidered. *British Journal of Psychiatry*, 137(1), 45–54.

Geertz, C. (1973). *The interpretation of cultures: Selected essays*. New York: Basic Books Inc.
George, D. R. (2010). The art of medicine: Overcoming the social death of dementia through language. *The Lancet, 376*, 586–587.
Gilleard, C., & Higgs, P. (2017). Social death and the moral identity of the fourth age. In J. Králová & T. Walter (Eds.), *Social death: Questioning the life-death boundary* (pp. 28–37). Abingdon: Routledge.
Glaser, B. G., & Strauss, A. L. (1965). *Awareness of dying*. Chicago, IL: Aldine.
Glaser, B. G., & Strauss, A. L. (1968). *Time for dying*. Chicago, IL: Aldine.
Goody, J. (1962). *Death, property and the ancestors: A study of mortuary customs of the LoDagaa of West Africa*. London: Tavistock.
Goffman, E. (1959). *The presentation of self in everyday life*. New York: Anchor Books.
Goffman, E. (1961). *Asylums: Essays on the social situation of mental patients and other inmates*. Garden City, NY: Anchor Books.
Goffman, E. (1963). *Stigma: Notes on the management of spoiled identity*. Englewood Cliffs, NJ: Prentice Hall.
Goss, R., & Klass, D. (1999). Spiritual bonds to the dead in cross-cultural and historical perspective: Comparative religion and modern grief. *Death Studies, 23*(6), 547–567.
Hallam, E., & Hockey, J. (2001). *Death, memory and material culture*. Oxford: Berg.
Hayes, A., Henry, C., Holloway, M., Lindsey, K., Sherwen, E., & Smith, T. (2014). *Pathways through care at the end of life*. London: Jessica Kingsley Publishers.
Heessels, M. (2012). *Bringing home the dead: Ritualizing cremation in the Netherlands*. Unpublished PhD thesis, Radbound University, Nigmegen, The Netherlands.
Hertz, R. (1960/1907). A contribution to the collective representation of death. Reprinted in R. Hertz, *Death and the right hand*. Aberdeen: The University Press.
Howarth, G. (2007). *Death and dying: A sociological introduction*. Cambridge: Polity Press.
Hughes, E. C. (1971). *The sociological eye*. Chicago, Il: Aldine.
Kalish, R. (1985). *Death, grief and caring relationships*. Pacific Grove, CA: Brooks Cole.
Kastenbaum, R. J. (1969). Psychological death. In L. Pearson (Ed.), *Death and dying*. Cleveland, OH: Western Reserve University Press.
Kastenbaum, R. J. (1988). 'Safe death' in the postmodern world. In A. Gilmore & S. Gilmore (Eds.), *A safer death: Multidisciplinary aspects of terminal care* (pp. 3–14). New York & London: Plenum Press.
Kellaher, L., Prendergast, D., & Hockey, J. (2005). In the shadow of the traditional grave. *Mortality, 10*(4), 237–250.
Klass, D., Silverman, P. R., & Nickman, S. (Eds.). (1996). *Continuing bonds: New understandings of grief*. New York: Taylor & Francis.
Komaromy, C. (2010). Dying spaces in dying places. In J. Hockey, C. Komaromy, & K. Woodthorpe (Eds.), *The matter of death: Space, place and materiality* (pp. 52–68). Basingstoke: Palgrave Macmillan.
Králová, J. (2015). What is social death? *Contemporary Social Science, 10*(3), 235–248.
Králová, J. (2016, June 29). Why we need to find a cure for "social death." *The Conversation*. Retrieved April 5, 2018, from http://theconversation.com/why-we-need-to-find-a-cure-for-social-death-59997
Leoman, O. (2001). Social death. In G. Howarth & O. Leoman (Eds.), *Encyclopedia of death and dying* (pp. 419–420). London & New York: Routledge.
Miller, E., & Gwynne, G. (1973). Dependence, independence and counter-dependence in residential institutions for incurables. In I. Gosling (Ed.), *Support, innovation and autonomy*. London: Tavistock.
Miller, J. (1990). Interview. In R. Dinnage (Ed.), *The ruffian on the stair*. Harmondsworth: Penguin.

Morley, J. (1971). *Death, heaven and the Victorians*. London: University of Pittsburgh Press.
Mulkay, M. (1993). Social death in Britain. In D. Clark (Ed.), *The sociology of death* (pp. 31–49). Oxford: Blackwell.
Mulkay, M., & Ernst, J. (1991). The changing position of social death. *European Journal of Sociology, 32*, 172–196.
Patterson, O. (1982). *Slavery and social death: A comparative study*. Cambridge, MA: Harvard University Press.
Prendergast, D., Hockey, J., & Kellaher, L. (2006). Blowing in the wind? Identity, materiality and the destinations of human ashes. *Journal of the Royal Anthropological Institute, 12*(4), 881–898.
Roques, T. (2014). The chemotherapy experience. *The Lancet, 383*(9936), 2202.
Sampson, C., Finlay, I., Byrne, A., Snow, V., & Nelson, A. (2014). The practice of palliative care from the perspective of patients and carers. *BMJ Supportive & Palliative Care, 4*(3), 291–298.
Seale, C. (1998). *Constructing death: The sociology of dying and bereavement*. Cambridge: Cambridge University Press.
Small, N. (1997). Death and difference. In D. Field, J. Hockey, & N. Small (Eds.), *Death, gender and ethnicity* (pp. 201–221). London & New York: Routledge.
Sudnow, D. (1967). *Passing on: The social organization of dying*. Englewood-Cliffs, NJ: Prentice-Hall.
Sudnow, D. (1982). Dying in a public hospital. In O. G. Brim, H. E. Freeman, S. Levine, & N. A. Scotch (Eds.), *The dying patient* (pp. 191–208). New Brunswick: Transaction Books.
Sutcliffe, T. (2007, August 9). Malcolm and Barbara: Flawed but virtuous. *Independent*. Retrieved September 8, 2007, from www.independent.co.uk/opinion/columnists/thomas-sutcliffe/thomas-sutcliffe-malcolm-and-barbara-flawed-but-virtuous-460792.html
Sweeting, H., & Gilhooly, M. (1991). Doctor, am I dead yet? A review of social death in modern societies. *Omega: The Journal of Death and Dying, 24*(4), 251–269.
Sweeting, H., & Gilhooly, M. (1997). Dementia and the phenomenon of social death. *Sociology of Health and Illness, 19*(1), 93–117.
Taylor, S. (2007). Approaches to health and illness. In S. Taylor & D. Field (Eds.), *Sociology of health and health care* (pp. 25–44). Oxford: Blackwell.
Thompson, S., & Thompson, N. (2008). *The critically reflective practitioner*. Basingstoke: Palgrave Macmillan.
Thompson, N., Allen, J., Caverhill, P. A., Cox, G. R., Davies, B., Doka, K. J., … Wittkowski, J. (2016). The case for a sociology of death, dying and bereavement. *Death Studies, 40*(3), 172–181.
Timmermans, S. (1998). Social death as a self-fulfilling prophesy: David Sudnow's "Passing On" revisited. *The Sociological Quarterly, 39*(3), 453–472.
Veil, D. J. (1964). The danger of dehumanization. *Mental Hospitals, 15*, 599–601.
Walter, T. (1999). *On bereavement: The culture of grief*. Maidenhead: Open University Press.
Walter, T. (2019). *Death in the modern world*. London & Thousand Oaks, CA: Sage Publications.
Walter, T., Hourizi, R., Moncur, W., & Pitsillides, S. (2011). Does the Internet change the way we die and mourn? Overview and analysis. *Omega: The Journal of Death and Dying, 64*(4), 275–302.
Woodthorpe, K. (2010). Buried bodies in an East London cemetery: Re-visiting taboo. In A. Maddrell & J. D. Sidaway (Eds.), *Spaces for death, dying, mourning and remembrance* (pp. 57–74). London & New York: Routledge.

CHAPTER 4

Discrimination, Oppression, and Loss

Neil Thompson

Introduction

If we are to develop an adequate understanding of those forms of loss and grief that are not directly connected with death, one important aspect of social life that needs to be considered is social justice—or, more specifically, social injustice. This chapter, therefore, explores the significance of discrimination and oppression and their relationship with loss and grief. The primary focus will be on discrimination and oppression associated with race and ethnicity, but there will be strong parallels with other forms of inequality, such as sexism and ageism. My aim is to highlight a number of key issues that connect discrimination and oppression on the one hand with loss and grief on the other, with a view to making a contribution to a fuller understanding of the complexities involved.

I begin by clarifying what I mean by discrimination and oppression before proceeding to explore how these relate to loss and grief.

Discrimination and Oppression

Discrimination, in the sense in which it is used in legal and moral-political contexts, is a two-part process: (1) identifying one or more differences between individuals, groups, or categories of people; and (2) treating those identified as "different" less favorably (e.g., through exclusion, marginalization, victimization, and other such discriminatory processes). Discrimination is the process (or set of processes) that leads to oppression, by which I mean:

> Inhuman or degrading treatment of individuals or groups; hardship and injustice brought about by the dominance of one group over another; the negative and demeaning exercise of power. It often involves disregarding the rights of an individual or group and is thus a denial of citizenship. Oppression arises as a result of unfair discrimination—that is, the disadvantages experienced as a result of discrimination have oppressive consequences.
>
> (Thompson, 2016, p. 50)

This definition introduces the key concept of power. Discrimination is premised on the exercise of power, while oppression involves the diminution of power (for those experiencing the oppression). When we are talking about discrimination and oppression, we are therefore talking about power and how it is used, misused, or abused.

There are different forms of power (Thompson, 2007), but the form I am interested in here is that of domination—that is, what is generally referred to as "power over," as when one group or individual is in a dominant position relative to others who are assigned to a subordinate position. This creates the opportunity for the latter group to be exploited, discriminated against, and thus oppressed by the former. Unfortunately, there has been a tendency in some quarters to oversimplify this into a straightforward binary, seeing some people as "oppressors" and some as "oppressed." This fails to recognize the multidimensionality of how such matters operate. The notion of "intersectionality" refers to the recognition that power, discrimination, and oppression interweave in different ways, reflecting the various connected pathways that different forms of discrimination can follow (May, 2015). For example, someone may be discriminated against by virtue of their gender and/or ethnicity while discriminating against others in terms of age and/or disability. In order to understand the complexities of discrimination and oppression, it is therefore necessary to develop a more sophisticated analysis than what is offered by a simple binary approach.

PCS Analysis

What can help us to develop this more sophisticated analysis is the PCS analysis framework I have developed in my earlier work (Thompson, 2016, 2017, 2018a). It is explained in the introductory section chapter in this book (Part I) as well, and so I will not repeat that discussion here, save to say that the key "message" of this approach is that we need to appreciate that discrimination operates at three different, but intersecting, levels: P (personal), C (cultural), and S (structural). Consequently, when we begin to consider losses associated with discrimination and oppression, it can be helpful to think of them in terms of the respective levels of P, C, and S. I shall return to this point later.

Discrimination: Beyond Personal Prejudice

For a very long time, when discrimination was considered, the emphasis was on personal prejudice (P) and efforts were devoted largely to educational programs to change negative and stereotypical attitudes towards minority groups. However, what was not given anywhere near the same level of consideration was the widespread cultural assumptions (C), transmitted from generation to generation (as part of the socialization process), from which such attitudes largely arose. And, what has tended to receive even less attention is the set of institutionalized power relations at a structural level (S) that feed, and are fed by, such cultural assumptions. For example, if an individual holds discriminatory, stereotypical attitudes towards ethnic minority groups, this is not simply a matter of his or her personal prejudice, in so far as that prejudice reflects wider cultural understandings (a discourse of white supremacy, for example), which in turn reflect structural relations of dominance and subordination in terms of positions of power predominantly being occupied by white people (and the fact that such people are predominantly men is an example of intersectionality).

The sociological underpinnings of PCS analysis have helped us to move away from a narrow, psychological perspective that reduces the complex, multilevel workings of discrimination and oppression to a simple matter of personal prejudice (see the discussion of "atomism" in the Part I introductory chapter). This approach can also cast light on aspects of loss and grief and thereby offer a form of bridge between such matters and discrimination and oppression.

Loss: Beyond Personal Responses

When it comes to the study of loss and grief, the major focus is very much on the individual, psychological level (Thompson & Cox, 2017). Relatively little attention has traditionally been paid to wider sociopolitical issues, such as social justice (Harris & Bordere, 2016), potentially giving newcomers to the field the impression that a focus on the individual is all that is required. Losses, whether death related or not, and our grief reactions to them, do not operate in a social vacuum; there will always be a wider social context that is highly likely to be influential in shaping the circumstances (and the reactions to those circumstances) at a personal and familial level.

The individualistic approach to loss and grief has encouraged a focus on the psychological aspects of grief (emotional, cognitive, and behavioral) which are, of course, important factors to consider. However, if they are not understood in their wider cultural and structural context, there is a danger that they will be misinterpreted, and/or key aspects of the situation may be missed or underplayed. For example, in certain cultures, men expressing grief openly through crying or other direct expressions of emotion is frowned upon and can leave the men within that culture open to sanction and disapproval (Doka & Martin, 2010). Similarly, a white person unaware of particular cultural norms that apply to people of color (Rosenblatt, 2016) may be unwittingly creating problems or unnecessary barriers to progress.

One particularly significant cultural factor in relation to losses that are not death related is that there is a tendency to fail to recognize such experiences as losses, and therefore to fail to acknowledge, or respond appropriately to, the grief involved, thereby making it a form of disenfranchised grief (Doka, 2002; Thompson & Doka, 2018). There will also be structural factors involved—for example, in terms of access to resources; the ability to have your voice heard; and the very fact that being in a structurally disadvantaged group or category (in terms of class, race/ethnicity, gender, and so on) is likely to lead to a higher number of personal losses (such as being a victim of crime or violence). In addition, there is the matter of what could be called identity-related losses—that is, losses associated with being assigned a marginalized status and identity. These can be highly significant in relation to discrimination and oppression, and so it is worth exploring these in more detail.

Identity-Related Losses

Once again, we are encountering a phenomenon that is traditionally understood in narrow, individualistic terms (as "personality," for example), with the wider cultural and structural dimensions often being pushed to the margins or left out of the picture altogether. The reality of identity is much more complex, as there are significant *sociological* dimensions to what gives us our sense of who we are (Lawler, 2013; Thompson, 2018b). Each person's identity is unique, of course, but what contributes to that uniqueness is the complex interplay of various social influences and constraints (especially the social divisions of class, race/ethnicity, gender, and so on) and how we respond to those influences and constraints (and, dialectically, how wider aspects of society react to our responses—for example, in the "punishment" of what are perceived as examples of deviance, of daring to be different in what are seen as socially troubling ways; Anderson, 2014). Identity is therefore a *psychosocial* phenomenon, involving both psychological and sociological dimensions, with a complex interplay between the two. There is no doubt that there are many losses associated with the various ways in which discrimination and oppression have an impact on identity, many ways in which social processes associated with social injustice can be harmful and disempowering. The following are just some of the examples that could be highlighted.

Racist Practices in Education and Employment

There is no shortage of literature and research documenting the prevalence of racist practices in education and employment. These generate significant (and cumulative) disadvantages for members of ethnic minority groups. The consequences of this are likely to include loss of employment and career advancement opportunities, as well as loss of personal development opportunities (with potential consequences in terms of quality of life, ability to form relationships, and so on). There can also be potential losses in terms of self-esteem, personal confidence, and ambition, all increasing the chances of encountering problems and obstacles in life.

Treatment of Aboriginal Peoples

The policies in Canada (Fontaine, 2010; Stanton, 2011) and Australia (AIHW, 2018) to place aboriginal children in residential schools or with white foster carers to "breed out" the aboriginal genes (to "kill the Indian in the child," as acknowledged in the Canadian Prime Minister's statement of apology to former residential school students; Harper, 2008) reflects a crude and racist eugenic ideology. This approach amounted to white supremacism garbed in a humanitarian claim to be improving the lot of "these unfortunate people." The losses involved for the children so affected would form a very long list and would include, of course, loss of family connections, cultural heritage, and stability—not to mention rights, dignity, and a sense of pride in one's ethnic roots.

While this cruel and unjust treatment of children has rightly come to an end, the concerns about the discriminatory treatment of aboriginal people in general continue to be of significant proportions (Healey, 2003), as do the many identity-related loses involved.

Language Suppression

In Wales, the Welsh language has equal legal status with English, but this has not always been the case. In the 18th, 19th, and early 20th centuries, there were deliberate attempts to suppress and even eradicate the Welsh language. Children heard speaking Welsh were forced to wear a sign around their neck that said, "Welsh not." It could be passed on only to anyone else heard speaking Welsh. The person wearing the sign at the end of the school day would be punished. This was a very insidious way to not only deny Welsh speakers the right to speak their own language, but also to pit Welsh speakers against one another. This oppressive abuse of power by the dominant group to undermine and stigmatize the identity of the less powerful minority was effective in its day, but it ultimately failed, as the affirmation of Welsh language, culture, and identity is very strong indeed today (Williams, 2011). Suppression of language is a powerful tool of domination, and one that invokes a number of losses.

Holocaust Denial

It is sadly the case that there remain people who, despite the overwhelming evidence to the contrary, deny that the Nazi Holocaust took place. The mass murder of Jews and Polish people as ethnic groups perceived to be less than human, alongside others likewise stripped of their humanity, remains a most horrific crime and atrocity. It is, quite understandably, a feature of the lives of the people so affected, an element of their culture. To deny that the Holocaust took place is to dismiss part of the Jewish people's cultural history, to seek to invalidate an important part of shared identity. To have your identity invalidated in this way is to be denied respect, dignity, and heritage.

It is important to stress that the social forces I have been describing here *can* (and often do) have a highly adverse effect on identity (and thus well-being), but it is not an automatic process. There are, of course, many cases on record of people who have flourished in their lives, despite the obstacles they had to face in terms of identity-related losses. Such losses are a challenge to resilience, but they can also be a spur to such resilience, rather than an obstacle to it.

I made the point earlier that identity is a psychosocial phenomenon. What we need to recognize in addition is that it is also a spiritual matter. A fundamental part of our spirituality is our sense of who we are and how we fit into the wider world (Holloway & Moss, 2012). People who face identity-related losses can therefore have to wrestle with a sense of being spiritually diminished, with considerable adverse consequences for their well-being and their mental health. Having to constantly fight to be heard, to be validated and affirmed, and to fend off marginalization and alienation is likely to be exhausting work, and so it is not surprising that many people in such circumstances will struggle to keep going.

Losses: Cathected and Non-Cathected

The classic understanding of grief derives from Freud's notion of "cathexis" (Freud, 1917), the idea that grief arises as a result of an emotional investment (cathexis) being made in a person, relationship, place, job, or other important part of life and that investment subsequently being lost (through death or other significant loss)—hence the notion that grief is the price we pay for love.

The types of loss that produce a grief reaction are therefore described as "cathected" losses—that is, losses that create a sense of emotional void and other related responses. But, not every type of loss is cathected. For example, losing a job that we hated could be a source of joy rather than grief or sorrow (although there may be some related losses that produce some degree of grief, such as losing touch with one or more people that we liked in that workplace).

This raises the question of whether it is possible to grieve for something that you have never had, something you have been denied. In at least one sense, it is possible to do so. I am thinking of anticipatory grieving, where we are aware that we are going to be losing someone or something important to us. However, in such cases, what we are actually grieving is the loss of hopes, aspirations, and plans, so, in that sense, the loss is actually of something we had, but no longer have—something that was important to us and thus cathected.

The question of whether identity-related losses can be mourned is more complex than this. Being aware that you are being denied something important (respect, dignity, a voice, rights, opportunities, and/or resources that are freely available to others can most definitely create a sense of void (an existential nothingness, to use the technical philosophical term) and thus longing. Whether it is appropriate or not to call this grief is a matter for debate, but what is clear is that identity-related losses due to discrimination and oppression can be sources of emotional distress and the other experiences we associate with grief.

This brings us back to the issue of cathexis. As a general rule, the greater the emotional investment, the more severe and far-reaching the grief reaction. Consequently, much will depend on the emotional investment made in those aspects of life that are denied by discrimination. People who "adjust" to their marginalized position as a coping method are likely to have less of an adverse reaction than those who are more fully invested in what they are being denied. However, it has to be recognized that such "adjustment" comes at a very high price at a number of levels (not least in terms of the disempowerment involved). This raises serious issues for those who refuse to "adjust" and choose to challenge the status quo, to campaign for rights, equality and social justice. This involves a much higher level of cathexis and thus a much higher risk of an adverse reaction. This fits with the more general picture of political activity—the more invested we are in it, the more there is to gain, but also the more there is to lose.

A Case in Point

The following is based on a conversation that took place on a training course on anti-racism that I was running.

> *First participant:* As a black woman I have two battles to fight, against racism in the wider society and sexism in my own family and community. But, sometimes I get so worn down that I just have to bow out for a while, otherwise I know it will all get too much for me and burn me out. And that would not be fair on me or my children.
>
> *Second participant:* That's why I've just given up, I've just learned to live with the hassles I get. Fighting the good fight all the time is just too exhausting, so I just get on with my life the best I can. It's sad, but that's how I cope.
>
> *Third participant:* "Bowing out" temporarily or altogether is a luxury I can't afford. As a disabled woman I am constantly struggling to get my rights and to get my voice heard, otherwise I just get ignored, patronized, and treated as a burden—and a second-class citizen to boot. When people are trying to deny me my independence, they are denying me my right to be a person in my own right, and I just can't live like that.
>
> *First participant [to third participant]:* All our circumstances are different and we've all got our challenges, so I respect your challenges and your courage in constantly rising to them, but there are times when I either bow out or go under; it's as simple as that. [To second participant]: But, I respect your right to do what you do too, but I couldn't do it. If I am not trying to get past the crap all this discrimination pushes on me, I start to feel like the dirt the bigots seem to think I am.

As with loss and grief issues generally, there is no set way of dealing with them—broad patterns will be discernible, but also aspects that are unique to each individual and each set of circumstances. To take our understanding forward, we therefore need to engage with the complexities involved (intellectually, emotionally, spiritually, and practically), rather than look for a simple solution or a formulaic response.

One further aspect of the question of identity-related losses is the significance of grief not just as our response to (cathected) loss, but also as a process of healing. Schneider (2012) rightly emphasizes the dangers of confusing grief with depression. The latter can be understood as a state when we are emotionally "stuck," as if paralyzed. While grief can superficially look just like depression, it is actually very different. This is because grief is a process of healing. While it is so often extremely painful, exhausting, and frightening, it is none the less a positive process, moving us through a gradual process of rebuilding our lives (intellectually, emotionally, spiritually, and practically) so that we can restore at least some level of well-being and continue with our lives. This is not to say that a person cannot be depressed and grieving at the same time, but it remains the case that it is problematic to assume that grief and depression are the same thing.

So, when it comes to the question of identity-related losses, the question of healing needs to be considered. What complicates the picture is that, in the case of other losses, they will generally follow the pattern of (1) cathexis; (2) a loss event; and (3) grief as a process of "meaning construction" (Neimeyer, 2001) to heal and rebuild (as far as possible). However, in the case of identity-related losses, the scenario is not quite so clear-cut. Each morning involves facing the losses again; they are more than a "loss event" that we can aim to "get over." In this regard, identity-related losses are "ambiguous losses" (Boss, 1999; see further description and examples of ambiguous loss in the chapters on this topic later in this volume), and we still have a long way to go to develop a fuller understanding of ambiguous losses in general and identity-related losses in particular.

What we are seeing, then, is a highly complex picture, and one that is in need of much further and much fuller investigation than has been the case up to now.

Addressing Identity-Related Losses

A key factor underpinning identity-based losses arising from discrimination and oppression is alienation, the process of being made to feel "other," to be less worthy, to not belong or be valued. It takes little imagination to recognize that, when we are looking at identity-related losses, we are in the realm of alienation and its destructive impact. Yet again, we are encountering a concept that is often discussed narrowly at an individual level, as if it is purely a personal experience and individualistic phenomenon. In reality, alienation can be better understood sociologically and more holistically as a process (or set of processes) that operate at personal, cultural, and structural levels. Efforts to address alienation (and, with it, identity-related losses) therefore need to focus on all three levels if the response is to be adequate. Of course, the structural level is bound to be the most difficult to address, given the institutionalized power interests that social structures represent. Moving towards a society that is inclusive and does not alienate certain minority groups or categories of people is fraught with difficulty, and there are no easy answers, but progressive movements can play a part in challenging the status quo as far as possible (Klein, 2018; Monbiot, 2018).

At a cultural level, much can be done to challenge discriminatory and oppressive assumptions and stereotypes (Bhatti-Sinclair & Smethurst, 2017). The actions need to rise above the simplistic level of what has come to be known as "political correctness" and offer much more sophisticated understandings of what is involved (Thompson, 2018c). Education in relation to social justice can play an important role in this (Barry, 2005; Harris & Bordere, 2016; Thompson, 2017), but much more than this is needed, as it is a matter not simply of challenging ignorance (for which education is well placed), but also of challenging an ingrained ideology that valorizes dominant groups and marginalizes others. We therefore need to include education but also to go beyond this to include whatever consciousness-raising tools are available to us (campaigning groups, for example).

At the personal level, there are (at least) two sets of issues to consider. One is that all individuals need to take responsibility for not contributing to discrimination, oppression, and alienation (bearing in mind my earlier comment that it is not simply a matter of dividing people into categories of oppressor or oppressed—someone who is oppressed in one way can be contributing to oppressing others in another way). The other is to recognize the need to support (in non-patronizing, non-paternalistic ways) those people engaged in a struggle to deal with the challenges presented by identity-related losses. This is about partnership and empowerment, not therapy. Of course, without change at the structural level, struggles at personal and cultural levels will continue to meet obstacles, resistance, and setbacks, but it is hoped that continued efforts at the personal and cultural level can contribute to eventual change at the structural level.

Conclusion

Discrimination, in its technical sociopolitical sense, involves isolating, marginalizing, and treating certain people less favorably, resulting in oppressive consequences for the significant numbers of people affected. Such discrimination does not occur at random; it follows the "fault lines" of society in terms of social divisions, such as language group, religious affiliation, sexual identity, age, and disability, as well as the more well-documented ones of class, race, and gender. The oppressive consequences of discrimination have implications in terms of loss and grief. We briefly focused on how the wider social context can shape grief reactions (gender and cultural differences, for example) but looked more closely at the significance of identity-related losses, in the sense that being a member of one or more marginalized groups can have profound consequences for our sense of who we are and how we fit into the world. We have noted that these are complex issues that require a sophisticated level of understanding and a sophisticated and well-thought-through plan of action for addressing them. As with all matters relating to loss and grief, there is no simple, one-size-fits-all way of dealing with them. These are issues that we need to wrestle with in all their subtlety and complexity and not allow the gravity of their oppressive consequences to lead us into simplistic, knee-jerk responses.

Key Terms

Cathected Loss: A Freudian psychoanalytic perspective on loss. This theory suggests that grief is the result of the loss of a psychological investment, which may be a person, relationship, place, job, or other significant life investment.

Intersectionality: This concept recognizes how power, oppression, and discrimination are interwoven within social frameworks and social categorizations such as race, class, gender, sexual orientation, disability, etc.

Social Justice: Full and equal participation of all groups which constitute a society that is mutually shaped to meet their needs. Social justice strives to materialize a vision of society in which the distribution of resources is fair and equitable such that all members are physically and psychologically safe and secure.

Oppression: The act of using power and/or resources to empower and/or bestow privilege to a group at the expense of disempowering, marginalizing, silencing, and/or subordinating another group.

Questions for Reflection

1. Utilizing the PCS analysis model, how would you define the experience of identity-related loss? Additionally, explore how identity-related loss relates to cathected loss.
2. Provide three examples that illustrate the concept of identity-related loss that are not specifically mentioned in the chapter. Furthermore, identify potential strategies for providing grief support to the situations described by your examples.
3. Provide an intersectional analysis of the case study in this chapter. What specific loss experiences do you think these individuals are experiencing due to discrimination and oppression? How can privileged individuals alleviate discrimination and oppression in their everyday lives to prevent others from experiencing identity-related losses?

References

Anderson, T. L. (Ed.). (2014). *Understanding deviance: Connecting classical and contemporary perspectives*. New York: Routledge.

Australian Institute of Health and Welfare. (2018). *Aboriginal and Torres Strait Islander stolen generations: Numbers, demographic characteristics and selected outcomes*. Canberra: AIHW.

Barry, B. (2005). *Why social justice matters*. Cambridge: Polity Press.

Bhatti-Sinclair, K., & Smethurst, C. (2017). *Diversity, difference and dilemmas: Analysing concepts and developing skills*. London: Open University Press.

Boss, P. (1999). *Ambiguous loss: Learning to live with unresolved grief*. Cambridge, MA: Harvard University Press.

Doka, K. J. (Ed.). (2002). *Disenfranchised grief: New directions, challenges, and strategies for practice*. Champaign, IL: Research Press.

Doka, K. J., & Martin, T. L. (2010). *Grieving beyond gender* (2nd ed.). New York: Routledge.

Fontaine, T. (2010). *Broken circle: The dark legacy of Indian residential school: A memoir*. Victoria: Heritage House.

Freud, S. (1917/2001). Mourning and melancholia. In *The standard edition of the complete psychological works of Sigmund Freud, Volume XIV (1914–1916): On the history of the psycho-analytic movement, Papers on metapsychology and other works* (pp. 237–258). New York: Vintage Classics.

Harper, S. (2008). *Statement of apology*. Retrieved from www.ainc.inac.gc.ca/ai/rqpi/apo/index-eng.asp

Harris, D. L., & Bordere, T. C. (Eds.). (2016). *Handbook of social justice in loss and grief: Exploring equity, diversity and inclusion*. New York: Routledge.

Healey, J. (Ed.). (2003). *Racism in Australia*. Rozelle, NSW: Spinney Press.

Holloway, M., & Moss, B. (2012). *Spirituality and social work*. Basingstoke, UK: Palgrave Macmillan.

Klein, N. (2018). *No is not enough: Defeating the new shock politics*. London: Penguin.

Lawler, S. (2013). *Identity: Sociological perspectives* (2nd ed.). Cambridge, UK: Polity Press.

May, V. M. (2015). *Pursuing intersectionality: Unsettling dominant imaginaries*. London: Routledge.

Monbiot, G. (2018). *Out of the wreckage: A new politics for an age of crisis*. London: Verso.

Neimeyer, R. A. (Ed.). (2001). *Meaning reconstruction and the experience of loss*. Washington, DC: American Psychological Association.

Rosenblatt, P. C. (2016). Cultural competence and humility. In D. L. Harris & T. C. Bordere (Eds.), *Handbook of social justice in loss and grief: Exploring equity, diversity and inclusion* (pp. 67–74). New York: Routledge.

Schneider, J. (2012). *Finding my way: From trauma to transformation: The journey through loss and grief*. Traverse City, MI: Seasons Press.

Stanton, K. (2011). Canada's truth and reconciliation commission: Settling the past? *The International Indigenous Policy Journal, 2*(3). doi:10.18584/iipj.2011.2.3.2

Thompson, N. (2007). *Power and empowerment*. Lyme Regis, UK: Russell House Publishing.

Thompson, N. (2016). *Anti-discriminatory practice: Equality, diversity and social justice* (6th ed.). London: Palgrave Macmillan.

Thompson, N. (2017). *Social problems and social justice*. London: Palgrave Macmillan.

Thompson, N. (2018a). *Promoting equality: Working with diversity and difference* (4th ed.). London: Palgrave Macmillan.

Thompson, N. (2018b). *Applied sociology*. New York; Routledge.

Thompson, N. (2018c). *Effective communication: A guide for the people professions* (3rd ed.). London: Palgrave Macmillan.

Thompson, N., & Cox, G. R. (Eds.). (2017). *Handbook of the sociology of death, grief, and bereavement*. New York: Routledge.

Thompson, N., & Doka, K. J. (2018). Disenfranchised grief. In N. Thompson & G. R. Cox (Eds.), *Handbook of the sociology of death, grief, and bereavement* (pp. 177–190). New York: Routledge.

Williams, C. (Ed.). (2011). *Social policy for social welfare practice in a devolved Wales* (2nd ed.). Birmingham, UK: Venture Press.

CHAPTER 5

Mourning in Trump's America: An Existential Account of Political Grief

Sheldon Solomon

For many Americans, myself included (see also Bochner, 2018), the November 8, 2016, election of Donald J. Trump as president of the United States engendered a poignant and profound sense of grief. We shared Meghan O'Rourke's (2016) view that

> We are experiencing not just the pain of political defeat but the grief of mourning something that feels irrevocably lost. There are two losses here, complementing and intensifying each other. First, the shocking defeat of Clinton, and the evaporation of a future in which a woman was the leader of the free world. Her defeat was a visceral reminder that misogyny and unconscious bias remain powerful forces . . . The second loss is the surreal election of a bigot like Trump. It brings with it a version of what psychologists call anticipatory grief—the emotion we feel while taking care of someone with a terminal illness and waiting for the worst to come.

Indeed, Trump's election was as ominously traumatic as other catastrophic landmark moments in recent history, such as the assassinations of John F. Kennedy (JFK), Martin Luther King (MLK), and John Lennon, or the September 11, 2001, attack on the Pentagon and World Trade Center. Each of these events produced a torrent of "grief of mourning something that feels irrevocably lost" (O'Rourke, 2016). JFK's, MLK's, and Lennon's assassinations divested us of the comforting illusion that our public figures are safe from domestic attacks. The events of 9/11 divested us of the comforting illusion that we are safe from foreign attacks. Trump's election divested many of us of the comforting illusion that the deep-seated racism baked into our collective identity has abated over the centuries. This election also challenged the belief that democracy is durable, and that people are amenable to persuasion by appeals to facts and reason. Some have compared the recent political events to the account given in Sinclair Lewis's 1935 fictional book *It Can't Happen Here*—where a mendacious businessman wins a presidential election and turns the United States into a totalitarian state.

Approximately 66 million Americans were appalled by Mr. Trump, agreeing with American historian David McCullough (2016; see *Historians on Donald*

Trump Facebook Page) that Trump was unfit to hold public office because of his lack of character, ability, responsibility, and experience (https://poll.qu.edu/images/polling/us/us09272017_Uphy49k.pdf/). Approximately 63 million other Americans, however, voted for Mr. Trump, despite, or even because of, these attributes. They viewed him in heroic terms, as a shrewd deal-making billionaire rich enough to be unencumbered by special interests and unrestrained by political correctness. They were heartened by Trump's swaggering promise to "Make American Great Again"[1] by revitalizing the economy, building a giant wall to repel hordes of rapists and drug dealers from the southern border, deporting millions of undocumented immigrants, prohibiting Muslims from entering the country, and to "bomb the shit out of ISIS" (www.cnn.com/videos/tv/2015/07/09/donald-trump-on-isis-cooper-sot-ac.cnn/video/playlists/ac360-donald-trump/).

No matter the perspective, Donald Trump's election was, and remains, extraordinarily divisive, inflaming longstanding racial, gender, and geographical tribal animosities that are antithetical to democracy and could prove exceptionally difficult to repair. It is important to consider that the same existential concerns that underlie Trump's political ascent are also operative in his detractors' mournful reaction to his presidency. This chapter will explore the common thread for both perspectives of the political climate in the United States.

Terror Management Theory

Terror management theory (TMT; Solomon, Greenberg, & Pyszczynski, 1991; Solomon, Greenberg, & Pyszczynski, 2015) was originally derived from cultural anthropologist Ernest Becker's (1971, 1973, 1975) interdisciplinary efforts to construct an overarching account of the motivational underpinnings of human behavior. Becker (1973) observed that while humans share with all forms of life a basic biological predisposition toward self-preservation, we are unique in our facility for abstract symbolic thought and self-consciousness. This mental agility has certainly enabled us to thrive in diverse and rapidly changing physical environments; in our finest moments, we are sublimely appreciative of being alive. Self-consciousness, however, also leads to the disquieting realization that life is of finite duration and that death can occur at any time.

The unvarnished awareness of death and tragedy produces potentially paralyzing existential terror that humans "manage" by embracing *cultural worldviews*: beliefs about reality that infuse life with meaning and purpose by providing an account of the origin of the universe, and prescriptions for appropriate conduct for the social roles individuals inhabit in the context of their culture. Meeting the standards for appropriate conduct yields *self-esteem*: the perception that one is a person of *value* in a world of *meaning*. Self-esteem affords psychological equanimity by buffering anxiety (in general, and of death in particular) in the present and increasing the prospect for immortality in the future. Literal immortality includes the concept of heaven, afterlife, reincarnation, resurrection, and the idea of indestructible souls central to most religions. Symbolic immortality can be obtained by having children, amassing great fortunes, producing great works of art or science, or being a member of a great and enduring tribe or nation. People are therefore highly motivated to maintain faith in their cultural worldviews and self-esteem as a psychological bulwark against existential dread.

One line of empirical support for TMT is derived from studies based on the *mortality salience* hypothesis; specifically, that if cultural worldviews serve to mitigate death anxiety, then reminding people of their own mortality should increase the need for those beliefs, and this should in turn be reflected by more positive evaluations of others who share or uphold one's beliefs, and increased hostility and disdain towards those who oppose one's beliefs or who embrace different beliefs. TMT researchers make mortality salient by having people write about death, view graphic depictions of death, be interviewed in front of a funeral parlor, or be subliminally exposed to the word "dead" or "death"; participants in control conditions write about something neutral or aversive but not related to death. For example, Rosenblatt, Greenberg, Solomon, Pyszczynski, and Lyon (1989) found that municipal court judges set a higher bond for an alleged prostitute in response to a mortality induction; and, that mortality salience increased participants' estimates of how much of a reward a private citizen should receive for thwarting a robbery. In another study, Greenberg, Pyszczynski, Solomon, and Rosenblatt (1990) found that following mortality salience, Christian participants had more favorable reactions to fellow Christians and less favorable reactions to Jewish targets (see Burke, Martens, & Faucher, 2010, for a meta-analysis of mortality salience studies).

In sum, TMT posits that humans manage the terror of death by subscribing to cultural worldviews that provide a sense of meaning and value, in pursuit of psychological security in the present and immortality in the future. Existential threats (in life as well as in the lab) instigate efforts to bolster faith in our cultural worldviews and boost our self-esteem.

How could these ideas help to explain the disparate reactions of Donald Trump's supporters and his detractors to the 2016 election (and thereafter)?

Fatal Attraction: The Allure of Charismatic Leaders

Trump's deportment, and his relationship with his followers, hews quite closely to that of charismatic populist leaders. German sociologist Max Weber characterized charisma as "a certain quality of an individual personality, by virtue of which he is set apart from ordinary men and treated as endowed with supernatural, superhuman, or at least specifically exceptional powers or qualities" (1922/1947, pp. 358–359). Moreover, Weber noted, charismatic leaders generally emerge in times of historical upheaval, when existential anxieties are apt to be prevalent. More specifically, Eric Hoffer, in *The True Believer: Thoughts on the Nature of Mass Movements* (1951), proposed that the primary impetus for all populist movements is grave economic and/or psychological insecurity, leaving people "in desperate need of something . . . to live for" (p. 15). Becker (1973) added that when mainstream worldviews are not serving people's needs for psychological security, resultant existential anxieties impel people to embrace charismatic leaders who bolster their self-worth by making them feel like they are valued parts of something great.

Such leaders, Hoffer (1951) observed, need not be intelligent or original. Rather, the primary qualifications

> seem to be: audacity and a joy in defiance; an iron will; a fanatical conviction that he is in possession of the one and only truth; faith in his destiny and luck; a capacity for passionate hatred; contempt for the present; a cunning estimate of human nature; a delight in symbols (spectacles and ceremonials) . . . the arrogant gesture, the complete disregard of the opinion of others, the singlehanded defiance of the world . . . [and] some deliberate misrepresentation of facts.
>
> (p. 114)

What charismatic leaders do exceptionally well is to transform their followers' fears into rage and righteous indignation and direct it toward people designated as all-encompassing repositories of evil who, once subdued or eradicated, will restore life to a glorious (albeit generally fictitious) golden era when life on earth was supposedly as it is purported to be in heaven.

Finally, once totally devoted to a charismatic leader, followers become impervious to facts and reason that could undermine confidence in the leader:

> All active mass movements strive . . . to interpose a fact-proof screen between the faithful and the realities of the world. They do this by claiming that the ultimate and absolute truth is already embodied in their doctrine and that there is no truth nor certitude outside of it . . . It is the true believer's ability to "shut his eyes and stop his ears" to facts . . . which is the source of his unequaled fortitude and constancy. He cannot be frightened by danger nor disheartened by obstacles nor baffled by contradictions because he denies their existence.
>
> (Hoffer, 1951, p. 78)

This is a stunningly accurate description of Trump and his supporters. When Trump entered the political arena, white Americans (particularly poorly educated males) were feeling economically and psychologically vulnerable. To a certain extent, these anxieties were justified in that one byproduct of globalization was the elimination of the vast majority of well-paying manufacturing jobs in the United States in the latter decades of the 20th century. Such jobs made it quite possible for white high school graduates to make a decent living, own a home, take vacations, and send their children to college.

Trump exploited these very real existential anxieties to his political advantage by (mis)directing them into grievances against foreign and domestic enemies. Foreign countries were accused of malevolent intent toward Americans by their trade policies, ignoring the fact that the wealthiest people in the United States (including Trump himself) profited handsomely from their investments in the multinational global economy. The dangers of domestic Islamic terrorism, while quite real, were grossly inflated, ignoring the fact that Americans are more likely to be killed by right-wing Christian extremists than Muslim marauders; and Islam was denigrated as a fundamentally and intrinsically violent religion antithetical to the

American way of life. Mexican immigrants, portrayed as rapists and drug addicts, were assailed as an existential threat to American lives and jobs, ignoring the fact that illegal immigration had declined during the Obama administration and that immigrants are less likely to commit crimes than American citizens. Then on the domestic front, Trump inflamed (preexisting) hostilities toward people of color by depicting them as lazy cheats jumping to the front of the proverbial line for government services, ignoring the fact that white people receive more government benefits than people of color—rich people in the form of tax deductions for mortgages and savings accounts for education and retirement, and poor people in the form of federal assistance to predominantly white (and Republican) states (Cole, 2018).

Trump then vigorously insisted that he was the only one capable of keeping us safe (thus reducing anxiety directly) and restoring America's greatness (thus reducing anxiety indirectly by giving people a renewed sense of meaning and value). Notably, Trump exudes confidence and defiance, is full of anger and contempt, disregards other's opinions, and makes claims that, although demonstrably untrue, support the narrative that he promotes at his rallies and disseminates widely through his Twitter feed.

Consistent with this existential account of the allure of charismatic leaders, Cohen, Solomon, Maxfield, Pyszczynski, and Greenberg (2004) found that mortality salience increased support for a charismatic candidate in a hypothetical gubernatorial election. Then, in response to the September 11, 2001, terrorist attack on the World Trade Center and the Pentagon, President George W. Bush's approval rating skyrocketed after he declared that the United States would rid the world of the evildoers and that he believed God had chosen him to lead the country during that perilous time. In a study conducted a few weeks before the 2004 presidential election, Cohen, Ogilvie, Solomon, Greenberg, and Pyszczynski (2005) found that, in a control condition, participants reported intending to vote for Senator John Kerry by a 4:1 margin; however, after a mortality salience induction, participants reported intending to vote for President Bush by a more than 2:1 margin. Similarly, studies conducted in 2015 and 2016 demonstrated that: (1) while Americans were more supportive of Hillary Clinton than Donald Trump in a control condition, their support for Trump increased in response to a death reminder; and (2) Americans asked to think about a terrorist attack, or a mosque being built in their town, or immigrants moving into their neighborhood had increased levels of non-conscious death thoughts that in turn increased their support for Trump (Cohen, Solomon, & Kaplin, 2017).

Mourning in Trump's America

It worked! Trump won the election with overwhelming support by white people (especially males) of all income levels by stoking xenophobia and racial resentment (Coates, 2017). "Who knew," mused Neil Gabler (2016),

> that so many tens of millions of white men felt so emasculated by women and challenged by minorities? Who knew that after years of seeming progress on

race and gender, tens of millions of white Americans lived in seething resentment, waiting for a demagogue to arrive who would legitimize their worst selves and channel them into political power.

And it's still working, despite the fact that, like many populist demagogues, Trump actually cares very little for, and is generally contemptuous of, his poorly educated, economically distressed religious supporters. Trump has by and large governed like a traditional Republican (except regarding free trade), determined to eliminate the Affordable Care Act, successfully providing tax reductions for wealthy Americans, and eager to use the resultant skyrocketing federal deficits to justify severely curtailing Social Security and Medicare (the two most important and popular anti-poverty programs from the New Deal). Yet in October 2018, less than two weeks before midterm elections, as Trump rallied his base by demonizing immigrants, people of color, victims of sexual assault, and Democrats who have the temerity to take issue with him, he had the highest approval rating of his presidency to date. Former President Lyndon Johnson anticipated this state of affairs in the 1960s when he observed: "If you can convince the lowest white man he's better than the best colored man, he won't notice you're picking his pocket. Hell, give him somebody to look down on, and he'll empty his pockets for you" (Beres, 2016).

While Trump supporters were jubilant after the election, a substantial proportion of his detractors were in a mournful state of shock and despair. Anger, too. After all, Trump lost the popular vote by three million votes and marginally won in the Electoral College by fewer than 80,000 votes in three crucial swing states. Moreover, James Comey's October 28, 2016, announcement that the FBI was reopening the investigation of Hillary Clinton's emails (Silver, 2017) and Russian efforts to release damaging hacked information and spread misinformation to bolster Trump (Jamieson, 2018) evidently had a decisive effect on the outcome of the election. Even after a substantial time since the election, the anger and despair had not subsided. Interestingly, anger is a normal part of the grieving process, covering vulnerable feelings of grief and despair.

Anger is also felt by many who see the current political milieu as a loss of the deepest values of a democratic society because of Trump's blatant corruption (Crane & Tabor, 2018), apparent incompetence (Woodward, 2018), mental instability (Lee, 2017), dictatorial aspirations (Browning, 2018), putting the country at risk by appointing political sycophants rather than knowledgeable professionals, and in leaving numerous important government posts unfilled or in a revolving door state as many of his appointees resign due to the inability to work with integrity within the Trump administration (Lewis, 2018). Despair is felt because Trump, while reducing his followers' existential anxieties by promoting his Make America Great Again worldview, poses a daunting existential challenge to his detractors' liberal/progressive worldviews derived from the Enlightenment tradition based on reliance on reason, admiration for democracy and civil society, faith in progress, and respect for the natural environment.

Shakespeare famously declared, "Macbeth doth murder sleep . . ." (*Macbeth*, Act II, Scene II, http://shakespeare.mit.edu/macbeth/macbeth.2.2.html) because of the king's egregious moral transgressions. Trump's transgressions are no less egregious. Trump doth murder truth. While all politicians bend the truth on occasion, Trump is a profligate and indiscriminate liar. (e.g., according to FactCheck.org (https://www.factcheck.org/2015/12/the-king-of-whoppers-donald-trump/), "In the 12 years of FactCheck.org's existence, we've never seen his match. He stands out not only for the sheer number of his factually false claims but also for his brazen refusals to admit error when proven wrong.") Like all totalitarians, Trump lies frequently and repeatedly. In a rational universe, as Daniel Patrick Moynihan put it: "Everyone is entitled to his own opinion, but not to his own facts" (Moynihan, 2010). In Trump's universe, alternative-facts (Kellyanne Conway) or histrionic declarations that "truth isn't truth" (Rudy Giuliani) routinely trump the real facts and real truth, in order to gaslight the public until they are no longer capable of making principled judgments based on rational argumentation or factual information (Arendt, 1951).

Trump doth murder intelligence. Although Trump has presented himself for decades as an exceptionally intelligent person and an accomplished student, this is, like most of his declarative statements about reality, a lie. Trump had an undistinguished career at Fordham University before transferring to the Wharton School at the University of Pennsylvania, where he falsely claimed to have finished first in his class, although his marketing professor, William Kelley, said that "Donald Trump was the dumbest goddam student I ever had" in 31 years of teaching (Dreier, 2018). As president, Wolff (2018) reported that many who worked closely with Trump have come to the same conclusion, referring to him as an "idiot," "dumb as shit," a "dope," and a "moron". Trump is openly contemptuous of knowledge and expertise, and he encourages his followers to share his dim view of intellectual inquiry, leading by example by speaking to them at a fourth-grade level.

Trump doth murder civility. He has gleefully shattered all norms associated with the presidency and public life in general. He has mocked sexual assault victims, disabled citizens, prisoners of war, and Gold Star families. He insults and demeans anyone who disagrees with him, and delights in inciting violence against the press and his political opponents, even offering to pay legal fees for his supporters who physically assault reporters or peaceful protestors (see, e.g., Finnegan & Bierman, 2016). Trump's rallies are horrific displays of boisterous collective cruelty, with cascading effects throughout the country as hate crimes against immigrants, people of color, Muslims, Jews, and members of the LGBT community have soared since the election (Rushin & Edwards, 2018).

Finally, Trump doth murder Planet Earth. Perhaps Trump's most egregious transgression is against the planet upon which we depend for our daily sustenance and long-term viability as a species. We are the only country on earth that ignorantly, selfishly, and arrogantly refuses to cooperate with other countries to mitigate the effects of human-induced climate instability, which the U.S. military views as the most serious challenge to national security in this century (see 2015 Department of Defense report at https://dod.defense.gov/News/Article/Article/612710/). Climate change will increase poverty and income inequality, accelerate the decline of vital environmental ecosystems, stoke social tensions and inflame ethnic conflicts. To hasten the moment that the earth will no longer be fit for human habitation on the grounds that addressing climate change is bad for business is absurd; anyone who doubts this should try eating money.

Collectively, Trump's transgressions against the majority of U.S. citizens and humanity in general have weakened or entirely obliterated liberal/progressive worldviews that value truth, reason, democratic institutions, civil discourse, respect for nature, and faith in progress. Whereas Trump's supporters were in despair prior to the election because they mourned the loss of better days in the past, the rest of the voting public are now in despair, mourning the impending losses in the future. In truth, there is grief on all sides of this issue, and the support of Trump in the midst of this challenging time in history complicates this grief rather than assuaging it.

Many were inspired by Barack Obama's *Audacity of Hope*; electing an African American president seemed like a propitious harbinger of peace, prosperity, and increasing opportunities for all Americans as well as others around the world. Many now yearn for the emergence of a new charismatic leader, although surely not another populist demagogue. A leader capable of convincing Americans that our collective identity as citizens of the United States must override our tribal affiliations. A leader who can help us forge a cultural worldview that provides all citizens with an enduring sense of meaning and value without demonizing and denigrating foreign enemies or designated in-house inferiors. A leader, perhaps like Abraham Lincoln, who can convince us that:

> We are not enemies, but friends. We must not be enemies. Though passion may have strained, it must not break our bonds of affection. The mystic chords of memory will swell when again touched, as surely they will be, by the better angels of our nature.
> (from Lincoln's first Inaugural Address, March 4, 1861, https://ap.gilderlehrman.org/resources/president-lincoln%C3%A2%E2%82%AC%E2%84%A2s-first-inaugural-address-1861)

Key Terms

Cultural Worldviews: Beliefs about existence that infuse life with meaning and purpose. These cultural beliefs provide explanations for the universe and/or models for appropriate behavior and social conduct for individuals to abide by.

Mortality Salience: A hypothesis suggesting that cultural worldviews can alleviate death anxiety, then threatening one's worldview or reminding individuals of their mortality will often generate psychologically defensive actions and/or behavior.

Self-Esteem: The subjective perception of self-worth that an individual creates. This notion is reliant on the fact that one is a person of value residing in a world of meaning.

Terror Management Theory (TMT): This theory posits that human beings alleviate existential anxiety surrounding death through cultural worldviews that offer a sense of meaning and value. These cultural perceptions offer psychological protection against the threat of perceived death both in the present and the future.

Questions for Reflection

1. What surprised you the most about this chapter? Has this chapter challenged some of your beliefs or assumptions? How would you characterize the relationship between Terror Management Theory and other theoretical models of non-death grief and loss?
2. What do you think are the social implications of Terror Management Theory? How can Terror Management Theory be utilized to create positive social change promoting equal opportunities and rights for all members of a society?
3. Reflect upon the following statement from the author: "Whereas Trump's supporters were in despair prior to the election because they mourned the loss of better days in the past, the rest of the voting public are now in despair, mourning the impending losses in the future." Have you ever considered how grief and loss overlap with the political process? Think of possible examples of how previous loss experiences could influence and frame one's perceptions surrounding politics.
4. What recommendations do you have for providing compassionate grief support in politically divided societies? How can we foster resiliency when considering politically based losses?

Note

1. Trump appropriated the phrase "Make American Great Again" from Ronald Reagan, without attribution. Perhaps this was because Trump wanted credit for someone else's ideas, as he is known to do fairly often. Also possible is that Trump and/or his advisers knew that Reagan famously campaigned in 1980 in Philadelphia, Mississippi—a town with a long history of segregation and racial violence, in an effort to lure rural southern white voters to the Republican Party. And although Trump may have been unaware that Hitler vowed to "Make Germany Great Again," my guess is that Trump's white nationalist supporters such as David Duke and Richard Spencer are aware of and appreciate the slogan's storied heritage. The important point here is that for Americans old enough to remember Reagan (i.e., a large chunk of Trump's base) there is no doubt that "Make American Great Again" implies "Make America White Again" (also see Devos and Banaji [2005] for an empirical demonstration that Americans implicitly associate the word "America" with "white").

References

Arendt, H. (1951). *The origin of totalitarianism*. New York: Schocken Books.
Becker, E. (1971). *The birth and death of meaning: An interdisciplinary perspective on the problem of man* (2nd ed.). New York: Free Press.
Becker, E. (1973). *The denial of death*. New York: Free Press.
Becker, E. (1975). *Escape from evil*. New York: Free Press.

Beres, D. (2016). *How LBJ foresaw the election of Donald Trump*. Retrieved from https://bigthink.com/21st-century-spirituality/lbj-lowest-white-man

Bochner, A. P. (2018). The Night of and the mourning after: Truth and transference in the election of Donald Trump. *Qualitative Inquiry*, 24(5), 309–317. http://doi.org/10.1177/1077800417745428

Browning, C. (2018). The suffocation of democracy. *New York Review of Books*. Retrieved from www.nybooks.com/articles/2018/10/25/suffocation-of-democracy/

Burke, B. L., Martens, A., & Faucher, E. H. (2010). Two decades of terror management theory: A meta-analysis of mortality salience research. *Personality and Social Psychology Review*, 14(2), 155–195. http://doi.org/10.1177/1088868309352321

Coates, T-N. (20187, October). The first white president. *The Atlantic*. Retrieved from www.theatlantic.com/magazine/archive/2017/10/the-first-white-president-ta-nehisi-coates/537909/

Cohen, F., Ogilvie, D. M., Solomon, S., Greenberg, J., & Pyszczynski, T. (2005). American roulette: The effect of reminders of death on support for George W. Bush in the 2004 presidential election. *Analyses of Social Issues and Public Policy*, 5(1), 177–187. http://doi.org/10.1111/j.1530-2415.2005.00063.x

Cohen, F., Solomon, S., & Kaplin, D. (2017). You're hired! Mortality salience increases Americans' support for Donald Trump. *Analyses of Social Issues and Public Policy*. http://doi.org/10.1111/asap.12143

Cohen, F., Solomon, S., Maxfield, M., Pyszczynski, T., & Greenberg, J. (2004). Fatal attraction: The effects of mortality salience on evaluations of charismatic, task-oriented, and relationship-oriented leaders. *Psychological Science*, 15(12). http://doi.org/10.1111/j.0956-7976.2004.00765.x

Cole, N. L. (2018). *Who really receives welfare and government entitlements*. Retrieved from www.thoughtco.com/who-really-receives-welfare-4126592

Crane, J., & Tabor, N. (2018). 501 Days in Swampland. *Intelligencer*. Retrieved from http://nymag.com/intelligencer/2018/04/trump-and-co-are-stealing-america-blind-timeline.html

Devos, T., & Banaji, M. R. (2005). American = White? *Journal of Personality and Social Psychology*, 88(3), 447–466. http://doi.org/10.1037/0022-3514.88.3.447

Dreier, P. (2018). Why Trump keeps telling the world 'I'm smart.' *American Prospect*. http://prospect.org/article/why-trump-keeps-telling-world-i%E2%80%99m-smart

Finnegan, M., & Bierman, N. (2016, March 13). Trump's endorsement of violence reaches new level: He may pay legal fees for assault suspect. *Los Angeles Times*. Retrieved from www.latimes.com/politics/la-na-trump-campaign-protests-20160313-story.html

Gabler, N. (2016). *Farewell, America*. Retrieved from billmoyers.com/story/farewell-america/

Greenberg, J., Pyszczynski, T., Solomon, S., & Rosenblatt, A. (1990). Evidence for terror management theory II: The effects of mortality salience on reactions to those who threaten or bolster the cultural worldview. *Journal of Personality and Social Psychology*, 58(2), 308–318. http://doi.org/10.1037/0022-3514.58.2.308

Hoffer, E. (1951). *The true believer: Thoughts on the nature of mass movements*. New York: Harper & Row.

Jamieson, K. H. (2018). *Cyberwar: How Russian hackers and trolls helped elect a president: What we don't, can't, and do know*. New York: Oxford University Press.

Lee, B. (Ed.). (2017). *The dangerous case of Donald Trump: 27 psychiatrists and mental health experts assess a president*. New York: St. Martin's Press.

Lewis, M. M. (2018). *The fifth risk*. New York: W. W. Norton & Company.

Moynihan, D. P. (2010). *Daniel Patrick Moynihan: A portrait in letters of an American visionary*. New York: Public Affairs.
O'Rourke, M. (2016, November). Mourning Trump and the America we could have been. *The New Yorker*. Retrieved from www.newyorker.com/culture/culture-desk/mourning-trump-and-the-america-we-could-have-been
Rosenblatt, A., Greenberg, J., Solomon, S., Pyszczynski, T., & Lyon, D. (1989). Evidence for terror management theory: I. The effects of mortality salience on reactions to those who violate or uphold cultural values. *Journal of Personality and Social Psychology, 57*(4), 681–690. Retrieved from www.ncbi.nlm.nih.gov/pubmed/2795438
Rushin, S., & Edwards, G. S. (2018). The effect of President Trump's election on hate crimes. Retrieved from SSRN: https://ssrn.com/abstract=3102652 or http://dx.doi.org/10.2139/ssrn.3102652
Silver, N. (2017). The Comey letter probably cost Clinton the election: So why won't the media admit as much? Retrieved from https://fivethirtyeight.com/features/the-comey-letter-probably-cost-clinton-the-election/
Solomon, S., Greenberg, J., & Pyszczynski, T. (1991). A terror management theory of social behavior: The psychological functions of self-esteem and cultural worldviews. In M. P. Zanna (Ed.), *Advances in experimental social psychology* (pp. 91–159). Orlando: Academic Press.
Solomon, S., Greenberg, J., & Pyszczynski, T. (2015). *The worm at the core: On the role of death in life*. New York: Random House.
Weber, M. (1922/1947). *Max weber: The theory of social and economic organization* (Trans. A. M. Henderson & Talcott Parsons). New York: The Free Press.
Wolff, M. (2018). *Fire and fury: Inside the Trump white house*. New York: Henry Holt & Company.
Woodward, B. (2018). *Fear: Trump in the white house*. New York: Simon & Schuster.

PART **II**

Understanding and Treating the Unresolved Grief of Ambiguous Loss: A Research-Based Theory to Guide Therapists and Counselors

Pauline Boss

Introduction

In this book, Darcy L. Harris brings together pioneers in the field of unresolvable loss and grief. Here, unending grief is due not to individual or family pathology but rather to more nuanced types of *loss* that lead to more complex types of *grief*. My contribution to this field is *ambiguous loss*, a term I coined in the late 1970s (see review in Boss, 2016). Back then, I researched families of military pilots missing in action (MIA) in Southeast Asia during the Vietnam War. Later, I studied families of veterans diagnosed with Alzheimer's disease—present physically but missing psychologically. As their families said, "both gone, and still here."

Then and now, ambiguous loss is defined as a loss that remains unclear and thus without resolution. Grief is ongoing, but the cause is not individual or family pathology, but rather, the external situation of a relationship ruptured by ambiguity—the lack of certainty about the loved one's presence or absence. Pathology emanates from the external situation of ambiguity and not from the individual psyche (Boss, 1999/2000, 2006, 2011, 2016). Because ambiguous losses remain unverified and often unacknowledged by society, there are not the usual rituals that provide comfort as after a death in the family. Grief is thus prolonged and often misdiagnosed as personal pathology instead of relational disaster. Examples range from the catastrophic—e.g., kidnapping, dementia—to the more common—e.g., divorce or adoption. Most often in such cases, the ambiguous loss never returns to status quo, so family members and friends have no choice but to adapt to the ambiguous loss and thus the change it implies.

Types of Ambiguous Loss

There are two types of ambiguous loss (see Figure II.1). The first type is *physical absence with psychological presence*. A loved one is physically missing, but the family left behind is preoccupied by not knowing—where the missing person is or

PHYSICAL ABSENCE with Psychological Presence	PSYCHOLOGICAL ABSENCE with Physical Presence
Examples: War, terrorism (missing soldiers, civilians) Natural disasters (missing persons) Kidnapping, hostage taking Desertion, disappearance Missing body (murder, plane crash, lost at sea) Incarceration Immigration, migration, expatriation Foster care, adoption Divorce Work relocation Military deployment Young adults leaving home Mate or child moving to care facility Children with sperm donor fathers	**Examples:** Alzheimer's disease or other dementia Traumatic brain injury Autism Coma Chronic mental illness Addictions: drugs, alcohol, gambling Depression Complicated grief Homesickness (immigration, migration) Preoccupation with lost person, with work Obsessions: computer games, Internet Gender transitioning (also physical absence)

Figure II.1 Two Types of Ambiguous Loss
Source: Adapted from Boss (2016).

whether they are alive or dead. Paradoxically, the loved one is "gone but still here," because without proof, there is no acceptance of death. Both coping and grief processes are frozen. The second type of ambiguous loss is *psychological absence with physical presence*. A loved one is "here but not here" due to memory loss or cognitive impairments caused, for example, by Alzheimer's disease or the 80 other types of diseases and conditions that cause dementia, or from addictions or serious mental illness. Paradoxically, the person is both here—and gone.

Basic Premise

The basic premise in the theory of ambiguous loss is this: ambiguous loss is the most stressful type of loss because it defies resolution. Unlike with death, there is no officially verified ending to the loss. As it continues, so does the immobilization of both grief and decision-making processes. Our interventions and treatments with ambiguous loss, then, are to help people move forward despite not knowing. Instead of focusing only on symptoms, we focus on context. This means reducing the stress of ambiguity and building the resilience to live with its unanswered questions.

Underlying Assumptions for Living With Unresolved Grief of Ambiguous Loss[1]

The underlying assumptions of ambiguous loss theory, based both on research and clinical observations by myself and by others, are essential to state. They include:

1. A phenomenon can exist perceptually even if it can't be measured.
2. People cannot cope with a problem until they know what the problem is. Naming the stressor as "ambiguous loss" therefore allows a mourner's coping process to begin.
3. With ambiguous loss, we assume that truth is often not attainable. Instead of the usual epistemological questions, then, we ask how people manage to live well despite the *absence* of truth. Many do, and we learn from them.
4. Ambiguous loss is a relational phenomenon; it assumes attachment to the missing person or object, such as a beloved pet or home.
5. Cultural beliefs and values influence how individuals, families, and communities tolerate ambiguous loss, as well as how they perceive it. We assume the primacy of perceptions, but we also know that facts matter.
6. With ambiguous loss, the source of pathology lies in the type of loss and not in the type of grief (Boss, 2010, 2012, 2015; Boss & Carnes, 2012; Boss & Dahl, 2014; Boss, Roos, & Harris, 2011).
7. With ambiguous loss, closure is a myth. Without finality, the loss and grief may continue for years or a lifetime, and even across generations (e.g., Native American uprooting and genocide, slavery, the Holocaust, genocides, wars, terrorism, forced migrations).
8. If a loss remains unclear and ambiguous, it is still possible to find some kind of meaning in the experience. This requires a new way of thinking, one that is not binary: "My kidnapped husband is probably dead—and maybe not"; "My grandmother who has dementia is still here—and also gone."
9. With ambiguous loss, resilience means increasing one's tolerance for ambiguity. Ambiguous loss theory, built on the Contextual Model of Family Stress (CMFS; Boss, 1987, 1988, 1999/2000, 2002, 2004, 2006, 2014; Boss, Bryant, & Mancini, 2017), assumes that people have a natural resilience (Masten, 2007, 2014). Yet, a person's resilience is highly influenced by the gendered divisions of agency and empowerment their culture allows.
10. Core to the theory of ambiguous loss is the primary assumption that families can be both physical and psychological entities and that *both* are sources of resilience in times of loss. A psychological family is the family in one's mind and heart. It can be loved ones near or far, related or not related, alive or dead—the persons we lean on (physically or symbolically) in times of adversity or joy. For example, brides or grooms often light a candle at their wedding to symbolically acknowledge the presence of a deceased parent or sibling; a traveler is invited to the home of strangers to celebrate a religious holiday they all value. Or close friends become "family" for one another in lieu of biological families who are unsupportive or in another country. To assess the

presence of a psychological family, we ask: *Who is there for you now? Who is there for you in times of sadness or joy? Who do you want to be present at your special events—birthday, graduation, wedding—or holiday gatherings? Who can you call when you need help?* Cross-culturally, the answers vary, and often they surprise. I just learned that many families who survived the earthquake and tsunami of 2011 in Japan find comfort in the belief that their ancestors are now looking after their missing loved ones (Boss & Ishii, 2015). The psychological family manifests itself in surprising ways across cultures.

How Does Ambiguous Loss Fit With Other Terms of Loss and Grief?

To clarify where ambiguous loss fits into the set of terms, which make up this book, I list the different types of *loss* and the different types of *grief* (see Figure II.2). Seeing the variation on both sides of this equation between loss and grief *allows* for greater nuance in assessment and intervention when there is ambiguity and uncertainty.

Figure II.2 suggests overlap in types of *losses* including Harris's (2010) *nonfinite, non-death* and Boss's (1999/2000) *ambiguous*. The general term, however, may be *ambiguous*. There is also overlap in types of *grief*, especially in Roos's (2018) *chronic sorrow* and Boss's (1999/2000) *frozen grief*, both of which tend to be disenfranchised. Doka's (1989) term *disenfranchised* may be the umbrella term here. Indeed, there are both tangible and intangible ambiguous losses; for example, a baby swept out of a mother's arms by the raging waters of a flood is a *tangible* loss, but missing out on the privilege of seeing her grow up into adulthood is an *intangible* loss.

As professionals, we must clarify for ourselves, as well as for the people we serve, whether a particular situation is a clear or ambiguous loss, whether grief is disenfranchised, and how to live well despite the paradox of absence and presence that comes with ambiguous loss. Elsewhere I have given extensive details (Boss, 2006), but here I summarize that both/and thinking is required, and I will present six non-linear guidelines for building the resilience to live well despite the ambiguity.

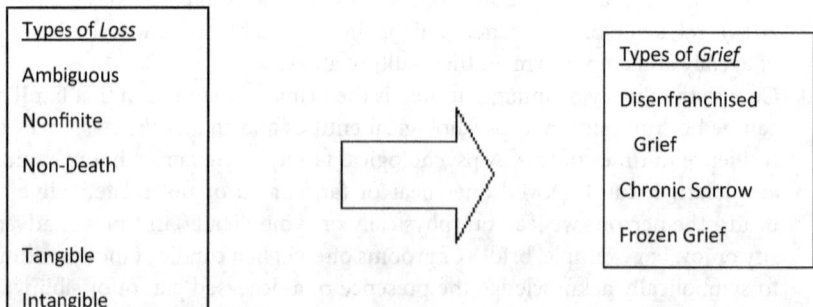

Figure II.2 Types of Loss Versus Types of Grief
Source: Boss (2016)

They include: (a) finding meaning; (b) adjusting mastery; (c) reconstructing identity; (d) normalizing ambivalence; (e) revising attachment; and (f) discovering new hope and purpose for life without the missing person (see Boss, 2006, for a full chapter on each guideline). Guidelines are psychosocial and are being applied by professionals from various disciplines. In addition, whether a loved one's body or mind has vanished, and whether we practice in rural or urban areas, or Eastern or Western cultures, these elements provide a flexible and inclusive guide for assessing and treating both types of ambiguous loss.

Standard Setting

Overall, the main standard or best practice cannot be the medical model and pathologizing the symptoms that people have with ambiguous loss. Rather, the model is stress-based for both assessment and intervention. The goal is not to cure the ailment but to build enough resilience to bear the ambiguity and uncertainty for years. (Note that there is triage for symptoms that require medical attention, but the overall therapy is for building resilience to deal with a problem that has no cure.) Unless, of course, someone is suicidal, homicidal, addicted, abusive, and/or incestuous, we cannot pathologize the people whose loved ones are missing. Rather, we intervene to ease the symptoms to a manageable level (see Boss et al., 2017, for guidelines and less binary ways of thinking for living well with ambiguous loss). Standards and guidelines of relevance require teaching people a new way of thinking (at least for Westerners)—less binary, more dialectic, more tolerant of ambiguity and paradox (being absent while present or vice versa), and less perfectionist. This means we, as professionals, must also shift our way of thinking from absolutes to both/and before we can be effective when counseling or treating people suffering with ambiguous losses.

Introduction to This Section

In the chapters that follow in this section, we see a sample of the variations of ambiguous loss that are being studied today and how this lens helps grief counselors, social workers, family therapists, hospice nurses, educators, and clergy to make sense of this confusing type of loss. This collection also represents both types of ambiguous loss. Type I ambiguous loss—physical absence with psychological presence—is illustrated by Darcy L. Harris's chapter on birth mothers' experience of loss after relinquishment of an infant and the chapter by Emmanuel Kassiotis, Liz Davies, and Keesha Quinn on missing persons. Type II ambiguous loss—psychological absence with physical presence—is illustrated by Dan Festa and Darcy L. Harris's chapter on living with spouses who have been or are diagnosed with dementia and Tom Dwyer's chapter on the loss and grief of addiction. Interestingly, the newest area of ambiguous loss research as of this writing focuses on an ambiguous loss that could illustrate both types of ambiguous loss. In this chapter, Mae-Lynn Germany, Anna C. Pederson, and Sara K. Bridges write about the ambiguous losses experienced from coming out and the process of trans*itioning.

What has emerged from early research and, more importantly, from these scholars and others around the world testing across cultures, is now called the *theory of ambiguous loss* (Boss, 2016). It is considered a socio-psychosocial model that lends itself to individual, couple, and family therapies as well as psychoeducational community-based interventions. This lens helps professionals—and the people they serve—to name and thus better understand the many unclear losses, which defy resolution and cause unending grief. The following five chapters represent the application and extension of ambiguous loss theory with the hope that readers will find this information useful in their own experiences and in work with clients from various cultures and communities.

Key Terms

Ambiguous Loss: Loss that does not have closure and as such remains unclear and cannot be fixed. Ambiguous loss can be physical or psychological. Individuals present symptoms of ambiguous loss in that they may be psychologically present but physically absent or vice versa.

Closure: An idea that the pain of grief will subside, such that an individual is no longer affected by a particular loss. As grief never entirely goes away throughout one's life; closure is always a false hope.

Resilience: The ability to go on with life after hardship and adversity caused by grief (instead of being paralyzed or destroyed by it). This theory represents a "return to baseline" in regard to functionality and one's perceptions of life.

Questions for Reflection

1. How is ambiguous loss distinct from other variations of grief? Identify three recommendations of how a person can practice resiliency while living with ambiguous loss and grief.
2. How can complex forms of grief such as ambiguous loss be perceived as pathological diagnoses? What clinical implications could potentially arise from medicalizing the grieving process?
3. Have you experienced any non-death losses in your life that were ambiguous in nature? What was your response to these loss experiences? How did others respond to your loss experience? Were you able to find acceptance with the ambiguous nature of the loss?

Note

1. Adapted from Boss (2017, pp. 271–273).

References

Boss, P. (1987). Family stress: Perception and context. In M. Sussman & S. Steinmetz (Eds.), *Handbook of marriage and family* (pp. 695–723). New York: Plenum.

Boss, P. (1988). *Family stress management*. Newbury Park, CA: Sage Publications.
Boss, P. (1999/2000). *Ambiguous loss: Learning to live with unresolved grief*. Cambridge, MA: Harvard University Press.
Boss, P. (2002). *Family stress management* (2nd ed.). Thousand Oaks, CA: Sage Publications.
Boss, P. (2004). Ambiguous loss research, theory, and practice: Reflections after 9/11. *Journal of Marriage & Family, 66*(3), 551–566. doi:10.1111/j.0022-2445.2004.00037.x
Boss, P. (2006). *Loss, trauma, and resilience: Therapeutic work with ambiguous loss*. New York: W. W. Norton & Company.
Boss, P. (2010). The trauma and complicated grief of ambiguous loss. *Pastoral Psychology, 59*(2), 137–145. doi:10.1007/s11089-009-0264-0
Boss, P. (2011). *Loving someone who has dementia: How to find hope while coping with stress and grief*. San Francisco, CA: Jossey-Bass.
Boss, P. (2012). The ambiguous loss of dementia: A relational view of complicated grief in caregivers. In M. O'Reilly-Landry (Ed.), *A psychodynamic understanding of modern medicine: Placing the person at the center of care* (pp. 183–193). London, UK: Radcliffe.
Boss, P. (2014). Family stress. In A. C. Michalos (Ed.), *Encyclopedia of quality of life and well-being research* (pp. 2202–2208). Dordrecht, Netherlands: Springer.
Boss, P. (2015). Coping with the suffering of ambiguous loss. In R. E. Anderson (Ed.), *World suffering and the quality of life* (pp. 125–134). New York: Springer.
Boss, P. (2016). The context and process of theory development: The story of ambiguous loss. *Journal of Family Theory & Review, 8*, 268–286. doi:10.1111/jftr.12152
Boss, P., Bryant, C., & Mancini, J. (2017). *Family stress management* (3rd ed.). Thousand Oaks, CA: Sage Publications.
Boss, P., & Carnes, D. (2012). The myth of closure. *Family Process, 51*(4), 456–469. doi:10.1111/famp.12005
Boss, P., & Dahl, C. M. (2014). Family therapy for the unresolved grief of ambiguous loss. In D. W. Kissane & F. Parnes (Eds.), *Bereavement care for families* (pp. 171–182). New York: Routledge.
Boss, P., & Ishii, C. (2015). Trauma and ambiguous loss: The lingering presence of the physically absent. In K. Cherry (Ed.), *Traumatic stress and long-term recovery: Coping with disasters and other negative life events* (pp. 271–289). New York: Springer.
Boss, P., Roos, S., & Harris, D. L. (2011). Grief in the midst of uncertainty and ambiguity. In R. A. Neimeyer, D. L Harris, H. R. Winokuer, & G. F. Thornton (Eds.), *Grief and bereavement in contemporary society: Bridging research and practice* (pp. 163–175). New York: Taylor & Francis.
Doka, K. (1989). *Disenfranchised grief: Recognizing hidden sorrow*. New York: Lexington Books.
Harris, D. (2010). *Counting our losses: Reflecting on change, loss, and transition in everyday life*. New York: Routledge.
Masten, A. S. (2007). Resilience in developing systems: Progress and promise as the fourth wave rises. *Development and Psychopathology, 19*(3), 921–930. doi:10.1017/s0954579407000442
Masten, A. S. (2014). *Ordinary magic: Resilience in development*. New York: Guilford Press.
Roos, S. (2018). *Chronic sorrow: A living loss*. New York: Routledge.

CHAPTER 6

Losses of Birth Mothers in the Adoption Triad

Darcy L. Harris

Introduction

Jenny sat down with her cup of coffee at her kitchen table. Picking up her tablet to read the morning news, she noticed a new message in her email inbox. Tapping on her inbox icon, she saw an email from the genetic testing company where she had sent in her saliva as part of a DNA analysis kit. She assumed the note was another invitation for her to participate in genetic research, as these tended to come every few months or so. But this time when she opened the notice, she froze. The email was from a man named Jonathan who contacted her as a genetic relative—more specifically, as her son. Jenny's hands began to shake as she read his note. He told her that he knew he was adopted as an infant and that he had completed the genetic testing in hopes of finding members of his birth family. Jenny got up from her chair and looked out the window. Nobody knew. She and her 35-year-old daughter had decided to do the genetic testing at the same time, hoping to learn more about their ancestry and any potential genetically related health conditions. It never occurred to her that in doing this test with her daughter, she would find the baby that she gave up for adoption so many years ago.

    It was the summer of 1972 when she was 16 years old, and Jenny and her family had gone to a cottage for an extended summer vacation together. She met Greg at a barbecue that was hosted by friends who also were vacationing in the area. She was immediately smitten. Greg was tall, handsome, and funny. He could tell stories that made people laugh until they cried. He seemed to know so much about everything. She didn't hesitate when he asked her to go fishing with him the next weekend. They hung out together the entire vacation, and said a tearful goodbye at the end, promising each other that they would continue their relationship through letters and phone calls, as they lived several hundred miles away from each other in different parts of the country. He was her first. Their intimacy was cumbersome, shared in a neighbor's barn loft, where they would both end up itchy and sneezing from the hay. Jenny's family was Catholic, and her devout mother had never discussed issues related to sex with her. The late-night talks with her girlfriends during sleepovers touched on their "crushes" with pop stars, but they were all naïve and wondered what sex would be like, usually with an idealized man who would be their husband. A month after Jenny and her family returned home, she began experiencing nausea and vomiting in the mornings. Her breasts were tender as well. Her mother made an appointment with their family doctor, who suspected Jenny might be pregnant and completed a pregnancy test that came back positive. He told Jenny and her mother the news together in his office.

Jenny's parents were beside themselves. Her Dad found Greg's phone number and called his parents, angrily accusing their son of taking advantage of his daughter. Jenny cringed as she heard the anger in his voice on the phone. Being unmarried and pregnant was a very shameful condition; being Catholic meant that she had sinned by engaging in sex outside of marriage. She felt she would be forever seen as damaged goods. Her parents decided that Jenny would go to a home for unwed mothers to have the baby, give it up for adoption, and she would then return home afterwards and resume her life. The home where Jenny went was unfriendly, and she was treated with scorn. When the baby was born, she was not allowed to see it. She was only told that it was a boy and that he was healthy. She was told that adoption was the best solution for her "situation" and that she needed to move on with her life. A week later, Jenny was sent back home to her family and to resume school. She married Roger four years later, and they had three daughters together. Every spring, Jenny would remember the baby that had been born to her in early April and wonder what happened to him, but she never told anyone why she would become sad and quiet during this time. Remembering being told by one of the sisters at the unwed mother's home that it would be best for her son if she let him live his life without interference, she never sought to contact him or find out more about him. And now, he had contacted her.

I decided to include a chapter about the experience of birth mothers after a woman who had a very similar experience to Jenny in the case study contacted me for grief counseling. She had been forced to relinquish[1] her baby when she was 16 years old. She was now 56 years old. The grief from losing her child had been a constant presence to her for 40 years. Interestingly, she sought grief counseling after her (now adult) child made contact upon finding her information in the adoption registry that had been opened after legislation that acknowledged an adoptee's right to information was passed.

In this chapter, I will explore the losses associated with birth mothers who relinquished a child through adoption. Frequently, there are references to the *adoption triad*, which includes the birth parent(s), the child who is adopted, and the adoptive parent(s). In this chapter, we will focus on the experience of the birth mothers.[2]

Jenny's story is an amalgam of many stories of women who relinquished infants that were considered "out of time" in the mother's lives. While the nature of adoption has dramatically changed since the time of Jenny's experience, what is relevant about her story now is the presence of many middle-aged women who relinquished infants when they were younger who may now possibly re-connect with these lost children as a result of legislation that has mandated the opening of adoption registries and the release of information to children who were adopted. In addition (as in Jenny's scenario), new commercially marketed DNA tests are readily available, allowing adopted children (and birth parents) to locate their biologically related relatives. For many birth mothers, the possibility of reconnecting with the child(ren) that were relinquished provides answers to many years of anxiously wondering and hoping that their children were loved and that their needs were met.

Birth Mothers' Experiences

Reviewing the literature related to the adoption triad reveals that the experiences of adopted children are frequently documented. There is also a sizeable body of literature that explores the experiences of adoptive parents/families. However, very little is written about the experiences of birth mothers, and the impact of the loss of a child through adoption placement (Brodzinsky & Smith, 2014). There are also significant changes in the demographics of birth mothers since Jenny's generation, as well as changes in how adoption arrangements may be put in place today versus during that time. In the past, most birth mothers relinquished their babies as a result of becoming pregnant outside of marriage and the strong social taboo surrounding out-of-wedlock children and their mothers. Birth mothers who choose adoption for their child today do so for many different reasons, including pregnancies that are considered to be out-of-time for the mother in varying ways. What seems to be a common thread for birth mothers, no matter the reason for placement of their child, is the entrance into a world of potential ambiguity and loss surrounding their decision to turn over the care of their child to an adoptive family.[3]

Most of the studies completed on the experiences of birth mothers indicated that most of these women continued to think about their children many years after they were placed in their adoptive families (Brodzinsky & Smith, 2014; March, 1997; Sachdev, 1989). Many of these women reported that they remembered not just birthdays and other special occasions, but on a regular basis, they would wonder about their child—what the child looked like growing up, if the child shared similar traits with them, hoping they were happy, and picturing them as they would move through developmental milestones (Fravel, McRoy, & Grotevant, 2000; Roles, 2007). Accompanying these thoughts and fantasies was an ongoing sense of grief and loss, with reminders of the lost child and lost relationship surfacing on a regular basis. In research that explores the experiences of women who relinquished a child several decades ago, and in studies that explore the impact of adoption on women more recently, the loss of a child through adoption and the grief that occurs afterward is a major life stressor in both scenarios (Brodzinsky & Smith, 2014). Birth mothers often experience ambivalence about their decision, with ongoing feelings of self-doubt, guilt, regret, self-blame, and despair (Aloi, 2009).

Pertinent to this discussion is the role of prenatal attachment and the reality that in the majority of pregnancies, there is a relationship already formed between the mother and child prior to the birth of the child. The emphasis in the adoption process has largely been on the entrance of the child into the adoptive family rather than the reciprocal loss of the baby for the birth mother. The bonding process for the birth mother, who carried the baby inside her during the pregnancy and experienced the birth of this baby into the world, had not been previously acknowledged. The relational bond that had been formed between the mother and the baby during the gestation period was viewed as transient and readily severed when the baby would no longer be physically present. In contrast to this view, research by Peppers and Knapp (1980) concluded that attachment between a mother and her unborn child usually begins long before the birth of the child. Rubin (1975) also noted that at birth there is already a sense of shared experience between the mother and the baby, as well as a shared history and the shared time together through the experience of the baby in utero. Severing this relational bond has implications. In contrast to earlier views that the birth mother can rest in the knowledge that her child has been given to a loving home and that she can move on with her life readily afterwards (often referred to as the "happily ever after" myth of adoption; Fravel et al., 2000, p. 426), many of these mothers feel a sense of betraying their child, shame for having given away or rejecting their child, and regret for not doing more to care for their child themselves (Aloi, 2009; Henney, Ayers-Lopez, Mack, McRoy, & Grotevant, 2007; March, 1997).

Birth Mothers' Ambiguous Loss

As described earlier, ambiguous losses occur in a relational context when there is uncertainty or lack of clarity about a loss experience. The hallmark of ambiguous losses is the psychological/physical absence/presence dichotomy (Boss, 2016). In the situation of birth mothers who choose adoption for their child, much research supports the ongoing sense of presence of the child in the birth mother's heart and mind. Fravel et al. (2000) completed interviews with 163 birth mothers, assessing for the participants' perceptions of the psychological presence of the adopted child. Their results provided "clear evidence that adopted children are psychologically present to their birth mothers" (p. 427). Indeed, in every birth mother who was interviewed in this study (n=163), some degree of psychological presence was documented. A passage from one of the participants' interviews was quoted:

> Special occasions, her birthday, a lot of memories come back on that day . . . I look at the clock and I think, "well it's [certain time] o'clock and I was in heavy labor, and [certain time] she was born, and it's weird because every year, I tend to look at the clock at that time. It's like all of a sudden I'm looking up at the clock and it's like, well, this is the time . . . Christmas and Thanksgiving I think about who's with the [adopted] family, and I close my eyes and envision grandparents and the new parents and siblings, what everybody looks like. This fall, she started kindergarten and that was . . . she's got new school shoes, and she's got a lunchbox. But those are positive feelings and there's probably not a day or week that goes by that I don't think about her.
> (p. 428)

Similarly, Aloi (2009) reported that birth mothers have long been assumed to "move on" in their lives, with the assumption that in doing so, they will eventually forget about the child—but instead of forgetting, their grief simply becomes suppressed. March (1997) reported that many birth mothers expressed unresolved grief over the loss of their child, with continued interested in the child years after the adoption. Some birth mothers also describe searching behaviors, similar to the attachment behaviors that are described in bereaved individuals (Kosminsky & Jordan, 2016). These birth mothers described that they would feel compelled to look at groups of children who would be similar in age to their child, wondering if their child might be present in these groups (Roles, 2007).

The ambiguous loss of birth mothers hinges on the ongoing uncertainty about the presence, emotional well-being, and outcome of the child's developmental processes. The child is typically very much psychologically present with these women, but physically either absent or inconsistently present. In adoptions where the birth mother and the adoptive family are known to each other, some of the anxiety over these concerns is alleviated; however, many birth mothers still express concerns about the child misunderstanding their decision to choose adoption, worrying that the child may reject or resent them, or that the ability to have contact with the child could be withdrawn at any time by the birth family (March, 1997).

The Social Context of Birth Mothers' Experiences

The adoption process is loaded with social norms, expectations, and assumptions. Adoptions that occurred before the last two decades were often seen as shameful events, where a woman who was sexually promiscuous paid the price for her actions by bearing an unwanted pregnancy. Charity organizations "relieved" her of the consequences of her actions by providing homes for unwed mothers that allowed them to be sequestered from their community during the time the pregnancy would begin to show, and then "taking care" of the baby by placing it for adoption in a "good" family. It was expected that the birth mothers would then walk away from the ordeal and be able to return to a respectable place in society (Andrews, 2017). Many of these women are like Jenny in our opening scenario; young when they became pregnant, not given choices about their care or the placement of their babies, and living their lives with an undercurrent of grief and anxiety over the child that was taken. Since the opening of adoption registries, access to vital statistical information, and the now widely available DNA testing kits, many of these women have been contacted by their (now adult) children. With the possibility of having direct contact that was not previously possible, new grief arises over the lost years with this child, in addition to fears about possible rejection, or deflated hopes about the relationship once contact is made but either does not continue or is experienced negatively by the birth mother and/or the adult adopted child.

While many of the social changes that have occurred in the past no longer involve a sense of shame for the birth mother, many birth mothers still experience feelings of inadequacy, regret, and self-doubt after they have chosen adoption for their child (March, 1997). Many women express the view that no mother gives up a child; not mothering a child is a breach of the social expectations for women's roles (Aloi, 2009). Even without the social mandate of legitimacy for children born to single women today, many birth mothers will still cite feeling pressured by family, the birth father, or professionals to part with their child (Triseliotis, Feast, & Kyle, 2005). The grief of birth mothers can be made more complex by the fact that they must consciously choose adoption for their child, which assumes that they chose to end the parental relationship (Roles, 2007).

Aloi (2009) describes how the grief of birth mothers is disenfranchised and dismissed. According to Doka (1989), disenfranchised grief occurs when a loss experience is not openly acknowledged, socially sanctioned, and/or not publicly mourned. The grief that is experienced by birth mothers is largely unheard and unacknowledged socially, even though the studies of birth mothers' experiences repeatedly describe significant effects that are profound and lasting. As stated in the previous section, it is assumed that the birth mothers have chosen adoption and thus they will not grieve (unacknowledged). There is also no death involved with the loss; the baby is alive and is assumed to be adopted into a loving family, and the birth mother continues with her life afterward (unrecognized). There are no rituals or public acknowledgment for the birth mother's grief (unsanctioned). Finally, there is the social stigma of becoming pregnant when it is assumed that modern women are educated and have access to birth control; thus, the birth mother is held responsible when an unwanted pregnancy occurs.

In the past five decades, major shifts have occurred in social norms, expectations, and the roles of women. Women are no longer socially shunned if they are single parents. They also have greater reproductive choices, including education about sexual health and access to reliable contraception and legal abortion (Grotevant, McRoy, Wrobel, & Ayers-Lopez, 2013). With these changes, the shroud of secrecy that surrounded women who became pregnant in less than ideal circumstances is no longer relevant. Adoption agencies began to recognize that unmarried women no longer felt the need to keep their pregnancy secret, and many who did become pregnant and were considering adoption for their baby were more likely to do so if their voice was heard in the process and there was the potential for contact with the child after placement (Grotevant et al., 2013). Thus, there are now have varying forms of adoption with different levels of contact.

Most adoptions today are no longer completely closed, recognizing the rights of adopted children to have access to information about their heritage and genetic health histories. Legislation has been enacted in most Western countries that allows adoptees to find identifying information regarding their birth parents. In studies that explored the outcome of open or mediated-contact adoption versus closed adoption, most birth mothers responded positively to the possibility of having some communication and participation in the lives of their adopted children. Negative outcomes for birth mothers in open or mediated-contact adoptions were reported in situations where the communication with the adoptive families and their child would wane or where there was contact that was later withdrawn for various reasons (Brodzinsky & Smith, 2014). Rather than if the adoption was closed, open, or mediated in the context of a third party, the overall satisfaction with the contact arrangements, regardless of the amount of contact, had the most positive impact for birth mothers (Henney et al., 2007).

Clinical Implications

It is important to recognize the central role of attachment within the losses that occur through adoption. In this chapter, we have focused upon the birth mothers' experiences; however, the central, common thread for all members of the adoption triad rests upon the importance of the primary attachment relationship and the potential consequences if there is a rupture in the attachment bond.

While a birth mother may feel that the decision to make an adoption plan is in the best interests of the child, she will still most likely experience the grief of losing that child because an attachment bond was formed with the baby over the nine months that she and the baby shared through gestation. Having this grief be recognized and acknowledged as real and valid are important first steps. Much of the birth mothers' anxiety about the child and recurring thoughts about the child will be present because of the attachment bond that has been formed. If, as Bowlby (1970) stated, attachment bonds exist to ensure the safety and survival of the young, then the attachment behaviors of searching, pining, seeking proximity, and frequent thoughts (and fantasies) about the child would be expected as a normal outgrowth of the bond that was formed between the mother and the baby in utero. Roles (2007) asserts that searching allows birth mothers to form a mental image of the child, validating that the loss indeed occurred; it also is an attempt to have reassurance that the child is doing well. In the absence of the attachment figure, attachment behaviors may intensify (Kosminsky & Jordan, 2016). It is also important to recognize that attachment behaviors are deeply rooted and are not under conscious control. So, while a birth mother may cognitively be aware of why the child is gone, the deeper attachment system signals a threat in this absence. In situations where the birth mother felt social pressure to relinquish, this sense of threat and anxiety may be greater.

Roles (2007) identifies therapeutic activities such as writing a letter to the child (which most likely will not be sent) or journaling to the child; explaining the reasons for the choice for adoption may be helpful. Letters/journaling may also express the birth mother's wishes for the child's future. Some birth mothers find it helpful to have a physical memento or linking object, such as the knit cap that the baby wore in the nursery, the identification band from the hospital, a footprint of the baby, or a picture taken as a newborn.

Many birth mothers seek out professional supports at varying points in their lives, and they are often disappointed that these professionals are not informed about the adoption process and don't understand their need to grieve. Aloi (2009) states that many health care professionals do not recognize the birth mother's need to grieve, and that some professionals have personal feelings and/or bias against a woman's decision not to parent her child. Many of these professionals simply don't know what to say or how to offer support to these women, and so they avoid them, further reinforcing the birth mothers' disenfranchisement. Additionally, focusing on the adoption decision rather than the grief that is present can reinforce social expectations that a choice is equated with agency, which may not be true in the birth mother's situation, especially if she felt coerced or pressured to make her decision.

Professionals who offer support to birth mothers should have a basic understanding about the nature of prenatal attachment and the role of attachment in primary relationships. It is also important to understand the experience of grief in situations where there is ambiguous loss (and thus ongoing grief that defies closure), and knowledge about the adoption processes in their locale. It is also important to note that not all birth mothers wish ongoing contact with their child; the level of openness in the adoption process is less a predictor of adjustment than the overall satisfaction with the contact arrangements that are in place (Brodzinsky & Smith, 2014). Many birth mothers find talking with other birth mothers to be helpful, sharing an experience that is often misunderstood but very profound in their lives (Roles, 2007; Brodzinsky & Smith, 2014. Another obstacle is financial, as many birth mothers cite the inability to afford professional support prevents them from seeking assistance.

Conclusion

The experience of birth mothers who have chosen adoption for their child is often greatly misunderstood and socially disenfranchised (Aloi, 2009). The fact that the adoption process involves a birth mother's active choice in determining the course of events sets this loss apart from death-related losses; however, the choice of the birth mother does not translate into a lack of grief, as these two aspects of the experience exist as separate entities from each other. Regardless of the contact arrangements with the adopted child and family, the grief of birth mothers needs to be acknowledged and supported in ways that match the particular needs of each woman (Brodzinsky & Smith, 2014). By attending openly to the layers of grief of birth mothers, both professionals and those personally affected by adoption can acknowledge, validate, and value this experience and its losses. While grief is painful, acknowledging what is painful can be hopeful as well, helping to break down the barriers of judgment, secrecy, and consequent shame that have been experienced by many birth mothers. Proper support can enable private grief to be publicly acknowledged, provide a context for the helpful expression of the grief, and ultimately increase respect for the voice of these women in the adoption process.

Key Terms

Adoption Triad: Three groups of people that are connected through the experience of adoption; the birth parent(s), the child who is adopted, and the adoptive parent(s).

Closed Adoption: A category of adoption in which information about members of the adoption triad is confidential, and communication does not occur.

Open Adoption: A category of adoption in which information about heritage, genetic health history, contact information, and a variable magnitude of personal information is accessible between the members of the adoption triad.

Prenatal Attachment: The relational bond between mother and child that begins prior to the birth of the child.

Questions for Reflection

1. Suppose a woman who comes to talk with you discloses that she is a grieving birth mother and was renounced by the adoptive family that is raising her biological child. Consequently, all communications have ceased, and the birth mother feels overwhelmed and alone. Identify major losses that the birth mother may be experiencing. After reading this chapter, how would you provide grief support to the birth mother?
2. How would you suggest educating a variety of health and social service professionals about birth mothers' grief to promote support and prevent further disenfranchisement to these individuals?
3. Explore the role of attachment in the grief experience of birth mothers whose child is adopted. Using an attachment-based model, how might you validate and facilitate the losses experienced by these individuals?

Notes

1. The term *relinquish* is used to represent women who were forced to give up their children to be adopted in previous years when there was profound social stigma surrounding unwed mothers and little choice was given to birth mothers regarding their child. Today, the more common terminology is that birth mothers *choose adoption* or *make an adoption plan*.
2. For more information regarding the experience of the adoptive family and adopted child, see Schacter and Schacter (2011), in *Counting Our Losses: Reflections on Change, Loss, and Transition in Everyday Life* (pp. 75–92). New York: Routledge. The experience of birth fathers has not been well documented in the literature; thus, this chapter's focus is upon the birth mothers' experiences.
3. While the experience of birth mothers whose children are lost as a result of intervention by child protective services may share many similarities to birth mothers who choose to relinquish a child for adoption, the scope of this chapter will be limited to the experiences of birth mothers who choose adoption.

References

Aloi, J. A. (2009). Nursing the disenfranchised: Women who have relinquished an infant for adoption. *Journal of Psychiatric and Mental Health Nursing, 16*(1), 27–31.

Andrews, V. (2017). *White, unwed mother: The adoption mandate in postwar Canada*. Unpublished Master's Thesis, York University. Retrieved July 31, 2018, from https://yorkspace.library.yorku.ca/xmlui/handle/10315/33571

Boss, P. (2016). The context and process of theory development: The story of ambiguous loss. *Journal of Family Theory & Review, 8*(3), 269–286.

Bowlby, J. (1970). Disruption of affectional bonds and its effects on behavior. *Journal of Contemporary Psychotherapy*, 2(2), 75–86.

Brodzinsky, D., & Smith, S. L. (2014). Post-placement adjustment and the needs of birthmothers who place an infant for adoption. *Adoption Quarterly*, 17(3), 165–184.

Doka, K. (1989). *Disenfranchised grief: Recognizing hidden sorrow*. Lexington, MA: Lexington Books.

Fravel, D. L., McRoy, R. G., & Grotevant, H. D. (2000). Birthmother perceptions of the psychologically present adopted child: Adoption openness and boundary ambiguity. *Family Relations*, 49(4), 425–432. doi:10.1111/j.1741-3729.2000.00425.x

Grotevant, H. D., McRoy, R. G., Wrobel, G. M., & Ayers-Lopez, S. (2013). Contact between adoptive and birth families: Perspectives from the Minnesota Texas adoption research project. *Child Development Perspectives*, 7(3), 193–198.

Henney, S. M., Ayers-Lopez, S., Mack, J. M., McRoy, R. G., & Grotevant, H. D. (2007). Birth mothers' perceptions of their parented children's knowledge of and involvement in adoption. *Adoption Quarterly*, 10(3–4), 103–129.

Kosminsky, P. S., & Jordan, J. R. (2016). *Attachment-informed grief therapy: The clinician's guide to foundations and applications*. New York: Routledge.

March, K. (1997). The dilemma of adoption reunion: Establishing open communication between adoptees and their birth mothers. *Family Relations*, 46(2), 99–105.

Peppers, L., & Knapp, R. (1980). *Motherhood and mourning: Perinatal death*. New York: Praeger.

Roles, P. E. (2007). *Birthparent loss and grief*. Retrieved March 29, 2019, from http://www.selfgrowth.com/articles/Roles1.html. Google Scholar.

Rubin, R. (1975). Maternal tasks in pregnancy. *Maternal Child Nursing*, 4, 143–153.

Sachdev, P. (1989). *Unlocking the adoption files*. Toronto: Lexington.

Schacter, S., & Schacter, J. (2011). Adoption: A life begun with loss. In D. L. Harris (Ed.), *Counting our losses: Reflecting on change, loss, and transition in everyday life* (pp. 75–92). New York: Routledge.

Triseliotis, J., Feast, J., & Kyle, F. (2005). *The adoption triangle revisited*. London: BAAF (British Association for Adoption and Fostering).

CHAPTER 7

Living in a Liminal Space: The Experience of Caring for a Spouse with Alzheimer's Disease

Dan Festa and Darcy L. Harris

Introduction

A looming public health crisis is the rising number of people with dementia, doubling every 20 years, due to global aging (Alzheimer's Disease International, 2015). Currently, there are approximately 47 million people with dementia in the world (World Health Organization, 2012), most of whom are cared for by family members in the community. A meta-analysis completed by Pinquart and Sörensen (2003) found dementia-related family caregivers to be significantly more stressed than nondementia caregivers and to suffer more serious depressive symptoms and physical problems. Of the approximately three million Americans with Alzheimer's disease (AD) living at home, it is estimated that 75% of the home care is provided directly by family and friends, and the remaining 25% represents services purchased by family members (Schultz & Martire, 2004). Regardless of which of these numbers are used for discussion, it is clear that caregiving family members with dementia is a public health issue of significance, and one that will become more prominent with the aging of the baby boomers, sometimes referred to as the "silver tsunami" (Perry, 2009).

The first author of this chapter (DF) chose to write about the caring for a spouse with AD from his own personal experience of caring for his wife, who was diagnosed with the disease several years prior. He has openly shared about the ins and outs of navigating many different territories, which will be described in this chapter. In writing from a first-person narrative, the author wished to provide readers with a sense of the "direct experience" of being the spouse to someone who loses bits and pieces of a life that had been shared together. The editor of this book (DH) will add commentary and referencing to the literature where appropriate in the text.

My Story

Lena was born into a military family in 1951. Her brothers were 15 and 17 years old, and by the time she reached her mid-30s, both of her parents were deceased. Her mother had suffered a post-partum psychosis when Lena was born, experiencing bouts of severe depression, becoming suicidal at times, and often struggling with untoward side effects frequently experienced in some of the early antipsychotic medications. Lena's mother ultimately died from Parkinson's at age 74. Lena's father was a career military officer, having served posts in foreign countries as well as in the United States. When he retired, he taught physics at a military college and experienced his first heart attack by the age of 65. He retired at age 67, and by the time he was in his mid-70s he was suffering from what, at that point, was called "hardening of the arteries." It was at that time that he became unsafe to drive a car. He died at age 75, having suffered a fatal heart attack following a phone call in which Lena conveyed the information that she had successfully defended her dissertation and thus had completed her doctorate. Lena's two brothers died respectively at age 68 and 72. One was diagnosed with Alzheimer's disease, and the other died of a sudden cardiac event, but prior to his death, he was struggling with issues of memory loss.

About eight years prior to Lena's diagnosis of Alzheimer's disease, I observed that she was struggling with some cognitive issues that first manifested as panic attacks when she was incapable of completing simple tasks that heretofore had never challenged her. Over the next few years she became more and more agitated while trying to complete fairly routine tasks. I also noted that she was having increasing difficulty in maintaining her focus, becoming more and more distractible and less and less able to utilize any form of technology. About six years ago, Lena was involved in two automobile crashes. In one, she fell asleep while commuting to her place of employment, side-swiping a bridge. In the second crash, her car flipped over into a culvert, totaling the car. Thankfully, Lena sustained only minor injuries.

Over the course of the next few years, Lena became increasingly anxiety ridden and bounced through several different professional positions, each time claiming that the technology was just not user friendly. She began having increasing difficulty remembering people's names. Finally, in her last position where she facilitated psychiatric groups, a patient complained about her inability to remember those in the group and their individual stories. In the summer of 2016 when Lena was asked to resign, she insisted that she was still capable of doing the work and she became very resentful and angry that she was being "forced out." That same summer, Lena was finally diagnosed with Alzheimer's disease, a crushing blow for one so bright—and an unwelcome journey for me as her spouse and primary caregiver.

Living with someone with Alzheimer's is like opening Pandora's Box each day, with more losses to confront and more challenges facing me as her primary caregiver, as well as for family and friends. Lena was still very much physically present, but I began to lose her emotionally, psychologically, and relationally bit by bit as the disease progressed. Lena moved from being quite independent and very capable professionally and personally to someone who was increasingly unable to function in everyday life tasks. Once bright and sharp-minded, her reasoning ability has become non-existent, and she now completely depends on others to accomplish routine, simple tasks and activities.

In the early stages of Lena's decline, her awareness of the losses associated with Alzheimer's was still intact, creating a great deal of sadness for her. As the disease has progressed, she has become less in touch with things around her and slipped into a morass of solitude, unable to extend herself to others, while at the same time craving contact with people. Recently, there have been greater declines. Lena is now no longer able to manage her own medications and is in tears several times a day. She oscillates between awareness of her loss of abilities and seeming to be totally unaware of her inabilities, continuing to act as if there is nothing different or wrong. She is quick to get angry with me and then later apologizes, stating that she is not angry with me but with the disease. As her disease advances, I find myself praying, not only for a quick death for her, but that she will quickly transition through this stage of quasi-awareness into oblivion where she will no longer be aware of the daily losses.

I find that my patience as a caregiver waxes and wanes. When I'm frustrated, I will try to say to myself, "how important is it anyway" or "this is a disease that is causing her to react in this way and her disruptive behavior is not being done on purpose or by intention." Sometimes I'm successful at reminding myself about this and at other times I become frustrated and lash out, which accomplishes very little other than making her feel greater self-loathing, of which there is already a great deal. Since her diagnosis, I have become more of a homebody, not by choice but by necessity. Lena no longer possesses the ability to focus and flits from one task to the next. It is almost like a form of ADHD. While still able to do some of her daily activities, I find that she has become less and less aware of her own toileting needs, and I now even have to prompt her to wash her hair. She has become more and more sloppy in everything she does, not seeming to notice when she spills something and even if she does attempt to clean it up, she is less than attentive to details.

(DH's note:) The topic of spousal caregiving in circumstances of dementia has been addressed widely in the literature. Many of the observations and feelings that the author describes in the previous section are well documented in studies that explore this experience. Of note here is the description of isolation of the caregiver as a result of the need to be close to home to monitor his wife's activities. The losses described here pertain to them both; Lena is losing herself in bits and pieces; Dan has lost the wife that he knew and loved, and he is also losing his ability to freely move in his own life. Much of the research on grief in caregivers of spouses with Alzheimer's disease focused on the multiple losses that are experienced over the course of the disease, including loss of socialization, intimacy, communication, roles, and relationships (Sanders, Ott, Kelber, & Noonan, 2008). This accumulation of losses often goes unrecognized by caregivers because they are so consumed with daily caregiving responsibilities.

Rossheim and McAdams (2010) discuss the stresses of long-term spousal caregiving. In their descriptions of spouses who provide long-term care to their partners, it is stated that caregivers are often overwhelmed by their duties; with their lives being consumed by endless tasks without boundaries, many have had to abandon successful careers as their spousal "patient's" progressing illness led to increasing demands for them to be present at home. As a result, there is often social isolation in addition to the burden of potential financial insecurity if family savings, insurance, and retirement are depleted by the loss of their income. "Time constraints, safety concerns, and exhaustion eventually force most spousal caregivers and their patients to retire from activities that once promoted connectedness, exploration, and personal meaning such as travel, social status, and community involvement" (Rossheim & McAdams, 2010, p. 478).

Unique Factors

I (DF) believe that there are many unique factors one can focus upon in confronting the ambiguous loss of Alzheimer's:

1. The indeterminate length of time for remaining in the midst of ongoing grief. As in the case of Alzheimer's, typically individuals live anywhere from 8 to 10 years, which can seem like an eternity for those trapped in this decline, living in the "already" the "not yet."[1]
2. The alteration in the natural trajectory of life. I believe that most of us grow and develop in life with certain key marker events to which we look forward. An example is that many people look towards retirement as a time to focus on doing the things that they have wanted to do or perhaps even doing things that have not been possible before because of the time commitments prior to retirement.
3. Even the celebrating of anniversaries and birthdays is disrupted. These kind of events, while only social constructs to which we've attached meaning, have become milestones within Western culture; when one partner loses awareness about dates or the significance of dates, those dates cease to carry the same importance, weight, or value; thus tending to fall by the wayside.

A part of the persona of the caregiver also ceases "to be." When your spouse no longer identifies you as their partner/spouse, that relationship is lost. While hopefully there are pleasant memories upon which to reflect, all that remains of the relationship are memories of what once was. These are not unlike the memories that a partner or spouse might have when one or the other dies; however, in a situation of ambiguous loss such as this, the individual is still physically present, even while that same person is cognitively and emotionally absent. The continued physical presence of the person who is dying cognitively and emotionally to you creates a unique scenario that most people couldn't comprehend. Sanders and Corley (2003) reported a strong sense of loss in caregivers' descriptions of their situation of a spouse with Alzheimer's disease. The descriptions of their grief included not just the loss of the companionship and ability to share with the partner as they had in the past, but the accumulation of multiple losses to both spouses that occurred throughout the disease process.

Social Context

(DH:) Alzheimer's disease is one of the most dreaded diagnoses in Western societies. We learn from an early age that having a sharp mind, being independent, and having the ability to control significant aspects of our lives are very important.

This disease robs people of some of the most valued aspects of our human existence. Because of the profound loss of faculties, there is a significant social stigma related to Alzheimer's (Werner, Mittelman, Goldstein, & Heinik, 2011). People fear the diagnosis as well as contact with those who are diagnosed, and the social network that once surrounded the family prior to diagnosis begins to dwindle away. One of the biggest challenges is that many people don't really understand what it is like to live with someone who has no short-term memory, in addition to other fading memories. Drentea, Clay, Roth, and Mittelman (2006) reiterate the experience described here; apparently, social isolation and loneliness are common due to inability of the caregiving spouse to leave the affected spouse alone, lack of availability of good supports that can navigate the ambiguity of the situation, and behavioral issues with the affected spouse that could readily be off-putting to others.

Those who have not lived with this kind of decline in a loved one are often unable to comprehend what the experience is like for the primary caregiver of a person with Alzheimer's disease. They may be kind and want to be supportive, but it is almost impossible to consider all of the ways in which memory affects our day-to-day lives and living. This lack of understanding further increases the sense of isolation for the individual living with the disease as well as the caregiver, both of whom are trapped in the midst of unpredictability and daily bizarre behaviors. Example (DF): My wife asks me daily, "What can I do to help you today?" If I don't give her things to do, she feels hurt and useless. If I give her things that would be helpful, she will write them down, forget where she put the list, and the items will go undone. So, in order to protect her desire to help, I will give her things that are insignificant to accomplish. While causing me additional work, she seems to feel better; then I simply either have to let these tasks go or I have to move more items to my "to do list."

I (DF) figured out about a year ago that my wife cannot cook anything that requires a recipe because she doesn't remember what she has already put in or left out; therefore, I've thrown out lots of food that she attempted to prepare because it was inedible. Even in cooking breakfast for herself, I've noticed that she burns the butter by putting it in a pan on the burner and then walking off and leaving it. I've also had to curtail her trips to the grocery store or any other store unless she is accompanied by me. She claims I am being controlling and that she has no rights, and to some extent that is true. She has no idea what items we may or may not have, and I found that she was spending lots of money on things of which we already had multiples. I got tired of returning unnecessary items to the store. In addition to no longer knowing where anything goes in the kitchen (or anywhere in the house), she also has no clue about what we already have or may need. I am constantly having to play hunt and seek to find routine items that she will place in strange locations and have no memory of where she placed them. She told me yesterday that she wanted to straighten up and organize our bedroom (on her own), which made me shudder. A few months ago, Lena was going to write thank-you notes to people who had sent us Christmas gifts. Together, we made a list of items received. She then lost the list, wrote several cards, but then couldn't remember what she was doing. For every card written, there were three that had to be thrown away because she became distracted and couldn't follow through on writing a coherent message of gratitude.

I have observed recently that Lena has begun experiencing more frequent delusions. She'll believe that I have asked her to accomplish some task or asked her to do something which I have not. This morning when she awakened, she asked if I had painted our bedroom because it looked more "peachy." Several times recently, she has envisioned critters climbing on our walls. Lena has also begun experiencing extreme mood changes. One minute she can be happy and blissfully operating in her own world, and the next minute I am being accused of all manner of things. I have been accused of asking her to move out because I had a new partner who was moving in. I have been accused of having affairs, taking away her ability to access her email, and many more.

(DH): The neuropsychiatric symptoms (NPS) of Alzheimer's disease (i.e., delusions, hallucinations, mood disturbances, agitation, aggression, disinhibition) probably create the biggest source of stress and grief for the caregiver. In a review of the determinants of caregiver burden and depression, including care demands, Cheng (2017) found that NPS symptoms were most predictive of increases in caregiver burden scores over time. NPS are more distressing because they are unpredictable, disruptive, difficult to manage, potentially embarrassing or abusive, and sleep-depriving. As a group, neuropsychiatric symptoms are most predictive of caregiver burden and depression regardless of dementia diagnosis. Disruptive behaviors are more disturbing partly because of the adverse impact on the emotional connection between the caregiver and the care recipient, and partly because they exacerbate difficulties in other domains (i.e., caring for activities of daily living; social situations).

Suggestions

One of the things that I (DF) found maddening at the outset of Lena's overt symptoms was that everyone had a host of suggestions about things that they thought might be helpful for someone with "memory" problems. They were great suggestions, but for someone with no short-term memory, they were a joke. We have one friend, a physician, who spent hours designing a chart so that Lena could check off all kinds of daily activities. The chart was lovely and totally useless. Lena thought it looked great and would be incredibly helpful; she spent time filling in all of the activities and never used it once because she didn't remember that she had the chart, where it was, or whether or not she had completed the task. I suggested labeling drawers in the kitchen; but Lena was opposed to that idea, not wanting everyone to know that she couldn't find anything. So, life is lived randomly; nothing is ever placed in the same location twice unless I do it. Every time she unloads the dishwasher, I have to spend time moving everything back to its original location so that when I am cooking, I can still find things.

A few weeks ago, someone posted a list on social media about things that one should or should not say to individuals with Alzheimer's. As I initially read the list, I became indignant. Once I had stepped back and returned to the list, I was able to take a second look. None of the suggestions were "bad" suggestions. My guess is they were written by a clinician who hasn't been living as a caregiver for someone with the disease. The addition that I thought should be included in the list is a strong message to caregivers to be able to forgive yourself. Living as a caregiver with someone who is suffering from this disease can be incredibly frustrating, anger engendering, and at best crazy making. So, letting myself "off the hook" when I lash out or don't respond in the most therapeutic fashion is an invaluable resource as I work to maintain my sanity.

I think another suggestion I offer is to take some breaks for self-care. I will be traveling to two conferences this year, which has necessitated a great deal of advance planning. For me to be able to attend both of these conferences has required the assistance of others. I've got some remarkable family and friends who will be coming in to stay with Lena while I'm traveling and provide some companionship and support while I am gone. That being said, there are probably times when I would benefit from being away more, but it is difficult to ask for assistance, and the amount of planning required and the costs to be gone for even short periods of time is daunting.

When Lena was first diagnosed, I told her that I was unwilling to live shrouded by a conspiracy of silence, so I have chosen to communicate Lena's condition to all that I meet; doing this seems to have prevented people from being angry at Lena when she says or does strange or bizarre things. And being open about Lena's challenges—and therefore my challenges—has allowed others the opportunity to provide some assistance, compassion, support, and relief. I have also alerted our financial agencies that Lena has Alzheimer's so that they can keep a close eye on any untoward activities to our accounts and alert me to that affect.

While many communities offer caregiver support groups, I have not chosen to avail myself of them at this point; it only feels like more work, something else I've "got to do." The Alzheimer's Foundation is a tremendous resource and has much great information. Many of the Foundation's activities are centered around fund raising, and while I'm very supportive of the idea of raising funds for Alzheimer's-related research, I'm also struggling to make ends meet because of added disease-related expenses. Because of these additional expenses, I have only just enough resources to maintain the day-to-day activities.

This experience underscores the importance of having an established health care proxy in place, so that as your loved one becomes less able to speak for themselves, you will have that power to advocate on their behalf. When Lena was first diagnosed, we completed a Living Will as well as naming me as her health care Power of Attorney. Lena's physician and I have a very good working relationship and share the belief that we want to make certain that Lena remains as healthy as she can, but we are not going to do anything heroic to prolong her life. We are also not going to worry about things like maintaining blood sugars, etc., that ultimately will not matter in the great scheme of things.

(DH:) What Dan describes has been referred to as *dual dying* because caregivers grieve the loss of the care recipient prior to the actual death, and they then grieve the loss of the person again when the actual death occurs (Sanders et al., 2008).

Factors that underscore his resilience are his network of friends and community supports, his willingness to ask for help when needed, and his openness in describing his situation.

Conclusion

While I (DF) may sound very clinical and cold in my observations, I am not. Daily, I grieve the losses of the partner I once had, who was capable of engaging in life and who now enjoys moments of levity and joy but much of the time doesn't remember having had these experiences. While I will mourn Lena's death, I believe that I will rejoice at a time when the losses are not daily and continuous. I am already mourning the loss of our relationship and the loss of the Lena that I knew in the past. I am no longer a spouse but a parent to another adult. The poet Robert Frost penned these words that I find helpful when thinking about Alzheimer's: "In three words, I can sum up everything I've learned about life: It goes on" (Fitzhenry, 1993, p. 261).

This segment from a book entitled *Night Light* by Amy E. Dean (1992) sums up the realities of living with someone who suffers from Alzheimer's:

> If we've ever dug in a garden and unearthed an ants' nest, we can recall their first reaction to our unintended destruction: they do everything possible to save their lives and supplies. The ants scurry around, moving the larvae to an underground room. Exposed contents are then relocated to unseen passages. In a matter of minutes, the ants are again safely underground and ready to resume their daily routines. How do we react when some catastrophe or unplanned event occurs? Do we want to crawl under a rock or are we as resilient as the ants? Instead of moaning over postponed plans or the loss of something in our lives, we can try to be like the ants and learn how to best work with circumstances that come our way.
>
> Life doesn't stop for us to lick wounds or add fuel to grievances. Hours pass, we grow older, nature continues. Every event is part of life's cycle. We can't run away from anything. We must meet life head-on and adjust to its ebb and flow.
>
> (p. 156)

This quote is a reminder that I (DF) can look at an unplanned event in my life as part of life's cycle. I need to trust that life will go on.

Key Terms

Alzheimer's Disease: A chronic neurodegenerative disease that causes difficulty and complications with memory, thinking, and behavior and is the most common cause of dementia.

Dual Dying: Grieving the loss of an individual preceding the actual death, and then grieving the loss of the individual when the actual death takes place.

Self-Care: A mindful practice of preserving one's own well-being. Self-care should always be congruent to a person's overall life situation and needs. Activities and practices may include: peer support, journaling, meditation, reflection/alone time, physical exercise, support from loved ones, eating well, pursuing interests/hobbies, and many more.

Questions for Reflection

1. Explore the role of non-death loss and ambiguous loss in the context of a spouse caring for a partner with Alzheimer's disease. What strategies would you suggest for a spousal caregiver who is grieving ongoing losses while caring for someone with Alzheimer's disease?
2. Do you know anyone who has suffered from Alzheimer's disease? How did it affect your relationship with them, and what losses occurred for you?
3. After reading this chapter, consider the aspect of social isolation and loneliness throughout the author's narrative. Why do you think many people fear those who are diagnosed with Alzheimer's disease? How can caregivers find social support when individuals avoid them, finances are limited, previous support systems fail, and their own spouse may not recognize them?
4. No cure currently exists for Alzheimer's disease. Do you empathize with the author when he feels the need to restrict Lena's responsibilities and autonomy, or when he's praying for a quick death for her? Why or why not?
5. Have you ever considered the significance of the role of memories in a person's life? To what extent do you believe that, as human beings, we are made of our memories? Building upon your previous answer, what, then, do you think is an appropriate way to provide grief support to those caring for a spouse who has been diagnosed with Alzheimer's disease?

Note

1. Life expectancy for patients with AD can vary between 3 and 10 years. The main predictor of life expectancy is the age at diagnosis. Therefore, caregivers, patients, and their families could plan on a median lifespan as long as 7 to 10 years for patients whose conditions are diagnosed when they are in their 60s and early 70s, to only about 3 years or less for patients whose conditions are diagnosed when they are in their 90s (Zanetti, Solerte, & Cantoni, 2009).

References

Alzheimer's Disease International. (2015). *World Alzheimer report 2015—The global impact of dementia: An analysis of prevalence, incidence, cost and trends*. London: Alzheimer's Disease International.

Cheng, S. T. (2017). Dementia caregiver burden: A research update and critical analysis. *Current Psychiatry Reports, 19*(9), 64–72.

Dean, A. E. (1992). *Night light: A book of nighttime Meditations*. Center City, MN: Hazeldon.

Drentea, P., Clay, O. J., Roth, D. L., & Mittelman, M. S. (2006). Predictors of improvement in social support: Five-year effects of a structured intervention for caregivers of spouses with Alzheimer's disease. *Social Science & Medicine, 63*(4), 957–967.

Fitzhenry, R. I. (1993). *The Harper book of quotations*. New York: HarperCollins.

Perry, D. (2009). In the balance: Silver tsunami or longevity dividend? *Quality in Ageing and Older Adults, 10*(2), 15–22.

Pinquart, M., & Sörensen, S. (2003). Differences between caregivers and noncaregivers in psychological health and physical health: A meta-analysis. *Psychology and Aging, 18*(2), 250–267.

Rossheim, B. N., & McAdams III, C. R. (2010). Addressing the chronic sorrow of long-term spousal caregivers: A primer for counselors. *Journal of Counseling & Development, 88*(4), 477–482.

Sanders, S., & Corley, C. S. (2003). Are they grieving? A qualitative analysis examining grief in caregivers of individuals with Alzheimer's disease. *Social Work in Health Care, 37*(3), 35–53.

Sanders, S., Ott, C. H., Kelber, S. T., & Noonan, P. (2008). The experience of high levels of grief in caregivers of persons with Alzheimer's disease and related dementia. *Death Studies, 32*(6), 495–523.

Schultz, R., & Martire, L. M. (2004). Family caregiving of persons with dementia: Prevalence, health effects, and support strategies. *The American Journal of Geriatric Psychiatry, 12*, 240–249.

Werner, P., Mittelman, M. S., Goldstein, D., & Heinik, J. (2011). Family stigma and caregiver burden in Alzheimer's disease. *The Gerontologist, 52*(1), 89–97.

World Health Organization. (2012). *Dementia: A public health priority*. Geneva: World Health Organization.

Zanetti, O., Solerte, S. B., & Cantoni, F. (2009). Life expectancy in Alzheimer's disease (AD). *Archives of Gerontology and Geriatrics, 49*, 237–243.

CHAPTER 8

Grief and Loss in Addictions
Thomas Dwyer

What I have lost is mainly an illusion of what I thought life would be.
—Anonymous

As a counselor specializing in addictions, I often read recovery literature to improve my professional skills. A few years back, I came across a simple one-page writing, not by a highly published leader in the field of addictions, but by a parent whose child was struggling with substance abuse. A sample of the parent's writing follows:

> When I first learned my daughter was chemically dependent, I felt as though she had died. All the dreams I had for her were gone. I was truly in mourning.
> (quoted in Families Anonymous, 2011, p. 167)

The writer continued, stating that in order for her to deal with the pain of her daughter's addiction, she had to allow herself to feel the pain of grief. The parent's quote, "I felt as though she had died" has resonated with me over the years and influenced my approach to addiction counseling ever since. Her daughter had not died, but to her, it felt as if she had. And what happens to all the hopes and dreams, not only for this parent but for all families grieving the loss of their loved one who is present in their lives but not the way they had envisioned? Lastly, and of equal importance, counselors need to explore the impact that grief can have on the substance abuser. When addiction grief is examined by counselors and families, the grief of the addict is often overlooked.

Case Study

Several years ago, I had a case that exemplified many of the issues associated with ambiguous loss (Boss, 1999). Mary[1] called my office seeking advice on dealing with her 21-year-old son who was dependent on opiates. During our initial session, Mary shared that she had been married for 23 years, most of which had been happy except for the past three years when her son, Ken, began using drugs. Mary said that she and her husband, John, were high school sweethearts. John went on to get an engineering degree at a prestigious university and she got a master's in education at a local college. She described John as very loving but very goal driven and scientifically minded. Mary worked as a teacher after college but decided to stay home when Ken was born, so she could be a "stay at home mom" until the kids became more independent, at which time she planned on returning to teaching. Mary had another son, Michael, age seventeen, who seemed to have adjusted well to high school. Mary said that Michael had always idolized his older brother, Ken. She explained that for many years she felt like she was living the "American dream." She had a loving husband, two beautiful children, a nice home in a safe neighborhood with good friends, and a cat and a dog. She reflected, "What could anyone else ask for?" She then added, "But then the accident happened, and life has never been the same."

Ken was an honor student and very popular among his peers. The two things he loved most, outside of his family, were his old Mustang car and baseball. When he was not playing and practicing baseball, he would be working on his car. Mary explained that Ken was an excellent pitcher, and college scouts started coming around to watch him pitch. Ken was hoping for a college baseball scholarship. Shortly before Ken's eighteenth birthday, through no fault of his own, he was "T-boned" in his Mustang crossing an intersection when another car ran a red light. He had to be extricated out of the car, which was totaled. Ken had several broken bones and permanently damaged his ankle. With several months of physical therapy, he recovered from most of his injuries, except for his ankle, which gave him continuous pain. When Ken was in the hospital, he was given oxycodone for the pain related to his injury. When he was discharged, he was given a thirty-day prescription. When he returned to school for his senior year, he had to walk, temporarily, with a cane. This caused him to be teased and led to the loss of his popularity. Since he no longer had his prized sports car, Mary had to drive him to school. It was at this time that Mary started to notice that Ken was asking for refills for his prescription before the thirty days were up. She also said that Ken started to become more moody and isolated in his room. Mary said that she truly hoped that he could still play baseball. She lamented, saying, "When baseball tryouts started, Ken could put little pressure on his ankle. He did not make the team, so he lost the second love of his life and any possibility of a baseball scholarship." Mary said that Ken then got very depressed, isolated himself even more, and started smoking marijuana. Ken's grades significantly dropped, and he just barely passed his final senior semester.

Mary admitted that she and John were looking forward to Ken going to college, not only for his benefit but for theirs as well, as he had become argumentative and moody most of the time. They had hoped that college would be a whole new positive experience for him to get a "fresh start." These hopes and dreams were not realized, as Ken flunked out his first semester. Mary said that this made her goal-driven husband furious and severely damaged his relationship with Ken. Things continued to get worse. Ken could not keep a job. He became addicted to the opiate pills, and when he started to run low on money, he switched to heroin. She said her life became a nightmare. There was never any peace. Ken would leave for a few days and never tell her where he was going. When Ken started into withdrawal, he would get agitated and at times become violent by breaking things and screaming in their faces. Mary said "we finally got him to a rehab facility. We were so hopeful that this would get him the help he needed." Mary continued saying that when he came home, he looked good and for a month "we had peace, but it didn't last." Ken picked up his drug habits where he left off. Not only were Mary and John arguing with Ken, but she said that she found herself in frequent conflict with John as to what should be done. Mary continued saying that with all this family drama, Michael had not been getting much of their attention. It was at this point that Mary called my office looking for help.

Sadly, Mary's story is all too common. As Mary continued her sessions, she shared multiple examples of ambiguous loss that most families experience when they have a loved one addicted to drugs and/or alcohol, such as: loss of a peaceful and loving household, attending her son's sporting events, college graduation, opportunity to return to work, family vacations, and possible grandchildren.

Family Addiction Grief—The Chameleon Effect

Boss (1999) discusses ambiguous loss as being a loss without death, when the loved one is physically not present but is psychologically present, such as a kidnapping, a solider missing in action, or that of a biological mother giving up her child for adoption. She also discusses a similar loss when the loved one is physically present but psychologically absent as in the case of a stroke, Alzheimer's disease, or addiction. Boss found "those with loved ones who were 'there but not there' were indeed more distressed than those who had a more ordinary loss" (p. 16). Through my experience, I would argue that addictions fall into both categories. In the case study, not only did Mary and John "lose" Ken psychologically when his personality changed from his opiate use, they had the additional physical grief when he would disappear for days without telling anyone where he was going. The family suffered every day, not knowing if the police would be calling to tell them that Ken had died.

So how does ambiguous loss affect family members? According to Barnard (2005), when a family member is found to be actively using drugs, the family unit is thrown into chaos. Initially, most families try to resolve the problem internally without outside assistance, but they are often overwhelmed by not knowing what to do. This strains family relationships. In research by Oreo and Ozagal (2007), parents often disagree on how to resolve the family crisis at hand. They suggest that families with an addicted loved one face the same ambiguous loss as those whose loved one suffered from a chronic illness or debilitating injury.

Families become so preoccupied in trying to resolve their loved one's substance abuse issues that through all the anger, anxiety, depression, conflict, and confusion, they never noticed that their worlds have been invaded by grief. Like a chameleon, grief entered their personal space, but the family members never noticed. I call this the *chameleon effect*. It is quiet, subtle, and blends into every family member's background. The grief begins to affect the family members' emotions and decision making. Part of human development is forming emotional bonds. When these bonds are disrupted, these affected bonds lead to grief (Bowlby, 2006). Before Ken's accident, Mary proudly discussed the strong family relationships existing among all her family members. Once the accident happened, grief found its way into her life and into the lives of the other family members.

Statements from other mothers I have counseled help to illustrate this grief:

> *Living with my addict son, felt like I was living bereavement every day he was using.*
>
> (Barbara G.)

> *After so many years of my daughter's active drug use, I grieved the loss of hope, which made me more depressed.*
>
> (Megan R.)

> *Seeing my son strung out on heroin made me feel like I was witnessing a slow suicide.*
>
> (Susan P.)

Boss (2006) talks about the conflict of emotions family members experience as illustrated below:

| Hopefulness | ⟷ | Hopelessness |
| Love | | Hate |

Boss states that the grief in ambiguous loss pulls families, especially parents, in different directions, from the hope that things will get better, to the reality and hopelessness when behaviors do not change. Parents are constantly conflicted. They love their child or other afflicted family member, but they "hate" their drug-affected behaviors. They are in a constant love/hate relationship.

Sibling Grief

So, what happens to the siblings during this time? When one of the children is dependent on drugs and/or alcohol, parents tend to focus most of their time and energy trying to rescue their addicted child. This leaves the other children in need of parental attention (Oreo & Ozgul, 2007). Barnard's (2005) study on the effects of drug use in the family showed that siblings, especially younger siblings, are negatively affected when an older sibling uses drugs. Barnard compared the relationship expectation of the younger sibling with the older sibling to the reality of the relationship when drug use became an issue. The common expectation before the older sibling's drug and alcohol abuse was that the older sibling would demonstrate a caring involvement, one that would often include confiding, protecting, and mentoring. The reality, all too often with drug use, was that the younger sibling became secondary to the substance use. The younger sibling then experienced the loss of the valued relationship. When the older sibling would disappear for days, they experienced high anxiety and fear that their older sibling would die in a drug-related activity. Despite all the disappointment, Barnard discovered that the younger siblings held on to strong hope that their addicted sibling would return to their drug-free self again. As Barnard noted, these hopes were often given up as the older sibling struggled to attain sobriety (2005).

Addict Grief

Do addicts grieve? Do they mourn the loss of the damaged relationships, especially family ones? Do they grieve the loss of what "could have been"? Bowlby (2006), in his study of attachment, stated that people build attachments to feel safe and secure. Using this as a starting point, one can conceptualize how drug attachment can lead to grief. Gervai (2009) suggested that the stronger the attachment, the more intense the loss if the bond is broken. Extending these concepts to addiction, Flores (2001) stated that addiction is a form of attachment disorder, and that addicts form strong emotional attachments to their substance of choice. Miller (1994) studied these drug attachments and suggested that addicts who decide to live a sober lifestyle often experience a significant amount of grief over the loss of the substance. Friedman (1984) asserted that alcoholics are in a perpetual state of grief. The conclusions of these studies are encapsulated in statements made by recovery clients in my practice.

> *My bottle [of alcohol] was my best friend. Whenever I needed companionship to make me feel better, it was always there. I knew it was killing me but I didn't care. I loved my bottle.*
>
> (Tracy G.)

> *When I first gave up using drugs, I felt I lost a part of me. Even though I knew that if I continued using, I would probably end up dead. I missed it and the world I knew.*
>
> (Peter R.)

The losses described by my two clients, Tracy G. and Peter R., exemplify only a small sample of the losses experienced by substance abusers. Active use of psychoactive drugs often leads to losses involving relationships, health, finances, and self-respect (Goldberg, 1985). Looking at the original case study from the beginning of the chapter, Ken experienced several ambiguous losses. Before the accident, he had a strong family relationship. His two favorite activities were working on his prized car and playing competitive baseball. This lifestyle motivated him to succeed academically and led to increased popularity among his peers. Unknown to Ken at the time, when the accident happened, he had experienced overwhelming grief. He lost his car, his ability to play baseball, and any possibility of a sports scholarship. His popularity lessened, which affected his motivation to continue school at an honors level. His grief led to depression and drug use, which eventually affected his loving family relationships. Not realizing the grief he was experiencing, Ken showed symptoms described by Denny and Lee (1984), who suggested that individuals actively using drugs and alcohol have difficulty expressing their feelings and dealing with the problems in their lives. This grief related to ambiguous loss is best described in a statement made by my client, Bob:

> When I was drinking I felt like a piece of garbage. I lost my marriage, my job, and relationships with my children. I lost it all because I loved my drinking more. Until I was ready to ask for help, I lived in a constant state of self-pity and grief.
>
> (Bob T.)

Clinical Strategies

Family Grief Treatment

Family addiction grief is not like mourning the loss of a person. It is a loss that you cannot physically touch or feel. It is an object that exists in one's expectations and dreams, and it is different for every family member, including the addict. As noted by Boss (2006), ambiguous loss negatively impacts the individual both physically and psychologically. Its stealth chameleon-like arrival affects the family unit and each family member or loved one, differently. There is no medication to cure grief; only treatments for some of the individual symptoms it creates. For the family unit, Boss states, "Family members of different genders and generations will often vary in how they interpret an unclear loss. The goal is to achieve some degree of convergence" (p. 19).

It has been my experience, as well as that of my peers who specialize in addiction, that it is rare for the whole family to initially seek a counseling session. Usually, an affected family member, quite often the mother, will be the first in session. The substance abuser will come in initially looking for ways to obtain or maintain his or her sobriety. The common ground that needs to be addressed at some point, amidst all the other addiction-related issues, is the grief from ambiguous loss that is affecting them all. The clinical strategies used in these two different sessions overlap in some areas and share a similar goal of restoring the family unit.

Affected Family and Loved Ones (AFLO)

For the sake of simplicity, I will include "loved ones," those who have a deep emotional relationship with the addict but not a family member, as part of this discussion. When AFLOs come for their initial session, they often want to learn how to "fix" the substance abuser, so sanity can be restored to the relationship. They are often shocked when they learn that the person that needs to be "fixed" is not their drug and alcohol-using family member but, surprisingly, themselves. I often hear, "I am not the one using drugs, why do I have to change?" I remind them that they are being negatively affected and that how they choose to respond to the chaotic environment directly correlates to their mental health. During our discussion on drug-related behaviors and their effects on the family members, I introduce them to the concept and symptoms of ambiguous loss that they may also be experiencing. These symptoms vary from one individual to another, and as Boss (2006) posits, "tolerance for ambiguity is related to our spiritual beliefs and cultural values, not just personality" (p. 18). Clinicians need to understand that parents of a substance abuser often feel anger, fear, shame, guilt, despair, and sadness (Oreo & Ozgul, 2007). The stigma affecting the family members from having someone in their household actively using drugs and/or alcohol can lead to judgments from non-family members. This often leads them to feeling ashamed, embarrassed, and isolated (Barnard, 2005; Butler & Bauld, 2005; Oreo & Ozgul, 2007). As counselors, we need to explore these emotions, especially in the context of the client's religious and cultural backgrounds.

Primary Needs

Counselors need to ensure their client's primary needs are being addressed. If violence and physical abuse are present, the proper authorities need to be involved. If the substance abuser is a minor, clients should be encouraged to call the police on their child. This can send a powerful message that threatening behavior will not be tolerated in the home. Once safety is assured, clinicians should assess their client's eating and sleeping habits, and whether the client is getting enough exercise. Clients should be encouraged to get a physical from their doctor to ensure the emotional strain of having an active substance abuser in the home has not caused any health issues. If the clients need encouragement, they should be reminded that if they are not healthy, their ability to help others could be greatly diminished.

Secondary Needs: Education and Spirituality

After the primary needs have been satisfactorily addressed, clinicians should focus on education and spirituality or personal growth. Boss (2006) states that families can learn to effectively manage their stress if given enough information. Using this as the foundation for educating families struggling with ambiguous loss from a drug-using family member, clinicians can ease their client's stress by providing information on the ambiguous loss and the associated grief symptoms and some scientific information on how the brain is affected by addiction. Barnard (2005) discussed the shock, fear, confusion, and overall disruption of the family unit when there is a substance abuser in the home. Oreo and Ozgul (2007) describe these feelings combined with the symbolic losses of the hopes and dreams that "could have been" as an ambiguous grief experience. Boss (2006) suggests that clinicians must help their clients identify their symptoms and label them as grief secondary to ambiguous loss, when applicable. This, she says, provides a sense of relief for the clients because they learn that what they are feeling is not unusual and that there is a label for it. According to the National Institute on Drug Abuse (2014), drugs affect many of the brain functions and cause the compulsions to use drugs despite the negative consequences. Educating the families on addiction can help ease some of the guilt and ongoing effort of trying to control the addict's behavior. In the 12-Step recovery programs, the Three C's concept is introduced, which includes Cause, Cure, and Control. The basis of this concept is that when dealing with an addicted loved one, family members need to remind themselves that they did not "cause" the addiction, they cannot "cure" the addiction, and they cannot "control" the addiction, so they need to focus on their own needs. This can provide some emotional relief for the clients and prepare them for their spiritual enrichment and personal growth. The process of emotionally detaching from the substance abuser does not mean one no longer loves him or her. It simply means that the client learns not to be as negatively affected as before when drug-affected behaviors occur. This, according to Boss (1999), creates an ambiguous paradox in that clients are asked to change when the situation remains the same. Victor Frankl, in his postscript 1984 edition of his famous book, *Man's Search for Meaning*, calls this *tragic optimism*. He states that absence of certainty allows for one to have hope for a positive outcome. Boss (1999) describes this status as moving forward into the fog, not knowing what the future holds.

So, how does one begin this spiritual and personal growth journey? I suggest that the journey should not be taken alone. Boss (1999) states that the human experience is never predictable, but with the support of family, friends, and community, and some spiritual beliefs, people can manage the ebb and flow of emotions that accompany these difficult times. Additionally, there are self-help support groups such as Al-anon and Nar-anon that are specifically run to help those who have a loved one suffering from drug and alcohol abuse. The community connection and fellowship that often come from these meetings can instill hope and self-care. It has been my experience that those who attend a self-help support group supplemented with the individual attention of private therapy generally have the most positive outcomes. Many of these groups are worldwide and can be found in most nearby towns.

Clinicians can help their clients redefine their relationship with their addicted loved one as an addict relationship. Once the relationship is identified, healthy boundaries and realistic expectations can be set. As difficult as it sounds, clinicians need to encourage their clients to look for positive things in the relationship and to try to instill hope and optimism. Guilt often is an anchor that inhibits a family member from moving forward with his or her life. Clinicians can help their clients learn to forgive themselves for any perceived actions or inactions that they feel they had or had not done. Knowledge is power, and by providing proper addiction education to their clients, clinicians can help them learn how to "move on" without their feeling that they are abandoning their loved one. In order for clients to "move on" in their journey, they need a goal, and in this situation, it is an ambiguous one. The goal is not to "fix" their loved one, but for the client to live a happier and healthier life, while their family member might still be actively abusing substances. According to Boss (2006), the path to human resilience, health, and survival is through meaning-making. She continues, saying that finding meaning happens when one can find some rational reasoning to what is happening. In a chaotic drug-affected household, searching for meaning in what appears to be a highly irrational environment becomes the lifeline to survival. If meaning-making becomes the compass to a healthier lifestyle, clinicians can provide many diversified suggestions that can make their client's journey a rewarding one.

Below are some ideas to discuss with clients that I have found useful in my practice:

- *Volunteerism*—find a cause that is meaningful. Helping others can be very rewarding.
- *Developing other interests and hobbies*—focus on things that are enjoyable.
- *Connecting with nature*—walk in the woods, or garden; all activities in nature can be very therapeutic.
- *Journaling*—racing intrusive thoughts can often be addressed by writing them down.
- *Creative activities*—write, paint, draw, build, spiritual reading, anything that puts the mind in a better place.
- *Building new dreams*—reassess one's life and set new goals that incorporate the new reality.
- *Meditation*—controlled breathing exercises often help in dealing with stress.

Addict Grief Treatment

As discussed earlier, Bowlby's (2006) attachment theory posits that people build emotional attachments not just to other people, but to things in order to feel secure. Jennings (1991) explains that the addict has to adjust to the loss and grieving process of life without their drug of choice. This is important for counselors to understand because addict grief is often forgotten in recovery. In the drug culture, addicts make social connections. They can become "experts" in their field. They develop a sense of belonging (Furr & Johnson, 2017). According to Goldberg (1985), overcoming addiction requires a complete lifestyle change. Applying Worden's *Tasks of Grief* (2008) to substance abuse, the individual seeking sobriety has to process the physical and emotional pain of the loss. The individual's ambiguous loss may intensify as s/he begins recovery and reflects on the lost relationships, jobs, money, and self-respect. Phillips (2017) states that an important part of recovery is for addicts not only to accept the past, but also to learn to forgive themselves and make amends when necessary. In addition to guiding their clients towards self-forgiveness and to processing the feelings of the past unhealthy lifestyles, clinicians can use the same clinical grief recovery suggestions that are made to the family members. Since the loss of the drug is much more personal to the addict, the counselor may ask the substance abuser to write a letter to his drug of choice and to process what he misses most about the drug relationship. Through this processing, hopefully, the counselor and client can discover the emotional void that the drug filled and supplant it with healthier coping skills.

According to the 2014 National Survey on Drug Use and Health conducted by the Substance Abuse and Mental Health Service Administration (SAMHSA,

2014), 21.5 million Americans, ages 12 and older, were considered to have a substance use disorder. According to the Pew Research Center survey conducted in August 2017, 46% of Americans have someone in their family or know of a close friend who has an addiction problem (Gramlich, n.d.). These alarming statistics mean that those in the field of counseling need to have a good understanding of addictions and be prepared to explore the ambiguous losses affecting the family members and the substance abuser.

Key Terms

> **Affected Family and Loved Ones (AFLO):** Individuals who have a deep emotional relationship with an addict; may be family, partners, friends, or other loved ones who are experiencing grief.
> **Chameleon Effect:** When grief occurs subtly from a loss and is not noticed by the individual experiencing it despite it affecting one's thoughts, feelings, and behaviors.
> **Tragic Optimism:** Hoping for a positive outcome in a situation that is uncertain, ambiguous, and even disastrous.

Questions for Reflection

1. Examine Mary's case study. How you would help Mary recognize non-death and ambiguous loss? Additionally, if Mary's son continually uses drugs, what strategies would you have for helping Mary?
2. Consider the parallels and nuances that exist within an addict's grief, a sibling's grief, a parent's grief, and other affected family and loved ones who could be grieving. What could be comparable between these grieving processes, and what would be unique?
3. In terms of clinical strategies, the author posits that secondary needs may be addressed only once primary needs have been met. Do you agree with the author's logic, and how would you define your primary and secondary needs? Could different cultures have different primary or secondary needs? If so, provide an example.
4. Addiction has been portrayed in an abundant amount of television programs and films in contemporary Western society. Select a film or television program that illustrates addiction, and examine the social messages surrounding addiction and loss. Additionally, explore how grief is illustrated, and whether this cultural piece would or would not be supported by the research provided in this chapter.

Note

1. For privacy and confidentiality reasons, the names of the individuals involved in all case studies and quotes have been changed.

References

Barnard, M. (2005). *Drugs and the family: The Impact on parents and siblings*. Glasgow: University of Glasgow, Joseph Roundtree Foundation.
Boss, P. (1999). *Ambiguous loss: Learning to live with unresolved grief*. Cambridge, MA: Harvard University Press.
Boss, P. (2006). *Loss, trauma, and resilience: Therapeutic work with ambiguous loss*. New York: W. W. Norton & Company.
Bowlby, J. (2006). *Attachment and loss*. New York: Basic Books.
Butler, R., & Bauld, L. (2005). The parents' experience: Coping with drug use in the family. *Drugs: Education, Prevention and Policy, 12*(1), 35–45. doi:10.1080/09687630042000275308
Denny, G. M., & Lee, L. J. (1984). Grief work with substance abusers. *Journal of Substance Abuse Treatment, 1*(4), 249–254. doi:10.1016/0740-5472(84)90003-5
Families Anonymous. (2011). *Today a better way*. Van Nuys, CA: Families Anonymous.
Flores, P. J. (2001). Addiction as an attachment disorder: Implications for group psychotherapy. *Group Psychotherapy and Addiction, 51*(1), 1–18. doi:10.1002/9780470713549.ch1
Frankl, V. E. (1984). *Man's search for meaning*. New York: Pocket Books.
Friedman, M. A. (1984). Grief reactions. *Alcoholism Treatment Quarterly, 1*(1), 55–69. doi:10.1300/j020v01n01_03
Furr, S., & Johnson, D. (2017, December). Grief, loss and substance use. *Counseling Today*, 35–39. Retrieved June 9, 2018, from https://ct.counseling.org/2017/12/grief-loss-substance-use/
Gervai, J. (2009). Environmental and genetic influences on early attachment. *Child and Adolescent Psychiatry and Mental Health, 3*(1), 12. doi:10.1186/1753-2000-3-25
Goldberg, M. (1985). Loss and grief. *Alcoholism Treatment Quarterly, 2*(1), 37–46. doi:10.1300/j020v02n01_04
Gramlich, J. (n.d.). *Nearly half of Americans have a family member or close friend who's been addicted to drugs*. Washington DC: Pew Research Center. Retrieved May 2, 2018, from https://www.pewresearch.org/fact-tank/2017/10/26/nearly-half-of-americans-have-a-family-member-or-close-friend-whos-been-addicted-to-drugs/
Jennings, P. S. (1991). To surrender drugs: A grief process in its own right. *Journal of Substance Abuse Treatment, 8*(4), 221–226. doi:10.1016/0740-5472(91)90042-9
Miller, J. R. (1994). Substance abuse: The role of depression and Trauma—A case report. *Journal of the American Academy of Psychoanalysis, 22*(4), 753–764. doi:10.1521/jaap.1.1994.22.4.753
National Institute of Drug Abuse. (2014). *Drugs, brains, and behavior: The science of addiction*. Retrieved May 1, 2018, from www.drugabuse.gov/publications/drugs-brains-behavior-science-addiction
Oreo, A., & Ozgul, S. (2007). Grief experiences of parents coping with an adult child with problem substance use. *Addiction Research & Theory, 15*(1), 71–83. doi:10.1080/16066350601036169
Phillips, L. (2017, May). The selfish act of forgiving. *Counseling Today*, 33–37. Retrieved June 9, 2018, from https://ct.counseling.org/brandingarea/selfish-act-forgiving/#
SAMHSA, Center for Behavioral Health Statistics and Quality. (2014). *National Survey on Drug Use and Health*. US Department of Health & Human Statistics.
Worden, J. W. (2008). *Grief counseling and grief therapy: A handbook for the mental health practitioner* (4th ed.). New York: Springer.

CHAPTER 9

Ambiguous Loss in Coming Out and Trans*itioning

Mae-Lynn Germany, Anna C. Pederson, and Sara K. Bridges

Like many trans people, I am learning to reattach to new words and new parts. I imagine what my body will be with immense joy and fear, worried and wondering what of "me" I've gained and what of "me" I've lost. Every year that passes, I fall more deeply in love with my name—Sam Dylan Finch, which rolls off the tongue like a tender incantation—while still wondering if the name I buried lives on someplace else. The unfamiliar becomes sweetly familiar, while the once familiar nips at my heels like a neglected dog.

It all had to mean something—and in a parallel universe, I think it still does, living on just as it was—because for this life to be bearable, I had to make meaning of these things. Because while the trauma of my assigned gender was at times like a clenched jaw around my body, it was, at first, the only thing I knew. And I created safety with what little kindling I had; I built a fire. Though it may have burned me and even, for a moment, engulfed me, it also kept me warm.

The truth of transition, they will tell you, is that it is pure and unadulterated joy and discovery. It makes for a touching story, to be sure. But quietly, I hold the space for something more—the messy reality that mingling with that joy is also raw and relentless grief, a letting go that too many of us struggle to make sense of.

—Sam Dylan Finch, "Capture Bonding: How I Both Need and Grieve My Gender Transition"

Introduction

When an event or change is perceived as desirable, expectations of excitement and celebration often leave little room for pangs of grief and loss that can accompany seismic life events (Harris, 2011). For transgender (trans*) and gender nonconforming (GNC) individuals, moving through the processes of coming out as trans* and transitioning are parts of one's experience in developing true self, often anticipated with joy. As with any transition, a parting from the familiar requires adjustment to new ways of living which can result in myriad nondeath losses ranging from the tangible, such as relationship loss or job loss, to intangible, such as the loss of safety and security or loss of identity. These grieve-able occurrences often go unrecognized, lacking social support and recognition, as they fall outside of traditional loss narratives and may be difficult for grievers to identify (Doka, 2002), particularly for losses where a person or aspect of self is both present and absent; the same, but different.

As trans* and GNC identity are negotiated within social and relational contexts, often bound in dichotomized gendered roles and expectations, ambiguity may arise regarding who is in and out of the social system, resulting in perceptions of loss, including valued relationships as well as aspects of self. Feelings of confusion or shame can also inundate the griever with the potential for reactions to be construed as ambivalence regarding trans* identity or ambivalence/regret about transitioning. Ambiguous loss has been used as a framework for understanding how families experience loss and make meaning of transition and gender (Norwood, 2012, 2013; Wahlig, 2014), but its applicability as a useful framework for understanding trans* individuals' own nuanced losses experiences and areas of resiliency has only just begun to be explored (Catalpa & McGuire, 2018; Dziengel, 2015; McGuire, Catalpa, Lacey, & Kuvalanka, 2016). This chapter seeks to review how ambiguous loss may manifest in gender transitioning and provide clinical recommendations for trans* individuals and families grappling with ambiguous loss. Our hope is that this chapter will shed light on the ways loss can manifest, not to reduce narratives or construe coming out and transitioning as loss, but in hopes of creating space for validating these experiences and avoiding further disenfranchisement.

Transgender and Transition

Language has been used as a means to marginalize and oppress groups while also holding the power to transform experience and empower, as can be seen in the narratives of transgender individuals, particularly surrounding gender. In Western societies, gender is traditionally viewed from a biological essentialist perspective that equates birth sex with discrete male or female gender identities that dictate norms and beliefs regarding appearance, behaviors, and attraction. The way that gender is conceptualized and reinforced in dominant social narratives can influence the way that an individual makes meaning of trans* identity as well as roles and expectations of self and others.

The term transgender, often denoted as trans*,[1] is an umbrella term used to describe individuals whose sex assigned at birth does not reflect their gender identity and who engage in gender crossing to align expression with identity. Transgender identity, in itself, subverts dominant social narratives surrounding gender as dichotomous and/or binary as exclusively male or female. Gender *identity*, a psychological construct, is one's internal sense or personal psychological experience of being male, female, a blend of both, or neither. This is something some individuals are born knowing, whereas for others this awareness develops over time. Gender *expression* is the external, perceived enactment and expression of identity, typically through dress, mannerisms, behavior, voice, and language, which may or may not conform to societally defined behaviors and characteristics associated with masculinity or femininity. Trans* and GNC individuals may engage in a process of affirming gender identity through transitioning. This can look like physical and/or behavioral changes, in order to align gender identity with gender expression, as well as social transition. Social transition may include coming out to self and others, changing name and/or pronoun, and the use of gender-congruent language within social groups (Erickson-Schroth, 2014). Perceptions of loss may arise in coming out and transitioning as this involves the acquisition of a stigmatized identity (Scott, 2011) as well as loss of cis-privilege leading to ambiguity in a sense of belongingness. At the same time, learning and navigating the ways that meaning is assigned to gender presentation and influenced by intersecting identities such as race, social class, spirituality, and sexuality may occur simultaneously (e.g., what does it mean to transition from a social location of being read as a cisgender, heterosexual African American woman to an African American gay transman; de Vries, 2012). Transitioning can result in the gaining and losing of social roles and identities, which may lead to questions of which parts of self are present and absent that shift depending on personal, interpersonal, social, and societal contexts.

Ambiguous Loss

Non-death losses are often difficult to name and claim, particularly when there is no verifiable death. For many transitioning, these losses are difficult to name or make sense of, as the idea of grieving for self can be confusing due to parts of self being both present and absent. This can be seen in the pull towards feeling that one must leave behind the person or name and what that personally represents. This becomes complicated by the belief or expectation that transitioning will be accompanied by feelings of joy and elation without feeling grief for parts of self. To acknowledge grief or give voice to grief may inadvertently be equated with doubt or regret around transition. Therefore conflicting thoughts and emotions may arise and persist due to the necessity of transitioning. The possibility of and implications surrounding grief may challenge the desire for and decision to transition.

Transitioning may not have a defined beginning or end with changes of gender expression happening gradually, over time, and in some cases throughout the lifespan. Thereby, grief may be ongoing, with it arising and subsiding in relation to changes in one's life along with transition. In narrative accounts of trans* individuals sharing their transition online, grief is described as occurring in waves during various periods of adjustment, such as coming out as trans, living socially in one's gender identity, engaging in hormone therapy and the process of gender-affirming surgery. One such account stated that feelings of grief were largely in response to "lost me" although he states that this was not to imply that he wanted to remain female-bodied (Games, 2013). In this, we can begin to see the tension between acknowledging grief and the concern that this may imply doubt surrounding transition. Additionally, feelings of loss may also arise in response to being misgendered. In being misgendered, uncertainty may emerge in how gender identity is being perceived in the context of gender expression resulting in lack of predictability and validation in social spaces. The unpredictability of when misgendering might occur further complicates the experience. The liminality experienced in transitioning along with being misgendered and not being read as one's gender identity may pose a challenge in establishing predictability and reconstructing identity. As frequent and unexpected social invalidation occur, hopes and expectations for living in the gender one is expressing are repeatedly dashed.

Losses accompanying transition may not be obvious to the griever and laden with difficulty in making sense of experiencing grief over past self and grief over a sense of knowing how to be. Similarly, even the most affirming of social supports may feel grief in response to a loved one transitioning, as it may feel like a loss of the person they once knew, necessitating a parting with dreams, hopes, plans, and expectations. As one mother describes grieving a future with her child as well as ongoing confusion about the loss:

> I realize now that I was grieving not the actual loss of my daughter but the idea of my daughter. I still wanted the hopes and dreams I had for her when she was born, you know—mother/daughter stuff, the prom dress, mani-pedi spa trips. That is where the shame set in—that grieving my daughter was wrong because I had a healthy son.
>
> (quoted in Key, 2014, p. 420)

Key aspects of ambiguous loss are reflected in the experiences of trans* individuals and their families across coming out and transitioning processes. Salient aspects include: the loss being difficult to describe or make sense of, the situation lacking a defined beginning or ending, hope being raised and dashed over time, experiences of ambivalence such as conflicting thoughts and emotions, a sense of feeling stuck or caught, difficulty in problem solving due to unknown parameters, no rituals or little validation of the loss, and feelings of relentless uncertainty due to ambiguity. As ambiguous loss serves as a stressor for the individual transitioning (Catalpa & McGuire, 2018), as well as social supports (McGuire et al., 2016; Norwood, 2012; Wahlig, 2014), boundary ambiguity arises from lack of clarity, leading those involved to question who is in and out of the social system due to varying degrees of physical and/or psychological absence (Boss, 2006). In efforts to move away from discrete narratives of acceptance and rejection that inundate trans* research, the ambiguous loss framework can be used as "a key analytic tool to queer the family acceptance and rejection narrative through an analysis of ambiguity, which dismantles and deconstructs discrete categories of presence and absence," (Catalpa & McGuire, 2018, p. 90). Similarly, this framework can be used to guide individuals to think dialectically, seeing parts of self and relationships through a lens of both/and.

Ambiguous Loss in Social Relationships

For family members and partners of trans* individuals, the processes of coming out and transitioning may be experienced as a catalyst for varied losses at the same time as offering the opportunity to know and affirm their trans* loved one's authentic self. Many of these losses center on the contradicting meaning of previously known parts of a loved one and/or a relationship being both present and absent, the same and different (Coolhart, Ritenour, & Grodizinski, 2017; McGuire et al., 2016; Norwood, 2012, 2013; Wahlig, 2014). Absent parts may include the trans* individual's former gendered identity and the accompanying gendered roles, relationships, and external presentation (Norwood, 2012). For example, while a parent's child may still be physically and relationally present after coming out and transitioning as a trans-man, their former gendered identity (female), familial role (daughter), and expectations for the future (motherhood) are absent. While some parents describe experiencing the loss of the future they envisioned for their child and the role they hoped to play in that future (Coolhart et al., 2017), others describe feelings of loss for the time when they did not yet know their child's authentic identity, having to wait so many years before getting to meet their authentic self (Bull & D'Arrigo-Patrick, 2018). Parents who share birth sex with their child may feel like part of their role as a parent is to serve as a model for their child, which may include teaching them gendered ways of being and ways of acting (e.g., how to "be a man").

At the same time as family members and partners are navigating what is present versus absent through the process of transition, they are developing an understanding of what remains the same and what will be different (Norwood, 2012, 2013). This struggle in meaning-making centers on the question of what else, if anything, changes when someone changes on the outside (how they look and behave). How one understands sex, gender, and identity strongly impacts the ways meaning is made of transition, (e.g., what is perceived as remaining the same or changing). For romantic partners, these meaning-making processes have an added layer of navigating what transition means for a continued intimate relationship and, potentially, renegotiating sexual orientation (Norwood, 2012).

In her research, Norwood (2013) identified four distinct ways that families and partners make meaning of transition (*replacement, revision, evolution, and removal*), each of which illustrates the presence-absence dialectic and how transition might be viewed as an ambiguous loss. Particularly for those who view gender as biologically determined and intrinsically tied to one's identity, transition in gender expression and/or sex characteristics can be understood as *replacement* whereby the trans* loved one is viewed as a different person following transition, with some family members viewing transition as a *living death* (Norwood, 2012, 2013). *Revision* involves family members seeing transition as changes to the trans* individual's gender presentation/others' perception of their gender. There is a sense that their gender has always been the same, with external presentation simply reflecting this reality; therefore, the core self is seen as constantly giving rise to fewer feelings of grief and loss. As a process of *evolution*, the loved one "post-transition" is understood as an updated version of the same self, shifting from one discrete gender category to the next. With *removal*, transition is viewed as a process where the trans* individual's personhood remains constant even though their external presentation and gendered way of living in the world (e.g., roles, mannerisms) changes, minimizing potential loss (Norwood, 2013).

Ambiguous Loss of the Individual Transitioning

Perceptions of acceptance or rejection, whether by institutions, social supports, or casual acquaintances, send powerful messages regarding the space for trans* identity in a given context. Through coming out and transitioning, ambiguity may be present for the trans* individual as questions arise regarding both who is in and out of the familial system and what aspects of self are in and out within a self-system of identities. Rejection or ambiguous responses from family members might be met with perceptions of physical absence, as relational changes occur by disconnection in relationships (e.g., moving out or being kicked out) and/or psychological absence (e.g., supports minimize or deny gender identity or transition; McGuire et al., 2016). In a recent study of boundary ambiguity among trans* youth, parents' reactions to gender variance and trans* identity disclosure were often seen as unclear and contradictory, leading to uncertainty about their familial membership and ability to express gender authentically (Catalpa & McGuire, 2018). As one participant noted: "I can't tell if [my parents] are supportive or not, because we don't talk about it that much" (p. 95). When ambiguous loss is present, perceptions of boundary ambiguity can create pressure to conform to gender expectations, potentially resulting in internal conflict or feelings of inauthenticity (Catalpa & McGuire, 2018). In this study, as ambiguity was found in relational, identity, and structural contexts, some trans* youth initiated family breaks in order to embrace authenticity, while others compromised gender congruence or maintained ambiguity to prevent familial breaks (Catalpa & McGuire, 2018). Although ambiguous loss in this context is traditionally conceptualized as relational (Boss, 2006) with problems existing in the cultural discourses surrounding binaried ways of viewing gender and how these influence meaning-making for families, we posit that these structures also influence the way that an individual experiences loss in coming out and transitioning, with some of these experiences appearing as more ambiguous, with varying dialectical tension stemming from presence/absence and same/different.

Ambiguous Loss and Past Self

As one transitions, ambiguous loss may arise within the system of self identities; important to this process is the consideration of which aspects of self are still present and which are absent. For some, it may feel essential for particular aspects of self to be relinquished in order to gain legitimacy and extinguish perceptions of doubt and uncertainty regarding transition. We can see this in trans* narratives among references to "past self":

> When your body is the captor, and your urge is to survive, how do you go on? For some of us, we dissociate, we separate, we detach. But I believe that some of us form attachments, too—to our dead names that our protectors used to coo as they cradled us in their arms, to our bodies that lovers used to gently trace with a finger or lusted after from across the room. And while we know

in our hearts that we must change, the intimacy and meaning of what we were was never lost on us. And it's this attachment that too many trans people are deeply ashamed of. How can I be seen as valid if I am not willing to abandon the entirety of what I was, of what that felt like? Am I truly transgender if I am unsure, afraid—or grief-stricken, even? If this is everything I need, but it hurts just the same? How can I hold this contradiction if it threatens my existence?

(Sam Dylan Finch, "Capture Bonding: How I Both Need and Grieve My Gender Transition")

Ambivalence can exist regarding the ability to claim grief as part of one's experience out of fear that this might diminish or challenge the necessity of transition. Confusion may arise regarding ways of interacting with the past self and the feeling that, in order to be comfortable with oneself as transgender, dissociating from the past self is essential. This narrative is reinforced by the necessity of living in discretely gendered ways prior to being granted approval for gender-affirming practices like surgeries. However, some reflect making meaning of transition and past self with a recognition of being both the same and different.

> Transition for me, though, sometimes feels like throwing my past self out the window. I've lived as a girl for 21 years. Birth Name, "me," accomplished a lot of great things. You know, "she" was a great student, "she" was a good person, "she" was a good musician, and "she" built this whole identity in this world as being this girl. In the end, "she" wasn't real. She was made up to paint the picture that the world wanted to see of me. But, I have and still have to go through this grieving process of losing my past self . . .
>
> I've been grieving my past self and I don't want to erase it. I don't want to cut off my past, where I lived as a girl, was perceived as a girl, and dealt with a lot of dysphoria and a lot of pain because that wasn't a separate person—that was me . . .
>
> Everyone changes as they grow up, not just trans people, so everyone is going to be different than they once were. I'm the same person I was 1 year ago, 5 years ago, 10 years ago. I was a confused kid sorting some shit out. And I finally feel like I'm growing into myself. I have a past that runs 21 years deep, not just the past year and a half I've known I'm trans . . .
>
> And so, at the end of the day, I personally don't want to forget my past. It wasn't just "her" who was a good person, a good student, a good musician. That was me. I accomplished and did those things and was that person.
>
> ("Grieving My Past Self 'Her' | FTM Transgender" MackMan)

Some may seek a relationship with their past self, incorporating this sense of self into current identity and future narratives, as this is recognized as history and a part of one's life narrative. However, the past self can also be a reminder of the pain experienced from feeling forced to live in a way that was not congruent with authentic self and associated with traumatic experiences. For some, distancing from past self can be a way of coping, functioning as an act of survival. Refusal to allow gender identity to be reflected on legal documents, refusing to use gender-affirming pronouns or chosen name, accidentally mislabeling, or deadnaming[2] can catalyze feelings of loss as the past self is made salient. Ambiguous loss can arise as references to and forced interactions with the past self creates a sense of physical presence reflected in institutional practices and documentation, although this part of self may have existed as more psychologically absent. One trans* youth shared his experience of his name being inappropriately documented on the card read for graduation as he crossed the stage Tiffany (Tye) Thomas: "I'm like okay, this is ridiculous, I'm like, technically Tiffany is nonexistent. Like this is not a person. Like come on, how do you screw that up? I was so pissed, and I took someone's pen and I had to search for a pen first of all because no one had one and I scratched out Tiffany" (Sinclair-Palm, 2017, p. 7). Tye describes a struggle with his trans* identity being supported by institutions, such as schools, that lead to making aspects of the self he wishes to distance himself from more visible. The lingering presence of aspects of the past self in social and institutional spaces can lead to feelings of erasure for trans* individuals, compounded by the lack of spaces for trans* individuals to work through a relationship with the past self or mourn the past self (Sinclair-Palm, 2017).

Ambiguous Loss Within Multiple Identities

In working with trans* clients, we must consider intersectional identities as they often influence how gender identity may be enacted and performed (Burnes & Chen, 2012). Learning new gendered expectations in the context of racial and ethnic cultural expectations and meanings may result in both gaining new roles and losing previously gendered expectations and spaces. In interviews gathered by de Vries (2012, p. 57), Jacobo (middle-class Latino transman) described gendered expectations of women serving, preparing, and cleaning after meals and the loss of these spaces after being told by other women "you don't belong in the kitchen anymore" and by men "you don't have to anymore." Changes in gender expression may also result in a sense of gaining or losing components of racial or ethnic identity. As reflected in de Vries (2012) for multi-racial or mixed-racial trans* participants, there was a sense of losing racial identity and learning to be Latina/o, resulting in gaining of ethnic pride. For Lance (a working-class, Lakota/white transman), changes through transition resulted in his being read as white, gaining aspects of white male privilege, and being excluded from communities of color (de Vries, 2012). For some, transitioning can include the loss of racial identity; impacting a sense of self with feeling that "cultural history and experiences were erased" (de Vries, 2012, p. 59).

By viewing transitioning through the lens of a singular social identity, as a process of navigating the continuum of man and woman or vice versa, we can miss the complex interplay of multiple identities (de Vries, 2012). As Fassinger and Arseneau (2007, p. 24) suggest, "identity enactment occurs within an overall contextual layer of temporal influences in which identity is shaped by the interactive influence of gender, sexual orientation, and cultural variables such as race, ethnicity, social class, disability, and religion." These areas are constantly being negotiated in personal health, including: mental and physical health; interpersonal realms (including relationships and family); social realms (including education and work); and the sociopolitical realm (including legal and political rights). Considering these contexts is essential as they influence how central or salient a particular social identity is at any given time. As Catalpa and McGuire (2018) found in the narratives of trans* youth, the interplay of personal identity and family identity resulted in feeling that trans* identity had made life harder for family members, leading the participant to contemplate de-transitioning to maintain family name:

> I have sort of been compensating, trying to get my family to be proud of me. Like, trying to get my middle name back . . . I have been online furiously trying to learn Chinese again too. Just hoping . . . if I disgrace them by being a girl, maybe I can make them proud of me by learning all of this stuff.
> (genderqueer/M-F; p. 97)

As concerns or fear arise in interpersonal, social, or sociopolitical realms, an individual in transition may feel it is necessary to make particular aspects of identity more salient, which we argue could also contribute to feelings of ambiguous loss. For example, it may feel necessary for trans* identity, which may be as a core aspect of self, to be invisible in some areas of life in order to maintain a sense of safety, security, or connectedness. Boundary ambiguity may arise from lack of clarity regarding what aspects of identity are in and out of the self system, depending on the context. Even in supportive environments such as therapeutic or support groups that may serve to develop resiliency and a sense of community, trans* individuals may feel disconnected, particularly when these supportive spaces are homogenous and may not reflect understanding or shared experiences with other cultural identities. In a case study presented by Burnes and Chen (2012), Tanya (28 years old, female-identified, African American, lawyer, assigned male at birth) was described as attending groups that were predominately white, leaving her feeling that others couldn't relate to how her African American identity impacted her ability to present gender and how "she felt her racial identity and gender identity were pulling her in different directions" (p. 120).

Clinical Implications

The ambiguous loss framework can assist practitioners in supporting trans* individuals and socials supports through grief that may arise in transition by: "1) recognizing their feelings as loss, 2) enhancing resiliency through redefinition and meaning making, 3) exploring how their own expectations may contribute to a belief that change is loss" (McGuire et al., 2016, pp. 373–374). Traditionally, this can be addressed by carefully guiding the naming and validating of the loss, finding meaning, tempering mastery, reconstructing identity, normalizing ambivalence, revising attachment, discovering new hope, and identifying resources (Boss, 2006;

Boss, Roos, & Harris, 2011).³ In working with ambiguous loss, treatment goals surround resiliency, i.e., learning to both tolerate ambiguity and change and move forward despite uncertainty (Boss, 2006). Underpinning these goals is the critical importance of clinicians continually considering the context of their clients' losses across personal, interpersonal, social, cultural, and sociopolitical realms. Below, we offer guiding clinical questions and techniques that can be used when working with families and trans* individuals in the coming out and transitioning process.

Naming and Validating the Loss(es)

As ambiguous losses are ongoing, marked with uncertainty, and lack societal support and recognition, naming the problem as the problem (namely grief and feelings of loss), can be ameliorative. It may be validating for clients to understand the nature of their loss as ongoing due to perceptions of inter- or intra-personal presence and absence. At the same time, conflicting feelings such as shame may arise when claiming feelings related to grief and loss. Therefore, clinicians are advised to use care when exploring meanings of grieving. The Loss Timeline (Dunton, 2012) presents itself as a useful tool for allowing clients to consider the ways that their personal loss histories have shaped their lives and experiences. At each point in the timeline, clients can explore if/how losses were grieved, what space they had, and what resiliency was developed. As Dunton (2012) describes, creating a loss timeline not only provides a sense of concreteness to the past but also fosters a recognition of the ways that life continues beyond the present timepoint, organizing towards a future and a restructuring of one's self that occurs in the aftermath of loss. When working with trans* clients, the technique could be modified by exploring the roles that have been gained and lost, or what aspects of identity have shifted over time. Utilizing this gain/loss framework can also have the benefit of fostering dialectic, "both/and" thinking.

Finding Meaning

For both trans* individuals and social supports, the ways that meaning can be made of transition can change over time, and the feelings of grief and loss along with them, particularly in the context of multiple losses. One way of making meaning in ambiguous losses is naming and identifying the problem loss or ambiguity, i.e., lack of clarity regarding who or what is in and out of the system (Boss, 2006). Externalization of the problem as ambiguity can minimize individual or familial blame and assumptions of dysfunction (Boss, 2016). Further, engaging in dialectical thinking helps to make meaning of changes surrounding gender transition. For example, "I'm experiencing both a sense of grief and suffering a loss, and I'm also discovering new relationships and connections (gains/loss)," "I feel both that my parent is gone and they are also still here (presence/absence)," "I feel both that I have lost the role of a daughter and still have the role of being a child (roles)." While recognizing feelings of loss can be challenging, yet healing at times, fostering this language can aid in sense-making (i.e., why loss is happening) or meaning-making (i.e., how this experience will be used; Harris, 2011).

Reconstructing Identity

As transitioning involves a change in roles and identity, trans* individuals and social supports may question a sense of identity in a self, social, or societal system, leaving one with questions of "Who am I now?" "How do I respond in light of these changes?" "What roles/identities have I gained and what have I lost?" Discussing family and societal gender roles, processing the intersectional nature of identity, and highlighting the stigma and discrimination that influence identity construction and enactment can be helpful (Boss et al., 2011). In looking at how loss events have shaped a sense of identity, we find self-characterization sketches (Kelly, 1991) or loss characterization sketches (Gerrish, 2012; Neimeyer, 2002) helpful. The following prompt can be used as a guideline, although the form that it takes will vary depending on the loss experience of each individual client. For parents, this may feel like the loss of their child in the birth-sex identity; for trans* individuals who are transitioning, this may be a characterization sketch surrounding loss or simply the experience of transition. Prompts may begin with: "Since the loss of...," "Since transitioning...," "Since saying goodbye to (past name or aspect of self), I..." As Gerrish (2012) describes, the instructions are intentionally simple and designed to minimize defensiveness while allowing the individual to focus on the experience of loss, without implying outcome. The technique allows clients and clinicians to begin to elucidate the ways that loss has shaped a sense of identity while also allowing space for the reconstruction of identity, redefining the self, and simply accessing "who they are in light of their loss." An example might be:

> Write in your own words a description of the kind of person you are following ___[the loss]_____. The exercise is one that I would like you to allow yourself whatever time you need to "speak for yourself" about the loss _____ and how this has affected you. You may wish to begin it as follows... "Since [transition, as I no longer feel like a _____, the loss of _____], I..."

Normalizing Ambivalence

Recognizing and articulating ambivalent feelings (e.g., uncertainty, lack of clarity, and lack of validation) can promote resiliency through redefining self and revising attachments (McGuire et al., 2016). Developing an awareness of and normalizing conflicting feelings can aid in mitigating these feelings and reducing further physical or psychological absence such as disconnected relationships, abuse, or neglect (Boss et al., 2011). One of the ways to create a space for the recognition of growth and change over time is by helping clients to develop an increased tolerance or comfort with ambiguity versus relying on, what Boss (2006) describes as, the myth of closure.

Revising Attachment

Learning the dialectic of continuing what is present at the same time as letting go of what is absent allows one to grieve what is lost and celebrate what is left. One technique that has been shown to help facilitate continuing bonds with the deceased is the Life Imprint (Neimeyer, 2012), which invites clients to reflect upon a person whom they have lost and trace the imprint of this person on their lives. As not all imprints are positive, an individual may come to see ways that less desirable traits or qualities continue to have an internal space in life after loss. We suggest this technique may be expanded and used for relationships where there is both the physical absence of a person/aspect of self and the recognition of psychological presence. Typically, the client identifies who they want to trace with careful reflection on the impact in their life through areas such as: mannerisms or gestures, ways of speaking and communicating, values and beliefs, and feelings about self and others. Responses may be a few sentences or paragraphs as time allows, with an invitation to discuss observations with their clinician or in dyads, if used in a group setting. Neimeyer (2012) suggests that a crucial aspect of this activity is to include two prompts: "What imprints would you like to affirm?" and "What imprints would you like to relinquish?" which allows for recognition that some imprints are ambivalent and that even the most positive of relationships may leave imprints that the individual desires to relinquish or vice versa. The importance of identifying areas of affirmation and those to relinquish can foster creative discussion surrounding ways of memorializing and fostering growth in imprints that are desired and the creation of rituals that commemorate the change and relinquishment of undesired imprints. For highly ambivalent or negative figures, more processing time to address conflicting feelings can be needed.

Discovering Hope and Identifying Resources

When individuals enter into therapy when ambiguous loss is present, often there may be a desire for resolution to the ambiguity with social supports wanting to return to the status quo (Boss et al., 2011), or the individual in transition hoping to return to a place where invalidating experiences are non-existent, and a sense of stability and predictability was felt. At times, these hopes serve to anchor individuals until new hope is found, which can be a lengthy process. Actively reconstructing views of gender, challenging dominant narratives of gender in Western culture and cis-normativity, may foster resilience and adaptive meaning-making for family members and partners of trans* individuals (Coolhart et al., 2017). These processes can be aided by the use of gender literacy (Catalpa & McGuire, 2018) and facilitating the expansion of norms, which can foster new hope and possibilities.

For clinicians, identification of appropriate resources is essential; careful attention should be paid to the ways that systems may inadvertently pathologize or misconstrue grieving as well as ambiguous loss. Resources should be tailored to the individual, considering their multiple, intersecting identities. This may foster a sense of shared experience as well as integrating these identities versus focusing on a sole social identity (e.g., what it means to be a gay trans* person of color versus just trans* support). As noted in this chapter, often physical breaks may occur in families and social supports throughout transition and coming out. We encourage clinicians to consider the idea of family of choice and how this may be used as a supportive resource for trans* individuals throughout transition.

Below is a list of questions to help guide clinical conversations when working with trans* clients throughout transition where ambiguous loss may arise with aspects of self, whether these are aspects of identity or the past self. Some may serve to illuminate areas of physical or psychological absence, allowing conversations to emerge surrounding ambiguity of what may feel like needs to be parted with and the meaning behind this transition. We would encourage clinicians to carefully explore subsequent responses with clients, as noted by previous researchers, areas of physical and psychological break may serve as ways of maintaining resilience or authenticity in some social relationship (Catalpa & McGuire, 2018).

Pre-transition

- As you contemplate transitioning, what do you anticipate being the hardest?
- What pieces of yourself do you fear losing?
- What pieces of yourself do you imagine leaving behind?
- Are there facets of yourself you feel you won't be able to converse with or find comfort in?
- Who are you no longer going to be forced to be?
- What aspects of who you were forced to be might be a little hard to leave behind?

During Transition or "Post" Transition

- What did you say goodbye to in order to be here today?
- What surprised you most?
- What was the hardest to leave behind?
- What might you want to carry with you as you begin to shift?
- What (if anything) have you lost to be here today?
- What rituals and tokens might be lost? What might you maintain?
- Given what you said goodbye to, what might you want to re-invite back into the picture?
- What roles/rituals/aspects of self have you lost to be here today? What roles/rituals/aspects of self have you gained?

Conclusion

All significant life events, even those that are desirable and celebrated, can be accompanied with perceptions of gains and joy while simultaneously holding space for and experiencing a sense of loss. As transition is perceived as a desired choice by many, recognizing, claiming, or vocalizing grief or feelings of loss may be construed as ambivalence or regret of transitioning. As societal space may be limited for non-death losses, which may result in disenfranchised grief (Doka, 2002; Harris, 2011), working with individuals and families in naming and validating feelings of grief and loss can begin to provide a sense of relief and comfort.

Key Terms

Cisgender: An individual whose sense of identity regarding gender correlates with their birth sex.

Gender Expression: An external expression of identity through dress, behavior, voice, language, and overall appearance.

Gender Identity: A psychological construct that is one's insight and subjective experience of being male, female, a blend of both, or neither.

Trans*: A superordinate term that can be used to characterize individuals whose sex assigned at birth does not reflect their gender identity, and who engage with gender crossing to align with identity. Examples may include: third gender, two spirit, neutrois, transmasculine/transfeminine, male to female (MtF), female to male (FtM), genderfluid, genderqueer, transgender, or gender neutral. Although not all individuals whom others might refer to as transgender identify with the term, and not all individuals who are gender nonconforming in presentation identify with trans* identity.

Questions for Reflection

1. Did you have misconceptions regarding trans* identities before reading this chapter? Why do you think that many individuals in society have difficulties supporting people who identify as trans*? Additionally, create a "dos and don'ts" list with suggestions for supporting trans* identities and gender diversity in relation to grief and loss.
2. Create your own Loss Timeline and concentrate on non-death-related losses that changed your perceptions about the world. How did these losses influence your concept of identity? How did you develop resiliency? Consequently, how do you think this exercise could help restructure one's identity positively and assist with meaning-making for an individual who identifies as trans*?
3. Search for online articles or videos that illustrates a trans* person's story regarding transitioning or choosing not to transition, and highlight the narrative surrounding grief, attachment, and ambiguous loss. Consequently, what factors such as gender identity, sexual orientation, ethnicity, socio-economic status, religious beliefs, disability, and age do you think affected this person's grief?
4. Suppose an individual who identifies as trans* comes to talk with you and discloses that they are struggling immensely due to family rejection and isolation. How would you provide support for this individual?
5. Explore specific trans* resources that exist within your community and investigate how they would be beneficial to trans* individuals.

Notes

1. It should be noted that numerous identities exist under the trans* umbrella (e.g., third gender, two spirit, neutrois, transmasculine/transfeminine, male to female MtF/female to male FtM, genderfluid, genderqueer, transgender, enderneutral) although not all

individuals who others might refer to as transgender identify with the term. Additionally, not all individuals that are gender nonconforming in presentation identify with trans* identity.
2. Deadnaming means referring to a trans* person by their birth name after they have adopted a new name.
3. For further discussion surrounding these themes in gender transition, see McGuire et al. (2016).

References

Boss, P. (2006). *Loss, trauma, and resilience: Therapeutic work with ambiguous loss.* New York: W. W. Norton & Company.

Boss, P. (2016). The context and process of theory development: The story of ambiguous loss. *Journal of Family Theory & Review, 8,* 269–286.

Boss, P., Roos, S., & Harris, D. L. (2011). Grief in the midst of ambiguity and uncertainty: An exploration of ambiguous loss and chronic sorrow. In R. A. Neimeyer, D. L. Harris, H. R. Winokuer, & G. Thornton (Eds.), *Grief and bereavement in contemporary society: Bridging research and practice* (pp. 163–175). New York: Routledge.

Bull, B., & D'Arrigo-Patrick, J. (2018). Parent experiences of a child's social transition: Moving beyond the loss narrative. *Journal of Feminist Family Therapy,* 1–21.

Burnes, T. R., & Chen, M. (2012). Multiple identities of transgender individuals: Incorporating a framework of intersectionality to gender crossing. In R. Josselson & M. Harway (Eds.), *Navigating multiple identities: Race, gender, culture, nationality and role* (pp. 113–127). New York: Oxford University Press.

Catalpa, J. M., & McGuire, J. K. (2018). Family boundary ambiguity among transgender youth. *Family Relations, 67,* 88–103.

Coolhart, D., Ritenour, K., & Grodzinski, A. (2017). Experiences of ambiguous loss for parents of transgender male youth: A phenomenological exploration. *Contemporary Family Therapy, 40,* 28.

de Vries, K. M. (2012). Intersectional identities and conceptions of the self: The experience of transgender people. *Symbolic Interaction, 35,* 49–67.

Doka, K. J. (Ed.) (2002). *Disenfranchised grief: New directions, challenges, and strategies for practice.* Champaign, IL: Research Press.

Dunton, A. (2012). Loss timelines. In R. A. Neimeyer (Ed.), *Techniques of grief therapy: Creative practices for counseling the bereaved* (pp. 184–186). New York: Routledge.

Dziengel, L. (2015). A be/coming-out model: Assessing factors of resilience and ambiguity. *Journal of Gay & Lesbian Social Services, 27,* 302–325.

Erickson-Schroth, L. (Ed.). (2014). *Trans bodies, trans selves: A resource for the transgender community.* New York: Oxford University Press.

Fassinger, R. E., & Arseneau, J. R. (2007). "I'd rather get wet than be under that umbrella": Differentiating the experiences and identities of lesbian, gay, bisexual, and transgender people. In K. J. Bieschke, R. M. Perez, & K. A. DeBord (Eds.), *Handbook of counseling and psychotherapy with lesbian, gay, bisexual, and transgender clients* (2nd ed., pp. 19–49). Washington, DC: American Psychological Association.

Finch, S. D. (2017, July). *Capture bonding: How I need and both grieve my gender transition.* Retrieved from https://letsqueerthingsup.com/2017/07/30/capture-bonding-how-i-both-need-and-grieve-my-gender-transition/

Games, F. (2013, March). *FTM-Grieving for my past self in early gender transition* [Video file]. Retrieved from www.youtube.com/watch?v=6hwsxFg9sHk
Gerrish, N. (2012). Using the loss characterization with bereaved parents. In R. A. Neimeyer (Ed.), *Techniques of grief therapy: Creative practices for counseling the bereaved* (pp. 169–171). New York: Routledge.
Harris, D. L. (Ed.). (2011). *Counting our losses: Reflecting on change, loss, and transition in everyday life*. New York: Routledge.
Kelly, G. A. (1991). *The psychology of personal constructs*. New York: Norton (Original work published 1955).
Key, A. (2014). Children. In L. Erickson-Schroth (Ed.), *Trans bodies, trans selves: A resource for the transgender community* (pp. 409–445). New York: Oxford University Press.
MackMan (2016, July). *Grieving my past self "her" | FTM transgender* [Video file]. Retrieved from www.youtube.com/watch?v=xZNO63x4eAY&t=98s
McGuire, J. K., Catalpa, J. M., Lacey, V., & Kuvalanka, K. A. (2016). Ambiguous loss as a framework for interpreting gender transitions in families. *Journal of Family Theory & Review, 8*, 373–385.
Neimeyer, R. A. (2002). *Lessons of loss: A guide to coping* (2nd ed.). New York: Brunner Routledge.
Neimeyer, R. A. (2012). The life imprint. In R. A. Neimeyer (Ed.), *Techniques of grief therapy: Creative practices for counseling the bereaved* (pp. 274–276). New York: Routledge.
Norwood, K. (2012). Transitioning meanings? Family members' communicative struggles surrounding transgender identity. *Journal of Family Communication, 12*, 75–92.
Norwood, K. (2013). Grieving gender: Trans-identities, transition, and ambiguous loss. *Communication Monographs, 80*, 24–45.
Scott, D. (2011). Coming out: Intrapersonal loss in the acquisition of a stigmatised identity. In D. L. Harris (Ed.), *Counting our losses: Reflecting on change, loss, and transition in everyday life* (pp. 171–183). New York: Routledge.
Sinclair-Palm, J. (2017). "It's Non-Existent": Haunting in trans youth narratives about naming. *Bank Street Occasional Paper Series, 37*, 1–15.
Wahlig, J. L. (2014). Losing the child they thought they had: Therapeutic suggestions for an ambiguous loss perspective with parents of a transgender child. *Journal of GLBT Family Studies, 11*, 305–326.

CHAPTER 10

Supporting the Families of Missing People: More Than an Investigation

Elizabeth Davies, Emmanuel Kassiotis, and Keesha Quinn

Introduction

The loss experienced when a loved one goes missing is outside the norm of losses experienced or anticipated in everyday life. While the loss of a loved one through illness or expected aging is no less significant for those left behind, such a loss can be partially understood in terms of cause, predictability, and timeliness. There might be the opportunity for some psychological preparation for a loss that is anticipated and clarity in terms of what has been lost, both physically and psychologically. There might also be the opportunity to say goodbye, and the ritual of a farewell in the form of a memorial or funeral that is both expected and socially affirmed. A loved one going missing is unexpected in its occurrence and traumatic in both its impact and the often ongoing and unresolved nature of the loss. When a loved one is missing, the ambiguous nature of the loss, in terms of what is lost, how long the loss will continue, and the meaning the loss has for those left behind, can be difficult to understand.

To date, the study of missing people has predominantly focused on the numbers of people who are reported missing, how many are located, and how many remain missing, as well as the reasons, sometimes speculative, for their becoming missing people, and the cost to the community in economic terms (Bricknell, 2017). While the experience of those left behind has received more attention in recent times, in terms of the lived experience of families when a loss is ambiguous, and how those left behind find meaning and hope in living with such a loss (Boss, 1999, 2006; Clark, 2006; Glassock, 2011; Wayland, 2015), little is written from the perspective of actively intervening with families to address the emotional and psychological impacts of living with missing.

The authors of this chapter have worked directly with those left behind when a loved one is missing. Their combined experience is more than 20 years working specifically with such families. While 20 years seems like a substantial amount of time, they have worked with families whose loved ones have been missing more than twice that time, and others whose loved ones have been missing a matter of days.

Almost 50% of families seek support in the first year of a loved one going missing (FFMPU, 2015). Because their priority is, understandably, to locate the missing loved one, it can be difficult to articulate the psychological and emotional needs for those left behind, waiting for news of their missing loved one. Families who do seek support from the limited available services might do so in relation to a practical issue that has arisen, or to a question that relates to a legal or financial difficulty. Support seeking might relate to the level of satisfaction with the investigative process, and the grief and frustration that ensue when a loved one has not been located (FFMPU, 2015). Families may seek reassurance that all that is within the power of investigators and families themselves has been done to find their missing loved one.

Case Studies

The case studies that follow have been de-identified and specific details, which may have identified the missing person or their family, have been changed.

> *Anne—A father missing for more than 30 years.*
>
>> We were sitting talking about the holidays; two 13-year-olds who were planning to just hang out together when dad came back from his trip. My friend said to me "but what happens if he doesn't come back?" That had never occurred to me. As we sat there a police car drove past and pulled up outside my house. I jumped up and ran home. The police were talking to my mother. My father's belongings had been found at a campsite near where he was thought to have been; but a search had revealed no sign of him. They told my mother they believed he had died.

Anne first approached a support agency when she was 40 years old. She was looking for support to understand and to find a way of living with a loss that remains ambiguous.

> *Lucy—A father missing for almost three years*
>
>> I didn't know at first that my dad was missing. I overheard a conversation. Now when I hear people talking, I'm not sure what they're telling me, and what they're not.

Lucy was 13 years old when her father went missing. She disclosed this information to one of the authors, after her mother and a grandparent sought assistance and support for Lucy and themselves.

> *Bill and Sharon—A son missing for more than 10 years.*

John was 30 when he went missing, leaving his parents' home to go for a walk. Initially Bill and Sharon reported their son missing and received a response from service providers and friends that caused increased distress and disappointment, being told, "*A 30-year-old should be okay on his own.*" They travelled extensively, actively searching for their son, but encountered difficulties relating to privacy legislation and having their concerns recognized. Bill and Sharon continue to access emotional support from within the missing persons' sector, through contact and connecting with other families in similar situations.

The Experience of Those Who Are Left Behind

It is not uncommon for individuals and family members to have different but equally valid reactions to living with a missing loved one. In the early days of missing, some family members may be able to be more proactive in searching than others. Supporting families to do "what feels right" in their individual situations considering their emotional, physical, and financial means is important.

> I trusted that they were out there searching for him over the years; following up on information and leads, when I couldn't be. I had three younger children at home to care for and support, and no time or support to be out there searching myself.
>
> (A parent of a missing young person)

In seeking to understand why their loved one has gone missing family members may blame themselves for actions they feel may have contributed to or caused their loved one to go missing. They may reach different conclusions about why their loved one has gone missing and what has happened to them. Guilt and self-blame are often reported by those left behind (FFMPU, 2016). As with other forms of loss, family members may express feelings of grief and sadness in different ways; this diversity may lead to disagreement and feelings of isolation, which may be exacerbated if those left behind do not have access to support, which recognizes and validates individual needs and differences. For some, recognition and support may come from within the family and community, while for others support is sought externally. Relationships may be strengthened by the shared experience, while for others, relationships may be strained. Some left behind report hesitation in articulating an opinion they fear is not shared by others within the family, and as a result they may feel that they are not understood and are silenced. It is important to note that individuals within families may have quite different capacities to tolerate living with not knowing.

Living With Not Knowing

While the experience of a loved one going missing is unpredictable, so is the outcome. Reassurances from friends and service providers of "he'll be back" are empty words. While the majority of missing people return or are located, a small but not insignificant number, most especially to their families and friends, remain missing (Bricknell, 2017). When a family makes a missing person's report to police, they have no way of knowing how long they will have to live in that difficult space of "not knowing." No one can tell them definitively, and while reassurances may offer a little comfort to some, a successful outcome is beyond anyone's control. A family member who reported a son missing makes the plea to investigators to *"understand that this family standing in front of you* [making the missing person's report] *may never know what happened to their loved one. They may never know if that person is alive and has moved on to another life, or if their loved one is dead."* The notion of an intensive search for a missing person yielding a positive result, in terms of their return to the family or community, cannot be guaranteed.

When a loved one goes missing, the impact on those left behind may not always be recognized, even by those close to the family.

> I bumped into my friend in the street. She asked me how I was, and I replied, "Not good, J [the son, whom the friend knew] is still missing." Her reply "but that was twelve months ago" told me she didn't understand at all.

Friends, family members, and service providers may fail to recognize that the loss is ongoing and traumatic. Family members report that the feelings do not ease or fade with time, as can happen with losses that are less ambiguous. Indicators of trauma, including anxiety, difficulty concentrating, disturbed sleep (and sometimes nightmares), hypervigilance, intrusive thoughts and images, and flashbacks can be overwhelming and difficult to understand (FFMPU, 2014). Family members are often hesitant to speak about such feelings, and the behaviors they engage in, as they try to cope with living with such a loss.

> I spoke to my GP about how terrible I was feeling, and she told me "you'll just have to learn to cope." I'm having a hard time, but that [coping] was what I thought I was doing.
>
> (A parent)

Naming the loss as ambiguous assists those who are left behind to understand the struggle they experience. Boss (2009) calls ambiguity "the real culprit" (p. 138) and, in explaining the challenges that result when ambiguity continues, feelings of embarrassment, shame, and failure to make sense of that struggle may be normalized and, at times, eased when the loss is explained in terms of ambiguity. Those left behind are better able to recognize their reactions as understandable in such difficult circumstances.

Much has been written about closure and its impossibility for those who are left behind when a loved one goes missing (Boss, 1999, 2006; Glassock, 2006). Missing defies the usual expectations of time, grief, and resolution and does not fit with traditional models of bereavement. While reassurance may be offered to loved ones who have experienced a death-related loss, that in time their grief may be less present for them on a daily basis, and in keeping with the aphorism that "time heals all wounds," the families of missing people report that the passing of time offers little comfort or respite from their feelings of grief. While others not directly impacted may expect or assume that family members reach a point of acceptance, this is unrealistic, and it disenfranchises the grief felt by those left behind. The expectations for those living with a loved one who is missing are often different and their grief not acknowledged in the same way a death-related loss may be.

The notion of achieving closure is a myth and cannot be applied in relation to ambiguous loss and the experience of living with having a loved one missing (Boss, 2009; Kreitler & Shanun-Klein, 2013). There may never be concrete or definitive answers, even if a missing person is located deceased or a coroner's investigation is finalized. Families are simply left in a space of not knowing some or all of the details of their missing loved one. While the loved one remains physically absent, loved ones left behind may continue to wonder, hope, or believe that their missing loved one is still alive. Boss (2009) suggests that instead of encouraging the notion of seeking closure, those offering support and those being supported should become more tolerant of the "still-open door"; that learning to hold a paradox—that someone we love can be both absent and present at the same time, is helpful.

> I read Pauline Boss's Ambiguous Loss and realised I didn't have "to know"; I didn't have to reach a conclusion, and I didn't have to hold the same opinion as my mother or anyone else. What is the harm in deciding to live with not knowing?
>
> (Anne)

Just as traditional grief models do not apply to the experience of families living with missing, the traditional social conventions that follow bereavement, such as viewing the body, planning a funeral or other ceremony, and having a place of remembrance, like a grave site, are customs and rituals that are mostly inaccessible when a loved one is missing.

Rituals and Acknowledgment of the Loss

In the case studies described earlier in the chapter, the three missing people were acknowledged or farewelled by their families in different ways and at different times in terms of the length of time they were missing. The ritual for one held great meaning, and her input as a young person was encouraged; for the other, the memorial service felt to her that it was for someone who had died. The funeral service that was organized felt premature, with little time to understand what had happened to her loved one and without any concrete evidence to support a funeral being held.

> It was too soon. He'd been missing a few weeks. I was not involved in the planning. I was told it was happening and that was it. I felt the door was being closed and there was an expectation that we would all move on.
>
> (Anne)

Families may seek assistance to establish meaningful rituals; and it can be most useful for them to be able to discuss with others what has been helpful in their own situation and with regard to accommodating differences in meaning-making and understanding. There may be disagreement about what the ritual means for each person within the family. After 10 years of their son missing, Bill and Sharon organized a memorial service for him. As time progressed, Sharon reported feeling more accepting of the possibility that their son might not be found alive, while her husband continued to hope that he might be alive and return one day. As a couple holding different positions, they spoke of facing challenges as a couple over the years. Ultimately, one was able to continue to hold his own views and beliefs and support the other in doing what she needed to do to honor and acknowledge their son's life and disappearance.

Recognition of the loss, despite the ambiguity that surrounds it, can be an important part of validating the experiences felt by families. The disenfranchised nature of the loss can lead to a lack of support, as well as a lack of acknowledgment (Doka, 2002). Anne's mother appeared to have little understanding of her daughter's needs. When Anne asked many years later, *"Why didn't you support me?"* her mother's response was, *"It never occurred to me that you needed support."* Lucy reported that friends and other people she knew failed to acknowledge that her father was missing or the impact of his absence on her. This was the experience reported by both young people in the case studies when they returned to school. When their experience was not acknowledged, they felt that their missing loved one's existence was ignored. For Lucy, like many others, the relationship with the missing person does not end with their disappearance or the passing of time. When others fail to recognize the ongoing nature of missing coupled with the ongoing nature of the relationship with the missing person, it is painful and deeply disappointing. This lack of recognition is reported by many who are affected by missing.

Anne has teenage children who have never met their grandfather, but they name and talk about him often. The need to acknowledge and celebrate her father's life, and to do with her own children what was not permitted for her, is of great importance and brings her comfort. Having conversations and performing simple rituals keeps his memory alive for her and allows her children who have never met him to make memories of their missing grandfather. The relationship to the missing person continues long after they are reported missing, regardless of differing personal and community opinions, and even legal coroner's findings.

Supporting Families

A sibling of a missing person contacted one of the authors enquiring about support. He expressed doubt about his suitability to be able to access a support service for the families of missing people. When asked about the reason for his doubts, he stated, "My sister has been missing for more than 30 years." As we talked, it became evident that he held the belief that the loss of his missing sister so many years earlier is a loss he should have dealt with. He expressed the belief that he should have been able to "move on."

Support for the loved ones of missing people may come from a variety of places, including agency contact or a local community group. In fact, any support is important (Boss, 2006). A person living with ambiguous loss needs their loss to be recognized as real, not something from which they simply "move on." Lucy, Anne, Bill, and Sharon, like other family members, all made contact at some point with agencies they hoped might offer them support and understanding about their experience and struggle. Social media played an important role in assisting them to locate and make contact with relevant agencies. Both Lucy and Anne had contact with a counseling service for support around living with not knowing, but at vastly different times in their lives and different periods of living with missing; one accessing support as a young person, within a few months of her father going missing, and the other almost 30 years later. Contact with support services and mental health service providers occurred at very different times, but what is unanimously shared in discussions with families is that the contact occurs at a time that feels "right" for the individual.

> No one knew what I was going through. I tried to be invisible at school.
>
> (Anne)

Within their school environments, both Lucy and Anne felt isolated, with little acknowledgment of what was happening for them. For Anne, no adult in her family ever explained to her school what the family was experiencing. She reports that it affected her academic performance at the time. Lucy initially did not want to disclose information about her father being missing to her peers. who, on learning of it made comments, including "worse things have happened to me" (FFMPU, 2013). While initially she did not want to talk to anyone, she participated in several media interviews and became the student at school who was able to talk about missing in an informed way with others. Like many who live with such a loss, Lucy developed strategies for tolerating the hurt of people's apparent lack of concern and unempathic responses. She identified those she felt she could trust and speak to if needed.

Families may hold different views about the importance of accessing support and the type of support they feel is helpful for them. Being offered access to a range of support options, which include counseling via different media, support groups, and events that facilitate the opportunity for contact with others in a similar situation, are important. The client being given the choice of frequency of contact with support agencies is important. While the loss of a missing person is ongoing, supports offered need to be available to those left behind in a manner they feel is timely and appropriate (Tubbs & Boss, 2000).

> Counseling was helpful. They talked to me about PTSD and being hypervigilant. We talked about the sadness and memories of John. I learnt that it's okay to put the burden [of grief] down sometimes.
>
> (Sharon)

Therapeutic Approach and Support Groups

Therapists not seeking solutions or working towards closure are placed in a difficult position because "ambiguity complicates loss, elongates trauma and threatens resiliency" (Boss, 2006, p. 27). When working with the families of missing persons, it is imperative to start "where they are at" and to identify their specific needs. Families are often met with those who do not know how to respond or do so insensitively. Supporting families is not about providing solutions or hypothesizing about what may have happened; rather it is recognizing that families are the experts where their missing loved one is concerned. The role of those supporting is to guide individuals and families to find meaning and hope, because without answers, meaning and hope shape how families and individuals cope, grieve, and work towards tolerance of their loss and find resilience (Boss, 2006).

To acknowledge a family's loss, having someone witness and validate their experience are key first steps in working with families experiencing ambiguous loss (Boss, 2009). In this space, it is paramount to allow families and individuals to share their experience and the attached emotions, normalizing these and doing so without judgment. For many families, holding onto hope can provide strength and an ongoing relationship with the missing loved one. However, for others, perhaps those seeking closure or seeking life to return to the way it was, hope can freeze responses to loss or hinder resilience (Boss, 2006). As a person remains missing, hope may change, from "*hope of a reunion, to hope of information, which finally became hope of resolution*" (FFMPU, 2005, p. 12). It is the hope that life can somehow continue despite the enormity of the loss, the hope that resiliency is possible, which is at the core of therapy (Boss, 2006).

Resilience is key to empowering clients in their ability to move forward. Building resilience despite ambiguity in a therapeutic context requires guiding individuals and families in realizing their own strengths and, more broadly, the resources available to them (Boss, 2006). Providing strategies to families or individuals that allow them to function, such as activities, reflections, or supports, guides clients from a space of finality to living in the space in between. It is common to feel a need to be in control; however, in the face of ambiguous loss, control is unattainable, so instead Boss suggests tempering mastery. Things that may help temper mastery include working towards understanding that the world is not always just and fair, externalizing blame, identifying past competencies, and accepting that some things will not change (Boss, 2006).

Lucy, and many of those left behind, describe those who care for and support them as those who "get it." Such support can help to validate and normalize a person's response to living with missing and the ambiguous nature of the loss they're experiencing. In acknowledging the loss and respecting that there is no closure or "moving on," people like Lucy are able to discuss their missing loved one and maintain a connection with them in a meaningful way. Support groups can provide a place for such validation and acknowledgment, encouraging members to share ways that, despite the complexity of their experiences, families can include their missing loved one in everyday routines, family events, and rituals.

> Sometimes, I talk to him while I am doing things; it's just a thing we do, like for others going to a grave and putting flowers there.
>
> (Bill)

Support groups can provide a combination of psycho-education, mutual aid, and therapy, where participants gain support and support each other (FFMPU, 2016). Such groups are an opportunity for those affected to meet others who are also living with a missing loved one and who, despite the varied responses that those left behind experience, are able to connect through a shared experience. Support groups help foster a sense of community and connection, where ambiguous loss and disenfranchised grief are known to often create disconnection.

> I think I see him most days. It even resulted in me having a car accident when I became distracted after I thought I had seen my son on the side of the road. From that moment on, I have had to remind myself to stop constantly searching for him, to concentrate on the present moment.
>
> (Sharon)

Support groups may help to empower participants, enabling them to better understand their experience and their response to missing through the provision and sharing of information. Facilitators can use the group setting to discuss and provide information about concepts, such as resilience, that may be helpful to those living with a loved one missing. For some, such as Sharon, her experience of having a missing son has led to years of poor sleep and hypervigilance. Support groups provide a forum for recognizing common experiences or responses such as these, and group members may benefit from sharing helpful management strategies with each other. These may include exploring ways of looking after themselves, including meditation, self-compassion (Neff, 2015), or exercise.

> The positive thing about it is that you get to listen to other people's experience and to realise that you are not alone.
>
> (Bill)

While support of an ongoing nature, such as support groups or individual therapy, may be what some individuals and families require, others may access support for more practical advice. In the beginning, such support may be sought about the police investigation and where to go to find more search information. Practically, families may at different times throughout the investigation require advice on the coroner's process or managing the financial affairs of their missing loved one. Such practical support and information may or may not lend itself to further therapeutic intervention, but it does allow for further discussion around the support services available. Contact with support services is best made in the early days of missing, but for individuals and families living with not knowing, there is reassurance in knowing that contact at any point in the missing person's experience is possible. It is helpful that those living with ambiguous loss are given opportunities to explore their feelings, as well as have their experiences and responses heard, affirmed, and normalized—whenever this is possible and in whatever setting is right for the individual or family at the time (FFMPU, 2016).

Conclusion

Nothing can prepare someone for the experience of missing. When a person is missing, the impact on those left behind is profound. The ambiguity and lack of resolution may create a barrier not only to the grief process but the ability to move forward (Boss, 2006). The physical absence is strongly felt, yet the grief is frozen (Boss, 1999). Families of missing people live with both the physical absence and psychological presence of their loved one, managing both the ambiguity surrounding their missing loved one and hope that they will return.

Missing impacts all aspects of an individual's experience. Emotionally and psychologically, it can be exhausting, with the potential to impact one's relational, practical, and financial well-being. The complexity and challenge of such a loss necessitates the availability of and access to support for those left behind, to find their own way to live with not knowing for as long as missing continues.

Key Terms

> **Not Knowing:** The difficult, strenuous, and uncertain space within which families of missing people must exist, as there may never be concrete facts or answers surrounding their loved one's disappearance.
> **Support Groups:** A group of persons with comparable situations, and who provide presence, support, encouragement, and validation to each other.
> **Tempering Mastery:** The ability to cultivate acceptance towards comprehending the imperfect nature of life, and to create a realistic sense of what one can control.

Questions for Reflection

1. Describe the ambiguous nature of loss for families of missing people. How can individuals offer grief support to someone who has experienced the complexity and uncertainty related to grief associated with missing persons?
2. Families who have a loved one that goes missing must live in the continuous state of not knowing. Why is not knowing so difficult for us as individuals? How can people learn to accept uncertainty, and the grief surrounding it? How can meaning be found in the state of unknowing?
3. What social messages exist surrounding the ambiguous loss of a missing loved one? Why do you think these types of losses are typically disenfranchised, and why is there often a societal pressure to "move on" when ambiguous loss occurs?
4. Traditional social conventions surrounding bereavement are typically inaccessible for individuals experiencing ambiguous loss. How could individuals

reconstruct traditional customs or create new rituals to fit the uncertain circumstance?

References

Boss, P. (1999). *Ambiguous loss: Learning to live with unresolved grief*. Harvard: Harvard University Press.

Boss, P. (2006). *Loss, trauma, and resilience: Therapeutic work with ambiguous loss*. New York: W. W. Norton & Company.

Boss, P. (2009). The trauma and complicated grief of ambiguous loss. *Pastoral Psychology*, 59(2), 137–145.

Bricknell, S. (2017). *Missing persons: Who is at risk?* Research Reports No. 8. Canberra: Australian Institute of Criminology. https://aic.gov.au/publications/rr/rr8

Clark, J. (2006). *Wanting to hope: The experience of adult siblings of long-term missing people*. Unpublished dissertation, University of Queensland.

Doka, K. J. (Ed.) (2002). *Disenfranchised grief: New directions, challenges and strategies for practice*. Champaign, IL: Research Press.

Families and Friends of Missing Persons Unit (FFMPU). (2005). *A glimmer of hope*. Parramatta: NSW Department of Justice.

Families and Friends of Missing Persons Unit. (2013). *In the Loop: Young people talking about missing*. Parramatta: NSW Department of Justice.

Families and Friends of Missing Persons Unit. (2014). *Missing people: A guide for family members and service providers*. Parramatta: NSW Department of Justice.

Families and Friends of Missing Persons Unit. (2015). *Data mining analysis*. Unpublished, Parramatta, NSW Department of Justice.

Families and Friends of Missing Persons Unit. (2016). *Conversations and connections: Support group meetings for the families of missing people*. Parramatta: NSW Department of Justice.

Glassock, G. (2006). Coping with uncertainty. *Bereavement Care*, 25(3), 43–46.

Glassock, G. (2011). *Australian families of missing people: Narrating their lived experience*. Unpublished doctoral thesis, Armidale, University of New England.

Kreitler, S., & Shanun-Klein, H. (Eds.). (2013). *Studies of grief and bereavement*. Hauppage, NY: Nova.

Neff, K. (2015). *Self-compassion: The proven power of being kind to yourself*. New York: HarperCollins.

Tubbs, C., & Boss, P. (2000). An essay for practitioners dealing with ambiguous loss. *Family Relations*, 49(3), 285.

Wayland, S. (2015). *'I still hope but what I hope for has changed': A narrative inquiry study of hope and ambiguous loss when someone is missing*. Armidale, Australia: University of New England.

PART **III**

Nonfinite Loss: Living with Ongoing Loss and Grief

Darcy L. Harris

Introduction

Angela had skated all her life. When she was eight years old, her coach told her parents that she had a great deal of potential, and they changed her into a competitive figure skating program, where she flourished. Angela loved being on the ice. By the time she was 12, she had won many championships at both the provincial and national levels. At age 14, her trainer introduced her to a senior women's skating coach who had been involved with many Olympic champions, and it was no secret that Angela was tracking for Olympic competition with her talent and abilities.

On Angela's 16th birthday, her boyfriend made plans to take her to a special restaurant to celebrate. On their way home, the car hit black ice and he lost control, with the car spinning off the road and hitting a tree head-on. The dashboard of the car was shoved into the passenger area, pinning Angela's legs. When the emergency workers arrived, they had to use special equipment to extricate Angela from the car. Angela's right leg was broken in many places. She required extensive surgery to re-set the broken bones. However, the bones in her ankle were shattered. The surgeons fused these bones to save her foot and to provide her with functionality so that she would be able to walk.

Angela's recovery was slow but steady. It took several months for her to be able to walk again. Over time, she painfully realized that she would perhaps be able to skate again with a special boot to stabilize her foot, but she would never be able to skate competitively. Angela's entire life had been devoted to skating and being on the ice. All her time outside of school had been devoted to her life on the ice. Her future had been planned around skating. Her parents had spent thousands of dollars on her training and competition.

This scenario has many losses in it. However, none of the losses are because someone died; rather, Angela's entire future as she had planned it is dead, including all the hopes, dreams, and passion that gave her life meaning and a sense of purpose. No doubt, while most people would sympathize with Angela, they would also have difficulties understanding the magnitude and significance of the loss and her grief because she is young and still able to function in the everyday world.

Most likely, the focus would also be upon the fact that she lived through the accident and still has a full life ahead of her. But it is not the life that Angela had planned and envisioned.

With losses that occur after the death of a loved one, there usually is a painful time of grieving the absence of presence of that loved one, and social support is offered to assist the bereaved individual(s) through this difficult time of adjustment. While the current thinking about grief is that the bereaved individual may continue to experience surges and uncover new layers of grief over time, the experience does change and evolve, as there is gradual adjustment to a life without the loved one who died. But what if the "death" and reminders of the loss occur over and over again on a daily basis? Or, what if the "death" was of a relationship where the people in the relationship continued to live after the relationship itself died? In Angela's situation, her daily routine of going to the skating rink and planning for competitions is no longer viable. She experiences regular reminders that her daily routine, schedule, plans, and purpose in life are permanently altered. Her future in competitive skating and all that it meant to her have died.

Development of the Concept

Elizabeth Bruce and Cynthia Schultz, clinician/researchers from Latrobe University in Melbourne, Australia, began considering the concept of loss and grief in the presence of non-death losses as they observed parents of children with disabilities. They noticed that the parents' grief became more and more evident as their children grew and repeatedly missed the developmental milestones that other children of their age achieved readily. Bruce and Schultz (2001) applied the term *nonfinite loss* to capture experiences where the loss itself continues and is ongoing in nature.

Nonfinite losses are enduring losses that are typically precipitated by a negative life event or episode where the loss itself retains a physical and/or psychological presence with an individual in an ongoing manner (Bruce & Schultz, 2001). Some forms of nonfinite loss may be less clearly defined in onset, but they tend to be identified by a sense of ongoing uncertainty and the need for repeated adjustment or accommodation. Several main factors separate this kind of loss experience from a death-related loss:

- The loss (and grief) is continuous and ongoing in some way. While the initial event may be time-limited, an element of the experience will stay with the individual(s) for the rest of life.
- An inability to meet normal expectations of everyday life due to physical, cognitive, social, emotional, or spiritual losses that continue to be manifest over time.
- The inclusion of intangible losses, such as the loss of one's hopes or ideals related to what a person believes should have been, could have been, or might have been.
- Awareness of the need to continually accommodate, adapt, and adjust to an experience that derails expectations of what life was supposed to be like. The term *living losses* is sometimes used to refer to nonfinite losses because of the

awareness that an individual will live with this loss or some aspect of it for an indefinite period of time, and most likely for the rest of that individual's life (Schultz & Harris, 2011).

An image that symbolizes the experience of nonfinite losses is when a mirror is held up to another mirror, with the resulting image displaying an infinite number of reflections for as far as the eye can see. There is no ending in sight. Like this image, nonfinite losses are ongoing in nature, and there is no known end to the experience and/or its ramifications. Essentially, this is your life now; the life you knew before is no longer accessible to you in the same way. In their writings, Bruce and Schultz (2001) describe several cardinal features of the experience of nonfinite losses:

- There is ongoing uncertainty regarding what will happen next. Anxiety is often the primary undercurrent to the experience.
- There is often a sense of disconnection from the mainstream and what is generally viewed as "normal" in human experience.
- The magnitude of the loss is frequently unrecognized or not acknowledged by others.
- There is an ongoing sense of helplessness and powerlessness associated with the loss.
- Nonfinite losses may be accompanied by shame, embarrassment, and self-doubting that further complicates existing relationships, thereby adding to the struggle with coping.
- There are typically no rituals that assist to validate or legitimize the loss, especially if the loss was symbolic or intangible.

Jones and Beck (2007) further add to this list a sense of chronic despair and ongoing dread, as individuals try to reconcile themselves between the world that is now known through this experience and the world that was originally anticipated.

Repeated Accommodation and Adaptation

The person who experiences or is affected by nonfinite loss is repeatedly asked to adjust and accommodate to the loss. At the same time, because nonfinite loss is often not well understood, others may be oblivious to the experience and its implications. Support systems may tire of attempting to provide a shoulder to lean on when they also see potential joy that should outweigh any lingering sorrow in a situation. For instance, a couple who went though many years of infertility treatment are finally able to conceive and have a baby. While the initial loss of fertility is resolved through successfully bringing a child into the world, the emotional and relational stress, financial strain, and the numerous times that hopes and dreams were built up and crushed before a successful pregnancy occurred would most likely have a significant and irreversible impact upon their assumptive worlds (Harris & Daniluk, 2010). Indeed, there is research that explores that difference in parenting between couples who have been through infertility treatment versus those who have not. In these studies, a diagnosis and treatment for infertility prior to parenting is related to increased incidence of depression, anxiety, and difficulties coping with parenthood for many couples (Hammarberg, Rowe, & Fisher, 2009; Hammarberg, Fisher, & Wynter, 2008; McGrath, Samra, Zukowsky, & Baker, 2010; Olshansky, 2009). Brian (2011) states that infertility never leaves the couple, no matter the outcome, whether the couple conceives, adopts, or remains childless.

For couples who parent after undergoing treatment, the intensity of the medical treatments preceding parenthood shapes their parenting decisions, how they view themselves as parents (and people), and their perceptions of parenthood in general. In terms of the assumptive world construct, expectations about conceiving a child and becoming a parent, misconceptions about the effectiveness of infertility treatments, changes in the couple's relationship, self-perceptions, and expectations about control over the future are often shattered, making it impossible to return to life as it was previously, even with the goal of parenthood having been accomplished. Well-wishers will stress the joy at having a new baby in the couple's life and most likely will not recognize, or perhaps even tolerate, any discussion of the mixed emotions or the suffering that the couple endured in the process of conception or adoption, so the ongoing losses and grief associated with the experience of infertility prior to the presence of a baby remain hidden and unacknowledged.

Viorst (1987) states that loss is a necessary part of life, and that many normal developmental milestones in life require adaptation and adjustment. However, the nonfinite losses differ from adjustment to change in everyday life by the degree that:

- Hopes, dreams, and the assumptive world are assaulted and/or shattered.
- The individual feels compelled to engage in a significant search for meaning in light of what has happened.
- The loss itself gathers significance over time rather than becoming integrated over time.
- There is a loss of coherence or meaning to previously held sources of meaning and purpose.
- The loss is ongoing in nature, with no clearly marked conclusion.

The individual affected by nonfinite loss continues in life in a way that is different from before; sometimes the change is internal and sometimes it is external, while in some situations the change is both internal and external.

The experience of the ongoing sense of loss may also be exacerbated because the circumstances surrounding the loss result in recurrent pain, grief, or distress involving, for example, shame, self-consciousness, or social isolation. It may be traced to a lost sense of self, the loss of a significant person, object, or lifestyle. The awareness of "who I believe I am" and "how I perceive that other people see me" are both upended with a new (and often ongoing) sense of turmoil, not knowing, and vulnerability. For further exploration and examples of nonfinite losses, the reader may be directed to the previous volume edited by Harris, *Counting our Losses: Reflecting on Change, Loss, and Transition in Everyday Life* (2011).

In nonfinite losses, it is important to note the difference between acceptance and adaptation. A loss may never be emotionally acceptable due to the deep wound created in the core of one's assumptive world when it occurs. However, inability to accept the loss does not preclude the ability to adapt to and accommodate the loss experience in an ongoing way. In this instance, the concept of adaptation means working towards the best-possible outcome, and this process can be incredibly hard. Adaptation involves conquering fears and dreads, redefining or modifying hopes and dreams, and asserting control in the face of extreme difficulties and vulnerability. It also means bridging the gaps and filling the voids. Finally, adaptation means respecting the place that grief will always have as counterpart to the loss from its onset, but in which the loss itself does not necessarily have to be accepted. Seeing the silver lining of a cloud doesn't preclude the fact that clouds still can block the view of the sun and that they bring rain.

Comparison to Bereavement After Death Losses

As described in the introductory chapter, most bereavement theories are focused upon experiences after the death of a significant person. With the exception of the constructivist focus on the need for meaning-making after the experience of significant life-altering events (Neimeyer, 2001), most theories of bereavement have not been readily applied to grief that results from a non-death loss. However, we can extrapolate how some of these theories may be applied to nonfinite losses.

Klass, Silverman, and Nickman (1996) proposed that bereaved individual's maintenance of a continuing bond with a deceased individual is a common and normative response to the death of a significant person. The basic implication for this theory is that grief may never really end, and that bereaved individuals frequently access their bond and associated relationship with their deceased loved ones internally. This ongoing aspect of their grief is often a conscious choice that provides comfort and reassurance. Nonfinite loss certainly implies that there is ongoing grief and adaptation to the loss that may also never really end. However, the focus in the continuing bonds theory is upon the continuation of the relationship with the deceased and the accompanying triggers of grief that may occur at specific times, and not upon the continuation of the loss experience itself.

The Dual Process Model of bereavement (Stroebe & Schut, 1999), which also is discussed in the introductory chapter, describes the unfolding of one's grief experience as an oscillation between focus upon the relationship with the deceased individual (loss orientation) with an alternate focus upon tasks of everyday life and distractions (restoration orientation). Although this model is built upon the experiences of individuals who are bereft after the death of a loved one, there are implications for how one may cope with losses that are less tangible as well. Instead of a focus upon a person or a relationship, the focus in the loss orientation may be upon the loss itself and the implications of that loss, whether it be a person, role, object, or some intangible aspect of one's life. This model allows for a wide range of diversity within responses to loss, including a coping in ways that are consistent with nonfinite losses.

Another area of interest in regard to bereavement research and the description of nonfinite loss is related to the research by Boelen and Prigerson (2007) and Prigerson et al. (2009) on prolonged grief disorder (PGD). The comparison here is relevant to the ongoing nature of the grief that is part of the definition of nonfinite loss. For example, is the long-term, ongoing experience of grief in nonfinite loss similar to what is described in the diagnostic criteria for PGD? The first criterion indicates that the event must be the death of a significant other. Thus, nonfinite losses that are intangible or non-death related would not fit into this diagnostic category. The focus in nonfinite loss is upon the *ongoing presence of the loss that requires continued adaptation and accommodation*; whereas the literature that sets out the criteria for PGD focuses on the protracted interruption in daily functioning for individuals after the death of a loved one. One further distinction between these two entities is that in nonfinite losses, the loss itself may be ongoing and not a definitive event, such as what is implied in PGD.

One further theoretical comparison is to examine the constructivist view of grief as a springboard to rebuild one's assumptive world and life narrative by making meaning of what has and is occurring through the loss experience (Neimeyer, 2001). Certainly, meaning-making as a form of coping with a significant loss experience that is nonfinite in nature would readily be identified in many instances. For example, the concept of the *wounded healer*, which is common in grassroots support organizations, embodies the idea that one can go through a very painful experience and later be able to draw upon that experience in a meaningful way to assist others who are in a similar situation (MacCulloch & Shattell, 2009).

One additional reference to the experience of nonfinite loss is to identify the frequent overlap with disenfranchised grief, which was discussed more fully in Chapter 2. Disenfranchised grief is described as grief that is not socially recognized or sanctioned, nor is the individual who is associated with these types of losses. Because the core of disenfranchised grief is the lack of social recognition or the stigmatization of the loss or grief in some way, many nonfinite losses would also fall into the category of disenfranchised loss, as these losses are often not recognized because they are often intangible, dismissed, not understood, or the grief is co-mingled with what is perceived as a positive event. For example, a mother whose son leaves home after graduating from high school may feel the loss of her son's daily presence in the house and everyday life even while she celebrates his moving forward in life to becoming an independent adult.

In summary, the *continuing presence of the loss* is the hallmark of what is captured in the description of nonfinite loss and its underlying conceptualization. It is important to remember that the perception of nonfinite loss and its accompanying ongoing grief is an entirely subjective and unpredictable experience. There is no return to the world as it used to be or to the person one was before, and the idea of closure is an unreasonable expectation. However, there is a realistic possibility of adaptation to the changed view of the world and self that emerges in an ongoing way. The grief response in this context will be ongoing, but this form of long-lived grief is not abnormal because the experience of loss is ongoing as well.

Examples of Nonfinite Loss

In this next section, we will explore specific examples of nonfinite losses. Each of the following chapters describes an experience where the lives of those involved have been changed/altered in a significant way as a result of an ongoing loss experience. It's important to note that some nonfinite losses overlap with ambiguous loss experiences, and many of these experiences involve chronic sorrow, which will also be discussed further in the next section. For many non-death loss experiences, some of the descriptions and features are similar. Comparisons and delineations between terms will be explored in more detail in Part VI, aptly entitled "Putting It All Together."

Key Terms

Living Losses: Losses that will remain as an ongoing presence in the life of an individual; the individual will continue to "live" with the loss experience. The ongoing response of the loss will require continual adaptation and adjustment.

Nonfinite Losses: Loss experiences that are enduring in nature, usually precipitated by a negative life event or an episode that retains a physical and/or psychological presence in an ongoing manner.

Prolonged Grief Disorder (PGD): A syndrome that focuses on the chronic interruption of daily functionality for grieving individuals after the death of a loved one.

Questions for Reflection

1. What are the core characteristics or experiences associated with nonfinite and living losses? Before you were aware of these concepts, how would you have responded to these variations of loss experiences?
2. Identify potential social implications of nonfinite losses for grieving individuals. How does this type of loss experience defy social norms?
3. Why do nonfinite and living loss experiences require consistent adaption and adjustment? What does adaptation and adjustment mean under these circumstances? Why is "closure" seen as a false hope and myth for these types of losses?

References

Boelen, P., & Prigerson, H. (2007). The influence of symptoms of prolonged grief disorder, depression, and anxiety on quality of life among bereaved adults. *European Archives of Clinical Psychiatry and Clinical Neuroscience, 257,* 444–452.

Brian, K. (2011). *Precious babies: Pregnancy, birth and parenting after infertility.* Essex, UK: Piatkus.

Bruce, E. J., & Schultz, C. L. (2001). *Nonfinite loss and grief: A psychoeducational approach.* Sydney, Australia: Jessica Kingsley.

Hammarberg, J. R., Fisher, K. H., & Wynter, K. H. (2008). Psychological and social aspects of pregnancy, childbirth and early parenting after assisted conception: A systematic review. *Human Reproduction Update, 14*(5), 395–414.

Hammarberg, K., Rowe, H. J., & Fisher, J. R. (2009). Early post-partum adjustment and admission to parenting services in Victoria, Australia after assisted conception. *Human Reproduction, 24*(11), 2801–2809.

Harris, D. L. (Ed.). (2011). *Counting our losses: Reflecting on change, loss, and transition in everyday life*. New York: Routledge.

Harris, D. L., & Daniluk, J. C. (2010). The experience of spontaneous pregnancy loss for infertile women who have conceived through assisted reproduction technology. *Human Reproduction, 25*(3), 714–720.

Jones, S. J., & Beck, E. (2007). Disenfranchised grief and non-finite loss as experienced by the families of death row inmates. *Omega: The Journal of Death and Dying, 54*(4), 281–299.

Klass, D., Silverman, P., & Nickman, C. (1996). *Continuing bonds*. New York: Basic Books.

MacCulloch, T., & Shattell, M. (2009). Reflections of a "wounded healer." *Issues in Mental Health Nursing, 30*(2), 135–137.

McGrath, J. M., Samra, H. A., Zukowsky, K., & Baker, B. (2010). Parenting after infertility: Issues for families and infants. *MCN: The American Journal of Maternal/Child Nursing, 35*(3), 156–164.

Neimeyer, R. A. (2001). The language of loss: Grief therapy as a process of meaning reconstruction. In R. A. Neimeyer (Ed.), *Meaning reconstruction and the experience of loss* (pp. 261–292). Washington, DC: APA.

Olshansky, E. (2009). Parenting after Infertility. *Zero to Three, 29*(5), 23–37.

Prigerson, H., Horowitz, M., Jacobs, S., Parkes, C., Aslan, M., Goodkin, K., et al. (2009). Prolonged grief disorder: Empiric validation of criteria proposed for the DSM-V and the ICD-11. *PLOS Medicine, 6*(8). Retrieved May 7, 2018, from www.ncbi.nlm.nih.gov/pmc/articles/PMC2711304/pdf/pmed.1000121.pdf/?tool=pmcentrez

Schultz, C. L., & Harris, D. L. (2011). Giving voice to nonfinite loss and grief in bereavement. In R. Neimeyer, D. Harris, H. Winokuer, & G. Thornton (Eds.), *Grief and bereavement in contemporary society: Bridging research and practice* (pp. 235–245). New York: Routledge.

Stroebe, M., & Schut, H. (1999). The Dual Process Model of coping with bereavement: Rationale and description. *Death Studies, 23*, 197–224.

Viorst, J. (1987). *Necessary losses*. New York: Fireside.

CHAPTER 11

Nonfinite and Cumulative Loss in Foster Care

Monique B. Mitchell

Introduction

"Open your eyes, Olivia. It's time to get up." Olivia, age 8, stretches out her arms and focuses in on the speaker. She does not recognize the person addressing her. "Who are you?" she asks. "My name is Dominick," the stranger replies, "I'm a social worker. It's time to go, Olivia. Come with me." Today is a day that Olivia will always remember, but one she wishes she could forget—the day she entered foster care. Olivia's identity as a "child" quickly changes to a "foster child" as her assumptive world shatters.[1] Experiencing removal from her home and placement into foster care is an event that can never be undone; a life-altering event which significantly disrupts a child's life, identity, and relationships. As Olivia is removed from her family and enters the foster care system, she will quickly experience the meaning of nonfinite loss (the ongoing experience of loss) and cumulative loss (multiple losses which occur simultaneously and/or subsequently). The foster care system is intended to be a temporary experience but, for most youth in foster care, it is considered anything but temporary. Olivia's world was turned upside down as she entered and lingered in a system that challenged her perceptions of family, permanency, and stability. As will be discussed in this chapter, the foster care experience is fraught with complex relational ebbs and flows; a life-altering experience troubled by impermanency, uncertainty, and loss.

Foster Care: The Numbers

More than 430,000 children are in the US foster care system. The number of children entering foster care in the United States has been steadily increasing since 2012. For example, in 2016, there were 273,539 children who entered the foster care system, an increase of 9% since 2012. More than 50% of children are placed into homes with people whom they do not know, and they will remain in foster care for one or more years (US Department of Health and Human Services, 2016). Although efforts are made to provide permanency, safety, and well-being to children while under governmental care, the outcomes for many of these children are disheartening. Compared to children in the general population, children with foster care experience are at a greater risk of negative long-term outcomes such as homelessness (Dworsky, Napolitano, & Courtney, 2013), unemployment (Barnow, Buck, O'Brien, Pecora, Ellis, & Steiner, 2015), low educational attainment (Zetlin, Weinberg, & Shea, 2010), and high-risk behaviors (Keller, Salazar, & Courtney, 2010). Furthermore, children in foster care report experiences of ambiguous loss, disenfranchised grief, and ongoing ambiguity (Mitchell, 2016a; Mitchell, 2016b; Mitchell, 2017; Mitchell & Kuczynski, 2010) which can negatively impact mental and behavioral health. These reported findings illustrate the need to better ensure that the psychological, social, emotional, physical, and spiritual needs of children in foster care are met to foster healing and healthy outcomes.

Social support is considered one of the most important predictors for positive outcomes for children and youth in foster care (Rutman & Hubberstey, 2016) and is considered a vital coping resource for grieving children and adolescents (Hooyman & Kramer, 2008). However, recent research suggests that the needs of grieving youth are not being adequately met while in the foster care system (Mitchell, 2017). This lack of support may be attributed to the insufficient training and education on grief and loss for individuals in the field. For example, Ober, Grenello, and Wheaton (2012) surveyed more than 350 counselors on grief training, and it was found that most counselors had not received adequate training on grief and loss. Because many of our helping professionals do not have the expertise to effectively counsel for grief and loss issues (Breen, 2010; Harris & Winokuer, 2016), it comes as no surprise that most child welfare professionals (who may or may not have a counseling, social work, or related human services degree) are not adequately prepared to attend to the specific needs of grieving individuals, let alone grieving children in foster care.

Loss and the Foster Care Timeline

The experience of becoming a "foster child" involves multiple foster care transition transactions, including the apprehension transaction (a child's removal from his or her original home and the home transfer; Mitchell & Kuczynski, 2010), the foster placement transaction (a child's entry to a new foster care placement; Mitchell & Kuczynski, 2010), and the "aging out" transaction (a child's transition out of foster care due to ineligibility to receive services based on age—usually 18 years old), among other transactions. Each transaction involves a life-altering event which can threaten children's relationships, beliefs, stability, and worldview. Therefore, children experience challenges at the beginning, the middle, and the end of their time in foster care. Multiple and various non-death losses ensue from these challenges: nonfinite losses, cumulative losses, and ambiguous losses. The latter, ambiguous loss, occurs when a person is psychologically present yet physically absent, or when an individual is physically present yet psychologically absent (Boss, 1999). Nonfinite and cumulative losses in foster care will be the focus for this chapter, as I have discussed ambiguous loss extensively in other publications.[2]

Nonfinite loss refers to a non-death loss that is often unexpected and ongoing. The loss can result in intangible losses, challenged beliefs, and an ongoing sense of confusion and despair. Nonfinite loss is often paired with disenfranchised grief, as this type of loss is typically overlooked and undervalued by society, resulting in grief minimization and disregard. Becoming a "foster child"[3] is an example of an event that creates nonfinite loss. This label, imposed on children by society, can cause children to question their identity, how long they will be a "foster child," and if they will ever be a "normal" child again. Being in foster care challenges the psychological and emotional well-being of children (Mitchell, 2016a; Mitchell, 2016b) and creates an ongoing struggle regarding relationships, belonging, stability, consistency, and ambiguity. To further complicate matters, the losses that children experience while in foster care accumulate; that is, children in foster care will experience *cumulative loss*. Cumulative loss, sometimes referred to as loss pileup, occurs when multiple losses are experienced by an individual successively and, at times, concurrently. As will be outlined in this chapter, losses occur the moment children are removed from their homes and placed into foster care, persist as children navigate the foster care system, and compromise children's futures as they transition out of foster care.

Loss at the "Beginning"

A child's transition, or entry, into foster care is an event filled with loss. Not only are children separated from their parent(s), they lose their homes and, often, also their friends, neighborhoods, and schools. In addition to these tangible losses, children experience losses that are less obvious—the loss of routine, the loss of stability, the loss of familiarity, and the loss of self. As one young person in foster care reports, "I felt like I lost myself when I went into care." (Mitchell, 2017, p. 3) Reports such as these challenge our traditional definitions of loss and encourage us to acknowledge the various losses that children will experience when they enter foster care. It is important to recognize that while some losses will be overt (i.e., the loss of one's family and home), other losses may be less tangible, or obvious, than others. For example, children's beliefs about family dynamics, social norms, routines and responsibilities, identity, and permanency are threatened when they are removed from their families and homes. Ultimately, these secondary losses (i.e., losses resulting from the primary loss of their family and home environment) contribute to confusion and nonfinite loss. Now labeled a "foster child," children question what that label means, how their role with the family unit will be affected, and how long they will be a "foster child" (Mitchell, 2016a; Mitchell & Kuczynski, 2010). Unfortunately, there are no easy answers to these questions and, as children have reported, these questions are often left unanswered (Mitchell, 2016a).

At the onset of placement, some children may try to cope with the foster care experience by convincing themselves that they will be returning home soon, whereas others may try to adjust to their new surroundings and family environments (Mitchell, 2016b). The majority of children who enter foster care are placed with people with whom they are unfamiliar (US Department of Health and Human Services, 2016). Children are expected to establish relational bonds with new care providers, peers, and other simulated families while the agency pursues case goals of reunification, adoption, or some other form of permanency, often with families other than those with whom the children are residing while in foster care. Ultimately, the foster care system is designed to provide children with permanent and sustainable relationships *after*, and not during, their foster care placement. As children linger in the foster care system, they are faced with the harsh reality that their identity as a "foster child" will remain until reunification or a permanent family is attained.

Loss in the "Middle"

Recent estimates indicate that more than 100,000 children remain in foster care for two or more years, while only 50% of children in foster care experience reunification with their parent or primary caretaker (US Department of Health and Human Services, 2016). These findings reveal that foster care is usually not a temporary experience and is one that involves ambiguity, family dissolution, and relational disconnection. Children in foster care are often challenged by family structures whose members can frequently come and go, homes (placements) which may dissolve at any time, and by communities which may be short-lived.

Despite efforts to minimize the number of placements experienced by children in foster care, it is not uncommon for children to move frequently while in foster care. Foster care alumni report: "You're bound to move . . . I never stay in one place. I moved four times in the past year. It does affect you. You don't know what to call home . . . I moved so much" (Unrau, Seita, & Putney, 2008, p. 1262), and "You're always moving, like I've been to like five different high schools." (Mitchell, 2017, p. 4). Multiple placements result in multiple losses, including the loss of care providers, peers, teachers, routines, stability, and normalcy. Experiencing inconsistency, lack of stability, and multiple placements can challenge a person's sense of normalcy. One foster care alumnus recalls, "Once I began to realize what normal people do and compare myself to them, I learned to lie to myself and others about who and what I was" (Unrau et al., 2008, p. 1261). As identified by youth in foster care, a youth's experience as a "foster child" can impact their perception of belonging and normalcy amongst their peers. It is important to consider how children are impacted when their peer relationships are constantly threatened and disrupted due to multiple placements.

Children in foster care who have developed trusting and accepting relationships with their peers may experience further emotional upheaval and trauma when these relationships are severed. As was reported by Hyde and Kammerer (2009), multiple placements can result in youth socially withdrawing from their peers. A 17-year-old youth in their study reports:

> At [Name #2] High School, I made so many friends. I think the whole school loved me . . . As I moved, I just didn't feel like making any more friends.

> Here I am just out of [Name#4] High School and I have two or three friends because I didn't even care.
>
> (Hyde & Kammerer, 2009, p. 271).

The cumulative loss of friendships is extremely problematic for children, especially during the adolescent years when peer relationships serve as a primary means of social support. Without stable and consistent friendships, an adolescent's natural disposition to bond with peers is compromised, and the experience of nonfinite loss is exacerbated.

In addition to experiencing the relational loss of friends, youth in foster care have reported how they are affected when they experience the relational loss of siblings. The sibling relationship has been reported by youth in foster care as one of the most important relationships in their lives (Herrick & Piccus, 2005; Mitchell, 2016b; Mitchell, Jones, & Renema, 2015; Unrau et al., 2008). It is not uncommon for youth to discuss how being separated from their siblings disrupts their lives, challenges their assumptive world, and results in grief and emotional turmoil (Mitchell, 2017). The sibling relationship can serve as a positive emotional and psychological resource for children as they navigate their way through the foster care system (Unrau et al., 2008). Experiencing the ambiguous loss of a sibling can be emotionally debilitating for children in foster care, especially when their sibling relationship provides one of the few forms of consistency in their lives.

Placement moves are not the only events that evoke loss for children during their time in foster care; losses also occur for children who have experienced stable placements. Recent estimates using a national dataset indicate that the median caseworker maintains employment in their position for less than two years (Edwards & Wildeman, 2018). Therefore, more than 100,000 children in foster care are likely to have at least two case managers. A child's relationship with his or her case manager has the potential to have great importance because it is one of the first relationships children will form with an adult when entering foster care. A child's case manager can provide comfort, security, and guidance as children enter an unfamiliar system that challenges their norms and expectations. As such, the bond that is created between children and their caseworker can be a significant relationship for children during this major life transition.

Children in foster care discuss how the relational loss of a case manager can negatively impact their desire to seek connection and support from adults. As one youth participant states, "When you keep losing caseworkers, it affects your ability to tell who you can and can't trust" (Strolin-Goltzman, Kollar, & Trinkle, 2010, p. 51). As stated by this youth, it can be challenging for children to establish a trusting and caring relationship with the adults in their lives when relational loss becomes normative. Given this, the emotional and psychological well-being of children can be negatively affected when their relationship with a case manager is severed, especially for those children who have established a caring bond.

As these experiences demonstrate, the ongoing losses and experience of not feeling "normal" while navigating the foster care system can continually cause despair and confusion for children as they wait for the day when the constant moving, displacement, and relational losses will subside.

Loss at the "End"

Although children can exit the foster care system at any age, on average, 20,000 children will exit foster care due to emancipation, also referred to as "aging out" (US Department of Health and Human Services, 2016). This transition involves multiple losses which can further impact an individual's sense of self and well-being. When exiting the foster care system, children are often placed with the great burden of achieving "self-sufficiency," which refers to the expectation that foster care alumni will successfully establish and maintain employment, housing, and healthy relationships. These expectations seem somewhat challenging and unrealistic when youth exiting foster care are simultaneously juggling multiple losses and expectations with little to no support.

An individual's 18th birthday is usually considered a time of celebration, but for many children in foster care, this can be a dreaded event which threatens their assumptive world and well-being. Some youth in foster care fear their 18th birthday due to a lack of support and being faced with having to leave their respective "home" on the day they turn 18. One youth reports:

> "When I turned 18, my caseworker was nowhere to be found. So when 12 o'clock hit, they was [sic] like, 'Oh well. We are closing her case.' So on Monday I was at home and I was like, what am I going to do?"
> (quoted in Goodkind, Schelbe, & Shook, 2011, p. 1042).[4]

Because financial payments to foster care providers are often terminated once a youth turns 18, youth can find themselves spending their birthday packing their bags while trying to figure out where they will lay their head that night. Not only is this experience disheartening, it is psychologically damaging. The people whom a youth called "family" can no longer financially afford to provide the youth with a home to live in, and this reality can cause deep psychological and emotional harm. Youth may question whether their "foster families" were only invested in their well-being for financial gain and if the memories and relationships they formed were ever authentic. As a result, the foster care system, designed to protect children from harm, can inadvertently produce young adults who struggle for connection, belonging, safety, and permanency.

Reports by youth in foster care illustrate their fear of what will happen to them when they transition out of foster care and the impending losses they will have to endure (Cunningham & Diversi, 2012; Dvir, Weiner, & Kupermintz, 2012; Mitchell et al., 2015). Youths' reports include, "I'm not sure of where to go and how to make it on my own" and "I am not ready to leave" (Mitchell et al., 2015, p. 297). Making matters even more complicated, youth often find themselves having to confront these losses and challenges alone. Supports, including social support, diminish as youth transition out of foster care and try to navigate their way to self-sufficiency

(Goodkind et al., 2011). Ultimately, children grapple with loss throughout their time in foster care, and as young adults, they often exit the foster care system with little to no support for safety, permanency, or well-being (the three main goals for children involved in the child welfare system).

Supporting Grieving Children in Foster Care

How do we, as individuals, systems, and society, better support grieving children in foster care? Although there is no easy answer to this question, there are practical steps which can be taken to better address children's experiences of nonfinite and cumulative loss. First, it is essential that a greater emphasis be placed on understanding how death and non-death loss, especially nonfinite, cumulative, and ambiguous losses, impact the psychological and emotional well-being of children in foster care. Publications such as these can contribute to this objective; however, publications alone will not adequately address children's grieving needs. Practical applications of this information also need to find their way into policies, programs, and the systems that serve children in foster care.

Currently, the foster care system views permanency as an "end goal" to the services it provides to children under its care. It is essential to recognize that this limited conceptualization of permanency is problematic to the well-being of children in foster care. As noted in this chapter, children's experiences of non-death loss accumulate throughout their time in foster care, and many significant relationships are either severed or estranged along the way. There is value in broadening our definition of permanency to include other significant relationships which can be nurtured and sustained throughout a child's time in the foster care system. For example, maintaining relationships with siblings, placements with the same care providers, and school systems with the same peers could all fall under the umbrella of achieving permanency outcomes for children while *in* foster care. Therefore, a consciousness shift is needed, which changes the focus from conceptualizing permanency as an "end goal" (i.e., permanency, with a caring and permanent adult, can be attained only after foster care) to an "ongoing goal" (i.e., permanency, which is fluid and multifaceted, can be attained while in and after foster care).

Another practical application of this information involves ensuring that child welfare professionals receive appropriate grief and loss trainings provided by a thanatologist or other grief and loss expert in the field. Without the proper training, programs and policies will not be created appropriately and implemented effectively to address the specific needs of grieving children. It is also essential to note that trauma training is not equitable to receiving training on grief and loss. Although there is overlap between trauma and loss, they are not synonymous. Therefore, the development and delivery of trainings that address the impact of grief and loss, developmental considerations, negative outcomes of unattended grief, and ways to assist grieving children is much needed in the child welfare system.

In addition to raising consciousness about grieving children's experiences and providing the needed training to meet the needs of grieving children, it is important to ensure that social support is ever-present for children as they navigate the foster care system. Children in foster care need to have opportunities to join social groups that include other children in foster care. Establishing peer connections with others who have shared lived experience can promote hope, reinstate normalcy, and assist youth with building confidence and personal empowerment (Schuurman, 2003). Furthermore, providing these types of primary supports may lead to secondary supports along the way, where children can build relational networks and supports which have the potential to blossom into lifetime friendships.

Specific and personalized plans are needed for youth who are preparing to transition out of foster care and prepare for their future. In the United States, these supports are often provided by a state's Independent Living Program (ILP), a federal program designed to assist youth transitioning out of the foster care system to achieve self-sufficiency. With the right supports, resources, and training in place, the ILP could be a vital resource to address the grieving needs of youth as they prepare for independent living and some of the fears and losses they may incur. For example, the ILP could assist youth by identifying their strengths and coping capacities and connecting them with the services and supports in the community that can not only assist them with self-sufficiency, but also ensure that their grieving needs are addressed during this significant life transition.

Conclusion

Although some losses can be prevented, nonfinite and cumulative loss are inevitable for children who are placed in foster care. Ultimately, it is essential that children's losses while entering, during, and while exiting foster care are recognized, acknowledged, and addressed. Intentional efforts to promote grief and loss education, training, and capacity building are first steps needed to support the many types of losses experienced by children in foster care and to move the child welfare community toward a grief-informed holistic model of care.

Key Terms

- **Cumulative Loss:** Multiple losses that occur continuously, or all at once; also known as "loss pileup."
- **Apprehension Transaction:** A child is removed from their initial home environment and transferred to a new government-sponsored foster care residence.
- **The Foster Placement Transaction:** When a placement in foster care dissolves, and a child is transferred to a new foster care residence.
- **The Aging Out Transaction:** Children in foster care eventually become ineligible to continue receiving services and support based on age (typically 18 years old). Subsequently, children are forced to live independently and vacate their foster care placement.

Questions for Reflection

1. Reflect upon the author's loss timeline for children in foster care. What surprised you the most about this timeline? Additionally, investigate the cumulative and nonfinite losses that can plausibly occur either in the beginning, middle, or end of the foster care timeline for children.
2. Provide an analysis on how foster care could influence a child's assumptive world and impact a child's identity. Specifically, how might being in foster care impact a child's cultural identity?
3. The author posits the question: "How do we, as individuals, systems, and society, better support grieving children in foster care?" Explore three of the author's resolutions to this question. Subsequently, develop your own answer as to how grieving children in foster care could be better supported.

Notes

1. For a detailed explanation and history of the assumptive world, see Chapter 1.
2. See Mitchell (2016a, 2016b, 2017).
3. "Foster child" is the term commonly used by society to refer to children in foster care and a term that I do not use, hence the use of quotations. My positioning is to use person first language, a value consistent with the NASW Code of Ethics and one to which I adhere.
4. As a mentor for youth aging out of the foster care system, sadly, I can personally attest that this youth's experience is not a rare event.

References

Barnow, B. S., Buck, A., O'Brien, K., Pecora, P., Ellis, M. L., & Steiner, E. (2015). Effective services for improving education and employment outcomes for children and alumni of foster care service: Correlates and educational and employment outcomes. *Child and Family Social Work, 20*, 159–170. doi:10.1111/cfs.12063

Boss, P. (1999). *Ambiguous loss: Learning to live with unresolved grief.* Cambridge, MA: Harvard University Press.

Breen, L. (2010). Professionals' experiences of grief counseling: Implications for bridging the gap between research and practice. *Omega: The Journal of Death and Dying, 62*(3), 285–303.

Cunningham, M. J., & Diversi, M. (2012). Aging out: Youths' perspectives on foster care and the transition to independence. *Qualitative Social Work, 12*(5), 587–602.

Dvir, O., Weiner, A., & Kupermintz, H. (2012). Children in residential group care with no family ties: Facing existential aloneness. *Residential Treatment for Children & Youth, 29*, 282–304. doi:10.1080/0886571X.2012.725368

Dworsky, A., Napolitano, L., & Courtney, M. (2013). Homelessness during the transition from foster care to adulthood. *American Journal of Public Health, 103*(S2), S318–S323.

Edwards, F., & Wildeman, C. (2018). Characteristics of the front-line child welfare workforce. *Children and Youth Services Review, 89*, 13–26. doi:10.1016/j.childyouth.2018.04.013

Goodkind, S., Schelbe, L. A., & Shook, J. J. (2011). Why youth leave care: Understandings of adulthood and transition successes and challenges among youth aging out of child welfare. *Children and Youth Services Review, 33*, 1039–1048. doi:10.1016/j.childyouth.2011.01.010

Harris, D. L., & Winokuer, H. R. (2016). *Principles and practice of grief counseling* (2nd ed.). New York: Springer Publishing Company.

Herrick, M., & Piccus, W. (2005). Sibling connections: The importance of nurturing sibling bonds in the foster care system. *Children and Youth Services Review, 27*, 845–861.

Hooyman, N. R., & Kramer, B. J. (2008). *Living through loss: Interventions across the life span.* New York: Columbia University Press.

Hyde, J., & Kammerer, N. (2009). Adolescents' perspectives on placement moves and congregate settings: Complex and cumulative instabilities in out-of-home care. *Children and Youth Services Review, 31*, 265–273. doi:10.1016/j.childyouth.2008.07.019

Keller, T. E., Salazar, A. M., & Courtney, M. E. (2010). Prevalence and timing of diagnosable mental health, alcohol, and substance abuse problems among older adolescents in the child welfare system. *Children and Youth Services Review, 32*, 626–634.

Mitchell, M. B. (2016a). *The neglected transition: Building a relational home for children entering foster care.* New York: Oxford University Press.

Mitchell, M. B. (2016b). The family dance: Ambiguous loss, meaning-making, and the psychological family in foster care. *Journal of Family Theory and Review, 8*, 360–372. doi:10.1111/jftr.12151

Mitchell, M. B. (2017). "No one acknowledged my loss and hurt": Non-death loss, grief, and trauma in foster care. *Child and Adolescent Social Work Journal, 35*, 1–9. doi:10.1007/s10560-017-0502-8

Mitchell, M. B., Jones, T., & Renema, S. (2015). Will I make it on my own? Voices and visions of 17-year-old youth in transition. *Child and Adolescent Social Work Journal, 32*, 291–300. doi:10.1007/s10560-014-0364-2

Mitchell, M. B., & Kuczynski, L. (2010). Does anyone know what is going on? Examining children's lived experience of the transition into foster care. *Children and Youth Services Review, 32*, 437–444. doi:10.1016/j.childyouth.2009.10.023

Ober, A. M., Haag Grenello, D., & Wheaton, J. E. (2012). Grief counseling: An investigation of counselors' training, experience, and competencies. *Journal of Counseling & Development, 90*, 150–159.

Rutman, D., & Hubberstey, C. (2016). Is anybody there? Informal supports accessed and sought by youth from foster care. *Children and Youth Services Review, 63*, 21–27. doi:10.1016/j.childyouth.2016.02.007

Schuurman, D. (2003). *Never the same: Coming to terms with the death of a parent.* New York: St Martin's Press.

Strolin-Goltzman, J., Kollar, S., & Trinkle, J. (2010). Listening to the voices of children in foster care: Youths speak out about child welfare workforce turnover and selection. *Social Work, 55*(1), 47–53.

Unrau, Y. A., Seita, J. R., & Putney, K. S. (2008). Former foster youth remember multiple placement moves: A journey of loss and hope. *Children & Youth Services Review, 30*(11), 1256–1266. doi:10.1016/j.childyouth.2008.03.010

US Department of Health and Human Services, Administration for Children and Families, Children's Bureau. (2016). The AFCARS report No. *24: Preliminary FY 2016 estimates as of Oct 2017.* Retrieved from www.acf.hhs.gov/sites/default/files/cb/afcarsreport24.pdf

Zetlin, A. A., Weinberg, L. L., & Shea, N. M. (2010). Caregivers, school liaisons, and agency advocates speak out about the educational needs of children and youth in foster care. *Social Work, 55*(3), 245–254.

CHAPTER 12

The Loss of Loneliness in Emerging Adults
Lara Schultz and Ann Laverty

Paige started her third year of university with familiar hopes and expectations that had been the backdrop of her transition to university and entry into emerging adulthood. A student in international relations and anthropology, she had envisioned these past years as the starting place to long-term meaningful friendships with like-minded persons and even the possibility of meeting a partner. In high school, Paige was a strong student. She participated on the debate team and ran for student council in Grade 12, yet she felt a chronic sense of not belonging and a deep sense of loneliness. She heard that university was the time one meets lifelong friends, and this probability had sustained her through her loneliest times.

Paige's first two years of university felt like a continual unraveling of the threads of hope and expectancy she had naturally developed. While she heard stories and read Facebook posts about her peers spending time together on weekends and attending on- and off-campus events, such relational opportunities always remained out of her reach. These losses were exacerbated by messages from her mother and older brother that she "just needs to meet people" and "be more approachable." Paige knew meeting people was not the issue. She was part of an International Relations club and had people in her classes with whom she could sit with and share updates. For Paige, her loneliness was the continual loss of expected relationships, of friends with whom she felt understood and could freely call to hang out, of dating experiences that could support imaginings of her desired future. Her grief was the loss of knowing if or how her loneliness could ever be different.

Listening to life stories invites a posture of reflection and recollection. In taking in Paige's narrative of loneliness, you may find yourself, as a reader, reflecting on your own experiences of loneliness when you were an emerging adult. Your recollections may be of a specific instance, an ongoing thread, an abrupt ending. We invite you to bring along your memories as you engage the chapter before you. Positioning oneself as a counselor requires awareness and integration of personal knowing and professional learning in carrying out informed and ethical practice.

Paige's story also speaks to us, as authors of this chapter, in our personal and professional experiences. We recall with some discomfort our own journeys as emerging adults, including silent awkwardness, seeking belonging, and wavering self-doubt. Our work as psychologists provides opportunities to engage conversations with clients about their experiences of loneliness. Understanding the complexities of this experience, how to make meaning, and finding ways forward has emerged through these counseling conversations. We begin our chapter by reviewing literature to situate loneliness as a nonfinite loss. Social contexts influencing the experience in emerging adulthood will be explored. We identify four broad themes that illuminate the experience of loneliness through the voices of emerging adults. Implications for counseling clients experiencing loneliness will be reviewed to support counselor reflection and learning. Understanding the nonfinite loss of loneliness in emerging adulthood will strengthen counseling practice in collaborating with clients who are navigating unrealized expectations in balance with efforts to create relational connections.

Contextualizing Loneliness

Loneliness is commonly defined as perceived discrepancy between desired and actual social relationships and is characterized by feelings of seclusion, void, and social pain. People who identify as being lonely report a lack of control over the quantity and, more importantly, the quality of their social activity (Lee & Goldstein, 2016; Luhman & Hawkley, 2016; Rokach, 2000). Research has identified the following specific factors that can initiate, exacerbate, or maintain feelings of loneliness: dissatisfaction with one's social relationships, expectations not meeting the reality of social status, and a deficit in emotional connectivity (Stoliker & Lafreniere, 2015). Importantly, researchers have identified late adolescence and young adulthood as two stages during which loneliness is arguably most prevalent across the developmental lifespan (Lee & Goldstein, 2016; Rokach, 2000). Normative transitions, such as moving away from home or starting new employment and school endeavors, often create physical separation from family and friends (Lee & Goldstein, 2016). These transitional experiences intersect with a phase of life during which social networks become more complex and integrated, with increased reliance on peer relationships outside the family system (Arnett, 2000; Erikson, 1997; Hopmeyer, Troop-Gordon, Medovoy, & Fischer, 2017).

Emerging adulthood represents a period with unique developmental tasks of relational growth (Arnett, 2000, 2001). Erikson (1997) referred to this phase of psychosocial development as intimacy versus isolation, highlighting the normative expectation for emerging adults to form and consolidate lasting relationships in order to successfully progress into adulthood with a sense of commitment, safety, and care. Loneliness may prevent this developmental task from being met, which can lead to isolation and further stall progress with future developmental tasks. In the context of post-secondary students, loneliness has been shown to hinder adjustment. The emotional experience of loneliness may reduce an individual's ability to self-regulate and manage cognitive processing, which can adversely influence academic performance. Furthermore, research has found students who experience loneliness develop negative perceptions of their environment and lose interest in positive exploration that may further restrict accommodation to the social and academic elements of post-secondary life (Hawkley & Cacioppo, 2010; Quan, Zhen, Yao, & Zhou, 2014; Stoliker & Lafreniere, 2015).

As seen with Paige, loneliness is a nonfinite loss that can be initiated by a specific event, such as moving or beginning post-secondary education, or it can be a continual experience of unmet innate needs and expectations to belong and feel loved within a community. The enduring loss of loneliness can preclude achievement of normal developmental expectations and involves the intangible loss of personal beliefs about what should, could, or might have been. Chronic loneliness requires adjustment and accommodation in different life contexts and in response to continual confrontation with disconnection from the mainstream of what is hoped for, expected, and envisioned. Furthermore, the magnitude and implications of this loss are frequently unrecognized and unacknowledged by others (Bruce & Schultz, 2001; Doka, 2008; Harris & Gorman, 2011).

Understanding Social Context

Loneliness in emerging adulthood is situated within the contexts of social media and disenfranchised grief. Engaging social media is common practice for emerging adults with over 90% of 18- to 29-year-olds using smartphones to engage social connections (Pew Research Center, 2015). In particular, post-secondary students report experiencing significant loneliness despite the availability of online and face-to-face social connections. (American College Health Association, 2016). Debate exists about the impact of social media on loneliness and mental health, with mixed research results. Findings range from social media being tied to negative mental health outcomes, with other studies reporting beneficial outcomes, and yet other investigations finding no evidence of harm or benefit to individuals (Berryman, Ferguson, & Negy, 2018; Nongpong & Charoensukmongkol, 2016; Ye & Lin, 2015).

Despite a lack of clear consensus, several considerations about Internet use to ameliorate loneliness exist. Interestingly, recognition is emerging about the nature of online relationships and what platforms are engaged as potentially more important than mere exposure (Ye & Lin, 2015). Song et al. (2014) found non-social online platforms (i.e., passive consumption such as downloading) pose a greater detriment to overall well-being and loneliness than social media applications (i.e., Facebook). As well, image-based social media (i.e., Instagram and Snapchat) seems to mirror the intimacy of face-to-face communication and can contribute to a decrease in loneliness; however, text-based media (i.e., Twitter and texting) appears to have a neutral effect in this regard (Pittman & Reich, 2016). It is also important to attend to individual differences and to consider other possibilities that may differ from research outcomes. For example, in contrast to previously noted research, Paige acknowledged using Facebook, yet it seemed to increase her experience of loneliness rather than foster connections.

Disenfranchised grief is another social context within which loneliness occurs. Losses are disenfranchised when they are not socially sanctioned, openly acknowledged, or publicly mourned (Doka, 2002). They include experiences that others may not know exist or, if known to exist, may not be recognized as a loss experience. As Paige shared, emerging adults expect to socially connect and build lasting relationships. Campus and work life are touted as providing a multitude of opportunities for involvement. Within these contexts, it is not easy to admit feeling lonely. Not talking about loneliness can deepen isolation, and feelings of failure, inadequacy, shame, self-blame, awkwardness, and embarrassment can continue to emerge and intensify (Rokach, 2004). In essence, the likelihood of loneliness becoming a disenfranchised loss increases over time as it becomes more privately held and reinforced through thoughts, feelings, and actions engaged by lonely individuals and those around them.

Lived Experience of Loneliness

While research literature validates the presence, impact, and contextual factors of loneliness in emerging adulthood, listening to individuals living with loneliness helps us more deeply understand this lived experience. We believe the integration of research, theory and client experience is an important practice for clinicians. In this section, we describe four themes that give voice to the nonfinite loss of loneliness. These themes are drawn together from a qualitative research study with emerging adults who identified as being lonely (Schultz & Laverty, 2017). Research participants were invited to tell us about their experience of loneliness to facilitate understanding of the loss of loneliness. Each participant provided written consent to include quotes from their interviews in dissemination of the research. Their narrative descriptions speak to elements of the experience that are important for us to know.

Lonely, Not Alone

Loneliness is more than being alone. The confluence of being surrounded by people and not belonging may be the nucleus of feeling lonely, as it highlights the significant gap between the mainstream of what is expected and hoped for versus what is.

> Being alone is when you are not surrounded by anyone—that is alone. Lonely is when you are surrounded by strangers or even by friends, yet you feel lonely. Loneliness is more of an inner feeling.
>
> It's not so much having company because I've been around people and I still feel lonely. It's more like not having a deeper connection with people.

An absence of felt connectedness, a sense of confusion, alienation, and grief can be part of loneliness. Even in the presence of other people, it can be difficult to know how to engage. Loneliness is an internal phenomenon shaped and co-constructed by relational opportunities or missed opportunities.

> I feel lonely. I'm with people but I can't talk with them. The feeling I cry about is not knowing who I can call as a friend or who loves me—that is the feeling of loneliness.

Yearning for Connection

Loneliness involves a continuous yearning for connection. Losses emerge and re-emerge as normative expectations of social belonging remain out of reach. The experience can transcend past hurt and isolation through hope of a different outcome.

> I remember thinking you'll belong . . . university is going to be different . . . and then realizing, no it is not. You are still going to be in the outside group. You are incapable of being in that inner circle. Thinking you're going to bond and then realizing you're not.

The absence of connection is reinforced when opportunities to be socially engaged arise. There is a persistent desire for meaningful connection and a need to continually adapt to disconnection.

> I have friends but no close friends. I go to work and go back home alone. Sometimes I feel so upset that I want to talk with someone but I can't find anyone. When someone asks me how I am doing, I don't want to say I'm fine because I'm not fine. I just don't know what to say.

Expectation of Mattering

Loneliness includes an expectation of mattering to someone in confrontation with continued experiences of not belonging and being unimportant to others.

> I feel if I dropped off the face of the earth, it wouldn't make a difference. I was around lots of people but didn't feel like I mattered or was really part of a group.

A sense of hope for belonging and the anticipation of developing lasting intimate relationships are precluded by the losses experienced with loneliness.

> It was a matter of coming to terms that I'd never meet anyone, like long-term best buddies. I was stressed about school, feeling hopeless, not connecting. I remember coming home, crying inconsolably not even knowing what would make it better because I just felt so lonely.

Making Room

There is also a continual process of adapting to the loss experience through creating room for the possibility of social belonging. Amidst the ongoing loneliness, relational strategies are used to help accommodate, adjust, or adapt. At times, connections occur.

> I got a lot closer to a student who was also doing her honor's project. I don't know as I stopped feeling lonely, but I do know I was grateful for the

connection. Some of the simplest things she would do were out of the ordinary for me. She just accepted my presence and I was really grateful for her.

Making room also includes taking steps outside comfort zones to initiate relational connections. These steps often hold risks of further or deepened loss in balance with hope for constructive change.

> I know I am hesitant to be closer to people and form deeper bonds because of my past experiences. But I am hopeful that I will meet people and to know they care about me. It's scary as hell because you never know.
>
> I've realized somewhere along the line I decided not to invest and I ended up with no connections. That was the way I was living my life. This year, I'm trying to be open to see what might happen.

Considerations for Counseling

Counseling conversations often include themes of loneliness. While clients may not identify loneliness as a primary concern, attentive listening by a counselor can often invite reflective and therapeutic dialogue about loneliness present within a variety of life circumstances. Counseling can provide both a supportive environment where loneliness can be openly discussed as well as a collaborative space to work with clients to navigate possible change in living with nonfinite loss. Drawing on our experience as counselors, we identify considerations to guide counseling practice, sharing additional quotes from the research participants and our own possible reflective responses as counselors, to support these ideas.

Validating Loneliness as Nonfinite Loss

Loneliness, as with many types of nonfinite loss, is often disenfranchised and not commonly recognized as a form of nonfinite loss (Doka, 2002; Harris & Gorman, 2011). Consequently, clients who are lonely may not have considered their loneliness and lack of connected experiences as a loss. Counselors may find that gently introducing the possibility of loneliness as a form of nonfinite loss may be novel to clients and helpful in validating their experience. For example, a client might say:

> I can't tell my family I am struggling. I am afraid it would make them more worried. I feel lonely because all of the things I've missed out on. I have so much to figure out about how not to be lonely and I feel like I am on my own to do it.

In response, a counselor might reflect:

> It sounds as if your loneliness feels unending. There is a concept called nonfinite loss, which means losses that are continuous and often not recognized by others. I'm wondering if we can talk a bit more about your loneliness and the losses you have experienced.

Deepening client understanding of loneliness as nonfinite loss can support the natural human need to make sense of one's experience, validating emotional, social, cognitive, and behavioral dimensions of the experience. Supporting increased awareness may help reduce distress and support hope for constructive adaptation (Harris & Gorman, 2011). Client feedback can affirm benefits of these efforts:

> My counselor asks questions I hadn't thought to ask or hadn't wanted to ask. Through counseling, I came to realize my losses, all of those connections I don't have. I know how much it affected my well-being and am starting to realize what I need to do.

Bridging Theory With Practice

Effective counseling is guided by conceptualizing client concerns within a framework of counseling theory. A variety of theoretical approaches and models exist within grief literature to support counselors working with clients experiencing the nonfinite loss of loneliness. This means that reconstruction theory supports clients in understanding their experience, moving from sense-making to meaning-making positions. Through relearning the world changed by their loss experience, assimilation and accommodation are possible (Attig, 1996, 2001; Harris, 2011; Neimeyer, 1998, 2001; Neimeyer & Anderson, 2002). As a young female client reflected on her process:

> There are people whom I used to call friends and at some point in my life they stopped talking to me. I messaged them, they don't reply. Sometimes people are busy—I understand that. But when weeks go by, I realize they don't care and it is hurtful. Counseling helped me make sense of what was happening and to realize I can make my own meaning in a way that works best for me.

Narrative therapy supports clients in developing a narrative or story about their experience that acknowledges the reality of the loss and invites possibility for hope and change (Neimeyer, 2004). It can include externalizing the problematized narrative and thickening client agency for living with nonfinite loss (White & Epston, 1990). With consent, a counselor might say:

> In listening to your experience of loneliness, I'm thinking about it as a chapter of your life. I am hearing a story of self-blame for not embracing opportunities. I wonder how this next chapter is different as you speak about making efforts to connect with chosen colleagues. How would you like this story to continue?

The Dual Process Model proposes that clients oscillate between loss-oriented and restoration-oriented coping engagement as they navigate grief (Stroebe & Schut, 1999). Within the introduction to this section, Harris proposed an adaption of this model to represent and validate the processes involved in coping with nonfinite loss. This model can be also effectively used to educate and support clients in recognizing choices in coping with the nonfinite losses of loneliness. A male client shared:

> Understanding I can feel sad about things I missed out on and still do fun things while I'm figuring this out was helpful. At first, I felt like it was all hopeless but then I started doing things that were meaningful to me—to bring some meaning back into my life. Knowing I can have both is really helpful.

Considering Client Diversity

Human beings cannot be understood in separation from their sociocultural context. Counselors need to attend to the interface between loneliness and the diverse locations clients inhabit. How might experiences of intersectionality and/or oppression heighten or exacerbate loneliness? Reflect for a moment on Paige, whom you met in our case study. Bring to mind your image of Paige. In meeting her as a client, how might your understanding of her loneliness as nonfinite loss differ if she was an Indigenous bisexual woman or an Asian man with a visual impairment? Recognizing larger ecosystems, especially for individuals from historically marginalized backgrounds and life realities, is essential in our work as counselors (Arthur & Collins, 2010; Bowleg, 2012; Ratts, Singh, Nassar-McMillan, Butler, & Rafferty McCullough, 2016). As an international student reflected:

> When I was 17, I realized I am not heterosexual. I am from Pakistan where being homosexual is punishable by law. I could not find anyone from the LGBTQ community in my life. I felt really lonely and trapped because I could not be myself. I couldn't tell people in my community and even though I know my family loves me and I love them, I couldn't be out to them. It was very lonely.

Cultural norms exist in the experience of grief and mourning following death-related losses (Rosenblatt, 2007). We believe it is also important for counselors to explore the influence or role of sociocultural norms in the experience and expression of non-death-related losses such as loneliness. A client speaks about her experience:

> I come from a culture where people don't talk about their feelings. If you tell people you are lonely or depressed, they would say you are crazy, what is depression, you have your family—you cannot be lonely. The same is true with grieving—even when someone dies everyone is pretty stoic. So this idea of loneliness as a loss would be doubly weird in my culture.

Assessing for Comorbidity

Counselors collaborate with clients in ongoing assessment about their experience of loneliness to develop a plan for counseling. This assessment should include exploration of any comorbid or co-occurring experiences that may contribute to, exacerbate, or complicate loneliness (Lim, Rodebaugh, Zyphur, & Gleeson, 2016). Loneliness has been found to be prevalent in emerging adults experiencing a variety of mental health concerns including depression and social anxiety (Teo, Lerrigo, & Rogers, 2013; Zawadzki, Graham, & Gerin, 2013). As a client confirmed:

> I became depressed in my first year because of my academic struggles. I had to keep this from my family. The more I became depressed, the lonelier I became and the lonelier I became, the worse my depression became.

When loneliness co-exists with other mental health concerns, it can be important to address both concerns (Lim et al., 2016; VanderWeele, Hawkley, Thisted, & Cacioppo, 2011). Counseling plans can be collaboratively developed and may begin with treatment of the mental health concern if it is primary. This may involve using evidence-based treatments, such as cognitive-behavioral therapy, acceptance and commitment therapy, and dialectical behavioral therapy, integrated with models of grief counseling. At times, clients may be unaware of their co-occurring concerns and counselors play a valuable role in helping to identity a complexity of mental health concerns:

> My counselor and I figured out part of the reason I was having issues was because of my mental illness, which led me to experience loneliness. I had to deal with both things at the same time. I learned how to trust my ability to make decisions that were right for me using different treatment methods.

Exploring Implications of Social Media

Given the interface of social media with loneliness in emerging adulthood, it can be valuable to explore clients' social media engagement and impacts on feeling lonely. Assessing the type of the loneliness experienced (i.e., lack of a social network, lack of a close significant relationship) is beneficial to understanding factors motivating online communication used to build connections (Hood, Creed, & Mills, 2017).

> If there is a person like you on Facebook, who understands what you are going through, you are on the same level. Maybe you can help each other out. So, I am hopeful to meet friends who will not leave me. If I learn to do that on-line, I may feel less anxious talking in person.

Exploring individual competence and confidence in social engagement is helpful, as loneliness can increase if social media sites are used to primarily develop social skills, despite their benefit in facilitating relational connections for the socially adept (Teppers, Luyckx, Klimstra, & Goossens, 2014). Finally, evaluating the amount of time spent engaging online relationships, to the exclusion of face-to-face interactions, is important, as excessive online use can contribute to increased loneliness and reduce potential benefits of online engagement (Ryan,

Allen, Gray, & McInerney, 2017; Shettar, Karkal, Kakunje, Mendosa, & Chandran, 2017).

Inviting Hope

Theories of grief and nonfinite loss commonly describe the potential for clients to experience constructive growth through navigating their loss experiences (Bonanno, 2004; Gorman, 2011; Neimeyer, 1998, 2004; Schaefer & Moos, 2001). While counselors explore and validate the losses and social pain of loneliness, it is also important to support clients in developing skills and knowledge to create desired change. This may include listening for, reflecting, and expanding upon the explicit or implicit voices of hopefulness within client narratives. For example, a counselor may inquire about advice clients can offer themselves to address their loneliness. To which a client may respond:

> If you are lonely, try to figure it out. There is no rush. You have all the time. It can be frustrating because it is human to want to know answers about your loneliness right away but just continue on at your own pace. See what life has to bring. Life is a mixture of good and bad.

Conclusion

As counselors, we have the privilege of working with emerging adults who experience the nonfinite loss of loneliness. Writing this chapter has given us opportunity to deepen our awareness of the complexity of this experience. Understanding the prevalence of loneliness and influence of sociocultural contexts illuminates the impacts of unmet developmental expectations for relational belonging. Listening to personal stories about experiences of loneliness adds depth and appreciation for individual losses. Considering counseling implications informs our practice in collaboratively working with clients to develop a meaningful narrative of loneliness and to create change. It is our hope this chapter will invite reflection on your own experiences and shape conversations with clients regarding the nonfinite loss of loneliness.

Key Terms

Emerging Adulthood: The period and development of a person between adolescence and full-fledged adulthood.

Loneliness: A complex emotional response that generally consists of social pain, emptiness, lack of control, and isolation due to dissatisfaction with one's relationships, expectations not meeting the reality of social status, and/or a deficit in emotional connectivity.

Social Media: Tools or applications that can be accessed through digital devices (smartphones, computers, tablets) that allow people to create, share, or exchange information, ideas, and pictures/videos in virtual communities and networks.

Questions for Reflection

1. How is loneliness the experience of nonfinite loss? Additionally, analyze the four broad themes of loneliness in emerging adults with respect to nonfinite loss. Which theme resonated the most with you, and why?
2. Explore both the positive and negative aspects of social media in relation to loneliness and nonfinite loss. What are your personal experiences and thoughts surrounding social media, loneliness, and nonfinite loss?
3. What nonfinite losses have you experienced or are experiencing in emerging adulthood? How were you able to find acceptance, healing, and/or meaning during this time? What guidance would you provide to a previous younger version of yourself regarding these experiences?
4. What are the most substantial barriers that emerging adults experience when seeking support for their loneliness? How can one invite hope back into their lives during periods of isolation and despair? How would you provide grief education and support to someone who is lonely?

References

American College Health Association. (2016). *National college health assessment: Canadian reference group*. Retrieved from www.acha-ncha.org/docs/ncha-ii%20spring%202016%20canadian%20reference%20group%20executive%20summary.pdf

Arnett, J. J. (2000). Emerging adulthood: A theory of development from the late teens through the twenties. *American Psychologist, 55*(5), 469–480.

Arnett, J. J. (2001). Conceptions of the transition to adulthood: Perspectives from adolescence through midlife. *Journal of Adult Development, 8*(2), 133–143.

Arthur, N., & Collins, S. (Eds.). (2010). *Culture-infused counselling* (2nd ed.). Calgary, AB: Counselling Concepts.

Attig, T. (1996). *How we grieve: Relearning the world*. New York: Oxford University Press.

Attig, T. (2001). Relearning the world: Making and finding meanings. In R. A. Neimeyer (Ed.), *Meaning reconstruction and the experience of loss* (pp. 33–54). Washington, DC: American Psychological Association.

Berryman, C., Ferguson, C. J., & Negy, C. (2018). Social media use and mental health among young adults. *Psychiatry Q. 89*(2), 307–314. doi:10.1007/s11126-017-9535-6

Bonanno, G. A. (2004). Loss, trauma, and human resilience: Have we underestimated the human capacity to thrive after extremely aversive events? *American Psychologist, 59*(1), 20–28.

Bowleg, L. (2012). The problem with the phrase *women and minorities*: Intersectionality—An important theoretical framework for public health. *American Journal of Public Health, 102,* 1267–1273. doi:10.2105/AJPH.2012.300750

Bruce, E. J., & Schultz, C. L. (2001). *Nonfinite loss and grief: A psychoeducational approach*. Baltimore: Paul H. Brookes.

Doka, K. J. (Ed.). (2002). *Disenfranchised grief: New directions, challenges, and strategies for practice*. Champaign, IL: Research Press.

Doka, K. J. (2008). Disenfranchised grief in historical and cultural perspective. In M. S. Stroebe, R. O. Hansson, H. Schut, & W. Stroebe (Eds.), *Handbook of bereavement research and practice: Advances in theory and intervention* (pp. 223–240). Washington, DC: American Psychological Association.

Erikson, E. H. (1997). *The life cycle completed*. New York: W. W. Norton & Company.

Gorman, E. (2011). Adaptation, resilience, and growth after loss. In D. L. Harris (Ed.), *Counting our losses: Reflecting on change, loss, and transition in everyday life* (pp. 225–237). New York: Routledge.

Harris, D. L. (2011). Meaning making and the assumptive world in nondeath loss. In D. L. Harris (Ed.), *Counting our losses: Reflecting on change, loss, and transition in everyday life* (pp. 239–246). New York: Routledge.

Harris, D. L., & Gorman, E. (2011). Grief from a broader perspective: Nonfinite loss, ambiguous loss, and chronic sorrow. In D. L. Harris (Ed.), *Counting our losses: Reflecting on change, loss, and transition in everyday life* (pp. 1–13). New York: Routledge.

Hawkley, L. C., & Cacioppo, J. T. (2010). Loneliness matters: A theoretical and empirical review of consequences and mechanisms. *Annals of Behavioral Medicine, 40*(2), 218–227.

Hood, M., Creed, P. A., & Mills, B. J. (2017). Loneliness and online friendships in emerging adults, *Personality and Individual Differences*. http://dx.doi.org/10.1016/j.paid.2017.03.045

Hopmeyer, A., Troop-Gordon, W., Medovoy, T., & Fischer, J. (2017). Emerging adults' self-identified peer crowd affiliations and college adjustment. *Social Psychology of Education, 20*, 643–667.

Lee, C. Y. S., & Goldstein, S. E. (2016). Loneliness, stress, and social support: Does the source of support matter. *Journal of Youth and Adolescence, 45*, 568–580.

Lim, M. H., Rodebaugh, T. L., Zyphur, M. J., & Gleeson, J. F. M. (2016). Loneliness over time: The crucial role of social anxiety. *Journal of Abnormal Psychology, 125*(5), 620–630.

Luhmann, M., & Hawkley, L. C. (2016). Age differences in loneliness from late adolescence to oldest old age. *Developmental Psychology, 52*(6), 943–959.

Neimeyer, R. A. (1998). *Lessons of loss: A guide to coping*. New York: McGraw-Hill.

Neimeyer, R. A. (2001). Reauthoring life narratives: Grief therapy as meaning reconstruction. *Israel Journal of Psychiatry and Related Science, 38*(3–4), 171–183.

Neimeyer, R. A. (2004). Fostering posttraumatic growth: A narrative elaboration. *Psychological Inquiry, 15*, 53–59.

Neimeyer, R., & Anderson, A. (2002). Meaning reconstruction theory. In N. Thompson (Ed.), *Loss and grief: A guide for human services practitioners* (pp. 45–64). New York: Palgrave Macmillan.

Nongpong, S., & Charoensukmongkol, P. (2016). I don't care much as long as I am also on Facebook: Impacts of social media use on both partners of romantic relationship problems. *The Family Journal: Counseling and Therapy for Couples and Families, 24*(4), 351–358.

Pew Research Center. (2015). *Social networking fact sheet*. Retrieved from www.pewinternet.org/fact-sheets/social-networking-fact-sheet/

Pittman, M., & Reich, B. (2016). Social media and loneliness: Why an Instagram picture may be worth more than a thousand Twitter words. *Computers in Human Behavior, 62*, 155–167.

Quan, L., Zhen, R., Yao, B., & Zhou, X. (2014). The effects of loneliness and coping style on academic adjustment among college freshmen. *Social Behavior and Personality, 42*(6), 969–978.

Ratts, M. J., Singh, A. A., Nassar-McMillan, S., Butler, S. K., & Rafferty McCullough, J. (2016). Multicultural and social justice counseling competencies: Guidelines for the counseling profession. *Journal of Multicultural Counseling and Development, 44*, 28–48.

Rokach, A. (2000). Loneliness and the life cycle. *Psychological Reports, 86*(2), 629–642.

Rokach, A. (2004). Loneliness then and now: Reflections on social and emotional alienation in everyday life. *Current Psychology, 23*(1), 24–40.

Rosenblatt, P. C. (2007). Culture, socialization, and loss, grief, and mourning. In D. E. Balk (Ed.), *Handbook of thanatology: The essential body of knowledge for the study of death, dying, and bereavement* (pp. 115–119). New York: Routledge.

Ryan, T., Allen, K. A., Gray, D. L., & McInerney, D. M. (2017). How social are social media? A review of online social behavior and connectedness. *Journal of Relationships and Research, 8*(e8), 1–8.

Schaefer, J. A., & Moos, R. H. (2001). Bereavement experiences and personal growth. In M. S. Stroebe, R. O. Hansson, W. Stroebe, & H. Schut (Eds.), *Handbook of bereavement research: Consequences, coping, and care* (pp. 145–167). Washington, DC: American Psychological Association.

Schultz, L. E., & Laverty, A. M. (2017). *Loneliness as nonfinite loss: Experiences of emerging adults*. Unpublished manuscript, SU Wellness Centre, University of Calgary, Calgary, Canada.

Shettar, M., Karkal, R., Kakunje, A., Dilip Mendosa, R., & Mohan Chandran, V. V. (2017). Facebook addiction and loneliness in the post-graduate students of a university in southern India. *International Journal of Social Psychiatry, 63*(4), 325–329.

Song, H., Zmyslinksi-Seelig, A., Kim, J., Drent, A., Victor, A., Omori, K., & Allen, M. (2014). Does Facebook make you lonely? A meta-analysis. *Computers in Human Behavior, 36*, 446–452.

Stoliker, B. E., & Lafreniere, K. D. (2015). The influence of perceived stress, loneliness, and learning burnout on university students' educational experience. *College Student Journal, 49*(1), 146–160.

Stroebe, M., & Schut, H. (1999). The Dual Process Model of coping with bereavement: Rationale and description. *Death Studies, 23*, 197–224.

Teo, A. R., Lerrigo, R., & Rogers, M. A. M. (2013). The role of social isolation in social anxiety disorder: A systemic review and meta-analysis. *Journal of Anxiety Disorders, 27*, 353–364. http://dx.doi.org/10.1016/j.janxdis.2013.03.010

Teppers, E., Luyckx, K., Klimstra, T. A., & Goossens, L. (2014). Loneliness and Facebook motives in adolescence: A longitudinal inquiry into directionality of effect. *Journal of Adolescence, 37*, 691–699.

VanderWeele, T. J., Hawkley, L. C., Thisted, R. A., & Cacioppo, J. T. (2011). A marginal structural model analysis for loneliness: Implications for intervention trials and clinical practice. *Journal of Consulting and Clinical Psychology, 79*, 225–235. http://dx.doi.org./10.1037/a0022610

White, M., & Epston, D. (1990). *Narrative means to therapeutic ends*. New York: W. W. Norton & Company.

Ye, Y., & Lin, L. (2015). Examining relations between locus of control, loneliness, subjective well-being, and preference for online social interaction. *Psychological Reports: Mental & Physical Health, 116*(1), 164–175.

Zawadzki, M. J., Graham, J. E., & Gerin, W. (2013). Rumination and anxiety mediate the effect of loneliness on depressed mood and quality of sleep in college students. *Health Psychology, 32*(2), 212–222.

CHAPTER 13

Families' and Children's Experiences of Loss in the Family Justice System

Rachel Birnbaum

A large body of empirical research confirms the negative risk factors associated with parental divorce for children. Divorce increases children's risk for psychosocial maladjustment and academic problems compared to children in intact families (Amato, 2010; Clarke-Stuart & Bretano, 2006; Kelly & Emery, 2003). The risks vary depending on the time since the divorce has occurred, the age and gender of the child, and pre-separation characteristics such as the severity of parental conflict, the conflict style of the parents, and the focus of the conflict (Kelly, 2012). Yet, not all children in high-conflict separating families have negative outcomes. Parental warmth, consistency, and a caring relationship with at least one parent figure can have a buffering effect (Amato & Gilbreth, 1999; Cummings & Davies, 1994).

This chapter focuses on children's experiences of the separation and divorce process and the losses they endure over time in discrete ways (i.e., loss of innocence, important relationships, and psychic pain) over the years (Hetherington & Kelly, 2002; Schwartz & Finley, 2005). A case vignette about a 12-year old girl[1] who wants to move with her mother to British Columbia will illustrate the tug of war that she experiences as a result of her parents' dispute before the court. She eloquently describes a retrospective account of her journey as her parents dispute her custody and access arrangements. How children's voices are heard during the family justice process will be outlined, and practical recommendations will be made for family justice professionals involved in the family justice system. Finally, a blueprint for social, legal, and political reform for children and families will also be highlighted for family justice reform.

Wallerstein (1985) wrote about the overburdened child and the long-term consequences of separation and divorce. That is, their seeming independence and maturity that characterize many of these children post separation and divorce, while underneath is the malingering grief over the loss of important attachment figures and relationships from their lives, which can have long-term consequences (Kelly, 2012). Wallerstein and Blakeslee (1989) state,

> Divorce is a different experience for children and adults because the children lose something that is fundamental to their development—the family structure.
> (p. 11)

Children and Loss in the Justice System 171

The outcomes for children and families are also intertwined with the family justice system. That is, to whichever lawyer can best champion their client's case will the spoils of victory go—or is it that easy? What are the emotional costs to children and their parents who battle it out in court? Justice Mackinnon, J., stated after a 15-day custody and access trial,

> Their [the names of the two children] parents have disputed the children's care and living arrangements since the fall of 2010, even prior to separating. A dysfunctional intact family became a highly dysfunctional separated family. None of the children has escaped unscathed.
>
> (para 2)[2]

Justice Quinn, J.W., stated after a seven-day custody and access trial,

> This is yet another case that reveals the ineffectiveness of Family Court in a bitter custody/access dispute, where the parties require therapeutic intervention rather than legal attention. Here, a husband and wife have been marinating in a mutual hatred so intense as to surely amount to a personality disorder requiring treatment.
>
> (para 2, 3)[3]

Justice Pazzaratz, J., went further after a 10-day custody and access trial and stated,

> As with most separations, these parties [the parents] started out with a small but manageable list of legitimate complaints and concerns.
>
> a. They could have worked together, followed some professional recommendations, obeyed some court orders, and tried to make this as painless as possible for their daughter.
> b. But instead they took a *scorched earth approach*. [italicized for emphasis]
> c. They became consumed not just with *winning*, but with making sure the other party *lost*.
> d. That's why more than two years after separation; after a five-day temporary hearing; after many more motions; and after a 10-day trial—they were each still asking that I force the other party to take a psychiatric exam.
>
> It is both easy and appropriate to say that this has become a "high conflict" file. But we need to do more than just label relentless litigants. We need to understand that parents like this are completely different—so as a court system we need to treat them differently.
>
> a. Like most high conflict couples, the Applicant and the Respondent have come to perceive our court system as an endless forum to advance complaints and criticisms of one another . . .

e. In the early stages of a family court file, it is quite legitimate for parties to fully outline the problems and concerns, *even at the risk of hurting one another's feelings.*

But eventually these high conflict disputes reach a tipping point where new complaints and accusations keep surfacing, not *at the risk* of hurting one another's feelings—*but for the express purpose* of hurting one another's feelings.

a. Court proceedings become an excuse—*an institutionalized opportunity*—to vent. To attack. To get in one more jab.
b. Individual court dates become perceived as pre-arranged skirmishes in an endless war. No matter the result, somebody will always make sure there's another day in court.
c. And in the process, the judge becomes relegated to irrelevant bystander. As if watching a car crash constantly reoccurring.

High conflict parents have their own agenda, and it rarely has anything to do with the law

a. They seek personal vindication. Not resolution.
b. They've got scores to settle. Grudges, pain, and retribution—legitimized under the banner of "best interests of the child."
c. Their mission is blame—or at the very least, deflecting more blame onto their ex.
d. Fundamentally, *they* view litigation completely differently than *we* view litigation.
e. And that's why we delude ourselves when we think it's possible to force high conflict couples to behave reasonably.

Perhaps high conflict couples keep coming back to court because—unwittingly—we provide them with a socially acceptable outlet for their maladjusted and destructive behavior.

a. Perhaps as a court system we are too nice. Too obliging. Too tolerant.

(para. 169–173)[4]

This particular court judgment describes how some high-conflict parents use the court system as their battleground to engage in their own feelings of the hurt and pain about separation and divorce. Tragically, their children are merely the pawns of that dispute in the name of children's best interests.

What happens to these children when their parents go to battle over their care and upbringing? At one end of the continuum are the losses for children that build up due to feelings of divided loyalty, split families, and losses of holiday times and family gatherings. Emery (1999) cogently summarized the effects on children as: (1) divorce causes a great deal of stress on children; (2) divorce increases the risk of psychological problems; (3) despite the increased risk, most children from divorced families function as well as do children from first-marriage families; (4) children whose parents divorce report considerable emotional pain, unhappy memories, and continued distress; and (5) the individual differences in children's post-divorce adjustment are influenced by factors such as the quality of the child's relationship with the residential parent, the nature of interparental conflict, the families' financial outlook, and the nature of the relationship between the child and nonresidential parent. However, at the other end of the continuum, the headlines have read,

> The deaths of two young girls in British Columbia who were previously the subject of a custody dispute have prompted debate about how judges decide cases involving allegations of domestic violence. Andrew Berry, 43, has been charged with two counts of second-degree murder in the deaths of his six-year-old daughter Chloe and her four-year-old sister Aubrey. The sisters' bodies were found on Christmas Day inside a Victoria-area home.
> (Roseby and Johnston, 1998, p. 1)

Roseby and Johnston (1998) have referred to children in locked battles because of their parents as "Children of Armageddon"—children sometimes pay the ultimate price for their parents' separation and divorce. Demo and Fine (2010) propose a theoretical model that focuses on both variability and fluidity. They argue that there is much diversity in the individual's divorce-related experiences. However, they all share interactions and intersections at the individual (i.e., self-esteem, mental health issues), community (i.e., lawyers, police, court, mental health professionals), family (new partner, friends), and structural levels (i.e., laws, traditions, religion), while children become the unintended victims of parental separation (Birnbaum, 2012).

Case Vignette

The following case vignette highlights these intersecting systems and the family justice process.

Jenny, age 12, is an only child. Her parents (Cathy and Tom) separated when Jenny was 6 years of age. Cathy works part-time at a bookstore and Tom is a stockbroker; they live and work two hours east of Toronto, Ontario. The parental separation was friendly from the beginning, and each agreed to a parenting plan with the assistance of their lawyers. They both wanted what was best for Jenny and did not argue over any of the childcare or financial matters. They agreed that Jenny would reside with her mother, who had sole decision-making about her education. They agreed that Jenny would visit with her father every other weekend from Friday after school to Monday morning and every other overnight Wednesday. He had sole decision-making about her health and religious upbringing. Tom is a practicing Catholic, and Jenny's mother had no religious affiliation.

Cathy met her new partner, Peter, at the bookstore where she worked when Jenny was nine years old. They had a relationship for three years and lived together for the last two years. Peter was a publisher with a national magazine and decided that since his parents were getting old and needed help with their house, and he was traveling more than he wanted to, the best option for them as a family would be for them to move to Victoria, British Columbia. After much discussion, Cathy agreed and told Tom what their plan was. Tom was not happy with the move and decided that he would go to court to stop Cathy from moving with his daughter. Both Cathy and Tom's relationship deteriorated as soon as the court process began. Each served documents on the other, raising issues about their past relationship that only got each of them angrier. The once happy and secure Jenny was thrust into her parent's conflict. Both Cathy and Tom tried to convince Jenny about their long-term plan for her as being the best option.

The court requested that a children's lawyer[5] represent Jenny to assist the court in determining what would be best for her. Over the next five months of the court proceedings, Jenny was subjected to multiple interviews; her grades began to decline, she regressed to child-like behaviors (i.e., clingy), and she began stuttering. Both her parents blamed the other for their daughter's emotional decline and only dug their heels in more to get what they wanted as they believed it was in Jenny's best interests.

Jenny was clear with her lawyer at every meeting that she wanted to live solely with her mother and Peter in British Columbia. She loved her father and suggested she could visit during the summer months for all of July and August and they could Skype and text as often as each wanted to. She saw the move as an adventure and was always in love with the ocean and mountains. She acknowledged that she would miss her friends, but they, too, could Skype and text often and visit each other during the summer breaks that she would be with her father.

Tom was hurt that Jenny wanted to move away from him and believed that Cathy and Peter were manipulating her to agree to the move. He wanted to go to trial. Cathy and Tom tried to meet with a mediator in the interim to resolve the dispute, to no avail. Jenny was so upset with her father that she began to stop eating as she believed she needed some control over what was going on. She lost so much weight that she required hospitalization. Again, both Cathy and Tom continued to blame one another. On one occasion in the hospital, Cathy and Tom were yelling so loudly at one another in front of Jenny that the hospital called child welfare. A social worker did meet with both parents and warned them if they did not resolve their conflict away from Jenny, they may have to take their own legal steps.

Cathy and Tom finally realized that Jenny was paying the price for their behavior. They decided that they would make one more attempt with the mediator to see what they could and could not agree on. Jenny was released from the hospital and began individual counseling. Jenny continued to tell her lawyer that she wanted to move with her mother and Peter. Tom began to realize that Jenny was old enough to make her own decisions, and he did not want to put her in the middle any more. He agreed to the move with the proviso that Jenny would be with him for the summer months, all of the Christmas holiday break every other year and every other March break.

Jenny moved to Victoria with her mother and Peter. She made new friends and visited with her father as they all agreed to. Jenny is now 21 years old. She received a telephone call from the author to participate in a research study about her experiences with the family justice system (Birnbaum & Bala, 2009). She agreed to participate and tell her story. Jenny reported that she never got over her parents' separation. She believed that the move would help her in making that final break with the idealized family. She reported that her father remarried when she was 15 years old, and every time that she went to visit her father, she felt like she was intruding in their space. She stopped visiting with him when she turned 16 years old. Jenny reported that she has not seen her father for over three years now and continues to struggle with her weight and her self-esteem, and she feels socially awkward. She has few friends that she can really confide in, and while she completed her university studies in drama, she has not worked for the last year. In response to what she had to say to other young people going through their parents' separation and divorce, she broke down and cried. She said that she had friends whose parents separated, and they were fine; but she also had friends, including herself, who she described as not being fine. She stated that children and young people need more help during these difficult times. She stated that while she liked her lawyer and he listened, he did not ask her a lot of personal questions, and she did not feel that she could open up to him as a result. She stated that every child and youth really need as much emotional support and time to work through the process. She reported that she had no control over what her parents decided about the separation, and that led her down a road that physically challenged her (i.e., weight issues and hospitalization) and emotionally took its toll over the years. She stated that while she supports that all children have a voice in their parents' separation, there also needs to be accompanying services for children and young people to engage with.

Conclusion

The chapter began with the literature on both risk and resilience of children post separation. There is much diversity in children's outcomes. Depending on whether you are looking at the forest (overall cases) or the individual tree (single case), there will always be different outcomes. In individual cases, outcomes are determined by the individual's risk and protective factors as to how well they adjust post separation. In the research literature, the differences in outcomes are determined by the discipline of the researcher, the methodology of the design, and the different theoretical lens used to assess the differences. Yet, at the end of the day, children need to be supported by their parents, family justice professionals, and the family justice system.

Children's views can be heard in the following ways: (1) parents provide their own testimony evidence about what their children told them; (2) a person other than a parent, such as a social worker, teacher, or doctor, testifies about what the child told them; (3) a video-recorded statement, letter, or email of the child presented to the court; (4) a custody and access assessment, prepared by a mental health professional, that will include reports on interviews with the child; (5) a lawyer appointed to represent the child and present the child's views to the court; (6) a judicial interview; and (7) views of the child report where children's views are only provided to the court (Birnbaum, 2017). While it is important that all children have their voice heard in a manner that is safe and helpful to them, not all children want to be involved, and those wishes should also be respected.

For professionals, this means that there needs to be familiarity with family law and the implications for children and parents, and knowledge of the services and programs available for children and families. For the family justice system, there needs to be an interdisciplinary partnership between all the systems involved. That is, family law must be more integrated, and collaborative as outlined in Figure 13.1

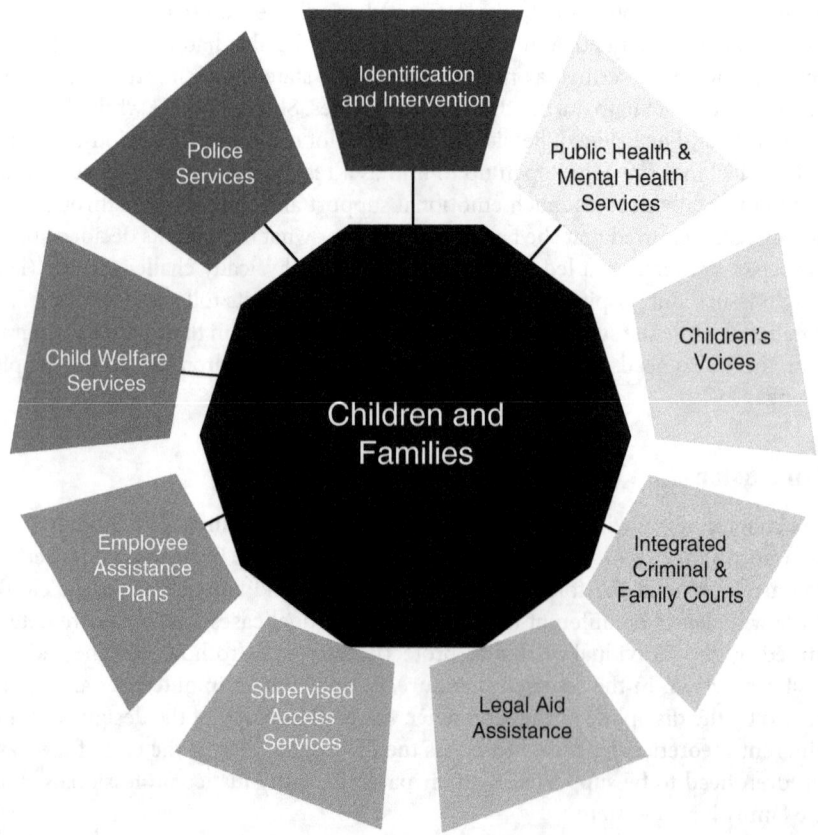

Figure 13.1 Need for a Multidisciplinary Family Justice Approach
Source: Birnbaum (2012).

(Birnbaum, 2012). Children and families must no longer go to siloed family justice services that are uncoordinated, forcing them to tell and retell their stories to multiple professionals.

Family law is special and unique because it involves not just the legal divorce, but also the emotional, behavioral, and physical caretaking arrangements of children's lives before, during, and post separation. Their well-being is inextricably linked to not just the parental relationship but the parent-child relationship. While every province and territory have government-funded services of one kind or another for separated families, not all services are equally available; some families must pay for these services while others are publicly funded (Birnbaum, 2009). A clarion call is needed on a broader systemic level that seeks uniformity and equality for all children and families across the country. These services and programs must be available not only when families engage with the family justice system, but also before and after. Research and follow-up with children and families must accompany services and programs if children's best interests are the goal of the family justice system.

Key Terms

Children's Lawyer: In Ontario, the Office of the Children's Lawyer is an independent law office that represents children before the court in child custody disputes, child protection matters, and estate matters.

Children of Armageddon: Refers to children whose parents are in intensive and lengthy courtroom proceedings for custody. The term illustrates how children can suffer because of these proceedings, and how children experience negative consequences when parents are engaged in heavy, overt conflict when separating.

Family Justice System: In most Western-oriented countries, the government (through specific departments or agencies) oversees matters such as separation and divorce through the legal category of Family Law. Disputes may be resolved by the courts, but may also be resolved through mediation, arbitration, and collaborative law.

Questions for Reflection

1. After reading this chapter, what losses can you identify that children may experience when exposed to the family justice system? How can children be better supported when parents divorce?
2. Why do you think loss and grief in childhood affects people significantly in adulthood like Jenny? Explore the role of attachment, the assumptive world, and some of the other theoretical grief models that were present in the case study of Jenny.
3. How do you think legal systems exacerbate or complicate an individual's grief? How can resiliency be fostered for both parents and children affected by these intensive proceedings?

Notes

1. This is a real case from a qualitative research study undertaken by the author for her Master of Laws degree. The names and places are changed.
2. *Fielding v. Fielding*, [2013] CarswellOnt 11117.
3. *Bruni v. Bruni*, [2010] ONSC 6568 (CanLII)
4. *Whidden v. Ellwood*, 2016 ONSC 6938 (CanLII)
5. In Ontario, the Office of the Children's Lawyer is an independent law office that represents children before the court in child custody disputes, child protection matters, and estate matters.

References

Amato, P. R. (2010). Research on divorce: Continuing trends and new developments. *Journal of Marriage and The Family, 72*, 650–666.

Amato, P. R., & Gilbreth, J. G. (1999). Non-resident fathers and children's well-being: A meta-analysis. *Journal of Marriage and The Family, 61*, 557–573.

Birnbaum, R. (2009). *Research on resources for children and youths undergoing parental separation and/or divorce: A literature review*. Ottawa, Canada: Family, Children and Youth Section, Department of Justice.

Birnbaum, R. (2012). Rendering children invisible: The forces at play during separation and divorce in the context of family violence. In R. Alaggia & C. Vine (2nd ed.). *Cruel but not unusual: Violence in Canadian families* (pp. 371–413). Waterloo, ON, Canada: Wilfrid Laurier University Press.

Birnbaum, R. (2017). Views of the child reports: Hearing directly from children involved in post separation disputes. *Social Inclusion, 5*(3), 148–154.

Birnbaum, R., & Bala, N. (2009). The child's perspective on legal representation: Young people report on their experiences with child lawyers. *Canadian Journal of Family Law, 25*(1), 11–71.

Clarke-Stuart, A., & Bretano, C. (2006). *Divorce, causes and consequences*. New Haven, CT: Yale University Press.

Cummings, E. M., & Davies, P. (1994). *Children and marital conflict: The impact of family dispute and resolution*. New York: Guilford Press.

Demo, D. H., & Fine, M. A. (2010). *Beyond the average divorce*. Thousand Oaks, CA: Sage Publications.

Emery, R. E. (1999). *Marriage, divorce, and children's adjustment*. Thousand Oaks, CA: Sage Publications.

Hetherington, E. M., & Kelly, J. B. (2002). *For better or for worse: Divorce reconsidered*. New York: W. W. Norton & Company.

Kelly, J. B. (2012). Risk and protective factors associated with child and adolescent adjustment following separation and divorce: Social science applications. In K. Kuehnle & L. Drozd, (Eds.), *Parenting plan evaluations: Applied research for the family court* (pp. 49–85). Oxford, UK: Oxford University Press.

Kelly, J. B., & Emery, R. E. (2003). Children's adjustment following divorce: Risk and resilience perspectives. *Family Relations, 52*, 352–362.

Roseby, V., & Johnston, J. R. (1998). Children of Armageddon: Common developmental threats in high conflict divorcing families. *Child and Adolescent Psychiatric Clinics of North America, 7*(2), 295–309.

Schwartz, S. J., & Finley, G. E. (2005). Divorce related variables as predictors of young adults' retrospective fathering reports. *Journal of Divorce and the Family, 44*, 145–163.

Wallerstein, J. S. (1985). The overburdened child: Some long-term consequences of divorce. *Social Work, 30*(2), 116–123.

Wallerstein, J. S., & Blakeslee, S. (1989). *Second chances: Men, women, and children: A decade of after divorce.* New York: Ticknor & Fields.

CHAPTER 14

Midlife Children Caring for Their Aging Parents

Darcy L. Harris

Introduction

Nancy was in her office, busily typing away at her computer. She had gotten behind in her work, and a looming deadline was hanging over her head. Her secretary gently knocked on the door and told her that her father was on the phone. It was the fourth call that week. When she picked up the phone, he was agitated and told her that his computer had frozen and he couldn't get it to work. He was anxious, saying that he had all his information on the computer and he couldn't access any of it. Nancy tried to problem-solve with him over the phone to no avail. She could ask her husband, Ron, to go over to her Dad's house to assist him; but she knew that Ron didn't have a lot of patience with her father, and she was concerned he might make things worse. All her father's neighbors were older as well and would most likely not be able to help him, either. Her 90-year-old father lived alone in the home that he had built 45 years ago, and he had chosen to stay in the home after her mother had died almost 20 years prior.

In this past week, her father had asked her to come over to his house several times (a 30-minute drive across the city, if traffic wasn't bad) to help him to sort out his medications, pick up things at the store, climb a ladder to replace a lightbulb, and to help him re-set his TV remote. The last time she went to his home, he was disheveled, needing a shower and to shave. He was also unsteady on his feet, with bruises on his arms and legs from where he had either fallen or hit a desk corner or door. His laundry was piled on the floor, overflowing from the laundry bin. The refrigerator smelled like something had died inside it, so Nancy cleaned it out. She noted that most of what was in the refrigerator was food that she had prepared for him, hoping he would be able to warm it up to eat without much bother. She now realized that even heating up food in the microwave was a challenge for him. Several times, she had tried to talk with him about getting some help in the home or assistance with his daily care, and he refused, saying he didn't want "some stranger in my home." He had also had two car accidents in the past six months. She knew he wasn't processing information well and that his reflexes were slower than they used to be. She had tried to talk with him about using a senior taxi company or having things delivered to his home, and he became angry with her, accusing her of trying to undermine his independence. Nancy just hoped he didn't drive and kill himself or someone else due to a lapse in judgment.

Nancy sighed. The man who stood in front of her now bore very little resemblance to the father she knew even a few years prior. He had always been meticulous and organized; he loved his food and was always heavier than he wanted to be. And now he barely weighed much more than her. She loved her father very much, but trying to help him, keep up with her own family at home (which included two teenage girls), and the demands of her full-time job were wearing her down. She was usually able to get her work done without any difficulties, and she had become pretty good at multitasking. However, she was spending so much time driving back and forth to her father's house and taking care of things for him that she was behind in everything. She worried about her father when he was alone. She didn't know how long she could juggle everything before she got sick herself, and if that happened, everything would fall apart.

Nancy's situation is common today; the scenario puts a human face to the information provided in this chapter. While we celebrate the advances in technology and medical care that have prolonged life expectancy considerably in the past several decades, a price is being paid. Living longer now includes living with more complex medical issues, chronic disabilities, and increased dependency upon family members and professionals to assist with many of the tasks associated with everyday living and functioning. The number of adults taking care of aging parents in the United States has tripled in the past 15 years, and a full 25% of grown children are helping their parents by providing either personal care or financial assistance (Arno, Viola, & Shi, 2011; Burke, 2017). Ironically, the difficulties associated with aging in elderly parents often occur at about the same time that adult children's careers are peaking. The aging population, higher life expectancies, and the shift in emphasis from institutionalized acute care to home care may suggest that more chronically ill, disabled, and frail people are relying on help from family than in the past. Results from the Canadian General Social Survey (GSS; Statistics Canada, 2013) show that between 2007 and 2012, the number of caregivers age 45 and over increased by 760,000 to 4.5 million caregivers, representing a 20% increase in the number of caregivers over those five years. It is estimated that approximately 34.2 million Americans have provided unpaid care to an aging parent in the last 12 months (National Alliance for Caregiving (NAC) and the American Association of Retired Persons (AARP), 2015). This pattern is similar across all developed countries (Haberkern & Szydlik, 2010). In this chapter, we will explore the losses associated with the gain of living longer on the aging population and the lives of their now middle-aged children.

Adult Children and Aging Parents

We live in a time when it isn't unusual for four generations of a family to co-exist at the same time. With life expectancies now well into the 80s for most developed countries, and the increase in the number of nonagenarians and centenarians[1] (Cullen, Hammer, Neal, & Sinclair, 2009), it is very likely that many young children have meaningful relationships with their grandparents as well as their great-grandparents. During this same time, there have been significant changes in family structure and social perspectives. In most developed countries, men and women both work and share the costs of living for their households. Women make up almost half of the labor force in most developed countries (International Labour Office, 2014; Statistics Canada, 2011; United States Department of Labor, 2017). What hasn't changed dramatically is that women still tend to take on the majority of responsibilities related to the informal (unpaid) care of both children and aging parents.

The role of caregiver to aging parents tends, at first, to be an outgrowth of the familial relationship, where practical help and emotional support have been offered over time in various ways. In response to a parent's developing disability, middle-aged children may increase the support they already give, and they may begin adding new types of assistance as well. Typically, increases in caregiving begin with either a health crisis or recognition of a significant change in functioning (Kim et al., 2016). Difficulties arise in these scenarios over many stress points:

- The amount of time and number of hours devoted to caregiving begins to interfere with the caregiver's other family and work commitments (Burke, 2017; Cohen, Cook, Kelley, Sando, & Bell, 2015).
- There is a need for more formal supports (i.e., professional support/assistance with parents who are confused or who need significant help with their activities of daily living), but the supports are too expensive or unavailable (Kim et al., 2016).
- The financial issues aren't a problem, but the parent refuses any help or assistance that is offered or will accept help only from the family member who is already struggling with the mounting pressures and responsibilities that are accruing (Cohen et al., 2015; Feinberg, Reinhard, Houser, and Choula (2011).
- There is a conflict between the elderly parent and the adult child regarding independence and autonomy. Adult children may, at times, step in and undermine parental independence and autonomy in situations where there is a perceived crisis, a time of relatively high degree of parental need, when there are concerns about safety, and/or if a decision needed to be made expeditiously at a time when the parent is not in a position to do so (Funk, 2010).

The term *caregiver burden* has been used to describe the adverse effects upon the caregiver's emotional well-being as well as social, occupational, and personal roles (Bastawrous, 2013; Cohen et al., 2015). Numerous studies explore the impact of caring for an aging parent on their adult children. The following aspects of the caregiver burden have been documented:

- *Emotional burden*—adult children who provide care for their aging parents commonly report feeling stressed, exhausted, and overwhelmed as they try to meet the demands of their families at home, their aging parents, and their work commitments. Many report symptoms that parallel burnout. In a study by Sallim, Sayampanathan, and Ho (2015), 30% of caregivers to aging parents fulfilled the criteria for clinical depression. Most caregivers stated that they frequently

feel overwhelmed because of the many demands for their time and attention; however, most of the negative feelings center around guilt for not doing enough for their aging parents (Losada et al., 2017).
- *Social burden*—an outgrowth of spending so much time and energy caring for aging parents in addition to other responsibilities is the lack of time available for sharing time with other family members in a meaningful way, lack of time for socialization with colleagues and friends, and not being able to attend social functions either due to lack of time or exhaustion. It is difficult for peers who are not in the same situation to comprehend the complexity of caregiving roles and responsibilities; in fact, many well-meaning friends and family members will often express concern and offer advice to the caregiver, which can begin to feel like more unmet expectations from them. These realities can readily create a sense of isolation, loneliness, and being "out of step" with peers.
- *Financial burden*—70% of caregivers report making work accommodations (i.e., cutting back working hours, coming in later or leaving early, taking leave from work, bringing work home, or quitting their jobs) because of increasing caregiver demands. In addition to the direct cost that occurs as a result of lost time at work, there is also the reduction in benefits and pension plans (or the loss of these if the individual leaves the labor market). In addition, many of the costs of caregiving land on the adult child who is the caregiver; costs for travel, meals, supplies, and other necessities begin to add up. Cohen et al. (2015) stated that the average adult child taking care of an elderly parent spends roughly $5,500 annually in out-of-pocket expenses. For women, the total individual amount of lost wages due to leaving the labor force early because of caregiving responsibilities equals $142,693. The estimated impact of caregiving on lost Social Security benefits is $131,351 per individual. A very conservative estimated impact on pensions is approximately $50,000. Thus, in total, the cost impact of caregiving for the individual female caregiver in terms of lost wages and Social Security benefits can run as high as $324,044 (National Alliance for Caregiving and the American Association of Retired Persons (hereafter NAC & AARP), 2015).

An issue that often arises when a parent's needs for care increase is the intensification of the relational dynamic that was present prior to the parent's need for assistance. An interesting study by Hansen and Slagsvold (2015) reported that caregiver stress and family conflict is lower in countries where public supports for both caregivers and their elderly parents are readily available. Increasing caregiving needs of elderly parents usually results in more time being devoted to their care by their middle-aged children, who have lived independently and have their own routines, values, and ideas about many aspects of life that may not be congruent with their elderly parents' views. Being thrust into close proximity for longer periods of time with their parent during a time when both the parent and the adult children feel stressed will most likely magnify the relational pattern that was present beforehand. In normal parent-child relationships of all ages, there are disagreements and differences that can usually be navigated because there is space and time that can serve as a buffer and allow for perspective-taking. Silverstein and Giarrusso (2010) state that in many family systems, parents and adult children may have mixed feelings about the other. For example, parents often express dismay over their adult child's busy schedule, choice of romantic partner, parenting style, and unfulfilled expectations. Adult children often feel misunderstood, judged, or that they have somehow disappointed or are not appreciated fully by their older parents. These authors state that ambivalence in family relationships is normal, and that it is possible to still have a loving, respectful relationship even in the presence of mixed feelings. However, in caregiving situations where issues of dependency and need arise, this ambivalence may become more antagonistic, further adding to the stress of both the aging parent and the adult child.

Underneath the stresses that an adult child experiences in providing care to an increasingly dependent parent is the loss of the original relationship they shared, where the parent was the child's provider, protector, confidante, and caregiver. In these situations, the adult child becomes the one who offers advice and provides practical (and sometimes financial) assistance and emotional support (Bangerter et al., 2017). Many of the losses that the aging parent experiences in terms of cognitive abilities, physical health, and general functionality are grieved by both the aging parent and the adult child; these losses are harbingers of an irreversible change in their relationship, as well as reminders that time is marching forward to the day when the parent will no longer be physically present. Parents often struggle with issues around autonomy and dependency as they experience a decline in functioning. In most developed countries, there is an emphasis on independence, functionality, and productivity. Many elders find their decreasing abilities to be humiliating, and they often worry about being a burden to their families, and most especially to the adult child(ren) who serve(s) as their primary caregiver(s). Previously, the emerging role of adult children as caregivers in the context of decreased functionality and increasing dependency needs of a parent was referred to as the *parent-child role reversal*. However, this reference is not used widely now because it is seen as infantilizing and shaming to parents, adding insult to injury during a time of vulnerability and stress (Walsh, 2012).

Social Context

If we consider the social context that surrounds the experiences of aging parents and adult child caregivers, many social norms and structural issues rise to the surface, including the assumption that caregiving is still seen primarily as women's work, that informal care is essentially unpaid labor that goes unrecognized, and in most Western developed countries, there is no paradigm that allows for dependence or vulnerability without shame being attached to the experience. In this section, we will explore each of these issues.

Caregiving as Women's Work

One of the most consistent findings in the literature related to family caregiving is that women provide more care than men (Ward-Griffin, St-Amant, & Brown, 2011). Pinquart and Sörensen (2011) completed a meta-analysis of several hundred caregiving studies and found that female caregivers provided more hours of care and were more likely to provide personal assistance, and women experienced a greater burden and more depression than men in their families. Adult siblings in families tend to negotiate amongst themselves as to who will provide care to their aging parent(s); it is almost always a female or set of female siblings who step forward to manage the primary caregiving duties. Pope, Kolomer, and Glass (2012) discuss the notion that "sensitivity to others" and "responsibility for caring" (p. 244) are often central themes in women's socialization, and these characteristics are often core aspects of women's self-concept and identity. Thus, women may have more of an internal motivation (and expectations by other family members) to provide care for their aging parents. The rub here is that the expectations for women to take the primary caregiving role of an aging parent are additive to women's work outside the home and responsibilities within the home. In their published review of caregiver demographics, the National Alliance for Caregiving and the American Association of Retired Persons (NAC & AARP, 2015) reported that 4 out of 10 female caregivers felt that they had no choice in taking on this role with their aging parents. This study predicted that as the population continues to age, and life expectancies continue to creep higher, women could end up spending more time caring for their aging parents than for their own children.

Financial Impact of Informal Care in the Social/Health Care System

Unpaid care provided by a family member is called *informal care*. Shortages of direct care workers (such as home health aides or personal support workers) and/or the inability to pay for adequate services at home leave many families with no alternative but to provide care themselves (Feinberg et al., 2011). Most aging parents wish to stay in their homes, and family support is integral to this desire. It is estimated that if family caregivers were no longer available to assist their aging elders at home, the economic costs to the health care system would dramatically increase. Feinberg et al. (2011) reported that in 2009, approximately 61.6 million family caregivers in the United States provided care to an adult who required assistance with daily issues related to aging. The estimated value of their unpaid labor amounted to roughly $450 billion in savings to the health care system. The impact of shorter hospital stays, limited hospital discharge planning, and the use of home-based medical technologies means that elderly people return to their homes even more sick, in need of not just basic assistance with their activities of daily living, but the monitoring of multiple medications and complex tasks such as tube feedings, catheter care and maintenance, injections, and operating medical equipment (NAC & AARP, 2015).

The savings to the health care/social service system from informal care may be offset by the increase in health conditions and hardships that occur to the adult children who are providing that care. Feinberg et al. (2011) reported that informal care provided to aging adults is now a public health concern, as the adult children who take on the role of caregiver experience profound stress, physical strains and injuries, competing demands for their time and attention, and financial stresses that begin to accumulate, leaving these individuals vulnerable themselves. Many caregivers end up utilizing health care services to address their stress-related maladies or to care for injuries that they received in their caregiving role. Others ignore their own health issues because they don't have time to make appointments for themselves or they don't have adequate insurance coverage (ibid.). For those caregivers who adjust their working hours in order to care for their aging parents, the financial hardship adds more stress to the situation. A survey of caregivers (Evercare and the NAC, 2007) found that 34% used their savings to help pay for expenses related to caring for their aging parents. Twenty-five percent of caregivers reported that they cut back on spending related to their own preventative health or dental care, and nearly 40% reported that they had reduced or stopped saving for their own future due to the increased expenses related to caregiving and/or their reduced ability to work outside of the home, potentially placing their own financial security at risk. In a similar survey of women who were caring for an aging parent, nearly 70% of these caregivers stated that they had significantly reduced their hours at work or had to leave the workplace entirely, with a direct impact upon their financial security (Pavalko & Henderson, 2006). Many caregivers who continue to work while acting as the primary caregiver for their aging parent report missed opportunities for promotions, business travel, relocation, and education as a result of providing care (NAC & AARP, 2015).

Socialization and Social Norms Related to Dependency

Two socially loaded issues intersect when adult children care for their aging parents. The first, as discussed earlier in this section, is the ongoing assumption that caregiving is "women's work" and thus is particularly devalued as menial, easy, and the responsibility of women in the family. The second issue relates to the shame and stigma that surround vulnerability and dependency in most Western industrialized countries. In these societies, aging is a process that is socially constructed as a problem. Older people are seen in a utilitarian light rather than for their potential and wisdom (Cruikshank, 2013). Aging is equated with the decline and loss of what makes a person valuable; most especially, the ability to be productive and independent. Tied closely into the devaluation of those who are elderly is the perceived drain upon public and personal resources when assistance is required. Caregivers of aging parents may perceive a loss of their social status if they leave the labor market or withdraw from social roles that are viewed as more important and/or more valued. Older individuals are viewed as less intelligent than younger individuals; they are often scapegoated and made fun of in popular media. They may internalize this devaluation and begin to feel that their presence is a burden and that they are inferior to younger individuals. Finally, they are often controlled and monitored in their movements as their bodies experience decline; thus, loss of ability becomes equated with loss of agency and value (Arroyoa, 2015).

Clinical Implications

Caregiver Supports

The burden of care is felt by both the caregiver and the aging parent; as discussed previously, there are numerous emotional, social, and financial stresses that accompany being in the role of primary caregiver to an elderly parent. The parent is often acutely aware of this burden on the adult child caregiver, and the loss of the ability to be the one to protect, provide, and support your child creates a unique form of grief and despair for many aging individuals. Caregivers are often so busy with the many responsibilities they carry that the time it takes to go to a meeting, access other supports, and/or even to explain what is needed to someone wanting to relieve their burden for a while takes up too much time and energy. Professionals involved in situations where the caregiver burden is concerning need to understand the situation and listen carefully to how the caregiver describes his or her needs, rather than making assumptions about where they should intervene.

The adult child caregiver needs to be integrated into the care team and engaged as a partner in care and with their parent and the team. Recalling the earlier discussion that most adult children who provide care to their aging parent(s) felt that they did not have a choice in the matter (NAC & AARP, 2015), the presence of ambivalence within the caregiver is important to address and explore. Feelings of tenderness and care toward the aging parent can coexist with feelings of resentment and frustration. A source of tension may stem from adult children who want to support autonomy in their aging parents yet feel uncertain about how to provide care without taking control in the relationship; taking control is often done by the adult child with a protective stance but may be met with anger and resentment from the parent. It is important to normalize the ambivalence for both parents and their adult children, and to provide outlets to relieve frustration wherever possible in practical measures (such as respite) as well as through compassionate listening (Igarashi, Hooker, Coehlo, & Manoogian, 2013).

Changing Nature of Families and Support

The changes in working roles and family structure in the last several decades have translated into many family members living a considerable distance from their parents. In addition, in the majority of families, women and men work full time outside the home, so taking time off work to care for an aging parent can have important financial ramifications. Childbearing is frequently delayed as women pursue educational and professional goals, so it is more common for women in midlife to still be responsible for the care of children at home when an aging parent begins to need assistance. The introduction of control over conception has also meant fewer children in families, with the result that fewer siblings are available to share the care needs of aging parents. Family systems also fluctuate more now than in the past; the de-stigmatization of divorce and the more common occurrence of blended families often leads to a lessening of a sense of connection between generations in families (Feinberg et al., 2011). Rather than look at adult children's needs separately from the needs of their aging parents, an approach that looks at the entire family system provides an opportunity for dialogue and problem-solving that is family-focused in nature. Programs that provide a combination of education, skills training, coping techniques, and counseling may be helpful rather than strictly care-oriented approaches, such as single-offering stress reduction techniques and limited interventions with individual family members (Feinberg et al., 2011).

Structural Support

At the level of policy making and implementation of broad-reaching programs, the psychological, physical, and financial cost of care needs to be acknowledged and addressed. Rather than individual companies implementing piecemeal plans for employees, there needs to be governmental direction and recognition of the significant impact of informal caregiving, with appropriate policies enacted to support both caregivers and their aging parents (Cohen et al., 2015). Employment leave policies that secure the caregiver's position in the workplace, and subsidies for those who are providing unpaid care, would be an important step to reduce the stress that employed caregivers face. Some states and provinces have enacted paid family leave programs, although many of these plans come with the caveat that the care is being provided to someone at the end of life and do not apply to chronic conditions.

Other policies that have been helpful to caregivers include the implementation of "family friendly" workplaces that allow for flexible hours, the ability to work from home with intermittent contact through the use of technology, and other forms of caregiver supports (Feinberg et al., 2011). With life expectancy now well into the 80s and 90s (and 100s) becoming commonplace, there needs to be adequate infrastructure in place to accommodate flexible care options for the elderly in society. Day programs, transportation services, quality meal preparation and delivery, as well as "stepped" programs that provide assistance according to the requirements of aging individuals need to be available and affordable. Most families do not have the ability to pay for the degree of assistance that is needed to keep an aging loved one in the community for a longer period of time; however, entrance into long-term care and institutional settings is another burden of cost that can be prohibitive.

Conclusion

The increase in life expectancy in Western-oriented industrialized societies comes at a price for those who are aging and their adult children. Aging individuals tend to live longer with more complex needs for medical and supportive care, and the burden of that care frequently falls upon their adult children, many of whom are already juggling responsibilities and commitments to their own families and workplaces. The stresses of caring for an aging parent frequently encompass emotional, social, and financial strains. Both the aging parent and the adult child experience significant losses during this time, and these losses need to be acknowledged. Supportive governmental and workplace policies need to be adequate and readily available. Finally, integrated care needs to be based upon compassionate listening and responding to all the family members involved.

Key Terms

Caregiver Burden: The stress that exists for adult children who are caregivers, and are burdened emotionally, socially, occupationally, financially, cognitively, and physically due to the home care situations and needs of their aging parents.

Informal Care: An individual who provides regular continuous support and assistance to another individual without being paid for these caregiving services.

Parent-Child Role Reversal: The swapping of roles between adult children and elderly parents. Aging parents often rely on their midlife children due to declining health and functionality, and thus require assistance to live. The term is not commonly utilized, as it is perceived to be demeaning to parents who are in a vulnerable and stressful situation.

Questions for Reflection

1. Compare both the loss experiences of midlife children caregivers and aging parents who have become dependent. What are the parallels and nuances between both grief narratives?
2. How do you think industrial Western societies view aging? Does this align with your own perspective on aging? Why do you think supports are lacking for the aging population? What policies would you like to see developed and/or implemented to minimize the burden for adult children caregivers, and to compassionately help the aging population?
3. What unspoken social rules did you recognize in this chapter? What surprised you the most about caregiver burden? What are your thoughts on why women caregivers are most at risk?
4. What supports should be available to midlife caregivers in order to mitigate their losses and decrease their caregiver burdens? How can we, as a society, provide more support to caregivers in order to mitigate their losses and burdens?

Note

1. A nonagenarian is an individual between 90 and 99 years of age; A centenarian is an individual over 100 years of age.

References

Arno, P. S., Viola, D., & Shi, Q. (2011). *The MetLife study of caregiving costs to working caregivers: Double jeopardy for baby boomers caring for their parents*. Westport, CT: The MetLife Mature Market Institute. Retrieved from www.aarp.org/content/dam/aarp/livable-communities/learn/health/metlife-study-of-caregiving-costs-to-working-caregivers-2011-aarp.pdf

Arroyoa, M. C. (2015). The body in old age and dependency: A territory of threat and uncertainty. *Sociology, 5*(7), 562–576.

Bangerter, L. R., Liu, Y., Kim, K., Zarit, S. H., Birditt, K. S., & Fingerman, K. L. (2017). Everyday support to aging parents: Links to middle-aged children's diurnal cortisol and daily mood. *The Gerontologist*, 1–9. doi:10.1093/geront/gnw207

Bastawrous, M. (2013). Caregiver burden—A critical discussion. *International Journal of Nursing Studies, 50*(3), 431–441.

Burke, R. J. (2017). The sandwich generation: Individual, family, organizational, and societal challenges and opportunities. In R. J. Burke & Z. L. M. Calvano (Eds.), *The sandwich generation: Caring for oneself and others at home and work* (pp. 3–39). Northampton, MA: Edward Elgar.

Cohen, S. A., Cook, S., Kelley, L., Sando, T., & Bell, A. E. (2015). Psychosocial factors of caregiver burden in child caregivers: Results from the new national study of caregiving. *Health and Quality of Life Outcomes, 13*(1), 120.

Cruikshank, M. (2013). *Learning to be old: Gender, culture, and aging*. Lanham, MD: Rowman & Littlefield.

Cullen, J. C., Hammer, L. B., Neal, M. B., & Sinclair, R. R. (2009). Development of a typology of dual-earner couples caring for children and aging parents. *Journal of Family Issues, 30*(4), 458–483.

Evercare and NAC. (2007). *Family caregivers—what they spend, what they sacrifice: The personal financial toll of caring for a loved one*. Minnetonka, MN: Evercare and Bethesda, MD: NAC.

Feinberg, L., Reinhard, S. C., Houser, A., & Choula, R. (2011). *Valuing the invaluable: 2011 update, the growing contributions and costs of family caregiving*. Washington, DC: AARP Public Policy.

Funk, L. M. (2010). Prioritizing parental autonomy: Adult children's accounts of feeling responsible and supporting aging parents. *Journal of Aging Studies, 24*, 57–64.

Haberkern, K., & Szydlik, M. (2010). State care provision, societal opinion and children's care of older parents in 11 European countries. *Ageing & Society, 30*(2), 299–323.

Hansen, T., & Slagsvold, B. (2015). Feeling the squeeze? The effects of combining work and informal caregiving on psychological well-being. *European Journal of Ageing, 12*(1), 51–60.

Igarashi, H., Hooker, K., Coehlo, D. P., & Manoogian, M. M. (2013). "My nest is full:" Intergenerational relationships at midlife. *Journal of Aging Studies, 27*(2), 102–112.

International Labour Office. (2014). *Global employment trends 2014: Risk of a jobless recovery?* International Labour Organization. Retrieved August 3, 2018, from www.ilo.org/global/research/global-reports/global-employment-trends/2014/lang--en/index.htm

Kim, K., Bangerter, L. R., Liu, Y., Polenick, C. A., Zarit, S. H., & Fingerman, K. L. (2016). Middle-aged offspring's support to aging parents with emerging disability. *The Gerontologist, 57*(3), 441–450.

Losada, A., Márquez-González, M., Vara-García, C., Gallego-Alberto, L., Romero-Moreno, R., & Pillemer, K. (2017). Ambivalence and guilt feelings: Two relevant variables for

understanding caregivers' depressive symptomatology. *Clinical Psychology & Psychotherapy*, 25(1), 59–64.
National Alliance for Caregiving and the American Association of Retired Persons (NAC & AARP. (2015). *Caregiving in the U.S.* Bethesda, MD: National Alliance of Caregiving. Retrieved August 3, 2018, from www.caregiving.org/caregiving2015/
Pavalko, E. K., & Henderson, K. A. (2006). Combining care work and paid work: Do workplace policies make a difference? *Research on Aging, 28*(3), 359–374.
Pinquart, M., & Sörensen, S. (2011). Spouses, adult children, and children-in-law as caregivers of older adults: A meta-analytic comparison. *Psychology and Aging, 26*(1), 1–14.
Pope, N. D., Kolomer, S., & Glass, A. P. (2012). How women in late midlife become caregivers for their aging parents. *Journal of Women & Aging, 24*(3), 242–261.
Sallim, A. B., Sayampanathan, A. A., Cuttilan, A., & Ho, R. C. M. (2015). Prevalence of mental health disorders among caregivers of patients with Alzheimer disease. *Journal of the American Medical Directors Association, 16*(12), 1034–1041.
Silverstein, M., & Giarrusso, R. (2010). Aging and family life: A decade review. *Journal of Marriage and Family, 72*(5), 1039–1058.
Statistics Canada. (2011). *The surge of women in the workforce*. Retrieved August 5, 2018, from https://www150.statcan.gc.ca/n1/pub/11-630-x/11-630-x2015009-eng.htm
Statistics Canada. (2013). *General Social Survey—Family (GSS)*. Retrieved August 1, 2018, from http://www23.statcan.gc.ca/imdb/p2SV.pl?Function=getSurvey&SDDS=4501
United States Department of Labor. (2017). *Data and statistics: Women in the labor force*. Retrieved August 3, 2018, from www.dol.gov/wb/stats/stats_data.htm
Walsh, F. (2012). Successful aging and family resilience. *Annual Review of Gerontology and Geriatrics, 32*, 153–172.
Ward-Griffin, C., St-Amant, O., & Brown, J. B. (2011). Compassion fatigue within double duty caregiving: Nurse-daughters caring for elderly parents. *Online Journal of Issues in Nursing, 16*(1), 1–13.

PART IV

Chronic Sorrow

Susan Roos

Chronic sorrow has without doubt existed throughout the entire history of the world. For this reason alone, it is both interesting and surprising that—so far as we can know—it was not until the 1960s (Olshansky, 1962, 1966) that the concept emerged—from the context of rehabilitation. Even then, the concept had a rocky course, and its existence and validity were (and can be, even today) questioned and resisted. A word does exist in Greek that may refer to chronic sorrow; the word is *parapono*. It refers to a "heavy heart" and to "the complaint without answer." In the 1960s, professionals working in the field of disabilities who dealt with parents, caregivers, and families of those with a wide variety of impairments—especially, at that time, intellectual or cognitive impairments referred to as "mental retardation"—often complained that families, especially mothers, were hindering and interfering with treatment and/or causing or worsening impairments. Parents were often seen as nuisances who were unable to accept their children. In the 1960s it was not at all unusual to hear references to "refrigerator parents," and labels such as "schizophrenogenic" and "autistogenic" were often used by professionals to describe family members, especially mothers. It was often even thought that "overprotective" and "overinvolved" parents were acting out unconscious death wishes toward their child.

Olshansky understood family and parental responses differently from most helping professionals at that time and identified what he referred to as "chronic sorrow." As he understood the presenting situation, chronic sorrow referred to grieving for losses that were ongoing and living and that could not be resolved or "gotten over" in the same way that grief related to permanent absence can be resolved or accommodated. The source of the loss is constant. Therefore, although chronic, this type of grieving is neither pathological nor subject to recovery or permanent adaptation in the way that losses due to permanent absence are. Olshansky saw chronic sorrow as a non-pathological, understandable, ongoing set of grief responses to a tragedy that is laden with symbolic meaning and whose effects are lifelong. He recommended that professionals demonstrate patience and that they be clear about goals.

Often seen as a maverick and as noncompliant with his peers, Olshansky had the courage to speak out and to express impressions and opinions that were at odds with customary and accepted ideas. He was an early advocate of "passing," a strategy for those with mental illness who could hide their psychiatric disorders and their past hospitalizations and treatment histories. At the time of Olshansky's introduction of the concept of chronic sorrow, he was in good standing with his professional peers. His recognition of chronic sorrow contributed greatly to a shift in how professionals perceived caregivers and family members of those with whom they worked so that relationships gradually have become more comforting and team-oriented. Family members, rather than feeling blamed and seen as nuisances, can usually now feel accepted, safe, respected, and valued in their roles as fully fledged team members working on behalf of their loved one.

Briefly defined, *chronic sorrow is a normal yet profound, pervasive, continuing, and recurring set of grief responses resulting from a loss or absence of crucial aspects of oneself (self-loss) or another living person (other-loss) to whom there is a deep attachment* (Roos, 2002a, 2018). Its essence is a painful discrepancy between perceived reality and what continues to be dreamed of; the loss is ongoing as it persists and is typically lifelong. Such losses would include permanent and disabling genetic defects and deformities, chronic mental illness, neuromuscular disorders, spinal cord injury, some cases of diabetes, and numerous other conditions. Today, cases of drug addiction and chronic pain are ever-increasing sources of chronic sorrow. Chronic sorrow can also apply to some cases of infertility or childlessness, as childlessness continues despite plans, costly and intensive fertility treatments, and persistent fantasies for parenthood. It can apply to disappearances of loved ones who have simply vanished, leaving no traces, and when it is not known (nor can it be known) whether they are alive or dead. Women who relinquished babies for adoption when adoptions were "closed" and who cannot know where their children are or even if they continue to exist are also prone to chronic sorrow. Some immigrants who have left their families, all friendships, their language, and all they've ever known, demonstrate chronic sorrow, although they have managed to make good lives for themselves. As a concept, chronic sorrow meets criteria posited by Penrod and Hupcey (2003), qualifying its legitimacy as a concept for consideration and study. The concept demonstrates such principles as pragmatism, epistemological maturity, logic, and conceptual components. Future reshaping of the concept can be expected as understandings and research shed new light on the phenomenon.

Characteristics of chronic sorrow include: (a) its non-pathological nature; (b) its essential disenfranchisement (Doka, 1989); (c) references to self- and/or other-loss; (d) its frequent traumatic onset; (e) its having no foreseeable end; (f) constant reminders and/or triggers; (g) unavoidable, periodic resurgences of intensity, (h) predictable and unpredictable stress points; (i) its *not* being a state of permanent despair, and (j) the continuation of functioning by the affected person.

Following Olshansky's introduction of chronic sorrow, studies validating and assessing the concept were forthcoming, followed by more than a decade when the literature was virtually devoid of consideration of the concept. During the 1990s, however, professional interest re-emerged. The Nursing Consortium for Research on Chronic Sorrow (NCRCS) was assembled primarily by nursing faculty members and led to a number of studies unquestionably validating the concept for a wide variety of conditions that seriously and permanently affect functioning. In the course of research, the nursing profession has developed research instruments (e.g., Burke, 1989; Eakes, 1995; Kendall, 2005). In nursing today, the concept is considered to be a middle-range theory. Middle-range theories are considered to be aimed at specific phenomena which, though limited in scope, are capable of generating research. Two antecedents have been posited by the nursing profession: the initial event of a living loss and the "unresolved disparity" resulting from the loss.

The role of fantasy is central to the existence of chronic sorrow. The pesky question arises: If we could not dream or fantasize, would chronic sorrow exist? The fantasy of what should and could have been and what was often unquestionably expected is predictably and unpredictably activated during the course of chronic sorrow, and the disparity between fantasy and reality can be cruel and wounding. Jacob Arlow, a psychoanalyst and contributor in a variety of ways to the analytic field (Arlow, 1964), explored the role of fantasy, especially unconscious fantasy, and understood its power in the construction of the self. He posited that when we experience outer reality, we simultaneously experience inner reality. The fantasy of what should or might have been and was expected can be activated numerous times during the course of chronic sorrow. It is the disparity between fantasy and reality that is at stake when sorrow is intensified or when there are triggers that activate intensity. The fantasy of what might have been (often a major factor and component in identity development) does not easily extinguish, if it ever does. After all, a self is made; it does not just magically appear. In his classic work on disability, Goffman (1963), in attempting to speak for the person who is disabled, referred to the loss as a social stigma and referred to the self-perception as a "spoiled identity."

As a form of disenfranchised grief, chronic sorrow is frequently launched by trauma. With very few exceptions, trauma occurs at the time of diagnosis, whether at birth (when there are obvious visible anomalies), when a devastating injury occurs, or when a condition that is not remediable is confirmed (e.g., Huntington's, ALS, etc.). For Bauby (1997), trauma occurred when he "graduated" from being a stroke patient with an uncertain prognosis to being profoundly quadriplegic (i.e., "locked in"). From that point forward, he would think of life as being "before" or "after" that "graduation." It is not at all unusual for a professional who engages in therapy with someone coping with chronic sorrow (or perhaps chronic depression when chronic sorrow has transitioned into this disorder) to encounter PTSD symptoms or other effects of trauma that require amelioration in order to address other major issues.

Professional Involvement

Professionals involved in working with those contending with chronic sorrow require certain expertise in areas such as trauma amelioration, existential therapy (including narrative and meaning co-construction), anger management, family therapy, identity clarification, strengthening, community resources (including advocating for these when none exist), and referral for psychotropic medication if or when necessary. There are several approaches to the problem of flashbacks, and professionals can usually readily avail themselves of training in techniques that ameliorate them. Foci of professional help also include, among other things, early onslaught, disorganization, disenfranchisement, triggers, stress management (both acute and chronic), symbiotic enmeshment, anger, depression, loss spirals, etc. In work with families, Rolland's (1989) psychosocial typology of illness can be helpful to clinicians by linking chronic illness to the family life cycle and to individual and family dynamics. Rolland's four broad distinctions (e.g., onset, course, outcome, and degree of incapacitation--each a part of a continuum), are all applicable to conditions related to disability.

It is critically important, perhaps vital, that professionals assume and communicate their understanding that chronic sorrow is a normal and understandable response, as helping clients to view themselves as non-pathological can alleviate negative assumptions and initiate a new sense of self as positive, capable, and resilient, while coping with issues that are sometimes fundamentally overwhelming but not insurmountable. Persons beset with chronic sorrow frequently report that simply knowing that chronic sorrow is recognized (is "real") and that it is non-pathological can be the source of immediate relief and comfort. As with all human distress, a feeling of being understood, accepted, and validated can go a long way.

Wolfelt's (1998) "companioning" model for the bereavement counseling relationship is proposed. The model is one of parity. Imagery inherent in "companioning" is very different from that involved in "treatment." The model implies collaboration and replaces the medical model and others with one that is growth-oriented and based on relationship. The basics of "companioning" include: (a) honoring the spirit (not focusing on intellect); (b) curiosity (not expertise); (c) learning (not teaching); (d) walking alongside (not leading); (e) stillness (not prodding forward); (f) discovering the gifts of sacred silence (not filling all vacancies with words); (g) listening with the heart (not analyzing with the head); (h) witnessing (not directing); (i) being present (not taking the pain away); (j) respecting disorder and confusion (not imposing logic and order); and (k) going with another into the soul's wilderness (not taking responsibility for mapping a way out).

Family Identity

Chronic sorrow conditions unquestionably represent a disruption of the family life cycle; however, the cycle is understood. When they learn that a family member is damaged to the extent of lifelong dependency, family members are normally extremely upset. Disorganization and chaos in the family may persist for a year and even for as long as two years following onset. Although family functioning may be erratic, disorganization during this time can be considered normal. New role demands are common even in constant-course conditions as family life cycle transitions are more complicated and often precluded. There can be a loss of privacy and frequent adverse effects on siblings as well as on the marital relationship, a disaffiliation with customary support resources, and many re-shapings of family functioning. Role flexibility is crucial for coping. Addressing problems as they arise, while no longer making adjustments on an assignment-of-priority basis, can become the new norm. Family members usually make every effort to "look good," and their efforts in this regard often mask how difficult life is and can be.

An especially stressful family transition occurs when caregivers can no longer carry the load due to aging factors or to their own disabilities, and when decisions and follow-through must occur in order to survive the vicissitudes of this kind of drastic change. Frequently, family members have assumed many things that do not stand up to disclosure. It has also been found that frequently the oldest daughter (or oldest sibling of the person with impairments) has been assumed to be the person who will take over the responsibility that the parents have carried. Active planning and open family discussion are critical, even when they reactivate old resentments, grief, and anger. Parent caregivers who are attempting to provide a secure future for their child with impairments may experience additional stress through complaints, accusations, and bitterness from other family members who may be verbalizing their feelings for the first time. Obtaining legal assistance in appointing guardianship, constructing trusts, and other arrangements is often an imperative; doing so is recommended.

Financial strain can be a significant factor in families. Finances are commonly further depleted by costly equipment and modification of the living quarters, as well as when parents must resign or withdraw from the workplace to be with the family member who is disabled. Studies are needed to increase early identification of families most at risk of permanent decompensation so that needs are met, and future stressors are planned for. Family functioning, the severity of the affected person's condition, and the person's "pre-injury" functioning are generally predictive of both family and individual functioning one year following onset. Early professional intervention may prevent family system collapse.

There is a paucity of research on the effects of chronic sorrow conditions on siblings. There are some indications that in adolescence and early adulthood, siblings benefit from parental mandates, permissions, and encouragement to disengage from family responsibilities and, when age-appropriate, to make lives for themselves separate from the family. Although siblings may suffer from an onslaught of stressors, there appear to be potential sibling benefits, especially in the context of character development. These include: (a) increased maturity demonstrated by empathic accuracy, insightfulness, and intuitiveness; (b) appreciation of wide human diversity; (c) appreciation for the good things in life; (d) keen awareness of prejudice and its damage; (e) patience, including serving and loving without expectations; (f) precocious independence and self-confidence; (g) incisive humor; (h) clear priorities and a sense of proportion; (i) vocational direction and clarity; (j) philosophical depth; and (k) creativity in meaning and life construction (Roos, 2002b). However, siblings are at risk of harboring guilt that can interfere with making satisfying lives of their own. On the one hand, parents may look to them for reassurance that they are managing the family and are parenting in a satisfactory way, as demonstrated by siblings' accomplishments. On the other hand,

and simultaneously, siblings may be prone to suffer from guilt when they accomplish things their disabled brother or sister can never accomplish. They are at risk of sabotaging themselves and falling appreciably short of what they are capable of.

When loss and grief are disenfranchised, such as in chronic sorrow, there are often no customary supports or expectations. There are no rituals, no expectations or assurances of recognition of the loss (as the person who is the source of the loss continues), and adaptations are usually drastic and disorienting. In some cases, the person who is the source of the loss may be essentially socially unrecognized so that s/he appears not even to exist. An enigma can ensue in which one might assume that if there is no existence, there is no loss. Therefore, grief is unacknowledged (and unaddressed) by those in the social context.

Disability and Social Justice

From time immemorial, people with disabilities and their families have had a very difficult existence. When babies have been born with obvious disabilities, infanticide has been an acceptable practice off and on from earliest days throughout history. Plato favored abandonment of an impaired infant in a mysterious, unknown place—i.e., passive euthanasia. Popular opinions, referring to a "lack of contribution" to society by impaired individuals, led to assumptions that they were not deserving of life or belonging with those who somehow "contributed." Contributions have been thought of in concrete and measurable terms (often economic). Reasoning that has led to conclusions or meaning of "contributions" has typically not included "immeasurables" or abstract thought of any kind. "Ugly laws" were enacted throughout the United States banning individuals with impairments that rendered them "unsightly" when in public places. People with disabilities, especially epilepsy, cerebral palsy, craniofacial defects, and other neurological and/or psychiatric disorders, were the focus of witch hunts, public floggings, and burning at the stake during early American history. These individuals were often seen as "devil-possessed" witches. Based on an unfortunate and inaccurate connection being made between low intelligence and criminality, a eugenics movement took place in many parts of the world, including the United States, Canada, England, and Europe, that resulted in the involuntary sterilization of many thousands of individuals who were determined to be of "poor stock." Those with disabilities were the ones who were subjected to the perfecting of the extermination practices used in the Holocaust. In Germany during this time, parents were praised and referred to as heroes when they killed their newborn infants who had obvious defects. Many infants and young children with impairments were taken from their families and sent to specialized clinics where they were put to death. Sem-Sandberg (2014) has written eloquently about the lives of these children.

A social contractarian philosophy has undergirded the great majority of social/political systems to date (Rawls, 1996, 2001). Social contracts have typically been based on the idea that there is a mutual advantage when people live together that does not exist when people live on their own. Classical theorists have assumed that social contracting individuals are men who are roughly equal in capacity and equally capable of productive economic activity. Although their interests may be represented, there have typically been no seats at the bargaining table for women, children, non-human animals, persons with disabilities, and (frequently) the elderly. Some omissions have been rectified in contemporary contract situations. However, according to Nussbaum (2006), no existing social contract doctrine includes people with severe and atypical physical and mental impairments in the group of those by whom basic political principles are chosen. People with disabilities have been stigmatized and excluded. Historically, people with severe mental impairments have not even been educated and have been excluded from the public realm.

From the viewpoint of justice, people with disabilities have not been treated as full equals, and their needs have frequently not been considered when basic principles are chosen. The social contract tradition presents basic questions such as, "By whom and for whom are basic social principles designed?" (Nussbaum, 2006). Those admitted to the bargaining table have typically included parties who design principles for citizens who are without serious mental or physical impairments. However, human (and even non-human) beings are primary subjects of social justice, although they may not be capable of participation in procedures that result in political principles. Perhaps it is time at last to consider that human (and even non-human) beings have dignity and worth, even when impaired, and deserve to be treated with respect and on the basis of equality with others. Primary subjects of social justice, even when incapable of participating in procedures through which political principles are chosen, deserve to be treated with respect on the basis of equality with others. Classical political theories emerge from the general idea that social and political beings find fulfillment in relations with others. These theories may result in more equal political justice; however, it may at last be time to consider outcome-oriented theory rather than procedural theory.

Existential Issues

It appears to be the nature of human beings to search for meaning in existence and to need stabilizing beliefs about living. To be affected by chronic sorrow is to be existentially molested. Professional helpers are better off in their delivery of services when they are comfortable dealing with existential issues. It can be a good thing to be endowed with a center of "existential knowing." That some of us endure catastrophic loss while others blunder along relatively unscathed is a quandary that can gnaw at us and cause us to question many aspects of our lives indefinitely. When we are beset with chronic sorrow, we struggle to find meaning and coherence in a world that no longer makes sense. Questions without sensible answers can include: How can a God who loves me allow such devastation to occur? Is this unbearable and profound loss a punishment? What crime has been perpetrated that can deserve such punishment? Is the universe so uncaring and so random that it metes out these tragedies? I am no longer the person I used to be; who am I now? Existential issues can become intrusively foreground. For some who are confronting chronic sorrow, the work of making sense of such a loss and of somehow integrating it can often be a lifelong endeavor—if it ever happens.

Self-Loss and Other-Loss

The terms self- and other-loss can be used to identify the primary locus of the loss. The subjective meaning of a self-loss may be different from what is experienced when the loss refers to vital aspects of someone we care for deeply (other-loss). From the viewpoint of other-loss, Doka and Aber (1989) used as a metaphor the horror movie *The Invasion of the Body-Snatchers*, in which the loss of the original personality is portrayed that includes its replacement by a "parasitic consciousness." This particular kind of loss can be extremely difficult to sort out. Taken on a case-by-case basis, this kind of loss is one of dimensionality, and the continuum of loss can range from comatose states to severe mental illness. Severe changes in personality can also result from some types of seizures and from other neurological disorders. For some, the person who is in an intractable coma can be perceived as the same as dead (a situation often referred to as "psychological death," or the concept of social death discussed in Chapter 3). This same person may be treated quite differently by others; i.e., as fully alive. In either case, there is a cessation of the individual personality that once existed. Ethical issues can loom large in cases of other-loss when the loss is of the mind or consciousness. Ethical decisions can be fraught with great difficulty.

Clark Elliott (2016), a professor of artificial intelligence in the Chicago area, has written about the aftermath of his concussion that was sustained in a car accident. Now recovered, he has written about his fears, his painful awareness, and his grief for the loss of his former competent self. He functioned measurably poorer as a brain-damaged person. His book, titled *Ghost in My Brain*, refers to his awareness of the presence of his former self as he was struggling to do simple, basic things. He has written about his reunification with his former self in the course of his recovery. It is easy to wonder what would have happened if Elliott had sought therapy and had he been pushed to let go of or say "goodbye" to his former self?

Beethoven can be a poignant example of self-loss experienced when the loss has been of the one attribute that is most treasured (i.e., Beethoven's hearing). He wrote, often in his letters, about his anguish and perpetual frustrations as well as about his search for treatment and restoration. Although he continued to produce music, he was never again the person he had been, nor could he enjoy activities that he once enjoyed and took for granted. He repeatedly experienced disappointment and could not stop wanting and seeking restoration and/or the miracle of recovery.

For caregivers coping with other-loss, there is usually no choice but to continue to care for the one who has sustained serious and permanent disabilities. The "no choice" rule predominantly applies to suicidal thoughts and feelings. There is reason to believe, however, that in cases of equivocal death of persons with severe disabilities, coroners and medical examiners should be exceptionally cautious and very thorough when evaluating the cause of death of someone who is fragile and unable to defend him- or herself. Common assumptions should be carefully ruled in or out. Killing the person with severe disabilities and then completing suicide are not unknown happenings. Situations such as these can surprisingly occur when it has been thought in social settings that the caregiver is managing well and that the one who is cared for appears to be happy and well taken care of. A community can be plummeted into confusion and disbelief.

When other-loss involves a person who has been idealized, the loss is of elements that have been real and those that have been fantasized. The dreamed-for future is no more. In chronic sorrow conditions, one is sometimes forced to take an untenable position. Letting go of unrealistic dreams and images of how things should be now and in the future is experienced as disowning a cherished part of identity. Since what has been cherished is often a unifying element, releasing it takes an effort of will. The effort is painful and feels very wrong, and it is like partaking in some sort of atrocity. Our children are often the repositories and conveyors of our idealizations. They can be our hopes for completeness and our dreams and aspirations for the future. When the child arrives and is seen as severely impaired, most of us will love that child with all our hearts. What is unacceptable is the serious impairment and how it will ruin our fantasies and how it can ruin the life of our child—the child we have.

Polarization

Some groups currently associated with those who have disabilities have recently begun to assume an opinion that those who perceive themselves as coping with chronic sorrow conditions are resigned to their circumstances and that these groups may be a barrier to efforts aimed at research (or more trials) in the direction of remedies or even cures. Many such groups are focused on efforts to identify causes (frequently thought to be genetic) of various conditions and to find ways in which conditions can be prevented or remedied. For some, identifying with chronic sorrow appears the same as being opposed to remedies, prevention, and cures. The thinking involved in these matters is bifurcated. The assumption is that chronic sorrow, or grieving in any manner, is equated with defeat and resignation—in general, a very wrong assumption. Those with chronic sorrow conditions in their lives are most likely to go to extreme lengths in order to help the person who is disabled, suffering, or prevented from having what is considered to be a normal life in some way. It is not at all clear that advantages always accrue to those whose goal is "finding cures." It is, however, frequently very difficult for people to think in a wholistic, integrated manner (i.e., "both/and"). It would be difficult, if not entirely impossible, to find someone who is struggling with chronic sorrow conditions who would opt out of finding and making use of most measures available to improve the condition of someone who is loved and the recipient of devoted care who is thought to be prime for benefiting from a newly developed intervention or cure. Becoming aware of chronic sorrow and its process and effects can be a benevolent process that is ultimately a clear benefit to entire social and family systems. Chronic sorrow and/or the awareness of its effects does not mean that cures, research, and benefits are not wanted or that there is opposition to cures and remedies.

Trends

Today people are living longer than ever in history and are subject to disabilities and disease processes typical of aging adults, including Alzheimer's and other dementias. Family members and others who are themselves aging and worn out are now becoming "early" caregivers for their parents or other family members. Those in their 70s are taking the reins to care for parents in their 90s while sometimes having adult children living in their homes. While helpful, government pension plans rarely adequately cover living expenses. This growing situation is fertile ground for increased chronic sorrow. As more and more "perfect" babies are introduced to the world, the intensity of chronic sorrow may increase for those who do not or cannot avail themselves of relevant technology. The numbers of people expecting "perfect" babies, including such specific details as eye color, certain facial characteristics, etc., appear to be increasing. The possibility exists that increasing numbers of abortions may occur when parents insist on choosing the sex, the appearance, and the attributes of a prospective baby, including whether there is a possibility that certain genetically based health conditions are potentially "programmed" into a fetus.

The increased availability of advanced imaging techniques allowing for definitive diagnoses of significantly increased numbers of conditions will also influence both the frequency and extent of chronic sorrow. Wartime conditions, appearing to worsen as they continue, are impacting the frequency and extent of traumatic (and permanent) injuries that are affecting ever-growing numbers of adults of military age. Increasing numbers of active military personnel are surviving horrendous injuries, including loss of limbs, craniofacial and permanent brain injuries, and other physical traumas that were once the causes of certain death. It is possible that our increasing technological advancements are serving to "de-humanize" us and render us less attuned and caring for those contending with permanent and severe disability. The extent and nature of chronic sorrow may be shifting, changing, and impacting the future.

A variety of viewpoints may influence the prevalence of chronic sorrow. For example, belief in eventual remedies may contribute to the fantasy that life can be perfect, that what was expected can occur, and what has been lost can be restored. Patterns of hope alternating with despair can increase both the intensity and frequency of distress that emerges from chronic sorrow conditions. Competence in dealing with chronic sorrow, as well as its recognition and understanding, will be needed far into the future.

In the future, helping professionals will face rapid shifts and expansions of technological innovations and concomitant positive and negative spinoffs. New professions will likely proliferate as a result of increased reliance on technology. Fears already exist that the United States will become more fragmented rather than multicultural. A patchwork of subgroups may appear in which the primary focus is on self-interests rather than on support and inclusion of those who are "different." As a result, grief may become a unifying force, globally and professionally. The ever-increasing numbers of support groups may serve to contain and inhibit conflicts while influencing a growing concern for others.

A sad speculation is that as the numbers of elderly grow, especially those with severe disabilities, so too will the likelihood of abuse. Professionals may need the skills of an investigator, and they will need to become more conversant in the law as it applies to diminished capacity and to abuse and violation of civil rights. Administrative competence may increase in importance in professional training as professionals take on more oversight and supervision of direct caregivers. Aspects of chronic sorrow conditions appear to be increasing. Now is the time for professionals to be tuned in and aware of all aspects of this type of grief.

Key Terms

Chronic Sorrow: An ongoing response to losses that are continual and unending in nature; the chronicity of the feelings and the ongoing nature of the loss differentiate chronic sorrow from other forms of grief.

Other-Loss: Refers to loss experiences in which vital aspects of someone we care for deeply are lost. Examples may include a loved one becoming comatose, experiencing drastic personality change, or losing oneself to severe mental illness.

Self-Loss: Losses that are focused on the change of one's identity and concept of self, such as the loss of an attribute with which one subjectively identified.

Questions for Reflection

1. Define chronic sorrow and explore what differentiates chronic sorrow from other variations of loss experiences. Additionally, why do you think awareness of chronic sorrow is important?
2. The author raises a philosophical question: "If we could not dream or fantasize, would chronic sorrow exist?" Explore your thoughts regarding this question and identify how you would answer it. Are dreams and fantasies of a different life a positive or negative experience (or both) for an individual's grieving process?
3. Provide an analysis that explores the role of self-loss or other-loss in one of the following aspects of chronic sorrow: the family identity, disability, social justice, or individual existential concerns. Furthermore, do you think there are any positive aspects that could co-occur with the experience of such devastating loss for a grieving individual?

References

Arlow, J. (1964). *Psychoanalytic concepts and structural theory*. Madison, CT: International Universities Press.

Bauby, J. (1997). *The diving bell and the butterfly*. New York: Alfred A. Knopf.

Burke, M. (1989). *Chronic sorrow in mothers of school-age children with a myelomeningocele disability*. Doctoral dissertation, Boston University.

Doka, K. (Ed.). (1989). *Disenfranchised grief: Recognizing hidden sorrow*. Lexington, MA: Lexington Books.

Doka, K., & Aber, R. (1989). Psychosocial loss and grief. In K. J. Doka (Ed.), *Disenfranchised grief: Recognizing hidden sorrow* (pp. 187–198). Lexington, MA: Lexington Books.

Eakes, G. (1995). Chronic sorrow: The lived experience of parents of chronically mentally ill Individuals. *Archives of Psychiatric Nursing, IX*, 77–84.

Elliott, C. (2016). *Ghost in my brain*. New York: Penguin/Random House.

Goffman, E. (1963). *Stigma: Notes on the management of a spoiled identity*. Englewood Cliffs, NJ: Prentice-Hall.

Kendall, L. (2005). *The experience of living with ongoing loss: Testing the Kendall chronic sorrow instrument*. Richmond, VA: Virginia Commonwealth University.

Nussbaum, M. (2006). *Frontiers of justice*. Cambridge, MA: Harvard University Press.

Olshansky, S. (1962). Chronic sorrow: A response to having a mentally defective child. *Social Casework, 43*(4), 21–23.

Olshansky, S. (1966). Parent responses to a mentally defective child. *Mental Retardation, 4*, 21–23.

Penrod, J., & Hupcey, J. (2003). Enhancing methodological clarity: Principle-based concept analysis. *Journal of Advanced Nursing, 50*(4), 403–409.

Rawls, J. (1996). *Political liberalism* (Enl. ed.). New York: Columbia University Press.

Rawls, J. (2001). *Justice as fairness: A restatement* (Ed. Erin Kelly). Cambridge, MA: Harvard University Press.

Rolland, J. (1989). Chronic illness and the family life cycle. In B. Carter & M. McGoldrick (Eds.), *The changing family life cycle: A framework for family therapy* (2nd ed.). New York: Allyn & Bacon.

Roos, S. (2002a). *Chronic sorrow: A living loss*. New York: Routledge.

Roos, S. (2002b). Chronic sorrow: Siblings of children with disabilities have needs too. *The Brown University Child and Adolescent letter, 18*(11), 1–6.

Roos, S. (2018). *Chronic sorrow: A living loss* (2nd ed.). New York: Routledge and Abingdon, Oxon, UK: Routledge.

Sem-Sandberg, S. (2014). *The chosen ones*. New York: Farrar, Straus and Giroux.

Wolfelt, A. (1998). Companioning vs. treating: Beyond the medical model of bereavement, Part 1–3. *Forum Newsletter of the Association for Death Education and Counseling, 24*, 4–6.

CHAPTER **15**

Parenting a Child With a Serious Disability
Annie Cantwell-Bartl

The grief that parents experience in supporting a child with a serious disability has many unique features. It also shares some characteristics with the grief experienced by individuals who have experienced other losses. Caring for a child with a serious disability is demanding and extends over a lifetime. It is also a privilege. The nature of the child–parent relationship in this situation is complex and does not follow the usual developmental trajectory. There is also greater-than-usual dependency and intensity within the relationship.

A range of factors influences the grief of any individual. These include a person's developmental history, relationships, styles of grieving, religious and cultural background, ethnicity, and experience of other losses. Grieving individuals also embody unique vulnerabilities and strength, all of which have an impact on their grief experiences. Grief is not only an intrapsychic response, because individuals exist within a social context (Harris, 2011; Harris & Winokuer, 2016). Within any social group, there is a dominant narrative. This dominant narrative influences how experiences are validated and also how they are interpreted (Harris, 2011).

To aid in understanding of the nature of the grief of parents of children with disabilities, I have incorporated a case study of Jennifer and Tom, a couple in their 30s. They already had a six-year-old child, Alice, when Jennifer became pregnant with baby Michael, who was born with a disability. This case study illustrates their experience, as told by Jennifer.

> We had longed for another baby. I found it hard to get pregnant again and I had four miscarriages. I came from a family where there was not much support and I hoped married life would be better. And then I lost all those babies. I felt so sad, and very few people recognized our sorrow. Our families were pretty disengaged and friends just suggested that we have another try. We felt alone. Tom did not talk much about how the losses affected him. In contrast, I talked a great deal, but I felt very few people wanted to listen. We wondered whether we would ever have another baby. Finally, I was pregnant again, and we were delighted. Our obstetrician told us that I was carrying a healthy child.
> When Michael was born, he was beautiful and looked strong. We celebrated and got ready to go home from the hospital. Suddenly, Michael

became blue, and the staff rushed him to the ICU (Intensive Care Unit). A cardiologist arrived. He had a business-like approach, without much feeling for us. He said our boy had a severe cardiac condition and he would need urgent surgery, or he would die. He told us that Michael would never have a healthy heart and that he would have other difficulties, and that one day Michael would die of his condition. He suggested that we should let Michael die, because he would have no quality of life and because caring for a child with such a significant disability would be too hard for us. He then said that if we decided to go ahead with surgery that we were fortunate because the hospital had quality cardiac surgeons. Finally, he added that we had to make an urgent decision about Michael's management.

We were devastated. It felt like something had torn away within me. I could hardly take in conversations and we both felt numb and overwhelmed. I was frightened and worried. We were so sad, but there was little time for sorrow. We had to organize care for our other child, let people know about Michael's condition, and make a decision about surgery. We decided that we had to give him the best chance of life and be good parents, and so we chose surgery.

We sat beside Michael's bed and watched him carefully. There was so much we had to do. We had to organize the home responsibilities and someone to walk the dog. There were doctors and other professionals to see and we had to talk to family and friends. Tom felt that he had to support me in the hospital and also deal with other demands in his day. He juggled home, hospital, and his career. We put one foot in front of another and got on with it. I do not know how we managed. In the hospital, nobody asked how we were and none of the staff talked about Michael.

Reactions like Tom and Jennifer's are common at the time of diagnosis. The diagnosis was unexpected and shocking and the parents experienced an intense wave of grief. A loss of this nature shatters the assumptive world (Harris & Gorman, 2011; Janoff-Bulman, 1992; Kauffman, 2002). It undermines the sense of how life should be and of the wished-for child. The common saying, "I don't care what gender my baby is, as long as the baby is healthy" has not manifested for these parents, and they experience deep distress. This loss, like any other type of serious loss, causes a narcissistic wound, a sense that part of the self is ripped away with the loved one (Neimeyer & Cacciatore, 2016). Grieving parents are likely to recall other life losses at this time, as is typical in any experience of grief. For Tom and Jennifer, loss was accompanied by trauma, which is common after a diagnosis of a serious condition in a child (Cantwell-Bartl & Tibballs, 2015), or in parents when a child is in the ICU (Cantwell-Bartl & Tibballs, 2013; Nelson & Gold, 2012; Ularntinon et al., 2010). Jennifer and Tom were numb, flooded with emotion, and hypervigilant, all symptoms of traumatic stress.

After any loss, individuals respond in the style that they have learned over the course of their lives. They have learned a style that is adaptive, even though it may not be the most effective or healthy way of responding to loss. Accordingly, Jennifer talked about her grief and Tom withdrew. Jennifer did not elaborate on this difference and the impact on her, but it could have been a cause of tension in their relationship. Not all parents who have a child with a disability have an initial loss and trauma trajectory like Jennifer and Tom's. Sometimes, parents have a sense that there is something not right in their child before the diagnosis, and the news can bring both grief and relief. Jennifer and Tom received little soothing and support. The cardiologist was not empathetic and other health professionals were preoccupied. There was little wider support for them.

Whatever the time of the diagnosis, parents of children with disabilities need empathetic care and a holding space (Winnicott, 1960), humane presence, attention, and someone to bear witness to their pain (Neimeyer, 2012a). The experience for Jennifer and Tom was that the focus was on the baby, leaving them emotionally isolated. The parents felt grief for their imperfect baby (Barnett, Clements, Kaplan-Estrin, & Fialka, 2003), and their grief was disenfranchised (Doka, 2002), just as it was after the miscarriages.

The Dual Process Model (Stroebe & Schut, 1999, 2010), a contemporary model of grieving, can serve as a guiding reference in understanding the parents' grieving. The model has been demonstrated to be helpful for parents whose child has a disability (Cantwell-Bartl, 2018). The theory holds that the most effective adaptation to loss involves an oscillation between stressors and coping processes: Loss orientation and restoration orientation (see also Chapter 1 in this volume for application of the Dual Process Model to non-death loss experiences). Loss orientation refers to the concentration on and coping with the stress of the loss, including grief-related feelings and behaviors. Restoration orientation coping refers to efforts to adjust to changed circumstances, new roles, and new challenges (Stroebe & Schut, 1999, 2010). Where one orientation alone is emphasized, complicated grief responses (including attachment difficulties) can result (Stroebe & Schut, 2010).

Early in a child's life after a diagnosis, parents have little time for grief. They experience an immediate wave of grief, but it is unprocessed and bypassed, and they concentrate on restoration coping. This mode of parental coping, with a restoration emphasis, does not indicate unhealthy grieving, because this mode is necessary to deal with the many tasks. Further, it has been demonstrated that short-term avoidance can be adaptive (Shear, 2010), allowing for a gradual integration of painful information (Bowlby, 1980).

> After some days, Michael had surgery. It was a dreadful experience and we did not know if he would survive. At home, we curled up in a fetal position on the couch. When we returned to the hospital to see him, we could hardly speak, as we were too overwhelmed. The surgeon told us that things went well, but Michael was still seriously ill. In the ICU, he looked dreadful. My beautiful baby was surrounded by tubes and he had a huge cut on his chest. I could see his beating heart. No parent should see that. I could not bear to leave Michael in case they hurt him again and in fear that he would die.
>
> In the days that followed, I felt that we were on the margins and had no part in our baby's care. Michael gradually recovered from his surgery

> and after a few weeks was discharged to the ward. It was a bit better there, but I still felt that I had no personal time with him, and the nurses were in charge of his care. I felt that he belonged to them and not to us. I do not know how we managed. We just kept going. As the weeks went by our friends stopped coming to see us. It wasn't fair that we were still in the hospital. Tom and I should have been at home with our healthy baby. No one asked about us.
>
> Michael was in hospital for many months. Tom went back to work and I had to deal with the staff. Tom felt that he had to be strong and silent, so I could lean on him. I wanted to talk, which was hard for him. I still felt keyed up and found it hard to absorb what the doctors were telling me. At times, I would cry in bed at night. When I felt very sad, I would look out and see the stars, and then I felt some hope.

Jennifer and Tom continued to experience waves of grief. Restoration tasks continued to have priority, as expressed though positive thinking, or in completing the many demands that needed attention, or, for Jennifer, in directly supporting Michael. Restoration and loss sometimes merged in the manifestation of their grief; for example, when sorrow was intermingled with hope. It is likely that Jennifer and Tom had traumatic stress symptoms throughout their baby's time in the ICU. There were many stresses for them, and trauma takes priority over the processing of grief.

Throughout their time in the hospital, parents need intervention that assists with stress reduction. This includes basic, clear information, practical support, understanding, and the opportunity to rediscuss information. This is not a time for complex psychological interventions, and parents do not have the personal resources to engage in these. The parents' traumatic stress symptoms need to be addressed before they can process grief.

> It was a huge relief to get Michael home. I felt very anxious. I worried that I would not be able to care for him and that he would die. Sometimes I would feel sad but then he would smile, and I would delight in him.
>
> The first twelve months were very demanding, and he needed to be tube-fed as he was not strong enough to feed normally. At home, I bonded with him more deeply. I could hold him, sing to him and enjoy him. He became "our baby." I learned a great deal about his care. My grief would sometimes break through and I would cry unexpectedly. I began to sleep a lot better, and so did Tom. Tom did not show his grief as much, but sometimes after putting Michael to bed, I could tell he had been crying.

The parents felt safer at home, with fewer traumatic stimuli and Michael was more stable. They experienced a more normal oscillation between the two domains of coping, and at times joy and sorrow manifested together. The couple grieved in a healthy manner. In their grieving, Tom and Jennifer manifested some gender-specific coping responses. Men frequently control their emotions (Schwab, 1996), bypass feelings, and believe that they need to be strong for their partners, as the wider societal narrative dictates.

> There was very little practical help. I think some people thought that Michael was contagious. At times, I struggled emotionally. I became alarmed if I heard an ambulance outside. We had no money because I could not go back to work and it was hard to pay the bills. A woman at the local financial aid office said that because Michael was healthy and could walk, we did not need help or financial assistance. I could not believe her insensitivity. I got angry and I heard that she told her colleagues that my anger was all about my grief. It was not about my grief, it was unfairness; and then I would feel more loss and more stress. We had to fight for everything.
>
> At school, we discovered that Michael had learning problems and he developed some difficult behaviors. Sometimes he had tantrums because he found the schoolwork hard. When it was time for holidays, if we went away, it had to be organized like a military operation, to make sure that things were suitable for him. We don't see many of our old friends. New friends can be compassionate, but very few offer to help. There are always issues in our lives. Sorrows go on. I think I live with ongoing exhaustion.

Jennifer described the way her traumatic stress symptoms were re-aroused by disturbing stimuli such as the sound of an ambulance. New losses also emerged, such as Michael's learning difficulties. The response of the wider social world had a significant impact on Jennifer and Tom's life and adjustment. When parents have a child with a disability, they move to the margins of the mainstream social group and the dominant societal narrative of productivity and functionality (Harris & Winokuer, 2016). The child is also marginalized because his or her developmental progress is different from what is considered normal. Marginalization then affects how their experiences are understood or validated by others, which has an impact on the availability of external resources (Harris & Winokuer, 2016). Parents often find that external resources and assistance are inadequate. Parents need to soothe, protect, and relate sensitively to the child (Winnicott, 1960). They are best able to do this when they are well cared for themselves (Winnicott, 1960). Disconnection from the mainstream disrupts security and safety (Harris, 2011) and can result in powerlessness and despair (Harris & Gorman, 2011).

> Alice, our other child, has always been a good girl and a great help, but I worried about the impact on her. I think she gets embarrassed about having a brother with a disability. My family has disappeared, and friends will say, "Is he better now?" I cannot stand it, and I just say, "Yes." I talk to a few people who care about me, but it is lonely. Tom listens without saying much. Sometimes I hear him yelling at the dog, and I think, "Poor old dog." No one has ever offered us family counseling.
>
> I am not always conscious of grief, but sometimes it hits me unexpectedly. I grieve for the healthy little boy that I thought was coming. I grieve for what

we have lost and I grieve for Michael and the losses that surround his life as well. I feel sad for the many things that have not been right about my life. I know when Tom is hurting. I see him struggling at the park when he sees that Michael cannot join in the rough-and-tumble play.

I am with Michael most of the day. Sometimes I think it is unfair that I do not get a break. It feels like we are standing on the outside of the world looking in, because our family is different. On occasions, Tom and I hold each other in our sadness, but at other times, I wonder about Tom's grief. He has spoken more about his grief now than he did in the early days.

In spite of all of these hardships, we love Michael deeply. I have learned many new skills. I think about how much strength I have found in myself and I feel good about how we have managed. Although the doctor said that we would have no quality of life supporting Michael, we have many good times. I do not know how long Michael will be with us, but I am glad we have the opportunity of loving him. I have always been a compassionate person, but now I am much more aware of others who are struggling. Caring for Michael has been very hard, and will remain hard. However, I feel proud of what we have achieved and proud of Michael and what he endures. He is a role model for some people and he is a lovely boy.

Having a child with a disability in the family affects all family members. It is common for the siblings of a child with a disability to be well behaved, because these siblings understand that their parents have much to deal with. Some siblings, on the other hand, become defiant and angry because their parents' attention is directed to the child with the disability.

There were many new losses for Jennifer and Tom. These involved ones of depleted finances, the impact on Alice, Michael's behavioral difficulties, and their social isolation, along with many others. Their experience is one of non-finite loss (Bruce & Schultz, 1998; Schultz & Harris, 2011), a phenomenon of ongoing, enduring loss where loss retains an presence over a lifetime (Bruce & Schultz, 2001). Their losses also include intangible losses, such as a loss of hopes and dreams (Bruce & Schultz, 2001). Michael will continually miss normal developmental milestones, and it is uncertain what the future will entail (Harris & Gorman, 2011). Most of the losses experienced by Jennifer and Tom were unknown or unrecognized by others. This can result in the phenomenon termed *chronic sorrow*, which has been regarded as a normal consequence of having a child with a disability (Olshansky, 1966; Coughlin & Sethares, 2017).

In spite of the difficulties of living with and supporting Michael, Jennifer described many positive experiences. This phenomenon contrasts with the common perception that having a child with a disability is tragic, awful, and/or pathological (Goddard, Lehr, & Lapadat, 2000). This one-dimensional attitude, which is based on stereotypes, adds another level of difficulty for parents (Goddard et al., 2000). Although these phenomena may manifest in some parents, or manifest on occasions, overall the picture is more robust, nuanced, and complex. Many parents make sense of their child's disability (Goddard et al., 2000), straddling joy and pain, demonstrating profound resilience. Many engage in meaning reconstruction. This is a phenomenon where after a loss, people find new ways of living (Neimeyer, 2012b, 2016), or renewed strength and wisdom (Maas, 2008). Some parents even experience post-traumatic growth (PTG; Bonanno, 2004; Gorman, 2011; Tedeschi & Calhoun, 2004), where individuals who have known trauma are able to rebound, or demonstrate what has been described as *ordinary* magic (Masten, 2001). This resilience and growth is common in parents of children with disabilities (Pelchat, Levert, & Bourgeois-Guérin, 2009), reflecting the vitality of the human spirit and the strength of love in parents.

The portrait of Jennifer and Tom demonstrates the importance of recognizing the grieving journey traveled by parents of children with disabilities. There are many parallels between this grief and the grief experienced by individuals in response to other types of losses. However, this grief has some unique features, too. For Jennifer and Tom, there was an initial wave of grief in response to the diagnosis, but restoration tasks were soon emphasized, and grieving bypassed. The parents needed to negotiate many demands in supporting the baby and the family, and this points to the value of short-term grief avoidance (Shear, 2010).

Jennifer and Tom's loss was interwoven with trauma, as is common in this cohort (Cantwell-Bartl & Tibballs, 2015), and a loss of this nature shatters the assumptive world (Harris, 2011; Janoff-Bulman, 1992; Kauffman, 2002).

When Jennifer and Tom returned home with their baby, their symptoms of traumatic stress were reduced. They had more resources and time for grieving, and they undertook a more normal oscillation between the two modalities of loss and restoration. At times, these modes intermingled. In spite of this oscillation, the emphasis upon restoration remained. Grief emerged in waves. The parents employed a dynamic activity of proximity regulation (Hooghe, Neimeyer, & Rober, 2012), where they circled around their pain and moved towards and away from it, as the grief over their losses was juxtaposed with adaptation to these same losses. This juxtaposition resulted in a titration of pain and allowed for a gradual integration of loss over time (Bowlby, 1980). Some events could provoke traumatic stress symptoms once again, but it was not a constant.

Although Tom and Jennifer had done well, some of their grieving was yet to be negotiated. Michael was alive and there was much to do. Adding to the burden, new losses appeared. The parents had limited time to consider their grief, and restoration coping continued to be strong but sat beside waves of grief. Later in the lives of these parents, the interval between the two domains of coping lengthens. Waves of grief will always emerge in response to loss awareness, but adaptation means that parents are not as raw, and there is a longer period of restoration before a wave of grief appears. Parents experience nonfinite loss and some features of *ambiguous loss* (Boss, 1999; Boss, Roos, & Harris, 2011). They live with many stresses and exhaustion. In time, most parents do well, adapt, and are resilient.

Parents need support over time, and their grief needs validation and understanding. They need to live within a caring community supported by a range of health professionals who will advocate for them and assist them in constructive and meaningful ways. Finally, parents need to feel that their loving commitment to their child has brought richness and strength to the community.

Clinical Implications

1. Early in the child's life after the diagnosis, think psychological first aid and strategies to help the parents feel safe. Think solid support, assistance with the tasks of living, and practical help. Always offer warmth, care, and understanding.
2. In the early time, parents will be in restoration mode, organizing life issues and care of the child. Allow the parent to choose what s/he would like to talk about, rather than setting an agenda involving grief.
3. As parents become more settled, they are likely to experience and express more grief. Be alert for this.
4. Assess whether parents are experiencing traumatic stress symptoms, and, if these symptoms are present, validate and educate the parents about these symptoms. Offer strategies that may assist with reduction in traumatic symptoms. They will need to talk about their trauma and feel safe before they will be able to speak comprehensively about their grief.
5. Be mindful of the wider picture of the parents' functioning and learnings over time, including the presence of other, additional losses. Assess previous life losses.
6. Ask about the wider societal influences in their lives, and ask how well supported they are. It is common for these parents to be emotionally or socially isolated, or both.
7. Advocate for wider psychosocial supports for them, or help them to find these supports, including financial support, respite, home help, child minding, and leisure activities.
8. Assess their experience of how the wider world relates to and treats them. This is likely to be another source of loss.
9. Listen for chronic sorrow and normalize their reactions to the ongoing loss experience.
10. Be mindful of the grief of fathers and assess the impact on the couple of different manifestations of the expression of grief.
11. Inquire about other family members. Ask about the impact of the child's disability on the extended family, and the presence or absence of child care. Think about their needs and offer supportive referrals if desired.
12. Listen for break-through traumatic stress symptoms and provide strategies for their remediation if present.
11. Be mindful of the complex picture of grief and strength in these parents and create a space where they can talk about new losses and taboo feelings, such as ambivalence about the child, anger that this has happened, and even at times wishing that the child would die.
12. Listen for strength, adaptation, resilience, and committed loving.
13. Be open to what you can learn from these parents.

14. Affirm the valuable contribution that parents make in caring for their child with a disability, in a society that affirms many contrary values.

Key Terms

Disability: An attribute that affects a person's life that could be developmental, sensory, physical, cognitive, intellectual, or some combination of these. The experience of disability is unique to each person, and it substantially affects a person's life activities.

Traumatic Stress: An overwhelming reaction which consists of intense emotions and physical responses to a deeply distressing or disturbing experience that is often sudden, unexpected, violent, disfiguring, and/or out of normal expectation.

Post-Traumatic Growth: The potential that individuals can have for transformation after exposure to trauma, highly stressful events, and/or crises.

Questions for Reflection

1. The case study of Jennifer and Tom in this chapter illustrates how they both felt alone in their grief. What might hinder people's ability to provide grief support to a friend or family member who was the parent of a child with a serious disability? How would it be possible to overcome or change these hindrances?
2. In terms of clinical implications, the author posits strategies for supporting the grief of a parent who has a child with a serious disability. Provide a reflection on three of these strategies and offer a further analysis on how these chosen approaches could be conducive in supporting the grieving process. Additionally, create and share your own clinical suggestion that would aid the grief process in respect to parenting a child with a disability.
3. Investigate the unique aspects surrounding the loss experiences shared in this chapter. How do these loss experiences shape one's grief? Furthermore, how can post-traumatic growth alter one's perceptions of these losses?
4. Consider the social and cultural context surrounding developmental milestones. How are parents and children with disabilities affected when developmental milestones are not achieved? What is the relationship between the notion of "normal," marginalization, and grief?

References

Barnett, D., Clements, M., Kaplan-Estrin, M., & Fialka, J. (2003). Building new dreams: Supporting parents' adaptation to their child with special needs. *Infants and Young Children, 16*(3), 184–200.

Bonanno, G. A. (2004). Loss, trauma, and human resilience: Have we underestimated the human capacity to thrive after extremely aversive events? *American Psychologist, 59*, 20–28.

Boss, P. (1999). *Ambiguous loss: Learning to live with unresolved grief.* Cambridge, MA: Harvard University Press.

Boss, P., Roos, S., & Harris, D. L. (2011). Grief in the midst of ambiguity and uncertainty: An exploration of ambiguous loss and chronic sorrow. In R. A. Neimeyer, D. L. Harris, H. R. Winokuer, & G. F. Thornton (Eds.), *Grief and bereavement in contemporary society: Bridging research and practice*. New York: Routledge.

Bowlby, J. (1980). *Loss, sadness and depression*. New York: Basic.

Bruce, E., & Schultz, C. (1998). Grieving nonfinite loss. *Journal of Family Studies*, 4(2), 215–220.

Bruce, E., & Schultz, C. (2001). *Nonfinite loss and grief*. Baltimore: Paul H. Brookes.

Cantwell-Bartl, A. M. (2018). The grief and coping of parents whose child has a constant life-threatening disability, Hypoplastic Left Heart Syndrome, with reference to the Dual Process Model. *Death Studies*, 42(9), 569–578.

Cantwell-Bartl, A. M., & Tibballs, J. (2013). Psychosocial experiences of parents of infants with hypoplastic left heart syndrome in the PICU. *Pediatric Critical Care Medicine*, 14(9), 869–875.

Cantwell-Bartl, A. M., & Tibballs, J. (2015). Psychosocial responses of parents to their infant's diagnosis of hypoplastic left heart syndrome. *Cardiology in the Young*, 25(6), 1065–1073.

Coughlin, M. B., & Sethares, K. A. (2017). Chronic sorrow in parents of children with a chronic illness or disability: An integrative literature review. *Journal Pediatric Nursing*, 37, 108–116.

Doka, K. J. (Ed.) (2002). *Disenfranchised grief: New directions, challenges, and strategies for practice*. Champaign, IL: Research Press.

Goddard, J. A., Lehr, R., & Lapadat, J. C. (2000). Parents of children with disabilities: Telling a different story. *Canadian Journal of Counselling*, 34(4), 273–289.

Gorman, E. (2011). Adaptation, resilience and growth after loss. In D. L. Harris (Ed.), *Counting our losses: Reflecting on change, loss, and transition in everyday life* (pp. 225–237). New York: Routledge.

Harris, D. L. (Ed.). (2011). *Counting our losses: Reflecting on change, loss and transition in everyday life*. New York: Routledge.

Harris, D. L., & Gorman, E. (2011). Grief from a broader perspective: Nonfinite loss, ambiguous loss and chronic sorrow. In D. L. Harris (Ed.), *Counting our losses: Reflecting on change, loss and transition in everyday life* (pp. 1–14). New York: Routledge.

Harris, D. L., & Winokuer, H. R. (2016). *Principles and practice of grief counselling* (2nd ed.). New York: Springer.

Hooghe, A., Neimeyer, R. A., & Rober, P. (2012). Cycling around an emotional core of sadness: Emotional regulation in a couple after the loss of a child. *Qualitative Health Research*. doi:10.1177/1049732312449209

Janoff-Bulman, R. (1992). *Shattered Assumptions: Towards a new psychology of trauma*. New York: Free Press.

Kauffman, J. (2002). *Loss of the assumptive world: A theory of traumatic loss*. New York: Brunner: Routledge.

Maas, V. S. (2008). *Lifestyle changes: A clinician's guide to common events, challenges, and options*. New York: Routledge.

Masten, A. S. (2001). Ordinary magic: Resilience process in development. *American Psychologist*, 56(3), 227–238.

Neimeyer, R. A. (2012a). Presence, process and procedure: A relational frame for technical proficiency in grief therapy. In R. A. Neimeyer (Ed.), *Techniques of grief therapy: Creative practices for counseling the bereaved* (pp. Part 1, Chapter 1). New York: Routledge.

Neimeyer, R. A. (2012b). *Techniques of grief therapy: Creative practices for counseling the bereaved.* New York: Routledge.

Neimeyer, R. A. (2016). *Techniques of grief therapy: Assessment and intervention.* New York: Routledge.

Neimeyer, R. A., & Cacciatore, J. (2016). Towards a developmental theory of grief. In R. A. Neimeyer (Ed.), *Techniques of grief therapy: Assessment and intervention* (p. 5). New York: Routledge.

Nelson, L. P., & Gold, J. I. (2012). Posttraumatic stress disorder in children and their parents following admission to the pediatric intensive care unit: A review. *Pediatric Critical Care Medicine, 13*(3), 338–347.

Olshansky, S. (1966). Parent responses to a mentally defective child. *Mental Retardation, 4*(4), 21–23.

Pelchat, D., Levert, M., & Bourgeois-Guérin, V. (2009). How do mothers and fathers who have a child with a disability describe their adaptation/transformation process? *Journal of Child Health Care, 13*(3), 239–259.

Schultz, C., & Harris, D. L. (2011). Giving voice to nonfinite loss and grief in bereavement. In R. A. Neimeyer, D. L. Harris, H. Winokuer, & G. F. Thornton (Eds.), *Grief and bereavement in contemporary society: Bridging research and practice* (pp. 235–287). New York: Routledge.

Schwab, R. (1996). Gender differences in parental grief. *Death Studies, 20*(2), 103–113.

Shear, M. K. (2010). Exploring the role of experiential avoidance from the perspective of attachment theory and the Dual Process mode. *Omega: The Journal of Death and Dying, 61*(4), 359–371.

Stroebe, M., & Schut, H. (1999). The Dual Process Model of coping with bereavement: Rationale and description. *Death Studies, 23,* 197–224.

Stroebe, M., & Schut, H. (2010). The Dual Process Model of coping with bereavement: A decade on. *Omega: The Journal of Death & Dying, 61*(4), 273–289.

Tedeschi, R., & Calhoun, L. (2004). Posttraumatic growth: Conceptual foundations and empirical evidence. *Psychological Inquiry, 15*(1), 1–18.

Ularntinon, S., Bernard, R., Wren, F., St. John, N., Horwitz, S., & Shaw, R. (2010). Traumatic stress reactions in parents in pediatric intensive care: A review. *Current Psychiatry Reviews, 6*(4), 261–268.

Winnicott, D. (1960). The theory of the parent-infant relationship. *International Journal of Psychoanalysis, 41*(41), 585–595.

CHAPTER 16

Environmental Grief

Kriss A. Kevorkian

Introduction

Between the years of 1965 and 1975, teams of men were sent to Penn Cove, Washington, to capture Southern Resident Orcas, also known as *Orcinus Orca*, that would be displayed for exhibition and entertainment in marine parks. Due to the harrowing capture of the orcas, the population of all three Southern Resident pods, J, K, and L, was reduced. At least 13 orcas were killed during these captures, while 45 orcas were delivered to marine parks around the world. Today, only Lolita (Tokitae) remains alive in captivity at the Miami Seaquarium (Center for Whale Research, n.d a). Since the orcas were captured, the population has never fully rebounded. According to the Center for Whale Research, in 1995, the total of all three pods was at its highest with 95 orcas (n.d. a). At the time this chapter was written, only 76 orcas remained.

In 2017, Howard Garrett, Co-founder, Director, and President of the Board of the Orca Network, read a letter at the annual Penn Cove Orca Capture Anniversary Commemoration from a community member who lived in the area during the time the Southern Resident Orcas were being captured. In the letter, the community member recalled the "screaming" from the older Southern Resident Orcas that could be heard all over Whidbey Island. The young Southern Resident Orcas were corralled into a sea pen while nets held the older adults back. It was traumatizing to hear, let alone see, what was being done to the orcas. Like those in the audience listening to Mr. Garrett read the letter, I was sobbing by the time he ended the letter and announced, "And now we will hear from Dr. Kriss A. Kevorkian who will speak about environmental grief."

The orca, Tokitae, now about 50 years old, remains the last known survivor of the group of more than 50 orcas that were captured 47 years ago. Since her mate died of a brain aneurysm in 1980, she has become the only solitary orca in captivity, where she lives in the smallest orca tank in the nation (Herrera, 2017). Groups of people around the world have been holding vigils to bring awareness of Tokitae's plight to those in power, in the hope that one day soon she will be returned to her native waters in the Salish Sea (Mapes, 2018). The Lummi People (Lhaq'temish), the original inhabitants of the northernmost coast of Washington and southern

British Columbia, have been working with the Orca Network to bring Tokitae back to her home in the Salish Sea so that she can be with her pod.

When Mr. Garrett learned about environmental grief, he shared, "I thought it was a bold new concept that was absolutely appropriate and needed in today's world." When I began my lifelong research into the realities of environmental grief in 2001, I felt as though I was the only one reacting to the phenomenon. Today, I rarely run into someone who isn't reacting to environmental grief, no matter whether that person is a scientist, lawyer, and/or layperson. So many people feel it as we see our planet being abused and diseased to no end.

Environmental Grief

Environmental grief is the grief reaction stemming from the environmental loss of ecosystems caused by either natural or human-made events (Kevorkian, 2004). It builds upon the concept of disenfranchised grief (see Chapter 2 in this volume) because it is not openly acknowledged or accepted in society (Doka, 2002). Pet loss is an example of this form of grief. Imagine telling your boss that you need time off because your animal companion died. We still have difficulty getting time off to grieve for human loved ones, let alone non-human ones. Some people believe that those of us who care for the planet threaten to endanger economic activity, but we're people passionate about protecting the beauty of nature as well as green spaces, clean water, and healthy air to breathe. It's hard to believe that there are cities in the United States where corporations have the right to spray pesticides so close to homes that not only cause human inhabitants to become ill but so, too, do the animals and plants (Gluckich, 2018). In Flint, Michigan, people must purchase drinking water because their own water is no longer safe to drink (Buncombe, 2018). These are just a few examples of the harsh realities that provoke environmental grief in those who experience or witness them.

My original research on environmental grief included interviewing scientists and conservationists utilizing the heuristic method to better understand their perceptions of people's experience of this phenomenon, as well as society's reaction to the idea of environmental grief (Kevorkian, 2004). I chose to focus on one species for my study: the Southern Resident Orcas in the Salish Sea. These are a unique species of orcas who have a distinct dialect from others and primarily eat Chinook salmon. According to the Center for Whale Research, current threats to the Southern Resident Orcas include:

- Reduced quantity and quality of prey (Chinook/King/Spring salmon).
- High environmental levels of persistent biochemicals, such as PCBs and flame retardants, that have known harmful effects on marine mammals (e.g., immune system repression and reproductive system dysfunction).
- Sound and disturbance from vessel traffic and shipping.
- Potential oil spills and the damage that these spills cause to waterways and the wildlife that are dependent upon them (Center for Whale Research, n.d. b).

Sadly, due to the ever-increasing amount of environmental destruction today, more and more people are experiencing environmental grief, as evidenced by the increasing appearance of peer support groups in various environmental organizations. One such organization is 350.org, an international action-based organization built on the work of Bill McKibben, an environmental activist, educator, and author. Although such groups might not explicitly use the term "environmental grief," they are beginning to recognize the phenomenon, even if they haven't named it yet.

During my initial research on environmental grief, one interviewee stated that I "put a name to a vague feeling" she'd had. "It was like when we learned about PTSD. You put a name to it, and now I can move on because I know what it is" (Kevorkian, 2004). Oftentimes, when an experience is labeled or named, a certain validation comes with it. People want to know that what they are feeling is real, valid, and acknowledged. The #MeToo movement has empowered victims of sexual assault and/or harassment to self-identify. Attaching a diagnosis to symptoms empowers people by enabling them to seek out information as well as support from fellow sufferers and medical professionals, which was not easily accessed before their condition had a name. The act of naming brings validation and a feeling that one is not alone (Thomas, 2017). When discussing environmental grief, those who are dealing with its repercussions no longer feel alone; support can be easily found, and action-based coping skills can develop. Understanding environmental grief also allows individuals to gather in associations that can lobby for policy changes that may help.

Nature as Healer

Richard Louv writes about our need for nature in the tech-filled, fast-paced world we live in. His book, *Last Child in the Woods: Saving Our Children from Nature-Deficit Disorder* (Louv, 2005), was the first book to discuss the benefits of nature on childhood development and child and adult mental, physical, and emotional health. Louv coined the term *nature deficit disorder* in that book, explaining that children are spending more time with technology and less time out in nature, which has detrimental effects on their health and well-being:

> Reducing that deficit—healing the broken bond between our young and nature—is in our self-interest, not only because aesthetics or justice demands it, but also because our mental, physical, and spiritual health depends upon it. The health of the earth is at stake as well. How the young respond to nature, and how they raise their own children, will shape the configurations and conditions of our cities, homes—our daily lives
>
> (Louv, 2005, p. 3).

I am not alone in thinking that nature can shape well-being. In "The Blue Mind Rx: Wild Waters Can Be Lifelong Medicine for All People," Wallace Nichols (2016) includes a list of information about the importance of "wild water" and adds, "Research shows that nature is therapeutic, promotes general health and well-being, and blue space in both urban and rural settings further enhances and broadens cognitive, emotional, psychological, social, physical, and spiritual benefits." We know the health benefits of being in nature, which is one reason why it is important to fight so hard to protect it.

When nature flourishes, all living species thrive. Nature provides respite and healing, and it enhances the mental and physical health of people. It is part of many people's spiritual traditions and awareness. In fact, one challenge that arises in counseling people reacting to environmental grief is that we often suggest that people go out in nature, either to take a walk in the park or just get some fresh air. But what happens when that special place in nature has been destroyed or the animals you once saw daily are now gone? How does one cope? Counselors have found guided imagery to be helpful for people who have experienced trauma in all its forms. When counseling a client dealing with environmental grief, a counselor can guide the client to that beautiful place s/he used to love, no matter how it might look today. People can draw strength from that session by recalling what once was to what it is today, spurring them to continue to "protect" what remains.

Implications for Counselors

When counseling people who are experiencing environmental grief, it is important, as with all forms of counseling, that the client is heard. Ethical expectations compel us to see any client's personal beliefs as a cultural aspect of their identity. Religious or spiritual beliefs, ethnic traditions, and social identities; counselors must be fluent and respectful when working with people who hold diverse value systems. Just as there are differences in the type and degree of religious beliefs among different people, there are also differences in the type and degree of attitudes held toward the earth and its ecosystems. Counseling must respect the client's belief and value systems, even when they differ significantly from those of the counselor. When environmental views are seen and understood as an aspect of culture when working with someone dealing with complex issues who needs to be heard, respected, and provided with a safe space to share feelings, then we aspire towards competency.

In the past, mass extinctions were caused by forces outside of human control. However, research shows that 99% of the species today that are threatened are considered at risk only because of humans (Center for Biological Diversity, n.d.). Among the growing list of environmental atrocities, humans have destroyed habitats, causing an increase rate of change in our biosphere. Because of this increase, and because every species' extinction potentially leads to the extinction of others bound to that species in a complex ecological web, numbers of extinctions are likely to snowball in the coming decades as ecosystems unravel (Center for Biological Diversity, n.d.).

Today, one could research any number of environmental issues or animal species in decline and come to the same conclusion that environmental grief is real and needs to be acknowledged and discussed. Hydraulic fracturing, also known as fracking, is a timely and precise example of such an environmental issue. Fracking is damaging land, causing earthquakes, and polluting water in many communities, causing serious health threats to people, livestock, and wildlife (Hoffman, 2018).

People dealing with fracking in their communities are seeing the destruction of their homes due to floods, wildfires, and earthquakes. Consider those individuals who are doing all they can to protect the land and/or water, and the valve turners willing to go to prison to stop the flow of oil. These people need support and empathy.

> The Climate Psychology Alliance (CPA) works with individuals who connect depth psychology and climate change, as we all face the difficult truths of climate change and ecological crisis. Central to the vision behind CPA is that we are seeking to place human science alongside natural science in the cause of ecologically informed living, through understanding and facing difficult truths.
> (Climate Psychology Alliance, n.d.)

Environmental grief and nature deficit disorder may not be mental or physical health diagnoses according to official diagnostic definitions or categories. Yet, many mental health and health care providers do counsel clients to seek health-enhancing activities in natural settings, to get away from their phones and computers and experience peaceful settings. Clients who spend time in nature reduce stress and enhance healing. Thus, there is an inherent acknowledgment that nature enriches our lives. Recommendations from professionals acknowledge the value of nature.

Call to Action

The reactions we experience to the environmental destruction, decimation, and ecocide that we see in our world today signal a call to action. One feels those reactions profoundly, and rather than allowing ourselves to suffer in silence, we empower ourselves when we move into action. Actions undertaken that heal complicated feelings of loss coupled with those that prevent further loss of the environment are optimal.

We understand that first responders, along with medical and mental health professionals, are at risk of compassion fatigue, vicarious trauma, burnout, and even post-traumatic stress due to the work they do. The same can be said for people who are reacting to environmental grief, whether on the front lines as protectors or those who are doing what they can from the safety of their own home. At the same time, there seems to be an increase in rhetoric, policies, and laws that are removing what environmental protections that have existed in the United States.

Alongside the increase in rhetoric is an increase in media attention and awareness to the damage that is occurring. Travel websites have articles on places to see before they disappear (Rough Guides, 2018). Downloadable images and photos on news websites show us the damage done to the environment and the differences before and after regulations protected it, and there is an increasing number of environmental documentaries available for streaming and in theaters. Environmental grief is not just for environmental activists anymore. People can readily see the dire consequences of environmental destruction on the places they love or want to visit.

At some point in the coming years, environmental grief may no longer be considered a form of disenfranchised grief. If that is the case, societies will have to make serious changes to how we choose to live and consume. We've known for more than half a century that we need to stop our addiction to oil, stop our overconsumption, and stop allowing corporations to pollute our planet. Sadly, those warnings have often fallen on deaf ears. Even though many of us have done the best we can, we cannot stop now. Progress, as we see, can be overturned by a new administration in power, which adds another level of grief to the mix. For now, we can identify environmental grief as one that holds in its innermost complexities the seeds of activism, which alone and collectively will help heal the planet and all its inhabitants.

Vicarious Trauma

The continual witnessing of the destruction, on film or firsthand, can result in vicarious trauma reactions. For some, stress from witnessing, seeing, and/or hearing stories of traumatic events or suffering, can come from watching a documentary like *Blackfish* (Oteyza & Cowperthwaite, 2013) about orcas kept in captivity. *Racing Extinction* (Stevens & Ahnemann, 2015) brought tears to many viewers in the audience. There are multiple, powerfully intense graphic scenes in the documentary. One particularly intense graphic scene in this documentary shows sharks with their fins cut off who are tossed back into the water where, unable to propel themselves forward, they gasp for air and drown. *The Messenger* (Jackson, Blake, Woods, & de la Fouchardiere, 2015), a documentary about birds, discusses the number of migrating birds dying due to pesticide use in the United States that is devastating for not just birds, but also the planet, and people. Media can affect viewers as deeply as seeing destruction occurring firsthand.

Laura Van Dernoot Lipsky (2002) came up with the term *trauma stewardship*. She defines the term as "a daily practice through which individuals, organizations, and societies tend to the hardship, pain, or trauma experienced by humans, other living beings, or our planet itself" (p. 11). She suggests we remain in the present, as she cites the work of Zen Master Thích Nhất Hạnh:

> We need enlightenment, not just individually but collectively, to save the planet. We need to awaken ourselves. We need to practice mindfulness if we want to have a future, if we want to save ourselves and the planet.
>
> (Hanh, n.d.)

It isn't always easy to identify the depth of an individual's experience of environmental grief. For the practitioner, accurate identification of the depth of trauma requires both the science of psychology and the art of caring.

> People who experience trauma do not always present to mental health professionals with symptoms of post-traumatic stress disorder... People frequently continue to live beyond the traumatic incidents and make adaptations in

their daily lives. Often the adaptation, rather than the trauma, is what brings a client in for services.

(Kaplan, 2007, p. 143)

Mental health professionals may look for a specific trauma event, as guided by standard diagnostic procedures.

Insidious Trauma

Trauma is often *not* limited to a single identifiable incident. For example, members of oppressed groups experience incidents of trauma, and they also experience the insidious trauma in daily life—news reports of violence against group members, denial of housing, public harassment, social institutions, and their representatives backing discriminatory policies (Kaplan, 2007). Therefore, considerations about the destruction of the environment, loss of nature, extinction of species, and threats against others are all ongoing traumatic experiences for those who seek solace in nature. The day-to-day media coverage of the effects of climate change, legislators' denial of the damage or causes of destruction, photos and videos, and even the sales pitches to "travel now before they are gone" are examples of these traumatic stressors.

For those people who are environmentally conscious, these stressors can be seen as examples of insidious trauma, wherein the client may present with feelings of sadness, depression, lack of energy, anger, loss of meaning, or a general sense of powerlessness or frustration in their lives. For many people, it is the insidious trauma—the ongoing reminders of the loss of their land, that they no longer can safely drink from the creek when hiking, the bare and flat mountaintop remains of coal mining, the plastics floating by in the ocean as they enjoy a vacation—that serve as reminders of environmental destruction. The sadness emerging from these experiences and the shock of seeing pictures of the remains of animals and/or forests may create a sense of loss. This is a key aspect of environmental grief—not that the loss is felt due to a specific traumatic event, but rather a slow and ongoing process of loss, a sense of what was once beautiful that brought joy is now ugly and ravaged—and it's profound. This experience fits the description of chronic sorrow, as the loss is ongoing without a foreseeable end and there are constant reminders of what has been lost and the potential of what will be lost with time (Roos, 2018).

Clinical Implications

As previously mentioned, I always thought of environmental grief as something to spur people to act. Advocacy and constructive action are appropriate and healing responses to this type of grief. When it comes to counseling, we often speak of empowering our clients to "take charge" and "take control." Let's enable, equip, and embolden ourselves to exert control over our own parts of the world. Together, we are unstoppable.

Suggestions for those reacting to environmental grief include the following:

- Purchase products produced by socially responsible companies.
- Purchase items that use less packaging.
- Before purchasing anything, consider how you will dispose of it.
- If you must purchase new, purchase items that are designed to be reused or recycled.
- Purchase used items and upcycle.
- Avoid single-use plastics such as plastic straws, water bottles, utensils, and bags.
- Talk with your friends about what you can do in your community to increase awareness of the destruction plastics and pollutants cause in our oceans and to wildlife.
- Investigate the Climate Reality Project (n.d.) (www.climaterealityproject.org) and attend a training.

These steps show clients that, though environmental grief may feel deep and insurmountable, there are things that can be done on a smaller scale that can truly make a difference on a larger scale.

When it comes to making a greater impact, organizations exist that help identify and preserve what they refer to as the "rights of nature" I learned about the rights of nature from a lecture I heard a few years ago by a community organizer through the Community Environmental Legal Defense Fund (CELDF, n.d.). I am working with CELDF and the Earth Law Center to get the rights of nature for the Salish Sea, which would include protections for the Southern Resident Orcas as well as salmon. In most countries, nature has the legal status of property. In contrast, Earth Law argues that nature has inherent rights and legally should have the same protection as people and corporations. Earth law enables the defense of the environment in court—not only for the benefit of people, but for the sake of nature itself (Lee & Bender, 2018).

In April 2018, with the help of CELDF, the Colombia Supreme Court of Justice declared that

> [the] Colombian Amazon is recognized as an entity, a subject of Rights, which includes the right to legal protection, preservation, maintenance and Restoration.
>
> (CELDF, 2018)

The rights of nature are often considered a paradigm shift in our thinking because we don't often view nature as having *personhood*. We have been taught to view nature as property. But why shouldn't nature, a living ecosystem, have rights—especially if corporations have rights of personhood? Environmentalists have been protesting and writing letters to their representatives in government, and to many public forums for decades, with limited effectiveness. Groups like CELDF forge a new path for the environment and humanity when protections are enshrined in law at whatever level of government possible. Often, momentum starts locally and, when successful, moves up to state and federal levels where the benefits to all increase exponentially.

Summary

In this chapter, a new term, environmental grief, was defined and discussed. Real-world examples illustrating causes of environmental grief were provided, as well as the implications of what this grief can mean for those who experience it, either directly or indirectly. Strategies were offered to assist counselors helping individuals coping with environmental grief. In addition, action tips were suggested for potential clients to understand there are things that can be done to heal oneself, as well as the planet. Most importantly, this chapter showed that environmental grief, once considered to be a reaction felt only by environmental activists, protectors, and conservationists, is now a reaction that more and more laypeople are experiencing. The number of people who find themselves struggling with environmental grief will increase as we continue to see those in power choose to focus their energy and attention on profits rather than look out for the health and well-being of present and future generations living on our fragile planet.

Key Terms

Environmental Grief: Grief relating to the natural world, such as the loss of ecosystems, animal life, plant life, and/or the destruction of the planet.

Insidious Trauma: A state in which ongoing and less-intensive traumatic incidents begin to add up, creating significant feelings of loss that have no foreseeable conclusion (can be categorized under chronic sorrow).

Nature Deficit Disorder: This concept posits that children are spending less time outdoors, which is disadvantageous and causes harm to human health.

Vicarious Trauma: A state of tension in which an individual can become overwhelmed and preoccupied by bearing witness to intense emotional experiences and/or traumatic events.

Questions for Reflection

1. Thoroughly explore the rationale that encompasses environmental grief and provide examples of how people could experience environmental loss in contrasting ways. What are some suggestions on how you could offer support to an individual experiencing environmental grief?
2. What are your thoughts surrounding the environment and its ability to promote human well-being? Why do you think nature is therapeutic? How could nature help to support grieving individuals in various types of losses?
3. How should clinicians and practitioners respond to the ongoing environmental crisis that is occurring within the world? Create recommendations on how to promote positive psycho-social change that promotes environmentalism and acknowledges environmental grief.

4. How would you constructively respond to individuals who openly minimize environmental issues, and thus disenfranchise environmental grief?

References

Buncombe, A. (2018, May 26). Four years on, the people of Flint are still fighting for that most basic necessity—clean drinking water. *Independent*. Retrieved from www.independent.co.uk/news/world/americas/flint-water-crisis-michigan-town-charges-when-rick-snyder-karen-weaver-michelle-wolf-flint-town-a8369546.html

Center for Biological Diversity. (n.d.). *The extinction crisis*. Retrieved from www.biologicaldiversity.org/programs/biodiversity/elements_of_biodiversity/extinction_crisis/

Center for Whale Research. (n.d. a). *Southern resident killer whale population*. Retrieved from www.whaleresearch.com/orca-population

Center for Whale Research. (n.d. b). *What are the current threats facing the Southern Resident Killer Whales?* Retrieved from www.whaleresearch.com/orca-questions

Climate Psychology Alliance. (n.d.). *Our history*. Retrieved from www.climatepsychologyalliance.org/about/our-history

Climate Reality Project. (n.d.). *Become a climate reality leader*. Retrieved from www.climaterealityproject.org/

Community Environmental Legal Defense Fund International Center for the Rights of Nature. (n.d.). *Rights of nature*. Retrieved from https://celdf.org/rights/rights-of-nature/

Community Environmental Legal Defense Fund. (2018, April 6). Colombia supreme court rules that Amazon region is "subject of rights." *Press Release*. Retrieved from https://celdf.org/2018/04/press-release-colombia-supreme-court-rules-that-amazon-region-is-subject-of-rights/t

Doka, K. (Ed.). (2002). *Disenfranchised grief: New directions, challenges, and strategies for practice*. Champaign, IL: Research Press.

Gluckich, E. (2018, February 12). Rural Lane county residents fight aerial herbicide spraying. *Capital Press*. Retrieved from www.capitalpress.com/Oregon/20180212/rural-lane-county-residents-fight-aerial-herbicide-spraying

Hanh, T. N. (n.d.). *Thích Nhất Hạnh Quotes*. Retrieved from www.brainyquote.com/quotes/thich_nhat_hanh_531607

Herrera, C. (2017, November 20). Lolita may never go free. And that could be what's best for her, scientists say. *Bradenton Herald*. Retrieved from www.bradenton.com/news/business/tourism/article185580673.html

Hoffman, J. (2018, April 5). *Potential health and environmental effects of hydrofracking in the Williston Basin, Montana*. Retrieved from https://serc.carleton.edu/67733

Jackson, J., Blake, S., Woods, D., & de la Fouchardiere, M. (Producers) & Rynard, (Director). (2015). *The messenger* [Motion picture]. Canada: SongbirdSOS & Productions á Cinq.

Kaplan, L. E. (2007). Insidious trauma and the sexual minority client. In M. Bussey & J. Bula Wise (Eds.), *Trauma transformed: An empowered response*. New York: Columbia University Press.

Kevorkian, K. A. (2004). *Environmental grief: Hope and healing*. Unpublished doctoral dissertation, Union Institute and University, Cincinnati, Ohio.

Lee, D., & Bender, M. (2018). *Why earth law will be good for Puget Sound in Washington State, USA*. Retrieved from www.earthlawcenter.org/blog-entries/2018/1/why-earth-law-will-be-good-for-puget-sound-in-washington-state-usa

Louv, R. (2005). *Last child in the woods: Saving our children from nature-deficit disorder*. Retrieved from http://richardlouv.com/books/last-child/excerpt

Mapes, L. V. (2018, May 10). Seeking to free Puget Sound orca, Lummi Nation launches trek to Miami. *Seattle Times*. Retrieved from www.seattletimes.com/seattle- news/environment/seeking-to-free-a-puget-sound-orca-lummi-nation-launches-trek-to-miami/

Nichols, W. J. (2016, September 14). *The blue mind Rx: Wild waters can be lifelong medicine for all people*. Retrieved from www.wallacejnichols.org/116/1097/the-blue-mind-rx-statement.html

Oteyza, M. V., & Cowperthwaite, G. (Producers), & Cowperthwaite, G. (Director). (2013). *Blackfish* [Motion picture]. USA: CNN Films & Magnolia Pictures.

Roos, S. (2018). *Chronic sorrow: A living loss*. New York: Routledge.

Rough Guides. (2018, February 15). *20 destinations to see before they disappear*. Retrieved from www.roughguides.com/gallery/20-destinations-to-see-before-they-disappear/

Stevens, F., & Ahnemann, O. (Producers), & Psihoyos, L. (Director). (2015). *Racing extinction* [Motion picture]. USA: Oceanic Preservation Society.

Thomas, F. (2017, November 5). Why giving your mental illness a name can help you recover. *Metro*. Retrieved from https://metro.co.uk/2017/11/05/why-giving-your-mental-illness-a-name-can- help-you-recover-7047403/

Van Dernoot Lipsky, L. (2002). *Trauma stewardship: An everyday guide to caring for self while caring for others*. Champaign, IL: Research Books.

CHAPTER 17

Grief and Mental Illness

Lauren J. Breen and Maria E. Fernandez

Annika is a 45-year-old shop assistant. Throughout college, she experienced issues with anxiety and depression. Two years after she started working as a teacher, she had a breakdown and was subsequently diagnosed with bipolar disorder. She started treatment and went back to work. She knew she was more irritable and easily distracted than before, but she was shocked that her colleagues were unsupportive and she felt they were spying on her in case she had another breakdown. She couldn't cope with the surveillance and, after a particularly negative annual performance review from the school's principal, she left the profession. Two years ago, Annika had another relapse, which led to a six-week stay in a psychiatric hospital. She took several months off work, moved in with her parents, and focused on her health. She tried for a little while to find another teaching job, but the process was exhausting, so she now works at the frozen yogurt stand at the mall. She is embarrassed about how her life has turned out and describes this as the reason she doesn't date. Although she feels she is now having more good days than bad, she mourns the loss of independence, her identity as a teacher, and opportunities to enjoy romantic relationships and have children.

Tom is Annika's father. Tom was so proud when Annika graduated—she was the first person in their family to complete a university degree—and he was devastated at her diagnosis. Even when Annika is symptom-free, Tom worries so much more about Annika than about his other daughter, and he always pays extra attention to Annika's moods and behaviors just in case she might relapse. He is concerned about what the future might look like for Annika, especially now that he and his wife are both in their late 70s. Who will look after Annika when he's gone? Why has life been so unfair to his beautiful baby girl? He loses sleep at night because of worries about Annika now and in the future.

Mental Health Challenges as Chronic Sorrow

Mental disorders are dysfunctional behavioral and/or mental patterns that cause significant distress and/or impairment in functioning and may be acute, chronic, or follow a relapse and remitting pattern (American Psychiatric Association, 2013). Approximately one in five adults will be diagnosed with a mental disorder in their lifetime. Worldwide, mental and substance use disorders are the leading cause of years lived with a disability (Hay et al., 2017), comprise the largest contributor to disability in young adulthood (Vos et al., 2017), and are associated with higher rates of premature death (Hay et al., 2017). Mental illness doesn't exist in a vacuum and instead intersects with numerous contextual variables such as family, culture, economic circumstances, and whether services are available and accessible. Approximately half of people with mental illness miss out on mental health services.

The diagnosis of mental illness is like a threshold for many, and while treatment may be effective, there can also be relapses, ongoing uncertainty about the future, and an accumulation of losses. Likewise, family members and friends of people experiencing mental health challenges might also grieve significant losses. These are examples of the "shattered glass" that is described in the introduction of this book. In this chapter, we outline the losses that might be experienced by people diagnosed with mental illness and their family members, and describe these as forms of chronic sorrow.

Social Contexts of Mental Illness

Despite the (increasingly) numerous mental illnesses that are recognized, and the various backgrounds of each individual diagnosed, it is common for people with mental disorders to report stigmatizing experiences from their family and friends, colleagues and workplaces, and health professionals. Studies using community surveys have shown that respondents perceive mental illness as largely intractable (Seeman, Tang, Brown, & Ing, 2016) and view people with mental illness as dangerous, have emotional reactions such as fear and pity, and desire social distance from people with mental illness (Angermeyer & Matschinger, 2003). Media portrayals of people with mental illness tend to emphasize inaccurate and unfavorable characteristics such as dangerousness, aggression, unpredictability, violence, and solitude (Wahl, 1992). People with mental illness might also internalize the stigma, identify as their diagnostic label and the stereotypical characteristics of the diagnosis, leading to poorer well-being (Cruwys & Gunaseelan, 2016) and reduced psychological help-seeking (Rüsch et al., 2014). Even more worrying, people with mental illness report that doctors and other mental health professionals are just as likely as anyone else to stigmatize them (Mental Health Council of Australia, 2011).

Stigma has long been of interest to psychologists and sociologists. In sociologist Erving Goffman's (1963) book, *Stigma: Notes on the Management of Spoiled Identity*, he articulated the concept of "passing"—a process whereby people successfully conceal their difference—and the ways in which stigma affects the stigmatized person's identity. Further, once a person's identity is stigmatized, the stigma can continue over time, irrespective of whether the person continues to show signs of disorder. This process was outlined in a study by psychologist David Rosenhan (1970), where eight "sane" people—three psychologists, a psychology student, a psychiatrist, a family doctor, a painter, and a housewife—had themselves admitted to various hospitals. To gain admission, each reported feeling empty, hollow, and hearing a "thudding" noise. All were admitted, and seven of the eight were diagnosed with schizophrenia. Once admitted, the "patients" stopped reporting these symptoms and acted in their normal or typical fashion. Interestingly, the other patients were quick to realize that these patients were imposters—several guessed they were in fact journalists or university professors—but the staff did not. The average length of hospitalization was 19 days and ranged from 7 to 52 days. All were discharged with a diagnosis of schizophrenia "in remission." That is, they still retained a stigmatizing diagnosis! Rosenhan concluded that these places are insane because, even when a person is behaving normally, the presence of the diagnostic label can itself be stigmatizing because individuals will from that point forward be viewed through a lens that assumes their behavior is interpreted as being abnormal.

People with mental illness commonly describe being under continual surveillance from family, friends, and colleagues. In a study of women with bipolar disorder (Fernandez, Breen, & Simpson, 2014), participants talked about symptom surveillance. For example, one participant stated, "I have actually had friends say, 'Are you symptomatic? You are talking a lot; maybe you have got some mania?'" (p. 895). Another participant reported that her work supervisor's surveillance "crossed the line":

> My boss was really worried that I might have been becoming unwell and, unfortunately, she contacted my psychiatrist before I got there. That was such a breach of confidentiality and just triggered a whole lot of stuff for me . . . My boss had said I was wearing different clothes, so it is this fear of I cannot look different, I cannot wear different things, I cannot have a lot of money or act in certain ways.
> (p. 895)

Losses From Living With Mental Illness

For people living with mental illness, their experiences of scrutiny create self-doubt and reduce their confidence and self-esteem. They may describe their identities as inextricably linked to their diagnosis and report numerous losses as a result of living with mental illness. We summarize these losses and provide illustrative examples in Table 17.1.

Family members and friends of people with mental illness might also experience losses and stigma. Parents and caregivers of people with mental illness are typically concerned with concealing the illness, feeling unable to disclose the illness to others or receive visitors to the home, experiencing stigma, and worrying about explaining illness to others (Link, Yang, Phelan, & Collins, 2004). For instance, parents and caregivers of adolescents and children with mental illness (e.g., schizophrenia, bipolar disorder) described the pervasive challenges of caregiving and diminished social and professional support (Richardson, Cobham, McDermott, & Murray, 2013). A study of mothers of school-aged children with mental health disorders (e.g., attention-deficit/hyperactivity disorder, oppositional defiant disorder, a mood or anxiety disorder) showed that the mothers were very careful about whether they disclosed their child's mental disorder, to whom, and under what conditions (Eaton, Ohan, Stritzke, Courtauld, & Corrigan, 2017). These decisions concerning disclosure versus concealment were complex and based upon considering the child's best interests as well as foreseeable reactions from others (including stigma and blame). We summarize these losses and provide illustrative examples in Table 17.2.

Table 17.1 Examples of Losses That Might Be Experienced by a Person With Mental Illness

Losses	Example
Loss of identity	"My biggest issue is coming to terms with the loss of who I am, and that I sometimes feel I cannot be the person I once thought I was" (Proudfoot et al., 2009).
Loss of independence	"Can't pay my bills like I need to. I have cut-offs. I'm going without electricity right now. I'm staying at my mom's house. My electricity is off. I can't pay it and that's stressful. I want my lights on. I only get so much a month" (Borba et al., 2011, p. 290).
Loss of employment	"My sleeping was not regular, my hours were not regular . . . my memory was shot, I was having trouble making decisions, and that did not bode well. And then I had an acute manic episode, the worst I've ever had, and that just more or less ended my career" (Michalak, Yatham, Maxwell, Hale, & Lam, 2007, p. 132).
Loss of relationships	"He ended up breaking it off 'cos of me, I guess. I was too intense. I reckon I was up and down and all over the place" (Inder et al., 2008, p. 126).
Loss of roles	"I am not able to be there for her when I have gone to hospital. I cannot really be a mother for her. That is a loss for me because she is very important to me, and to not feel that I can be a parent to her—it is difficult" (Fernandez et al., 2014, p. 894).
Loss of credibility	"I think people do treat me differently because I have an illness. I think they see me as weaker and I think that they're afraid to give me as much responsibility and often times don't give me as much credit as I deserve" (Sajatovic et al., 2008, p. 721).
Loss of status	"You have got this big stamp on your forehead that everyone else sees . . . All this stuff about equality in our society is just a load of rubbish" (Fernandez et al., 2014, p. 894).
Loss of daily functioning	"If I wasn't mentally ill I believe I would be more into taking care of better of myself. Well because the mind plays tricks on me, and sometimes I get depressed and I don't wanna do anything. If I didn't have those symptoms I believe that I would be more active or more motivated to do more" (Borba et al., 2011, p. 290).
Loss of control	"For years I had been going around in a sort of circle. The circle got bigger and bigger, it turned into a cyclone. The storm was devastating, and afterwards you have to pick up the pieces" (Mauritz & van Meijel, 2009, p. 255).
Loss of confidence	"For me [depression] has always been more than a disease: it has taken my self-esteem, confidence, and pride, heaved them into a swamp of worthlessness, confusion, and frequently, utter hopelessness" (Wisdom, Bruce, Saedi, Weis, & Green, 2008, p. 491).
Loss of social connectedness	"Because I know you can't tell by looking at me, so at first it won't even occur to people. But that does tend to make life very complicated, and it sometimes makes me extremely lonely" Mauritz & van Meijel, 2009, p. 254).
Loss of the imagined future	"I think I would have had my degree by now. I think I would have been able to get the qualifications I wanted much earlier and have a job" (Inder et al., 2008, p. 128).

Table 17.2 Examples of Losses That Might Be Experienced by a Person With a Family Member or Friend With Mental Illness

Losses	Example
Loss of the idealized person	"I miss him, every time when I walk past his [old school] picture I wish I [could] go back (crying) . . . [to a] long time ago" (Richardson et al., 2013, p. 728).
Loss of freedom	"Our life has become totally altered due to the situation, which one does willingly because he's our son and we love him dearly, but there's got to be an element of us attaining our lives as well" (Osborne & Coyle, 2002, p. 313).
Loss of financial security	"I can't work Monday to Saturday and it's, you know, [an] hour and twenty [minutes'] drive each way, so yeah, it's trying too financially, lot more petrol, lots of money [to] take her to appointments to psychologists and psychiatrists so it's affected things" (Richardson et al., 2013, p. 729).
Loss of social connectedness	"I felt like I needed to try and explain all that [child's symptoms]. Especially when we were having a playdate. We didn't know these people very well, and you'd catch the old [facial expression of disgust], so of course I had to say something. I had to explain it" (Eaton et al., 2017, p. 1632).
Loss of social status	"It's basically that you are stupid. My daughter says . . . 'it's no use saying anything because they [mental health professionals] don't believe me' . . . it leaves you with no foot to stand on, it's like banging your head against a wall, you don't get anywhere. They don't trust or believe her or me, especially not my daughter" (Johansson, Andershed, & Anderzen-Carlsson, 2014, p. 500).
Loss of control	"You have control to a certain degree as a parent, about how to raise your children, but when you have a youth with a mental illness you have no idea what to do" (Richardson et al., 2013, p. 727).
Loss of confidence as a parent	"You feel like it's your fault, and, and then you start to believe that it is your fault, even though you know it's not . . . It still creeps into your mind, in the way you think and you process stuff, and then I, even now, I still feel, um, that it, I feel guilt . . . Did I cause this in some way?" (Richardson et al., 2013, p. 727).
Loss of childhood	"She was lying in the bed crying and sad. I was alone at home, when she attempted suicide. Nobody took care of me, and I was only six years old, I was totally lonely" (Dam, Joensen, & Hall, 2018, p. 82).
Loss of a family life	"The whole family thing was very disrupted . . . I'd go to work, I'd leave work, I'd go to the hospital, I'd leave hospital for a meeting, I'd be up there until 9 o'clock at night and she wouldn't want to be alone so (husband) said he'd sleep up there, and then I'd be exhausted" (Richardson et al., 2013, p. 729).
Loss of the imagined future	I can try and guide him the best way I can, but when I go, his brother gets married, has a family, what happens to Sam? How's he going to cope? . . . I do worry about the losses he's going to have in his life, he's going to lose his brother, because his brother's going to get married and have a family, and then Sam's going to have the loss of no children, no wife, maybe no job that inspires him (Richardson et al., 2013, p. 726).

The losses documented in the literature, and summarized in Tables 17.1 and 17.2, demonstrate that living with mental illness is a form of non-death loss and grief. These losses tend to be ambiguous (Boss, 2000) and nonfinite (Bruce & Schultz, 2001) and precipitate chronic sorrow (Roos, 2002). Many of them are reminiscent of the concept of shattered assumptions articulated by Janoff-Bulman (1992). However, these losses can also be disenfranchised, meaning that people experiencing might not be supported in the ways offered to other grieving people (Doka, 1989).

Despite these losses, however, not all is lost; the grief resulting from these losses is both adaptive and necessary in order to rebuild the assumptive world after its destruction from significant loss experiences. For instance, in the study described earlier about women with bipolar disorder, the women described recovery as an ongoing process comprising acceptance of bipolar disorder as their new reality, using self-help strategies to reclaim control, connecting and identifying with people who are supportive, and redefining their identities in relation to a definition of recovery that did not necessarily mean reverting back to former functioning. These processes evoke Neimeyer's (2001) concept of meaning-making and is best exemplified by the following quote from a woman living with bipolar disorder:

> I found a poster in a magazine and I stuck it in my wardrobe. There is a girl with a small hump on her back with a little bit of downy hair; she has got long hair and big eyes. The poster reads, "I am not like other girls" . . . and I think that is how I see myself. I feel that I might be even a subtype of the human species basically. Not in a bad way—just that I am different. . . . In wanting to be like everyone else I had missed that there was maybe something special about me. In a way, that is something that can be celebrated.
> (Fernandez et al., 2014, p. 897)

Suggestions and Clinical Recommendations

Living with mental illness, and being the family member or friends of people with mental illness, are forms of living losses. Below, we have included some points that might be helpful for clinicians to support people living the losses of mental illness.

Clinical Interventions

It is common in many countries for mental health services to be offered only on a short-term basis. For instance, in Australia, the national health system allows people with a clinical diagnosis to access up to six subsidized sessions with a mental health service provider per calendar year; an additional four subsidized sessions are available to patients who require additional assistance or who present with a new disorder or issue. However, the enduring and multiple living losses that may be experienced by a person with mental illness and/or their family members are neither captured in clinical diagnoses, nor are they likely to be amenable to being addressed in a short number of sessions. Further, these living losses may not be recognized by treating mental health professionals, many of whom have little to no training in grief and loss issues (Breen, Fernandez, O'Connor, & Pember, 2013). It is therefore important that clinicians seek out training opportunities to bolster their knowledge and skills for working with loss and grief.

We recommend that treatment should entail a collaborative, client-centered approach and include the client's perspective concerning the symptoms and issues of loss upon which they want to focus. For instance, treatments that incorporate holistic approaches and encourage clients to explore how they wish to accommodate losses into their lives such as utilizing the Dual Process Model of coping with bereavement (Stroebe & Schut, 1999) and promoting meaning-making after loss experiences (Neimeyer, 2001). Working from a client-centered and holistic perspective may reduce the stigmatizing effects of living with mental illness and increase a client's sense of agency in treatment, which is important because people living with mental illness tend to experience loss of control. Furthermore, a client-centered approach would facilitate the exploration of one's core beliefs, which is essential when grieving the loss of one's assumptive world.

Additionally, clinicians should explore attachment styles during clinical assessments to help identify how adapting to loss may be complicated by one's assumptive world. For instance, individuals with an anxious/avoidant attachment style may benefit from exploring their somatic responses to loss, rather than forcing them to explore affective states that are likely to result in client resistance and more emotional dysregulation. If it is identified that a client's grief process is complicated by earlier attachment disruptions, clinicians could adopt an attachment-focused approach to the treatment of grief and loss (Kosminsky & Jordan, 2016).

Engagement and Advocacy

Initiatives such as Mental Health Week have a role in raising awareness and reducing stigma. However, it is important to do more than talk about it; instead, we need to actually do something about the stigma and discrimination faced by people with mental illness, the families who often bear the brunt of the care required, the workplace that might not be as supportive as it could be, and the difficulty in accessing and affording services. The World Health Organization (2013) advocates for the promotion of mental health and well-being in combination with the identification and treatment of mental illness. We would do well to consider how our work promotes and protects mental health in the context of living losses that result from mental illness.

Key Terms

> **Mental Disorders:** According to the American Psychiatric Association, mental disorders are dysfunctional behavioral and/or mental patterns that cause significant distress and/or impairment in functioning and may be acute, chronic, or follow a relapse and remitting pattern.

Stigma: Negative stereotypes, conceptions, behaviors, and attitudes that are directed towards a person who is perceived to have "shameful" qualities.

Questions for Reflection

1. What stigmas exist surrounding mental illness? Why do you think these stigmas exist? What types of losses can these stigmas cause for individuals living with mental illnesses? How can we, as a society, remove these stigmas and "do more than talk about it," as the authors suggest?
2. Suppose an individual who is caring for a family member or close friend with mental illness comes to you and shares that s/he is feeling overwhelmed, burned out, and hopeless. Examine the role of chronic sorrow and living losses that this individual may be experiencing. How would you provide grief support to this person, and how would you foster a sense of hope in a difficult situation that has no foreseeable end?
3. Provide an analysis on how the grieving process might overlap and differ from the diagnosis of a mental disorder. As mental health challenges can prompt numerous losses for an individual, why do you think so many mental health professionals have little to no training in grief? What negative effects can or do occur when mental health practitioners do not acknowledge losses surrounding mental illness? Develop suggestions for bridging this knowledge gap within the field of mental health.

References

American Psychiatric Association. (2013). *Diagnostic and statistical manual of mental disorders* (5th ed.). Washington, DC: Author.

Angermeyer, M. C., & Matschinger, H. (2003). The stigma of mental illness: Effects of labelling on public attitudes towards people with mental disorder. *Acta Psychiatrica Scandinavica, 108*, 304–309.

Borba, C. P., Depadilla, L., Druss, B. G., McCarty, F. A., von Esenwein, S. A., & Sterk, C. E. (2011). A day in the life of women with a serious mental illness: A qualitative investigation. *Womens Health Issues, 21*, 286–292.

Boss, P. (2000). *Ambiguous loss: Learning to live with unresolved grief.* Cambridge, MA: Harvard University Press.

Breen, L. J., Fernandez, M. E., O'Connor, M., & Pember, A-J. (2013). The preparation of graduate health professionals for working with bereaved clients: An Australian perspective. *Omega: The Journal of Death and Dying, 66*, 313–332.

Bruce, E. J., & Schultz, C. L. (2001). *Nonfinite loss and grief: A psychoeducational approach.* Baltimore, MD: Brookes Publishing.

Cruwys, T., & Gunaseelan, S. (2016). "Depression is who I am": Mental illness identity, stigma and wellbeing. *Journal of Affective Disorders, 189*, 36–42.

Dam, K., Joensen, D. G., & Hall, E. O. C. (2018). Experiences of adults who as children lived with a parent experiencing mental illness in a small-scale society: A qualitative study. *Journal of Psychiatric and Mental Health Nursing, 25*, 78–87.

Doka, K. J. (Ed.). (1989). *Disenfranchised grief: Recognizing hidden sorrow.* Lexington, MA: Lexington.

Eaton, K., Ohan, J. L., Stritzke, W. G. K., Courtauld, H. M., & Corrigan, P. W. (2017). Mothers' decisions to disclose or conceal their child's mental health disorder. *Qualitative Health Research, 27*, 1628–1639.
Fernandez, M. E., Breen, L. J., & Simpson, T. (2014). Renegotiating identities: Experiences of loss, coping, and recovery for women with bipolar disorder. *Qualitative Health Research, 24*, 890–900.
Goffman, E. (1963). *Stigma: Notes on the management of spoiled identity*. Englewood Cliffs, NJ: Prentice-Hall.
Hay, S. I., Abajobir, A. A., Abate, K. H., Abbafati, C., Abbas, K. M., Abd-Allah, F., . . . Murray, C. J. L. (2017). Global, regional, and national disability-adjusted life-years (DALYs) for 333 diseases and injuries and healthy life expectancy (HALE) for 195 countries and territories, 1990–2016: A systematic analysis for the global burden of disease study 2016. *Lancet, 390*, 1260–1344.
Inder, M. L., Crowe, M. T., Moor, S., Luty, S. E., Carter, J. D., & Joyce, P. R. (2008). I actually don't know who I am: The impact of bipolar disorder on the development of self. *Psychiatry: Interpersonal and Biological Processes, 71*, 123–133.
Janoff-Bulman, R. (1992). *Shattered assumptions: Towards a new psychology of trauma*. New York: Free Press.
Johansson, A., Andershed, B., & Anderzen-Carlsson, A. (2014). Conceptions of mental health care—from the perspective of parents of adult children suffering from mental illness. *Scandinavian Journal of Caring Sciences, 28*, 496–504.
Kosminsky, P. S., & Jordan, J. R. (2016). *Attachment-informed grief therapy: The clinician's guide to foundations and applications*. New York: Routledge.
Link, B. Q., Yang, L. H., Phelan, J. C., & Collins, P. Y. (2004). Measuring mental illness stigma. *Schizophrenia Bulletin, 30*, 511–541.
Mauritz, M., & van Meijel, B. (2009). Loss and grief in patients with schizophrenia: On living in another world. *Archives of Psychiatric Nursing, 23*, 251–260.
Mental Health Council of Australia. (2011). *Consumer and carer experiences of stigma from mental health and other professionals*. Canberra, Australia: Author.
Michalak, E. E., Yatham, L. N., Maxwell, V., Hale, S., & Lam, R. W. (2007). The impact of bipolar disorder upon work functioning: A qualitative analysis. *Bipolar Disorders, 9*, 126–143.
Neimeyer, R. A. (Ed.). (2001). *Meaning reconstruction and the experience of loss*. Washington, DC: American Psychological Association.
Osborne, J., & Coyle, A. (2002). Can parental responses to adult children with schizophrenia be conceptualized in terms of loss and grief? A case study analysis. *Counselling Psychology Quarterly, 15*, 307–323.
Proudfoot, J. G., Parker, G. B., Benoit, M., Manicavasagar, V., Smith, M., & Gayed, A. (2009). What happens after diagnosis? Understanding the experiences of patients with newly-diagnosed bipolar disorder. *Health Expectations, 12*, 120–129.
Richardson, M., Cobham, V., McDermott, B., & Murray, J. (2013). Youth mental illness and the family: Parents' loss and grief. *Journal of Child and Family Studies, 22*, 719–736.
Roos, S. (2002). *Chronic sorrow: A living loss*. New York: Brunner-Routledge.
Rosenhan, D. L. (1970). On being sane in insane places. *Science, 179*, 250–258.
Rüsch, N., Müller, M., Ajdacic-Gross, V., Rodgers, S., Corrigan, P., & Rössler, W. (2014). Shame, perceived knowledge and satisfaction associated with mental health as predictors of attitude patterns towards help-seeking. *Epidemiology and Psychiatric Sciences, 23*, 177–187.
Sajatovic, M., Jenkins, J. H., Safavi, R., West, J. A., Cassidy, K. A., Meyer, W. J., & Calabrese, J. R. (2008). Personal and societal construction of illness among individuals with

rapid-cycling bipolar disorder: A life-trajectory perspective. *The American Journal of Geriatric Psychiatry, 16*, 718–726.

Seeman, N., Tang, S., Brown, A. D., & Ing, A. (2016). World survey of mental illness stigma. *Journal of Affective Disorders, 190*, 115–121.

Stroebe, M., & Schut, H. (1999). The Dual Process Model of coping with bereavement: Rationale and description. *Death Studies, 23*, 197–224.

Vos, T., Abajobir, A. A., Abbafati, C., Abbas, K. M., Abate, K. H., Abd-Allah, F., . . . Murray, C. J. L. (2017). Global, regional, and national incidence, prevalence, and years lived with disability for 328 diseases and injuries for 195 countries, 1990–2016: A systematic analysis for the global burden of disease study 2016. *Lancet, 390*, 1211–1259.

Wahl, O. F. (1992). Mass media images of mental illness: A review of the literature. *Journal of Community Psychology, 20*, 343–352.

Wisdom, J. P., Bruce, K., Saedi, G. A., Weis, T., & Green, C. A. (2008). 'Stealing me from myself': Identity and recovery in personal accounts of mental illness. *Australian and New Zealand Journal of Psychiatry, 42*, 489–495.

World Health Organization. (2013). *Investing in mental health: Evidence for action*. Geneva, Switzerland: Author.

PART V

Tangible and Intangible Losses
Darcy L. Harris

Introduction

Margaret and Jason came to Father James for premarital counseling after their engagement announcement. Father James knew Margaret well. She and her family had been parishioners in the Catholic church where he was the priest for many years. Margaret's husband had died in a horrible highway accident 10 years ago, less than a year after they were married. This loss had completely broken her in many ways, but she had later turned the tragedy into a gift by starting a bereavement ministry in the parish that had served many others whose lives had been shattered by loss. When she told Father James that she had met someone and that they were beginning to consider the possibility of a future together, he was so very happy for her. She introduced Jason to him one Sunday when he had joined her for the service, and Father James noted the sparkle in her eye as she held Jason's hand. Both Margaret and Jason were in their late 40s. Margaret was planning to cut back her hours at work after they were married so they could travel together, which is something she never dreamed she would do again after her husband had died. Jason lived out of town and was planning to become a private consultant, which would allow him flexibility to move to Margaret's community so they could live there together.

As they talked in the first counseling session about their backgrounds, their hopes, and their dreams, Father James had to stop them, as Jason shared that he was divorced. That meant that Father James would not be able to marry them, and their union would not be recognized by the church. Not understanding the problem since he wasn't Catholic, Jason shared that he and his former wife mutually agreed upon the divorce, and he didn't understand why this was an issue. But it was. Once it became known that that Father James could not sanction the wedding, Margaret's Catholic relatives began taking sides. While they were glad to see that Margaret was finally happy again, most felt that she should have chosen someone who was "available to her in the eyes of God." Jason felt very hurt by the family's reaction and took their judgment of his divorce personally. Margaret's dismay over Father James's position turned into despair as she realized that in marrying Jason, she would most likely be creating a rift in her family that would continue to fester. Both her parish and her family had solidly stood by her after the death of her husband and she felt that she never would have gotten through this painful period of her life without them; now it felt they were abandoning her at a time when she was inviting them to share her joy. Jason began to withdraw and they began to have frequent arguments. Jason didn't understand why Margaret was so personally affected by the church's position about their relationship. Margaret felt paralyzed by the inevitable losses that she knew would occur both if she married Jason and if she did not. Father James felt bound by the laws of the church, despite his personal feelings of wanting happiness for Margaret.

After several months, Margaret and Jason split up, unable to navigate the polarization in Margaret's family and the parish community that their pending marriage had created. Margaret withdrew from her involvement in the church, feeling bitter, sad, and alone. When her husband died, she wondered how a merciful God could allow such a cruel thing to happen to her. When she found new love, she began doubting her faith at a deeper place, as the gift of the new love she had found was rejected by her faith community as well as her family. Jason ended up moving across the country to start his consulting career and to nurse his wounded heart. Father James often thought of this situation, wondering about devoting his life to an institution that seemed far removed from the love and compassion that motivated him to become a priest in the first place. In this situation, all the individuals involved probably appeared fine on the surface. Margaret was obviously very caring and strong as she developed the bereavement ministry at her church after suffering the loss of her husband years prior. Jason was successful in his business and had found someone to love again. Father James had a thriving parish and cared deeply for his congregation. Under the surface of each of these individuals' outward appearances were profound hurt, despair, and painful questioning of previously held assumptions and beliefs that now gnawed at each of them. For Margaret, the lack of support from the church and her family after she found love again resulted in an ongoing and crippling sense of despair, isolation, and hopelessness.

For many years, I worked as a therapist in a downtown counseling center where the mission statement included "honoring the spiritual dimension of life." I counseled several men whose sense of faith and purpose no longer provided them the impetus for the work they did as parish priests, and they sought support as they made the difficult choice to leave their vocation. All of them described enduring a great deal of misunderstanding, stigma, and blame after making the painful decision to leave the calling that they once felt would carry them throughout their lives. Very few people understood the devastation that these men felt when their belief in God and their commitment to the church not only didn't sustain them, but actually eroded their sense of hope and compassion for themselves and others. Outwardly, they appeared to be healthy, intelligent, and well compensated for their work. Below the surface, however, many of them often experienced feelings of debilitating anxiety, uncertainty, betrayal, anger, and pain all melded together in a terrible, excruciating knot. Many people did not recognize the losses that these individuals faced because they chose their vocation, and now they were choosing to leave that same vocation; the assumption was that it was all about their choice and, for some, a presumed weakness and failure in their commitment. Many of these men grieved silently and in isolation. The grief was both profound and unacknowledged by most of the people around them.

Intangible/Tangible Losses

The use of the terms *tangible* and *intangible* in reference to loss originates outside of the realm of social science. When searching for these terms in the literature, their use will often be in relation to insurance companies and to legal cases, both of which will discuss the tangible, physical losses that occur in the context of an event in addition to the intangible aspects of the experience, such as in the consideration of compensation for emotional pain and suffering that have also occurred. The two scenarios introduced at the beginning of the chapter can set the groundwork to discuss living losses that are both intangible and tangible in nature.

Tangible losses are those losses that are readily apparent, obvious to the observer, and/or physically evident. Many people who experience tangible losses are reminded that while their loss is acknowledged, it is often diminished, or there are attempts to refocus on the positive aspects of life that are still present. Often, the grief that is experienced is reframed by others into language that focuses on rebuilding after the loss, reframing what has happened, or reminders that "it could have been worse." Thus, the person who loses a job will be given pointers and information about finding new employment. The individual whose home was engulfed by a wildfire will be reminded that s/he can use the insurance money to rebuild a new home. The individual with an amputated leg after a car accident will be advised that s/he can go through physical therapy and become functional again, most likely along the way being reminded to focus on gratitude for still being alive.

Examples of tangible losses:

- Loss of a relationship that had been socially recognized (i.e., marriage).
- Loss of home or homeland.
- Loss of health or body parts that are readily identifiable.
- Loss of job (associated with loss contact with co-workers and loss of income).
- Loss of ability (such as due to accident or illness).

Tangible losses can be personal (i.e., loss of one's vision, hearing, sexual activity, or mental capacity; infertility; chronic pain or illness; rape, domestic violence and abuse; or political torture), interpersonal (i.e., divorce, ending a friendship, or death of a loved one), and material (i.e., losing a job, leaving one's country, wartime trauma, changing residence, or becoming homeless; Harris, in press). Intangible losses are not obvious or overtly apparent to others; however, these unseen losses can still be profound and debilitating to those who experience them.

Intangible losses are also sometimes referred to as *invisible losses*, because of the lack of physical signs or something obvious to the casual observer. Intangible losses are often more abstract or symbolic in nature. These losses frequently include the loss of hopes or dreams; they may be existential in nature, involving a loss in beliefs about the world or others, loss of meaning, loss of faith, or a sense of spiritual connection. These losses also can include changes in self-worth, a sense of threat to personal safety, the loss of a sense of control or self-efficacy, and profound demoralization. Intangible losses frequently occur in situations of abuse, neglect, and where there are imbalances in power and/or a control dynamic that is maintained at the personal expense of some of the individuals involved (Bordere, 2017; Goldsworthy, 2005).

Intangible losses and the grief related to them are very real and, unfortunately, rarely recognized or discussed. There is a tendency to devalue experiences that don't have an obvious, tangible aspect that can be readily identified. Intangible losses are often hard to put into words and describe accurately. They are also very highly subjective, and they are often kept private due to difficulties with language and, in many circumstances, a sense of shame or perception of personal weakness. This tendency to not acknowledge these types of losses often causes a great deal more pain for those who experience them; this lack of recognition and acknowledgment compounds these losses by shrouding them in secrecy and/or stigmatization.

Intangible loses may include things like:

- Loss of sense of innocence.
- Loss of dignity.
- Loss/change in sense of self or in a sense of identity.
- Loss of social status or roles.
- Loss of faith or hope.
- Loss of familiarity.
- Loss of connection to self, others, or a transcendent being.

This list is far from comprehensive, as there are likely a myriad number of different types of intangible loss experiences.

Tangible and intangible loss can sometimes occur together:

- A violent attack leaves a woman unable to have children (tangible) and a new feeling of being unsafe (intangible).
- A miscarriage results in the loss of a baby (tangible) and the loss of sense of identity for a parent or sibling (intangible).
- Moving to a new country can result in the loss of one's actual home and closeness of friends (tangible) and loss of familiarity or a sense of belonging (intangible).

In the literature, reference to tangible and intangible loss experiences can be found in several studies. Wang et al. (2012) explored the adjustment patterns in Chinese university students who traveled to the United States to study abroad. In their findings, both tangible and intangible losses were seen to have an impact upon the overall stress and adjustment patterns of these students. Tangible losses were described as the loss of in-person access to their homes, families, and friends, and intangible losses were described as diminished sense of self-efficacy, loss of a sense of belonging, and loss of the ability to freely navigate social activities in their new place of residence. Murphy (2012) discussed the losses that accompany stillbirth as consisting of the tangible loss of the baby as well as the intangible losses, such as the loss of hopes and dreams for that baby and for the role of being parents if there weren't other children in the home. Shear et al. (2011) examined reactions among survivors of Hurricane Katrina in areas that were in the direct path of the storm. The study explored the impact of both tangible losses (i.e., home, possessions, memorabilia), as well as intangible losses (i.e., quality of life, sense of well-being, control, security, way of life) to capture the entire scope of the victims' experiences. In another study of immigrants to the United States, Casado, Hong, and Harrington (2010) explored various aspects of grief for immigrants as they arrived and began to settle in their new country. In this study, the loss of personal identity (an intangible loss) was identified as one of the most significant predictors of adjustment.

Conclusion

We live in a world that is very materially oriented. Value is often determined by what can be measured physically and observed directly. The need for demonstrable proof and outcome transfers into how we perceive and interpret the events in our everyday lives. Experiences with physical evidence that can be known through our physical senses (i.e., sight, sound, touch, taste, and smell) are considered real and valid over experiences that manifest in one's psyche, in one's spirit, or in symbolic ways. Robson and Walter (2013) describe a hierarchical description of grief based upon the degree of social validation and acknowledgment for different loss experiences. For example, it would be assumed that acknowledgment (and social support) is highest for losses that occur as a result of the death of a loved one, followed by tangible, physical losses of various types where the loss is overt or obvious. Intangible losses, which involve an internal, subjective appraisal and may be more symbolic in nature, are often either completely unrecognized or, at times, attributed to some perceived weakness or flaw in the individual. Despite this unspoken hierarchy of validation, the bottom line is that no form of grief is unimportant. All grief serves to call us to attention that we need to tend to our assumptive world and engage in reparative work in some way. By acknowledging all types of losses and the grief that accompanies them, we open the potential for rebuilding and healing to occur. Grief doesn't just disappear because we (or others) tell ourselves that it shouldn't be an issue. It is important to keep in mind that grief, in response to whatever type of loss, is an important response that needs to be embraced so that the adaptive work that it facilitates in our lives can occur.

Key Terms

Intangible Loss: Invisible losses that are often hidden and are more abstract, figurative, or existential in nature. Examples of intangible loss experiences may include but are not limited to the loss of identity, social roles, control, sense of well-being, or trust.

Tangible Loss: Losses that are often physical, relational, or distinguishable. Examples may include loss experiences surrounding physical health, work, resources, or home in addition to many other losses.

Questions for Reflection

1. Reflect upon a situation in your life which has consisted of varying tangible and intangible loss experiences. In what ways did these losses affect your well-being and challenge your assumptions about life?
2. Provide an analysis on the loss experience for either Margaret, Jason, or Father James. How can Margaret, Jason, or Father James adjust to the loss in their lives? What clinical strategies would you utilize based upon the losses you have identified as to support either Margaret, Jason, or Father James?
3. Do you perceive all grief as equal? Why or why not? Additionally, what effects can living in a materially driven society have for how grief is valued for individuals?

References

Bordere, T. C. (2017). Disenfranchisement and ambiguity in the face of loss: The suffocated grief of sexual assault survivors. *Family Relations, 66*(1), 29–45.

Casado, B. L., Hong, M., & Harrington, D. (2010). Measuring migratory grief and loss associated with the experience of immigration. *Research on Social Work Practice, 20*(6), 611–620.

Goldsworthy, K. K. (2005). Grief and loss theory in social work practice: All changes involve loss, just as all losses require change. *Australian Social Work, 58*(2), 167–178.

Harris, D. L. (in press). Grief after non-death losses: An exploration of living with loss. In R. A. Neimeyer (Ed.), *Techniques of grief therapy: Bereavement and beyond*. New York: Routledge.

Murphy, S. (2012). Reclaiming a moral identity: Stillbirth, stigma and 'moral mothers.' *Midwifery, 28*(4), 476–480.

Robson, P., & Walter, T. (2013). Hierarchies of loss: A critique of disenfranchised grief. *OMEGA: Journal of Death and Dying, 66*(2), 97–119.

Shear, M. K., McLaughlin, K. A., Ghesquiere, A., Gruber, M. J., Sampson, N. A., & Kessler, R. C. (2011). Complicated grief associated with Hurricane Katrina. *Depression and Anxiety, 28*(8), 648–657.

Wang, K. T., Heppner, P. P., Fu, C. C., Zhao, R., Li, F., & Chuang, C. C. (2012). Profiles of acculturative adjustment patterns among Chinese international students. *Journal of Counseling Psychology, 59*(3), 424.

CHAPTER 18

The Threshold of Shattered Dreams
Ted Bowman

Words About Words

The task of writing about shattered dreams reminded me of the long-time scholarly and public discussion about the number of words Eskimos have for snow. As author, I chose shattered dreams as my filter for this discussion. Alternative choices included: loss of the assumptive world; altered and lost expectations; reordering of a person's world; adjusting one's personal theory of reality; working models that require change; and re-learning one's world (see Bruce & Schultz, 2001; Janoff-Bulman, 1992; Harris, 2011; for general discussions, Attig, 1996; Becker, 1997; Bowman, 1994, 2018; Koch, 1994; Parkes, 1996).

Another filter for this discussion could be threshold times or places. Sometimes called thin or hinge places, these are times or places that include any information which seriously affects an individual or family's view of one's or someone else's future. Some refer to such experiences as times when individuals, families, or communities move through the "borderlands" or from one "worldview" to another." While linked most often to transitions from living to dying to death and bereavement, threshold moments occur throughout lives. One daughter wrote: How does a family grieve the loss of a person whose body lives, and whose death occurs, as one writer puts it, "too late for grief?"(Konek, 1991, p. 112).

In the following pages, specific examples, perspectives, and responses for shattered dreams will be discussed. Whatever the description for a disruptive change that results in loss or an accumulation of losses, it will be asserted that finding meaningful words is part of a healing response. Further, failure to address such losses can compromise a person's, family, or community's ability to move forward.

Some cautionary comments about the words used in this chapter are needed. Years ago, at a national conference, I presented a session on shattered dreams. Near the end, a participant asserted that while she appreciated my use of and discussion of shattered dreams, she found the term inadequate for her experience of the Holocaust. She needed and wanted something stronger. Of all that I included, she was drawn most to the interruption and altering of future stories. Words have power. I was reminded then and now that this chapter is about losses for which the preferred choice of words may differ both because our experiences vary, and the meaning attached to losses can be widely different.

Accounts found in literary resources will be utilized to highlight and personalize the impact of shattered dreams. Stories not only evoke stories; they also can test and inform perspectives, paradigms, and practices. In the later section on responses to shattered dreams, the rationale for bibliotherapeutic approaches will be elaborated.

Accounts of Personal/Family Shattered Dreams

Three accounts reveal aspects of shattered dreams: loss of a future story; loss of being able to plan and dream; loss of dignity, self-respect, and related identities; and the losses of memory, organizational skills, even what to do next. Each of these persons has also crossed, perhaps again and again, a threshold from one world to another. Poet Norita Dittberner-Jax, upon learning of her husband's diagnosis with Lou Gehrig's disease, wrote:

> A shock so deep
> the dreaming shut down,
> or the memory of dreams—
> half of me is dumb
> And dream's companion
> the nudge from underground
> that I count on to give me
> direction, where are you? (2017, p. 4)

Writing about and to her addiction, a woman asserted that she was left with many scars and bruises, internal and external. She discerned that among those injuries, her self-respect, dignity, and much more had been taken. (Herbert, 2017, p. 19).

The title of Wendy Mitchell's poignantly painful and hopeful memoir—*Somebody I Used To Know*—described in a few words her account of early onset Alzheimer's. She later used the metaphor of Christmas tree lights for her condition: each year, noting that they must be unwound and untangled. Then, after untangling, one must plug them in to check for loose connections by assessing which lights flash and which do not. Finally, she asserted: "you can't predict which ones are missing" (2018, p. 131). Loss refers to being deprived of or ceasing to have something that one formerly possessed or to which one was attached. This broad definition is a recognition that shattered dreams can include one's assumptive world, their working models.

Here are some key components of shattered dreams: (1) losing an emotionally important image of oneself, one's family, one's life, one's work, even one's death; (2) losing the possibilities of "what might have been"; (3) abandonment of plans for a particular future; or (4) the dying of a dream (see Anderson & Mitchell, 1983; Bowman, 1994). Shattered dreams are common losses.

Some losses are conspicuous, resulting in changes in a person's appearance or abilities. Others are hidden losses. People who have experienced a colostomy don't typically announce it in the market or at a social gathering. And if friends or others do not see their equipment, their change and loss may go unacknowledged. "You look so good," can be experienced as painful, not a compliment. Shattered dreams can go undetected, out of sight, until and unless those living with shattered dreams name or are invited to name the losses of health, body image, diet, or being inconspicuous.

A professional confession: while leading support groups for people facing disruptive changes, my early commitment was to acknowledge their losses and to help them experience support and find resources that would aid, inform, and enrich coping. Participants, when asked to introduce themselves, led often with their conspicuous losses (the focus of the group—vision loss, cancer diagnosis, parent of a child with special needs, going through an undesired divorce). In the midst of those details, several participants often added words like "I didn't expect this," or "This wasn't part of the plan," or "This is not fair; I played by the rules."

Embarrassed, looking back, I was naïve about a particular loss that deserved attention, the loss of their dreams, their future story. They were describing a threshold in their lives that I did not understand they had crossed. Then, someone responded with something like: "It sounds to me that you had some pictures of your life and those pictures no longer fit, you had dreams and those dreams have been shattered."

I was being taught that shattered dreams, assumptions, expectations, working models, whatever they are called, are as important, perhaps for some, more important than burying the dead, doing the rehabilitation, moving from role as a spouse to that of caregiver, and raising a child with conditions never contemplated. Unless and until someone faces shattered dreams, there will be difficulty in dreaming new dreams—creating new pictures, or what Attig called relearning one's world (1996). A mother personalized it:

> When our baby was born we lost something we were already in love with—our idea of what she would be. No baby could ever completely fulfill that idea or be that fantasy, but most babies approach or overlap our dream baby, because our dreams come from what we know, from our idea of the norm. A child with a disability was not in our picture at all, except maybe as an occasional fear. We who have a child with a disability lost not only our fantasy baby, but our reliance on having a "normal" baby.
>
> (Gill, 1997, p. 16)

The emphasis on acknowledgment of any loss has been reinforced by family therapist Kenneth Hardy. It's one thing to lose something that was important to you, but it is far worse when no one in your universe recognizes that you lost it. The failure to acknowledge another's loss is to deny that person's humanity (2005). Hardy's assertion reinforces Doka's descriptions of disenfranchised grief or hidden sorrow (1989, p. 28).

An important clarification is, as with all losses and ways of grieving, one size doesn't fit all. The meaning and response to disruptive changes will vary among members of families or a similar cohort group. What is a shattered dream for one may not be the same, even for an intimate partner, parent, or friend. A question to ask is, whose dream is it? Parental wishes for children may not be chosen by the older child or young adult. Social pressures can lead to expectations that, when true discernment occurs, may be rejected.

A further important nuance is the distinction between disappointments and shattered dreams. All experience disappointments: the too-rainy, long-planned vacation with the family; the partner chosen by your child, while kind and acceptable, doesn't match with your hopes; a job turns out to include elements that conflict with your core values. Plans, hopes, and goals that started in childhood or recently get thwarted in some way. The distinction between disappointments and shattered dreams has to do with the degree of investment in the plan. Disappointments deserve review and response, but they typically are not *as* important as a shattering of one's core pictures.

Many persons may also invest and "lock in" to naïve and unrealistic dreams. Those that are shattered can cause as much unease, distress, and loss as those that are more realistic and achievable. Loss is loss and deserves its own form of grief. The axiom to meet people where they are, not where you want them to be or at a place you think they should be, applies as one listens for dreams that have been shattered.

This schema shows variations of shattered dreams this writer has heard over many years. It is not complete, nor has it been researched or written about at length. It is offered to stretch consideration of a wide range of shattered dreams.

Variations of Shattered Dreams

Hindsight dreams:
Dreams you did not know were dreams at the time, but did later or now do

Interrupted/postponed dreams:
Events or experiences that partially occurred (these dreams may still be present, but shelved for the present)

Dreams denied:
Events or experiences you expected but which were in one way or another denied you

Dreams ended:
Events or experiences which should/could have continued, but are gone forever

Missed dreams:
Opportunities, especially those for which we were too afraid to take the risk. Now, it is too late.

Stolen dreams:
Events or experiences which because of life circumstances (poverty, violence, oppression) were never conceived as possible

Rejected dreams:
Dreams which are let go of in response to too many losses, oppression, or informed choice

Frozen dreams:
Dreams still held onto in spite of previous losses or circumstances including the resources/ability to bring them to fruition

Developed by Ted Bowman

Historical and Collective Shattered Dreams

The impact of shattered dreams for individuals and families can be exacerbated when their perceptions and experiences are similar to historical or current cultural events or norms. A common example is suggested by the comment made by many after an unwanted medical or mental health diagnosis: "I've joined a club I did not want to be a member of!" For many, such a statement is about not only the personal impact of the diagnosis but also a perception, rightly or wrongly, about how they will now be seen.

Claude Steele called these perceived labels identity contingencies: things one has to deal with in a situation because you have been given a social identity because you are old, young, gay, a white male, a woman, black, Latino, politically conservative or liberal, diagnosed with a bipolar disorder, a cancer patient, and so on (Steele, 2010, pp. 3–11). There are, of course, layers to identity contingencies. As discussed earlier, not everyone's experience will prompt loss, even a loss of dreams. But, it may. Personal losses can become tainted by cultural biases. Nancy Mairs described her experience living with multiple sclerosis (MS):

> I don't want to denigrate people in the helping professions. I admire my brilliant neurologist; I literally owe my life to my supportive psychotherapist; and I respect the urge to love and heal which drives most helpers. All I'm trying to say is that they are trained to look at the world in a particular way—as a structure of problems and solutions—and that their view may not be the most useful one to an MS person and her or his family.
>
> (Mairs, 1990, p. 121)

An identity contingency can be exacerbated when there is a stereotype attached to one's identity or circumstance that threatens well-being. Claudia Rankin's racial example of two friends is telling, not only about race in America, but also about the continuing power of stereotypes.

She described exchanges between two friends, one black, one white, whose bonds include mutual interests and compatible personalities. "Sometimes," she wrote, "your historical selves, her white self and your black self, or your white self and her black self, arrive with the full force of your American positioning" (Rankin, 2014, p. 14). A loss of dreams may occur when a well-intentioned person who, without personal experience, steps into or is perceived to confirm a historical pattern that is charged for another because of historical patterns of perceived and real bias and oppression.

My then middle school son was having difficulty moving words from a page to his brain in ways that led to ease of comprehension and use. To access resources within the school, he would have to be labeled "special needs." My son begged me to not allow that to happen. He perceived that once those words were inserted into his school file, he would forever be labeled. He asserted that he would do anything: accept a tutor, go to school on Saturday (there was no school on Saturday), and, most impressive in relation to the impact on him, he would allow me, his father, to help him with his homework. My son knew at a young age the relationship between that identity contingency, school historical practices, and the shattering of his dreams.

Three other forms of collective or historical impact on shattered dreams deserve mention even while not being fully discussed. Historical trauma has been defined as "a constellation of characteristics associated with massive cumulative group trauma across generations." Lakota social worker Brave Heart asserts that there are three primary indicators:

- Traumatic events are widespread.
- There are high levels of collective distress.
- The trauma is usually perpetrated by outsiders (Brave Heart, 1999, pp. 1–21).

Leslie Silko, a Laguna woman, described the trauma of attempts of occupying peoples to destroy or take personal or tribal stories. "Their evil is mighty," she wrote, "but it can't stand up to our stories" (Silko, 1977, p. 2). Assimilation, even when well done, too frequently means that those being assimilated are to conform to the majority culture. Consider family examples related to adoption, foster care, and the son or daughter-in-law and their partner's family culture. The "new" or "different" person is supposed to fit in with the dominant narrative.

Another, moral injury, results from committing, witnessing, imagining, or failing to prevent acts or events that can be judged as evil or harmful and that violate foundational social and ethical taboos. When this occurs, Nakashima-Brock (2017) asserts that one's existing core moral foundations are unable to justify, process, or integrate the trauma into an identity or meaning system. Her assertion sounds similar to Parkes and Janoff-Bulman's assumptive world model. Moral injury has most often been used to describe war experiences. This cry of grief from a father also addresses moral and historical injuries. The poem is addressed to the police officer interacting with his Latino son. "My son deserves to live as all young people/He deserves a future and a job. He deserves contemplation . . ./My son speaks in two voices, one of a boy/the other of a man. One is breaking through,/ the other just hangs" (Rodriguez, 1998, pp. 38–39). The inextricable overlay of shattered dreams and perceived or actual prejudice deserves attention.

Finally, mention must be given to torture and shattered dreams. The definition used by the Center for Victims of Torture (CVT) to describe torture is: the intentional infliction of physical or psychological pain and suffering by or at the behest or acquiescence of any member or official of the state in power (go to www.cvt.org). A clinical psychologist at CVT personalized the definition in this way:

> There is no "post" in posttraumatic stress disorder (PTSD) for them, nor any national identity or security waiting in the future. They live stateless for years during which the life or death of their family is unknown. Some are deported back and killed; others lose family members while waiting; some are granted asylum and bring some of their family members to safety where they must cope anew with profound ambiguity about remaining disappeared family members, family roles, and national and cultural identity. Without information on the status of their asylum claim from the U.S. government, these clients and their

scattered family members in hiding or refugee camps around the globe have no choice but to learn how to live with the paradox of absence and presence (Boss, 2006). This often lasts for years and sometimes decades. As one of my clients once said, "I am no longer sure the sun itself will rise tomorrow." This is a taste of what we mean by ambiguous loss for the asylum seeker.

(Utrzan & Northwood, 2016, p. 2)

Each of the categories named in this section deserve focused attention which is not possible in this chapter. Even so, the inclusion here was mandatory in order to better understand some reactions to shattered dreams that may be influenced by collective, stereotypical, historical, traumatic, and moral injuries. If and when clinicians overlook experiences such as these, shattered dreams can get magnified.

Responses to Shattered Dreams: Narrative/Bibliotherapeutic Approaches

When dreams are shattered, stories also change. A cancer patient described it this way:

That night I knew I would never be the same . . . Surgery and chemotherapy would irrevocably break my body's continuity with its past. I did not dread what I would become, but I needed to mourn the end of what I had been. It was like saying goodbye to a place I had lived in and loved.

(Frank, 1991, p. 38)

Family therapist Karl Thom (1990) called storying and re-storying normative life processes. Stories are constantly changing, especially when thresholds are crossed. The distinctive stories addressed in this chapter are related to what narrative therapist Michael White (2007) called re-authoring stories, a phrase that mirrors Attig's relearning one's world and Parkes and Janoff-Bulman's assumed worlds.

White's early development of the re-authoring approach began as he perceived the parallels between literary stories and those he saw in therapy. Effective therapy is about engaging people in the re-authoring of the compelling plights of their lives (White, 2007, p. 75).

White's therapeutic method, similar narrative approaches, and classic bibliotherapy/poetry therapy are complimentary. Literary resources (poetry, song lyrics, memoir, fiction, etc.) can be used as a prompt for stories, including accounts of loss. Grieving persons can often more easily access a story outside themselves with greater clarity than their own story.

Spinal cancer survivor Reynolds Price wrote: "I needed to read some story that paralleled, at whatever distance, my unfolding bafflement" (1994, p. 180).

The effectiveness of bibliotherapy depends on the facilitator's ability to choose material that speaks to the individual participant's needs and interests; to make accurate, empathic interpretations of the participant's responses; and, through literature and dialogue, to draw out deeper self-understanding.

(Hynes & Hynes-Berry, 1994, pp. 10–11)

If, for example, someone is both grieving the impact of a severe medical or mental health condition on a family member and concerned that the person does not "get it," I might choose this from Kay Redfield Jamison:

> Some of my reluctance, no doubt, stemmed from a fundamental denial that what I had was a real disease. This is a common reaction that follows, rather counter-intuitively, in the wake of early episodes of manic-depressive illness. Moods are such an essential part of the substance of life, of one's notion of oneself, that even psychotic extremes in mood and behavior somehow can be seen as temporary, even understandable, reactions to what life had dealt. In my case, I had a horrible sense of loss for who I had been and where I had been. It was difficult to give up the high flights of mind and mood, even though the depression that inevitably followed nearly cost me my life.
> (1995, p. 91)

When used, tears of sadness and smiles of recognition are often evoked, allowing for further discussion of the grieving process, especially the ambiguities of grief, and how family members may differ widely in their response.

Choices of literary resources are delicate. Chavis advocated using the isoprinciple taken from music therapy. It involves selecting materials that match the client's mood or state of being. In short, a good bibliotherapist is a skilled listener and observer (Chavis, 2011).

Responses to Shattered Dreams—Following Metaphors/Listening for Embedded Pictures

Consideration of responses to shattered dreams includes awareness of metaphors. Each of the terms used at the beginning of this chapter, even though they are categorical phrases, could be metaphorical: assumed world, working model, loss of a future story; and shattered dreams. Grieving persons frequently choose metaphoric words to describe their experiences of loss (Nadeau, 2006). "All motion stopped when he died . . . I couldn't move" (Spenser, 2004); "suffering is the smallest room, and there the sufferer lives" (Berger, 1996, p. xvii); "No matter what the grief, its weight,/we are obliged to carry it" (Laux, 2005, p. 23) "disaster sucks all the air from the room" (Erdrich, 2010, p. 53); "the beloved died/ . . . he's reborn as words" (Orr, 2013, p. 89). Failure to listen and acknowledge metaphors can compromise grief and bereavement care.

Because misunderstanding can exacerbate losses, acknowledgment of and clear actions to hear more about metaphors conveys the intent to understand. Grief scholar Paul Rosenblatt asserted that when a metaphor is used for loss, even intimates may not know the meaning a metaphor has; hence the admonition to follow metaphors. To do so, one must practice respectful curiosity to gain insights into the metaphor used by a grieving person. (Rosenblatt & Bowman, 2013, p. 85). Following a metaphor can be helpful, whether for relatively common, recognized metaphors or for more rarely articulated ones. Falling into a hole, riding a roller-coaster, hitting a wall, an ongoing emptiness, the light going out, and ghosts or visitations are common metaphors used to describe the experience of a severe diagnosis, divorce, or death. Metaphors, not unlike narrative accounts, deserve curiosity and exploration. Moving too quickly away from metaphors to declarative speech or other seemingly clearer utterances disenfranchises the griever and empowers the clinician. Further, by exploring metaphors, practitioners can listen for shattered dreams (see Campbell, 2012; Kopp, 1995).

Here are examples of prompting questions one can use to elicit and invite expectations and plans that may have been disrupted by recent or past disruptive changes.

> When you pictured this time in your life, what did you picture?
> When you thought about being (a mom, alone, ill), what did you picture?
> If and when you thought of losses in your family, how did you think it would be, how would it happen?
> After release from the hospital, how did the next months look to you? What did you see ahead?
> Tell me about the plans you and (the name of the now-dead or severely ill person) had?

Questions such as these can include both what Rando called physical and psychosocial losses. Listen for dissonance between pictures, expectations, or dreams *and* the way their life currently is. Listen for thresholds being crossed. As discussed earlier, that will clarify whether there is disappointment or a shattered dream. Here is an example of continuing thresholds:

> By the time, my father's heart stopped, I'd been mourning him for years. And yet, when I consider his story, I wonder whether the various deaths can ever be separated, and whether memory and consciousness have such secure title, after all, to the seat of selfhood. I can't stop looking for meaning in the two years that followed his loss of his supposed "self," and I can't stop finding it.
> (Franzen, 2002, p. 30)

Franzen's essay is about Alzheimer's disease and related conditions. While that was his focus, the ambiguity he described could apply also to other mental health or medical conditions, and addictive behaviors.

Responses to Shattered Dreams—New or Altered Dreams

Havemann's medical memoir title, *A Life Shaken: My Encounter with Parkinson's Disease*, previews his threshold experience.

> After living for many years as an independent adult and planning to continue doing so for many more, you have to accept your newfound status of dependence. At the same time, you must resist the temptation to believe your

disabilities make you less than human . . . Parkinson's wins if it makes me focus on the long term—and give up. My strategy is to concentrate on the short term—and keep going.

(Havemann, 2002, pp. 155–161)

In order to move forward, shattered dreams must be acknowledged and grieved, in part, so that new or adapted dreams can emerge. For some, this can take a long time; for others, the transition occurs quickly. An example, which includes multiple choices of adapted dreams, may help.

A woman had a severe case of rheumatoid arthritis. As she described its particular impact for her, she volunteered that she woke up every day in pain. This was her conspicuous health loss. As she continued she beamed with pride about her ways of coping with the arthritis. "I've learned pain control," she said, as she described changes in diet, careful exercising, planned use of medications, even tools to help her relax. Here was a person who was coping well with a huge change. Then, her face dropped, tears flowed, as she said, "Ted, inside I am still a dancer and that is so very hard to let go of."

This was her loss of dreams. Dancing for her was exercise, body image, her social outlet, even a significant part of her way of life. And no one had helped her grieve or adjust to this loss.

I asked if she had grieved her shattered dreams. She was taken aback. She knew about funerals, retirement events, not grieving for dancing. I suggested that she go to the dance hall at least one more time with her friends. Use the occasion, I suggested, to tell each other stories about the dancing and its meaning for each. Honor the richness of that part of her life by a rite of passage to mark the change. It would also be, I submitted, a time for grieving.

Then, after some grieving, it seemed that she had at least three options. One, to put the dancing on the imaginary shelf, never to be done again, but kept alive as a rich part of her story telling life. (We all tell stories of things we no longer do but which we keep alive through our stories.) A second option was to continue dancing using her canes, wheel chair or other mobility aids. It was important to note that consideration of this option involved grieving because the dancing to be done this way would be different than the way she wanted to dance. Still a third choice was for her to become a coach or teacher of others who wanted to dance, thereby keeping the dancing alive.

(Bowman, 2018, pp. 22–23)

Dreaming new dreams and creating altered pictures, after disruptive change and loss, involves grieving old dreams.

The case study included in that account includes these options that may apply to other losses:

1. The grieving of some shattered dreams must include acknowledgment that while what was lost cannot continue, it may be possible to honor the

experience, memories, and dream through reminiscence, life review, and story-telling.
2. The grieving of other shattered dreams, while important, can lead to adapted ways to continue links to the previous dream. Musicians with fine-motor skill losses teach and mentor other musicians. Mothers Against Drunk Driving was started by the mother of child killed by a drunk driver.
3. The grieving of still other shattered dreams, while important, can lead to continuation but adapted versions of the previous dream. A mother, who dreamed of a perfect family, faced her son's diagnosis with autism, grieved her loss, saw the other side, champions every intervention, and now rises in hope (Linthorst, 2011, p. 94).

Each of these could be called wounded healers. They are wounded *and* they choose to continue living life to the fullest. Sam Keen wrote about grief related to fathers:

> One of the standard themes in mythology is the promise of the wounded healer. In our hurt [can lie] the source of our healing ... One of men's greatest resources for change is our wound and our longing for the missing father. We can heal ourselves by becoming the fathers we wanted but did not have ... Our best map for parenting is outlined like a photographic negative in the shadow side of our grief. Get in touch with your disappointment, your rage, your grief, your loneliness for the father, the intimate touching family you did not have, and you will find a blueprint for parenting. Become the father you longed for. We heal ourselves by learning to give to our children what we did not receive.
> (Keen, 1991, p. 226)

Closing Comments

Shattered dreams are real experiences of loss. Too many frameworks for losses overlook or minimize their significance. The intent of this chapter was to shine a light on this particular loss and to discuss viable responses. Acknowledgment, followed by permission to grieve shattered dreams, followed by support for respectful endings or adaptations of earlier dreams, are key tasks for grief care.

Key Terms

Identity Contingency: Stereotypes determined by others to an aspect of an individual's identity.

Moral Injury: Refers to a loss experience observed under the pretense of committing, grappling with, debating, witnessing, imagining, or failing to prevent acts or events or thoughts that are perceived as ethical transgressions. This generates social, psychological, cultural, or spiritual shame and distress for the individual.

Wounded Healer: Implies that we allow painful life experiences that we have endured to increase empathy towards the pain of others when they are in similar emotional states.

Questions for Reflection

1. Given the intangible, wide-ranging, and subjective nature of this loss experience, how would you define shattered dreams? How does the loss experience of shattered dreams differ from everyday disappointments in life?
2. Have you ever experienced any of the author's iterations of shattered dreams? If so, what was this experience like for you? If not, can you identify a shattered dream that you may currently be subject to losing?
3. After reading this chapter, which case studies surprised you in terms of loss experiences, and why? What might hinder people's abilities to acknowledge or support shattered dreams? How would you now respond to other's who have experienced losses associated with shattered dreams, and which of the author's strategies would you utilize?
4. How does the stigmatization of identity contingency prompt losses related to shattered dreams? How then does this relate to assimilation, traumatic experiences, historical narratives, cultural biases, or moral injuries?

References

Anderson, H., & Mitchell, K. (1983). *All our losses/all our griefs*. Philadelphia: The Westminster Press.

Attig, T. (1996). *How we grieve: Relearning the world*. New York: Oxford University Press.

Becker, G. (1997). *Disrupted lives: How people create meaning in a chaotic world*. Berkeley: University of California Press.

Berger, S. (1996). *Horizontal woman: The story of a body in exile*. New York: Houghton Mifflin Company.

Boss, P. (2006). *Loss, trauma, and resilience: Therapeutic work with ambiguous loss*. New York: W. W. Norton & Company.

Bowman, T. (1994). *Loss of dreams: A special kind of grief*. St. Paul: Self-Published. Retrieved from www.bowmanted.com

Bowman, T. (2018). *Finding hope when dreams have shattered*. Columbia, SC: CreateSpace.

Brave Heart, M. Y. H. (1999). Gender differences in the historical trauma response among the Lakota. *Journal of Health & Social Policy*, 10(4), 1–21.

Bruce, E., & Schultz, C. (2001). *Nonfinite loss and grief: A psychoeducational approach*. Baltimore: Paul H. Brookes Publishing Co.

Campbell, G. (2012). *Mining your client's metaphors*. Bloomington, IN: Balboa Press.

Chavis, G. (2011). *Poetry and story therapy: The healing power of creative expression*. London: Jessica Kingsley Publishers.

Dittberner-Jax, N. (2017). *Crossing the water: Poems*. Minneapolis: Nodin Press.

Doka, K. J. (Ed.) (1989). *Disenfranchised grief: Recognizing hidden sorrows*. New York: Lexington Books.

Erdrich, H. (2010). Phosphorescence. In T. Bowman and E. Johnson (Eds.), *The wind blows, the ice breaks: Poems of loss and renewal*. Minneapolis: Nodin Press.

Frank, A. (1991). *At the will of the body*. Boston: Houghton Mifflin Company.

Franzen, J. (2002). *How to be alone: Essays*. New York: Farrar, Straus & Giroux.

Gill, B. (1997). *Changed by a child: Companion notes for parents of a child with a disability*. New York: Doubleday.

Hardy, K., & Laszloffy, T. (2005). *Teens who hurt: Clinical interventions to break the cycle of adolescent violence*. New York: Guilford Press.
Harris, D. L. (Ed.). (2011). *Counting our losses: Reflecting on change, loss, and transition in everyday life*. New York: Routledge.
Havemann, J. (2002). *A life shaken: My encounter with Parkinson's disease*. Baltimore: The Johns Hopkins University Press.
Herbert, D. (2017). A letter from me. In N. Granger Jr. & L. Hoffman (Eds.), *Silent screams: Poetic journeys through addiction and recovery*. Colorado Springs: University Professors Press.
Hynes, A., & Hynes-Berry, M. (1994). *Bibliotherapy—the interactive process: A handbook*. St. Cloud, MN: Northstar Press.
Jamison, K. (1995). *An unquiet mind: A memoir of moods and madness*. New York: Alfred A. Knopf.
Janoff-Bulman, R. (1992). *Shattered assumptions: Toward a new psychology of trauma*. New York: Free Press.
Keen, S. (1991). *Fire in the belly: On being a man*. New York: Bantam Books.
Koch, T. (1994). *Watersheds: Stories of crisis and renewal in our everyday lives*. Toronto: Lester Publishing Limited.
Konek, C. W. (1991). *Daddyboy: A memoir*. St. Paul: Graywolf Press.
Kopp, R. (1995). *Metaphor therapy: Using client-generated metaphors in psychotherapy*. New York: Brunner-Mazel.
Laux, D. (2005). *For the sake of strangers in what we carry: Poems*. Brockport, NY: BOA Editions.
Linthorst, J. (2011). *Autism disrupted: A mother's journey of hope*. Spring Hill, TN: Cardinal House Publishing.
Mairs, N. (1990). *Carnal acts: Essays*. New York: HarperCollins.
Mitchell, W. (2018). *Somebody I used to know*. New York: Bloomsbury Publishing.
Nadeau, J. (2006). Metaphorically speaking: The use of metaphor in grief therapy. *Illness, Crisis & Loss, 14*(3), 201–211.
Nakashima-Brock, R. (2017). Moral injury and paths to recovery and spiritual resiliency, a handout used for a workshop May 7, 2017 in Minneapolis, MN.
Orr, G. (2013). *River inside the river: Poems*. New York: W. W. Norton & Company.
Parkes, C. M. (1996). *Bereavement: Studies of grief in adult life*. New York: Routledge.
Price, R. (1994). *A whole new life: An illness and a healing*. New York: Atheneum.
Rankin, C. (2014). *Citizen: An American lyric*. St. Paul: Graywolf Press.
Rodriguez, L. (1998). *To the police officer who refused to sit in the same room as my son because he's a 'gang-banger' from Trochemoche: Poems*. Willimantic, CT: Curbstone Press.
Rosenblatt, P., & Bowman, T. (2013). Alternative approaches to conceptualizing grief: A conversation. *Bereavement Care, 32*(2), 30–33.
Silko, L. M. (1977). *Ceremony*. New York: Penguin Books.
Spenser, D. (2004). Moment of inertia in Pomegranate. Santa Cruz, CA: Hummingbird Press. Retrieved March 9, 2008, from http://writersalmanac.publicradio.org
Steele, C. M. (2010). *Whistling Vivaldi: How stereotypes affect us and what we can do*. New York: W. W. Norton & Company.
Tomm, K. (1990). Foreword. In M. White & D. Epston (Eds.), *Narrative means to therapeutic ends*. New York: W. W. Norton & Company.
Utrzan, D. S., & Northwood, A. K. (2016). Broken promises and lost dreams: Navigating asylum in the United States. *Journal of Marriage and Family Therapy, 10*(1111), 1–13.
White, M. (2007). *Maps of narrative practice*. New York: W. W. Norton & Company.

CHAPTER 19

Sexual Assault, Loss, and the Journey to Justice

Tashel C. Bordere and Laura Danforth

Justice delayed is justice denied.
—William E. Gladstone (Speech in House of Commons, March 16, 1868)

Sexual assault is a major source of trauma, loss, and grief. Recognizing that both men and women experience assault, sexual violence remains gendered as females across social locations (e.g., geographic regions, ethnicity, sexuality, race, ability status, religion/spirituality, careers, military, prison systems) are uniquely preyed upon and disproportionately impacted by this abhorrent act. For example, in 2016 a male physician traveled to a female patient's floor 12 times, visiting her room three times, before sexually assaulting her while she was sedated, tethered to machines, and receiving breathing treatments for asthma (Banks, 2018; Phillips, 2018). Although found guilty as charged, the perpetrator privileged by occupation status (i.e., physician) was granted probation and will not serve a prison sentence (see *USA Today*, 2018).

One in three women in the United States experiences sexual violence, and 99% of those accused of sexual assault will not go to prison (Rape, Abuse, and Incest National Network [RAINN], 2015). For a small percentage of assault survivors, justice may be achieved but grossly delayed as a function of social inequities. For example, despite nearly 60 women (e.g., Andrea Constand) disclosing corroborating stories of assault by Bill Cosby (high-profile actor-comedian), it took nearly 15 years for him to be held accountable through a conviction of 3 to 10 years in prison.

In our writing this chapter, I (TB) endeavored to include the most current illustrations of diverse women's experiences with sexual violence employing cases highlighted in the media, a quest that proved to be daunting. Consistent with the alarming statistics on gendered sexual violence, national and international news coverage of women's assault experiences was endless, imbalanced by disparagingly low reports of perpetrator convictions or restorative justice for survivors.

The path to healing and vindication for a large population of women remains elusive and wrought with limited protections and therapeutic options as survivors cope with "suffocated grief" or penalties around their responses (Bordere, 2014, 2016) to multiple disenfranchising non-death losses (Bordere, 2017). This is particularly so for adolescent and young adult women in which we find the highest sexual assault victimization rates (Humphrey & White, 2000). Forty percent of women who have been sexually assaulted experienced this violation prior to 18 years of age (Smith et al., 2017). Adolescent and young adult survivors are charged with navigating normal developmental processes such as identity development, intimacy in friendships, dating, and independence from parents in preparation for adulthood roles and responsibilities (e.g., careers; Arnett, 2004; Erikson, 1968). Sexual assault leaves them dually grappling with grief complicated by post-assault trauma, loss, and grief, largely in the face of unjust outcomes.

Researchers found that 35% of females assaulted under age 18 were also assaulted in adulthood (CDC-NISVS, 2014). Thus, based on assault and conviction rates, a high percentage of young females may experience multiple assaults by multiple perpetrators at pivotal developmental periods without repercussions for assailants. The perpetrator's behavior is dismissed while the survivor carries trauma and loss and the adjustments they necessitate throughout adulthood into intimate relationships, employment, parenting, and grandparenting. Due to the pervasiveness of sexual violence against young adult women and the ongoing disparities and injustices in their survivorship journey, female sexual assault survivors are the focus of this chapter.

In this chapter, we provide a critical examination of non-death losses and grief for female sexual assault victim-survivors from a contextual (Bronfenbrenner, 1977) and social justice perspective (Bordere, 2016, 2017). We describe sexual violations committed against women largely by male perpetrators accounting for privilege, oppression, marginalization, and alliance-building in loss and grief enfranchisement for survivors. Heterosexual white males have the highest sexual assault rates (Planty, Langton, Krebs, Berzofsky, & Smiley-McDonald, 2013). The chapter is written with attention to the marginalized positionality of women existing in patriarchal cultural contexts in which heterosexual men conversely experience privilege or unearned advantages (e.g., legal protections; McIntosh, 1995) that allow for high assault rates and low convictions. Attention is given to common patterns and unique adjustments and issues around coping that may arise for survivors occupying privileged racial identity status, and for survivors representing multiple intersecting marginalized identities (e.g., gender—female, race—African American, stage of development—young adulthood).

In terms of language, in this chapter, "victim" refers to "one that is injured, destroyed, or sacrificed; subjected to oppression, hardship, or mistreatment" (Merriam-Webster's Dictionary, 2014. The descriptor "survivor" is utilized to capture the post-assault experience of functioning and surviving life (Bordere, 2014) in its aftermath. In this chapter, "sexual assault" refers to "any type of sexual activity or contact that you do not consent to" (U.S. Department of Health and Human Services, 2019). We acknowledge that individuals impacted by sexual violence may not employ these labels, and we honor their right to self-identify. Further, we illuminate the complexities and strengths involved in coping and resisting oppression following assault within broader social and political contexts largely unsuited to facilitate such resilience. We outline barriers to healing and enfranchisement, losses associated with sexual violations, and provide illustrations of resistance and resilience. The chapter concludes with implications for research and practice.

Barriers to Healing and Enfranchisement

Survivors may be confronted with multiple barriers to assault and loss recognition that circumvent the healing process and attainment of justice.

Identifying the Assault

It is a basic right that sexual assault survivors have access to language and concepts that are clearly and uniformly operationalized. The ability to name our experiences has implications for self-care, self-advocacy across settings (family, education, workplace, legal system), and help-seeking in identifying support services. Although death, as a loss, is most often utilized allegorically, the concept has a standard operationalization across institutions. Conversely, language related to sexual violations, as non-death loss experiences, is inconsistent and ambiguous. An array of labels is used interchangeably and uniquely, including "rape," "abuse," "battery," "assault," and even descriptors as obscure as sexual "misconduct" and as minimizing as "20 minutes of action" (Crimesider Staff, 2016) and "the incident" (The Guardian, 2016). For example, in explaining his sentencing during the Brock Turner sexual assault trial, Judge Aaron Persky repeatedly referred to the survivor's sexual assault experience as "the incident" to the omission of any concepts remotely indicative of sexual violations ("So I acknowledge the devastation. And—and to me, not only the—*the incident*, but the criminal proceedings"; Levin, 2016).

Inconsistent and overlapping definitions are found across geographic locations. According to the National Institute of Justice, rape is defined differently based on the state (e.g., NIJ, 2017). The U.S. Department of Justice defines sexual assault as "any nonconsensual sexual act proscribed by Federal, tribal, or State law, including when the victim lacks capacity to consent" (2018). On one government site, a section is titled "Rape and Sexual Violence" as if they are distinct experiences, and then describes rape as a type of sexual violence in the paragraph that follows. Sexual assault is then defined differently from rape, and yet these concepts are utilized interchangeably. These inconsistencies found through an extensive review of the scholarly literature (see Bordere, 2017) and on government sites (e.g., NIJ, 2017) have important implications for policy development and practice in federally funded institutions (e.g., universities, workplaces), clinical practice, research, and program development.

Communities have recognized issues around operationalization of sexual violations in just practice. In protest of a court decision in Pamplona, Spain, favoring five alleged perpetrators (i.e., La Manada) who sexually assaulted a young woman, protestors carried signage such as—"It is not an abuse. It's rape" (Minder, 2018). Media headlines reinforced this sentiment—"La Manada ruling sparks fierce debate over definition of sexual violence" (see El Pais, 2018)—illustrating community understanding of the significance of language and objective definitions of concepts in proper representation of experience and justice.

Ambiguity allows for subjective decision-making, favoring systemic oppression and patriarchal justice in legal systems. For example, the five alleged perpetrators, who ironically self-identify as a "wolf pack" or la manada, were released on bail due to insufficient evidence of "intimidation or violence"; part of the criteria for rape in Pamplona. In rendering the verdict, the victim-survivor was subjectively described as possessing an "attitude of submission and subjugation" which they did not deem indicative of "intimidation" (Rosell, 2018). The defense lawyers critiqued the survivor for not using self-protective measures (i.e., "biting their penises"; see El Pais, 2017) to defend herself against a group of five men.

Survivors exist in cultural contexts that may recognize neither the assault nor the losses, trauma, and grief emanating from it. Due to a lack of clarity about what constitutes sexual assault, survivors may similarly struggle with recognition that an assaultive act was committed against them.

Making the Connection: Assault as Non-Death Loss Experience

Family members, friends, and institutions that recognize a reported sexual violation may not view it as a source of loss and grief for several reasons. Lack of recognition may be related to the common assumption that grief is limited to death loss. This misassumption may be reinforced by resistance among professionals in death and grief to validate the connection of non-death loss to grief; the ever-expanding but limited research on non-death loss; and the scarcity of scholarly literature connecting sexual assault, non-death loss, and grief (Bordere, 2017; Schultz & Harris, 2011; Whiston, 1981). Over 30 years ago, Whiston (1981) provided a thorough delineation of non-death losses in assault but mentioned "grief" only once in the article. Another article, similarly published 25 years ago, outlined losses in sexual abuse with a focus on childhood (Bourdon & Cook, 1993).

Some possible explanations for these glaring omissions include the need for greater interdisciplinary research, gaps in research and practice when scholars and clinicians exist in distinct silos and miss out on collaborative opportunities, the prevalence of dominant discourses in literature in which women's experiences are framed from deficit perspectives (victim-blaming—e.g., a woman's use of alcohol caused the assault and re-victimization), and utilization of methodologies that discount the valuable roles of marginalized communities as vital informants in basic and translational research and writing. Bordere's (2017) article is the only known scholarly publication in existence, integrating sexual assault as a non-death loss experience with suffocated grief and social injustice. Limitations in the literature are costly for survivors who consequently may be offered few or no opportunities, even by well-meaning, cared-about persons, researchers, educators, and helping professionals (e.g., social workers, therapists) to process and receive research-based support grounded in socially just practice for a myriad of common losses and adjustments for women in sexual victimization (Bordere, 2016, 2017).

A beginning step towards enfranchisement of women in sexual assault is awareness and acknowledgment of the violation and its impact on women's post-assault lived experiences. Statistically, we have long known that sexual assault disproportionately impacts a large percentage of women, particularly in young adulthood (Department of Justice, 2014; Humphrey & White, 2000), yet it was through recent social and political actions that this violation has received more widespread attention. Several individual and collective actions were pivotal in raising awareness on national and international fronts including movements on social media (e.g., #MeToo—Facebook, Twitter), student activism (Krause, Miedema, Woofter, & Yount, 2017), former President Obama's White House Task Force on Sexual Assault in 2014, marches (e.g., Take Back the Night), and activism attire (T-shirts—Resisterhood, She Persisted). It is promising that sexual victimization has recently garnered greater attention. However, less credence has been given to the daily, and often lifelong, struggles and issues of disenfranchisement and suffocated grief among women coping with multiple complicated visible and nonvisible losses, trauma, and grief as victim-survivors.

Identifying Loss and Giving Voice to Grief/Loss and Grief in Sexual Assault Survivorship

A plethora of disenfranchising losses are associated with gendered sexual violence. The primary loss is that of the survivor's pre-assault life or loss of life as it was prior to the assault. Andrea Constand, victim-survivor of Bill Cosby's assault, emphasized this point in her victim impact letter (2018) stating:

> To truly understand the impact that sexual assault has had on my life, you have to understand the person that I was before it happened . . . [With the assault] life as I knew it came to an abrupt halt . . . I was a young woman brimming with confidence and looking forward to a future bright with possibilities. Now, almost 15 years later, I'm a middle-aged woman who's been stuck in a holding pattern for most of her adult life, unable to heal fully or to move forward.

Survivors may cope with assault-related physical, cognitive, emotional, social, and economic changes and adjustments that were not a part of their previous life tasks or lived experiences. The extensive life-altering secondary losses related to the assault may be unanticipated, interconnected, and unsupported, posing even greater challenges to an already arduous survivorship journey. Some losses may be obvious (e.g., peer group losses), while many others may be less transparent (e.g., loss of trust). Survivors may struggle with the non-finality or sustained presence of losses that are not visible or easily identifiable (Schultz & Harris, 2011) to entities that may have otherwise served a support function.

The countless non-death losses create "bereavement" or a sense of being "robbed" (DeSpelder & Strickland, 2015) for sexual assault survivors and cared-about persons (family, friends) as secondary survivors (Bordere, 2017). Bereavement is illustrated in two recently publicized victim impact statements in sexual assault cases. One case involved Brock Turner's sexual assault (utilizing objects) of an unconscious young woman (Emily Doe) who described ways in which she was robbed—"my worth, my privacy, my energy, my time, my safety, my intimacy, my confidence, my own voice" (Doe, 2016). Similarly, bereavement is apparent in Andrea Constand's victim impact statement regarding Bill Cosby's sexual assault—"He robbed me of my health and vitality, my open nature, and trust in myself and others"—(The Associated Press—CBS News, 2018).

Secondary losses in sexual assault may include losses and challenges in all domains of life. Survivors may experience losses and changes in physical and mental health (e.g., appetite loss, sleep loss, anxiety, depression). There may be a loss of a sense of safety (Frazier, Conlon, & Glaser, 2001) coupled with environmental mistrust in places that were previously (pre-assault) deemed secure. This may particularly be the case for Caucasian women, who although marginalized by gender, have consciously or unconsciously benefited from "hierarchies of social power" that exist within marginalized groups (Greene, 2012, p. 84). Caucasian women may have benefited from privileges around safety (e.g., police protection) and justice as a function of unearned advantages associated with white racial identity status. Navigating educational, medical, and legal systems with an additional marginalized social identity status (sexual assault survivor) in which women across social locations (e.g., Anita Hill in 1991; Christine Blasey Ford in 2018) experience discrimination, may be uniquely challenging for Caucasian women in the absence of protections that they may have been accustomed to in their pre-assault lived experiences. Care plans for this population should include attention to issues of loss, trauma, and grief involved in this shift from the protections of privilege to marginalization, discrimination, injustice, and invalidation following sexual assault.

Comparatively, female populations with intersecting marginalized identities (e.g., gender and racial minority) may possess an understanding of historical and contemporary issues of safety. For example, African American youth are aware of African American female and male exploitation as a part of ongoing familial racial socialization processes and education around safety and survival. Their already-heightened awareness and environmental mistrust may be further intensified by a sexual assault experience. Further, African American female grief around assault and secondary losses may be disenfranchised or go unacknowledged (Doka, 1989) both within the broader culture and within segments of their more immediate culture as a sacrifice for the collective sustainability of African American communities. Survivors may be held to expectations for silence for the protection of African American males (Neville & Pugh, 1997; Washington, 2001) who, like African American women, are sexualized and unjustly overrepresented in prison systems (Alexander, 2012). For example, in the 1991 Anita Hill sexual assault case against Clarence Thomas, Hill (victim-survivor) was publicly re-victimized in the televised Senate trial. She was also criticized by some African Americans who deemed her assault disclosure an attempt to hamper the upward mobility of an African American male in his plight to be a Supreme Court judge. In an interview, Meena

Harris (co-founder of the Black Lives Matter Global Network) recounted community responses such as, "*How dare you tear down this black man who had the chance to be one of the most powerful men in the country on the Supreme Court*" (Whaley, 2018).

Numerous aspects of the assault create losses of privacy for survivors. The costs of breaches in privacy leaves survivors unduly charged with pondering the implications of disclosure. Survivors justifiably fear stigmatization (Miller, Canales, Amacker, Backstrom, & Gidycz, 2011) victim-blaming, and discrimination grounded in the objectification of women (Collins, 2000; Hooks, 1989) and rape myths (e.g., false reporting—see Weiser, 2017). Survivors may elect to limit or avoid disclosure so that other's assumptive views about them and relationships are not altered or dissolved as a consequence. Khan, Hirsch, Wamboldt, and Mellins (2018) examined the social risks of labeling and reporting sexual assault among college students and found that ambiguity allowed for "social continuation" rather than "social rupture" (p. 452). Survivors were more likely to disclose the assault experience exclusively to a close friend. They did not want the assault experience to detract from their ability to matriculate through college or to risk the loss of social networks. Further, participants avoided disclosure because they did not want to attach a perpetrator label to the cared-about person who committed the assault.

Loss of privacy, time, and control continue with each assault disclosure (to family, friends, teachers, law enforcement, medical staff, legal system) and steps taken toward enfranchisement of survivors. For survivors who elect to complete a rape kit, the process involved in securing DNA evidence from assault survivors through rape kit testing is invasive and painful. Survivors participate in this lengthy process (4–6 hours) completed by unfamiliar medical professionals. Staff completing the exam may lack education and training in the psychological issues and losses associated with assault and the exam. Survivors may experience trauma and re-victimization through "evidence" collection which includes oral, vaginal, and anal swabs, blood draws, urine samples, and pubic hair combings (Ritter, 2011). Survivors experience a loss of time as they wait for responses to rape kit testing, often without being informed that rape kit completion does not insure that it will be processed. A nationwide inventory of untested rape kits revealed that tens of thousands of rape kits were never tested (see Reilly, 2015). In a NIJ special report, Ritter (2011) underscored issues of social injustice associated with untested rape kits.

> Delays in evidence being sent to a lab—as well as delays in analyzing evidence—result in delays in justice. In worst-case scenarios, this can lead to additional victimization by serial offenders or the incarceration of people wrongly convicted of a crime.
>
> (p. 14)

When rape kits are not processed, survivors experience losses in opportunities to seek convictions or participate in practices such as restorative justice that hold perpetrators accountable and promote healing around losses and grief in sexual assault. When processed, Quinlan (2017) highlights that sexual assault kits rarely lead to convictions. It is a basic right for survivors to complete sexual assault kits in the pursuit of justice. However, there may be a loss of opportunity to complete a sexual assault kit. In Canada, for example, rape kits are not easily accessible to women in rural communities where there are transportation barriers (Quinlan, 2017). Law enforcement officers are less likely to trust the veracity of minority women's sexual assault disclosures and are thus less likely to offer the opportunity to complete sexual assault kits.

Economic and educational losses consequent of assault produce costs for survivors and for women and allies (advocates for survivors) who worked to secure women's rights to receive an education and pursue career opportunities that allow for economic independence. In cultural contexts dominated by patriarchy, when losses are highlighted, attention is focused on losses for male sexual assault perpetrators. Particular attention is paid to losses impacting their financial and educational opportunity structures notably detached from the egregious acts of sexual violence precipitating the losses. One news article, "Weinstein Effect: Sexual Misconduct Claims Led to Losses for These Men" (e.g., loss employment from company; *USA Today*, 2017) with no mention of losses for over 70 women coping with shifts in their opportunity structures as they *survive life* (Bordere, 2014) following the assaults. This is problematic as sexual assault victimization costs approximately $151,423 (DeLisi et al., 2010),

In a study of economic losses and economic well-being with survivors and rape crisis service providers, Loya (2015) found that assault may produce long-term financial consequences. The four primary economic consequences related to the trauma of assault include decreased job performance, time off (e.g., medical and legal appointments, PTSD), inability to perform job duties (PTSD, difficulty concentrating), and job loss (being fired or quitting). In capitalistic contexts, survivors are provided limited time off for dealing with loss (Bordere, 2017; Harris, 2009–2010) and may return to work before they are mentally, physically, or cognitively ready to successfully function in a work environment. Consequently, they may experience job loss related to changes in job performance. These financial consequences produce suffocated grief (Bordere, 2014, 2016) for survivors who are penalized for normal trauma and grief reactions in institutions that do not appropriately provide accommodations for their experience of loss and bereavement. Further, Loya (2015) found that mental health challenges had the longest impact on survivors' ability to work. However, without an income, the survivor's ability to afford needed mental and physical health care is compromised. Survivors who can afford care may encounter helping professionals untrained in the interconnections among sexual assault, non-death loss, grief, and issues of social injustice, and hence lose the opportunity to get culturally responsive mental and physical health care support.

Through the myriad of experiences with barriers, delays, and disenfranchisement, there may be both a loss of self-confidence and a loss of confidence in social, legal, and political institutions. Loss of institutional trust may be reinforced for populations such as African American women, representing multiple marginalized identities, who may also have historical memories and present-day experiences of systemic injustices.

Survivor Resistance and Resilience Through Loss

Despite long journeys that all too infrequently lead to justice in legal and educational institutions, bereaved sexual assault survivors have found ways to acknowledge and resist oppression. They have been able to persist through the trauma and losses of assault through the support of allies, survivor-to-survivor support, and through healing work with other vulnerable populations. Allies are invaluable to healing and coping for assault survivors. For example, when Clarence Thomas was appointed to the Supreme Court in 1991 despite Anita Hill's candid sexual assault disclosure and testimony about his deviant behaviors, over 1,600 African American women united in purchasing a full-page ad entitled, "African American Women in Defense of Ourselves" (November 17, 1991) in the *New York Times* and other print media targeting African Americans (see Phillips, 2018).

In the face of stigma and invalidation, survivors have found public ways to acknowledge and validate the experiences of other survivors. In her victim impact statement regarding the Brock Turner assault, Emily Doe included a message of support and unity to other survivors—"On nights when you feel alone, I am with you. When people doubt you or dismiss you, I am with you. I fought every day for you. So never stop fighting, I believe you" (Doe, 2016). The #MeToo movement, which has gone viral on social media, was created over 10 years ago by Tarana Burke as an outreach effort targeting young women of color coping with sexual assault (Garcia, 2017; Vagianos, 2017). Burke created the #MeToo campaign as healing space for survivor-to-survivor disclosure and support for young women representing racial and ethnic minority status. The campaign gained increased momentum through social media and has been pivotal in increasing social and political awareness, education, and action around this formidable violation. Female survivors across diverse social locations (e.g., socioeconomic status, age, religion, race, ethnicity, nationality, sexuality) overwhelmingly embraced the #MeToo hashtag and social forums as safe spaces for disclosure, making social media (e.g., Facebook, Twitter) a major platform for sharing experiences of sexual assault. The #MeToo movement also inspired the hashtag #Cuentalo (tell your story) campaign in Spain. For some survivors, providing therapeutic services to others aids in personal healing around losses and grief in sexual assault. In Andrea Constand's victim impact statement (i.e., Bill Cosby assault), she explained—"I like my work. I like knowing that I can help relieve pain and suffering in others. I know that it helps heal me too." (The Associated Press, 2018).

Conclusion and Implications

Sexual assault remains a serious cultural issue disproportionately impacting young adult women across diverse backgrounds. Despite increases in awareness, gendered sexual violence persists at profoundly high rates with convictions occurring at consistently low rates. Greater uniformity and clarity are needed around language and the operationalization of concepts related to sexual violations so that survivors are better equipped to name their loss experiences and grief, advocate for themselves in different settings (school, work, home), and experience outcomes in criminal justice systems that are favorable to survivors. A myriad of losses are associated with sexual assault victimization and survivorship that warrant greater attention in the scholarly literature and in clinical practice. More interdisciplinary research is needed to better understand the loss, grief, and coping experiences of female sexual assault survivors and areas of resistance and resilience in oppressive cultural contexts. This can be accomplished through more participatory action research and activism among researchers (Cancian, 1993). In socially just practice, policies related to sexual assault must be implemented, regularly updated and enforced (e.g., educational settings, medical facilities, workplaces).

Key Terms

Allies: Individuals who actively recognize the value and importance of socially just causes, wish to end marginalization, and consciously support those who lack privilege and have suffered injustice.

Enfranchisement: Providing acceptance and permission for one to grieve in an autonomous way that is congruent with their needs, values, lived experiences, and overall situation.

Sexual Assault: Any sexual contact, attempt, or interaction that occurs without consent.

#MeToo Movement: A social movement against sexual assault and sexual harassment that has been fruitful on social media and communication-based platforms. Demonstrates the prevalence of sexual misconduct and the need for societal corrective action(s).

Questions for Reflection

1. How would you define "suffocated grief"? How is this term complimentary and different in comparison to Doka's disenfranchised grief (see Chapter 2)? Why do you think the varying experiences of sexual assault and the accompanying non-death losses associated with it are so difficult for others to accept, recognize, and support?
2. What barriers prevent sexual assault survivors from being able to find healing or meaning in their loss experiences? How can these barriers be addressed, altered, or removed?
3. Suppose an individual discloses to you that she/he has experienced sexual assault and is feeling overwhelmed by injustice. What strategies would you implement for supporting this individual's grief? Additionally, how can you become an ally on a societal level for people who have experienced sexual violence?
4. Conduct an online search for resources in your area that assist individuals who have experienced sexual assault. Which resources did you think were the most helpful, and how does the resource support survivors' grief experiences? Further, generate ideas and approaches on how sexual assault can be reduced on a societal level.

References

Alexander, M. (2012). *The new Jim Crow: Mass incarceration in the age of colorblindness*. New York, NY: The New Press.

Arnett, J. J. (2004). *Adolescence and emerging adulthood: A cultural approach*. Upper Saddle River, NJ: Pearson Prentice Hall.

Banks, G. (2018, August 17). Ex-Baylor doctor found guilty of raping patient at Ben Taub Hospital. [Website—The Chron] Retrieved from www.chron.com/news/houston-texas/houston/article/Ex-Baylor-doctor-found-guilty-of-raping-patient-13162171.php

Bordere, T. C. (2014). Adolescents and homicide. In K. J. Doka & A. Tucci (Eds.), *Helping adolescents cope with loss*. Washington, DC: Hospice Foundation of America.

Bordere, T. C. (2016). Social justice conceptualizations in grief and loss. In D. L. Harris & T. C. Bordere (Eds.), *Handbook of social justice in loss and grief: Exploring diversity, equity, and Inclusion* (pp. 9–20). New York: Routledge.

Bordere, T. C. (2017). Disenfranchisement and ambiguity in the face of loss: The suffocated grief of sexual assault survivors. *Family Relations, 66(1)*, 29–45.

Bourdon, L. S., & Cook, A. S. (1993). Losses associated with sexual abuse: Therapist and client perceptions. *Journal of Child Sexual Abuse, 2(4)*, 69–82. doi:10.1300/J070v02n04_05

Bronfenbrenner, U. (1977). Toward an experimental ecology of human development. *American Psychologist, 32*, 513–530. doi:10.1037/0003–066X.32.7.513

Cancian, F. M. (1993). Conflicts between activist research and academic success: Participatory research and alternative strategies. *The American Sociologist, 24*, 92–106.

Collins, P. H. (2000). *Black feminist thought: Knowledge, consciousness, and the politics of empowerment* (2nd ed.). New York, NY: Routledge.

Crimesider Staff. (2016, June 6). Father's defense of convict Brock Turner in Standford sex [ibid assault] case draws outrage [CBS News]. Retrieved from www.cbsnews.com/news/stanford-sex-offender-brock-turner-dad-steep-price-for-20-minutes-of-action/

DeLisi, M., Kosloski, A., Sween, M., Hachmeister, E., Moore, M., & Drury, A. (2010). Murder by numbers: Monetary costs imposed by a sample of homicide offenders. *Journal of Forensic Psychiatry & Psychology, 21(4)*, 501. Retrieved from http://proxy.mul.missouri.edu/login?url=http://search.ebscohost.com/login.aspx?direct=true&db=edb&AN=52646389&site=eds-live&scope=site

Department of Justice. (2014). Office of Justice Programs, Bureau of Justice Statistics, Rape and Sexual Victimization Among College-Age Females, 1995–2013. Retrieved from www.rainn.org/statistics/victims-sexual-violence

DeSpelder, L. A., & Strickland, A. L. (2015). *The last dance: Encountering death and dying* (10th ed.). Boston, MA: McGraw Hill.

Doka, K. J. (Ed.) (1989). *Disenfranchised grief: Recognizing hidden sorrow*. Lexington, MA: Lexington Books.

Erikson, E. H. (1968). *Identity: Youth and crisis*. New York, NY: W. W. Norton & Company.

Frazier, P. A., Conlon, A., & Glaser, T. (2001). Positive and negative life changes following sexual assault. *Journal of Consulting and Clinical Psychology, 69*, 1048–1055. doi:10.1037//0022–006X.69.6.1048

Garcia, S. E. (2017, October 20). The woman who created #MeToo long before hashtags. *The New York Times*. Retrieved from www.nytimes.com/2017/10/20/us/me-too-movement-tarana-burke.html

Greene, B. (2012). Intersections of multiple identities and multiple marginalizations: Clinical and paradigmatic considerations. In R. Nettles & R. Balter (Eds.), *Multiple minority*

identities: Applications for practice, research, and training (pp. 81–91). New York, NY: Springer Publishing.
The Guardian. Retrieved from www.theguardian.com/us-news/2016/jun/14/stanford-sexual-assault-read-sentence-judge-aaron-persky
Harris, D. L. (2009–2010). Oppression of the bereaved: A critical analysis of grief in western society. *Omega: The Journal of Death and Dying, 60*, 241–253. doi:10.2190/OM.60.3.c
hooks, b. (1989). *Talking back: Thinking feminist, thinking black*. Boston, MA: South End Press.
Humphrey, J. A., & White, J. W. (2000). Women's vulnerability to sexual assault from adolescence to young adulthood. *Journal of Adolescent Health, 27*(6), 419–424. doi:10.1016/S1054-139X(00)00168-3
Jabois, M. (2017, November 28). Pamplona gang rape victim: Don't leave me alone, please" [Website—EL PAIS] Retrieved from https://elpais.com/elpais/2017/11/28/inenglish/1511867397_302207.html
Khan, S. R., Hirsch, J. S., Wamboldt, A., & Mellins, C. A. (2018). "I didn't want to be that girl": The social risks of labeling, telling, and reporting sexual assault. *Sociological Science, 5*, 432–460.
Krause, K. H., Miedema, S. S., Woofter, R., & Yount, K. M. (2017). Feminist research with student activists: Enhancing campus sexual assault research. *Family Relations, 66*(1), 211–223. https://doi-org.proxy.mul.missouri.edu/10.1111/fare.12239
Levin, S. (2016, June 14). Stanford sexual assault: Read the full text of the judge's controversial decision.
Loya, R. M. (2015). Rape as an economic crime: The impact of sexual violence on survivors' employment and economic well-being. *Journal of Interpersonal Violence, 30*(16), 2793–2813.
McIntosh, P. (1995). White privilege and male privilege: A personal account of coming to see correspondences through work in women's studies: In M. L. Andersen & P. H. Collins (Eds.), *Race, class, and gender: An anthology* (2nd ed.). Belmont, CA: Wadsworth.
Merriam-Webster's Dictionary (11th ed.). (2014). Victim—*Merriam-Webster.com*. Retrieved from www.merriam-webster.com/dictionary/victim
Miller, A. K., Canales, E. J., Amacker, A. M., Backstrom, T. L., & Gidycz, C. A. (2011). Stigma-threat motivated nondisclosure of sexual assault and sexual revictimization: A prospective analysis. *Psychology of Women Quarterly, 35*, 119–128. doi:10.1177/0361684310384104
Miller, R. (2018, August 18). Former doctor who raped heavily sedated patient will serve no prison time. *USA Today*. Retrieved from www.usatoday.com/story/news/nation-now/2018/08/18/no-prison-time-ex-houston-doctor-who-raped-heavily-sedated-patient/1031665002/
Minder, R. (2018, June 21). Five men in 'wolf pack' Pamplona sexual assault case are released on bail. *The New York Times*. Retrieved from www.nytimes.com/2018/06/21/world/europe/spain-pamplona-sexualassault.html
National Institute of Justice. (2017). *Rape and Sexual Violence*. Washington, DC: U.S. Government Printing Office. Retrieved from www.nij.gov/topics/crime/rape-sexual-violence/Pages/welcome.aspx
National Intimate Partner and Sexual Violence Survey (NISVS). (2014, February 19). An Overview of 2010 Summary Report Findings. Centers for Disease Control, National Center for Injury Prevention and Control, Division of Violence Prevention. Retrieved from www.cdc.gov/violenceprevention/pdf/cdc_nisvs_overview_insert_final-a.pdf
Neville, H. A., & Pugh, A. O. (1997). General and culture-specific factors influencing African American women's reporting patterns and perceived social support

following sexual assault: An exploratory investigation. *Violence Against Women, 3*, 361–381. doi:10.1177/1077801297003004003

Phillips, K. (2018, August 19), A jury convicted a doctor of raping a patient at a hospital—sentenced him to probation. *Washington Post.* Retrieved from www.washingtonpost.com/news/true-crime/wp/2018/08/19/a-jury-convicted-a-doctor-of-raping-a-patient-at-a-hospital-and-sentenced-him-to-probation/?utm_term=.5dd0bfb8e624

Planty, M., Langton, L., Krebs, C., Berzofsky, M., & Smiley-McDonald, H. (2013, March). Department of Justice Office of Justice Programs, Bureau of Justice Statistics, Special Report—Female Victims of Sexual Violence, 1994–2010 (Revised May 31, 2016). Retrieved from www.bjs.gov/content/pub/pdf/fvsv9410.pdf

Quinlan, A. (2017). How rape kits failed women. *Herizons*, 20–23.

Rape, Abuse, and Incest National Network [RAINN] (2015). The Criminal Justice System: Statistics. Retrieved from www.rainn.org/statistics/criminal-justice-system.

Reilly, S. (2015). Tens of thousands of rape kits go untested across USA [Media—*USA Today*]. Retrieved from www.usatoday.com/story/news/2015/07/16/untested-rape-kits-evidence-across-usa/29902199/

Ritter, N. (2011, May). *The road ahead: Unanalyzed evidence in sexual assault cases.* U.S. Department of Justice, Office of Justice Programs, National Institute of Justice. Retrieved from www.ncjrs.gov/pdffiles1/nij/233279.pdf

Rosell, V. (2018, June 26). The "wolf-pack" case showed the world how Spanish law is mired in misogyny. *The Guardian.* Retrieved from www.theguardian.com/commentisfree/2018/jun/26/wolf-pack-case-spain-law-misogyny

Doe, E. (2016). *Victim impact statement—Emily Doe-Brock turner case.* Retrieved from www.sccgov.org/sites/da/newsroom/newsreleases/Documents/B-Turner%20VIS.pdf (Note—Link to Victim's Impact Statement was found in news release on Brock Turner's Sentencing; see www.sccgov.org/sites/da/newsroom/newsreleases/Pages/NRA2016/Turner-Sentencing.aspx)

Schultz, C. L., & Harris, D. L. (2011). Giving voice to nonfinite loss and grief in bereavement. In R. A. Neimeyer, D. L. Harris, H. R. Winokuer, & G. F. Thornton (Eds.), *Grief and bereavement in contemporary society: Bridging research and practice* (pp. 235–245). New York: Routledge.

Smith, S. G., Chen, J., Basile, K. C., Gilbert, L. K., Merrick, M. T., Patel, N., et al. (2017). *The national intimate partner and sexual violence survey: 2010–2012 state report.* Atlanta, GA: National Center for Injury Prevention and Control, Centers for Disease Control and Prevention. Retrieved from www.womenshealth.gov/relationships-and-safety/sexual-assault-and-rape/sexual-assault

The Associated Press. (2018, September 25). *Andrea Constand's impact statement: Bill Cosby "robbed me" of my health, vitality and trust* [Website—*CBS News*]. Retrieved from www.cbsnews.com/news/andrea-constands-impact-statement-bill-cosby-robbed-me-of-my-health-vitality-and-trust-2018-09-25/

Urra, S., & Hunter, S. (2018, April 26). "Running of the bulls" defendants escape rape convictions. *El Pais.* Retrieved from https://elpais.com/elpais/2018/04/26/inenglish/1524730809_875632.html?rel=mas

USA Today. (2017, November 13). *Weinstein effect: Sexual misconduct claims led to losses for these men.* Retrieved from https://www.usatoday.com/picture-gallery/money/business/2017/10/25/weinstein-effect-sexual-misconduct-claims-led-to-losses-for-these-men/106990250/

U.S. Department of Health and Human Services. (2019, March 14). *What is sexual assault?* Washington, DC: U.S. Government Printing Office. Retrieved from https://www.womenshealth.gov/relationships-and-safety/sexual-assault-and-rape/sexual-assault

U.S. Department of Justice. (2018). *Sexual assault.* Washington, DC: U.S. Government Printing Office. Retrieved from https://www.justice.gov/ovw/sexual-assault

Vagianos, A. (2017, October 17). The "me too" campaign was created by a black woman 10 years ago. *HuffPost—Women.* Retrieved from www.huffingtonpost.com/entry/the-me-too-campaign-was-created-by-a-black-woman-10-years-ago_us_59e61a7fe4b02a215b336fee

Washington, P. A. (2001). Disclosure patterns of Black female sexual assault survivors. *Violence Against Women, 7,* 1254–1283. doi:10.1177/10778010122183856

Weiser, D. A. (2017). Confronting myths about sexual assault: A feminist analysis of the false report literature. *Family Relations, 66*(1), 46–60.

Whaley, N. (2018, September 25). *Women advocates to recreate 1991 Anita Hill 'New York Times' ad—but with 1,600 men's names instead.* [Website—*The Movement*]. Retrieved from https://mic.com/articles/191489/women-recreate-1991-anita-hill-nyt-ad#.ZRWl4B8XR

Whiston, S. K. (1981). Counseling sexual assault victims: A loss model. *The Personnel and Guidance Journal, 59,* 363–366. doi:10.1002/j.2164-4918.1981.tb00570.x

White House Task Force to Protect Students from Sexual Assault. (2014). *Not alone report.* [Website]. Retrieved from www.nccpsafety.org/resources/library/not-alone-report/

CHAPTER **20**

Loss and Forced Displacement

Athir N. Jisrawi and Carrie Arnold

Introduction

Loubna and Karim lived in a small town in northwestern Syria where they had both grown up in a close-knit community of their extended family and childhood friends. They had been married for eight years and had two young daughters, Khadijah and Yasmine. While they were not rich by any means, they enjoyed a comfortable and self-sufficient life as teachers. In early 2011, they heard rumors of protests occurring in several Syrian towns, amidst uprisings happening across the Middle East as part of the Arab Spring. When the government's response to the protests turned violent, Loubna and Karim began hearing stories about family and friends being abducted or going missing. Karim's nephew, Ali, was only 13 years old when government-linked mercenaries abducted him. He had not been seen since. By late 2011, their town was routinely being targeted with attacks, and destruction of homes was increasing in frequency. Many families escaped to neighboring countries. In 2012, Loubna and Karim decided to pack up the few belongings they could carry (e.g., clothes, documents) and flee to Turkey. They left behind their home, friends, and extended family to seek out a safer life.

Upon arrival in Turkey, they were assigned to a tent in a refugee camp near the border. Life in the camps could not be described as anything but abject poverty and extreme discomfort, and there was a total lack of privacy. Hundreds of tents were packed close together. The summers were hot and dry, and the winters experienced flooding. Karim struggled to find employment that would allow him to provide for his family. What work he could find was temporary and highly insecure. The family was entirely reliant on humanitarian aid for their daily meals and rare health checkups. It was common for women to be sexually exploited and pressured to exchange sexual acts for aid. Loubna felt helpless in being able to provide food for her girls and was pressured into participating in these cruel and exploitative exchanges to avoid starvation. Understandably, this caused tremendous strain on Loubna and Karim's marital relationship. The girls were too young to understand the loss of their home, friends, and family (at the start of the conflict, Yasmine and Khadijah were two and five years old, respectively), yet the experiences in the camp were shaping their lives in profound ways. For example, the girls had never been to a proper school, and by the time they left the camp they were already years behind in their education.

In 2016, Loubna and Karim applied for asylum through the United Nations High Commissioner for Refugees (UNHCR) and were approved for resettlement in Canada. Upon arrival, they received help with housing, groceries, and daily tasks by community organizations and religious institutions. They began to frequent the local mosque where they experienced a feeling of belonging and a social environment they wanted their daughters to experience. Despite the safety and community support, the family had been severely affected by the deplorable conditions of the refugee camp and the horrors of the conflict, and they struggled to adjust to life in Canada. Loubna found it easier to learn English, while Karim wanted to find employment but was not mastering the language as quickly. Karim felt feeble in his attempts to learn English and ashamed that he had to rely on government assistance to provide for his family. He felt frustrated when he found out that his teaching degree would not be accepted in Canada, and he would have to spend years learning English before attending university all over again.

The couple could see the opportunities to build a new life in Canada, but Karim expressed his belief that the conflict would be temporary, and they would be able to move back to Syria in the near future. Yet they continued reading details about the ongoing conflict, hearing stories from family and friends about those who had died or gone missing and were grieving their own losses. Like many who are forced to leave their country, they felt a sense of *living here, and there*, at the same time, and were acutely aware of the innumerable losses that accompanied this indeterminate state.

After being in Canada for two years and with no end in sight to the conflict, they resigned themselves to focusing on settling down, which seemed to be the best long-term choice for their daughters. Khadijah and Yasmine were quickly learning English and enjoying their new school. As the months passed, they began to acclimate to life in Canada, but the complications of their new life still emerged occasionally. For example, Karim yearned to have another child, but Loubna feared backlash because they were still reliant on government assistance and could not provide for their family on their own. She had heard on the news that many Canadians viewed Syrians with suspicion, so she did not want to be seen as taking unnecessary advantage of the hospitality of her new country. She wondered if she would ever be able to make decisions in which her family's status as refugees would not be prominent.

Social Context of Forced Displacement

The story of Karim and Loubna is not unlike that of many millions of others forced to leave behind their homes and everything that was once familiar to them. According to the UNHCR, in 2016 there was a record high of 65.6 million forcibly displaced people globally, 22.5 million of whom were refugees under UN mandates (United Nations, 2017). As described by McLellan (2013), migration can be broadly divided into two categories:

1. Immigration, which entails permanently moving to a foreign country, usually by choice and with potential to maintain social connections and return to the homeland (e.g., a Jordanian doctor applies for Canadian immigration as a skilled worker and moves with her family to complete her residency at an Ontario hospital).
2. Forced displacement, which refers to the involuntary movement of refugees and internally displaced people. This is imagined as temporary but can end up permanent, and usually occurs due to conflict (e.g., a Syrian family such as the one in the opening case study are forced to leave everything behind in order to make a dangerous journey to safety).

Describing people who have left their countries of origin, whether by choice or by force, is a challenging task because the definitions of the most common terms seem to overlap and are often misused. Using the proper terminology, however, is quite crucial because some have important legal definitions and others carry stigmatizing connotations (http://ccrweb.ca/sites/ccrweb.ca/files/glossary_en.pdf). For example, the UNHCR defines a refugee as "someone who has been forced to flee his or her country because of persecution, war, or violence" (www.unrefugees.org/refugee-facts/what-is-a-refugee/). This is distinct from asylum-seekers, internally displaced persons, or economic migrants. The confusion in terms partly arises due to media portrayal of immigrants and forcibly displaced people. News outlets often use terms such as *refugee*, *immigrant*, and *migrant* interchangeably, making it more difficult for the average person to identify the differences between these categories and thus conflating the often-willing immigrant with the often-unwilling refugee. Additionally, politicians motivated to use refugees as scapegoats cast doubt on who these people are and what their motives are for coming to Western countries. Moreover, reference to these groups in dehumanizing terms such as "flows of refugees" and "floods of migrants" (Esses, Medianu, & Lawson, 2013) affect this discourse by generating a climate of fear and uncertainty.

The categorization of displaced people and the associated imagery profoundly influence how they are regarded by society. Instead of viewing refugees as humans in need of protection, who have experienced unimaginable horrors, and are simply seeking a safe place to live, the residents of host countries may view them with suspicion rather than compassion. In a study of media depiction of refugees, Esses et al. (2013) determined that dehumanization of refugees in the Western media, for example by portraying them as invaders or their asylum claims as fake, helps to

> justify their exclusion and mistreatment. By perceiving immigrants and refugees as not completely part of the human in-group, one can more easily believe that they deserve negative outcomes and that perceptions of the national in-group do not need to shift to accommodate their inclusion.
>
> (p. 531)

This occurs under the backdrop of an almost two-decades-long "War on Terror" (launched in the aftermath of the September 11, 2001, attacks), of which many of the refugees in question are victims, and which influences views of Muslims around the world. The perception of fleeing Muslims as being responsible for their own plight shapes the context in which refugees may be discriminated against, viewed as a potential economic, physical, or cultural threat, and thus considered exempt from humane treatment.

Consequently, representations and perceptions in the host society may shape how refugees view themselves, how they respond to loss, and what resources are available to facilitate their adaptation process. For example, prevailing views of refugees as an economic burden on host countries may influence their reluctance to live fully despite being in a position to do so in a safe country. Negative views directed from society at large may seep into refugees' own views of themselves, leading to self-stigmatizing behavior and the placement of constraints on confronting their losses. For example, as some semblance of normalcy began to creep back into their lives, their status as refugees still affected Karim and Loubna's life decisions, such as how their desire to have another child would be perceived. Ryan, Dooley, and Benson (2008) discussed the kind of dynamics that affect these decisions in their idea of a "resource pool," the personal, material, social, and cultural "means by which individuals satisfy needs, pursue goals and manage demands" (p. 7). The act of migration itself, combined with the social context within which it occurs, leads to lost resources (e.g., financial stability, emotional security), and adaptation depends on individuals' abilities to learn new things (e.g., English language proficiency) and attempt to regain what is lost. Within this context, the seemingly normative decision to have another child becomes fraught with political, cultural, and social implications. The next section expands upon the specific types of concerns and losses that are experienced by refugees before, during, and after displacement.

Losses Resulting From Forced Displacement

For individuals forcibly fleeing their homes, tangible and intangible losses occur over many years and can be delineated within the context of pre-migration, migration, and post-migration experiences (Pacione, Measham, & Rousseau, 2013). Tables 20.1 and 20.2, while not exhaustive, provide a few examples of the types of losses that would be experienced by Loubna, Karim, and their two children.

Further, it is necessary to remember that such losses are situated alongside the near-constant fear and worry for family and friends left behind in the conflict-ridden country. Grief responses could include anguish related to any deaths that occur, ambiguous losses (Boss, 1999) regarding those who are reported missing or abducted, and complications related to the intersection of grief and trauma. Additionally, the continual need to adjust to new people, places, and environments would require ongoing reorganization of one's violated assumptions (Janoff-Bulman, 1989) and a need to relearn the world (Attig, 2001) following abhorrent political, cultural, and social injustice. Chronic sorrow (Olshansky, 1962; Roos,

Table 20.1 Examples of Tangible Losses Associated With Forced Migration

Losses	Description
Loss of employment and education	Loubna and Karim lost their jobs as teachers in Syria; could not hold status as teachers in Canada due to lack of recognition of professional credentials; had to spend years learning English; their children missed several years of schooling.
Loss of social support	Forced to leave behind a strong, close-knit community of family and friends in Syria; lack of family upon arrival in Canada.
Loss of loved ones	Due to violent crimes such as abduction and murder.
Loss of physical safety	Exposure to conflict; forced to make a dangerous journey across the border into Turkey; deplorable conditions in the refugee camp resulted in poor nutrition and medical care; fear of abduction; sexual exploitation.
Loss of country	Connection to culture, customs, language, food.

Table 20.2 Examples of Intangible Losses Associated With Forced Migration

Losses	Description
Loss of emotional security	Overall loss of well-being associated with war and displacement; susceptibility to depression and other mental health issues.
Loss of relationships	Many shattered assumptions regarding marriage and family life; marital strain caused by the stresses of displacement and exploitation in the camps.
Loss of homeland	Loss of a sense of rootedness and belonging; left behind their marital home that had been in the family for generations.
Loss of dignity	Stripped of a sense of control over one's own life due to exploitative work in camps and inability to provide for family even after resettlement.
Loss of identity	Confusion related to old and new cultures; reconciling multiple identities including cultural, religious, and national; potential family clashes as the children learn English faster and assimilate more than their parents.
Loss of status/roles	Loubna was excelling in ESL while Karim struggled to learn English and to regain his primary role as provider; frustration and shame over losing status as teachers.
Loss of familiarity & confidence	Changes in all aspects of daily life, from small things such as how and where to buy groceries to large ones such as an unfamiliar workforce, may lead to loss of confidence in one's own abilities and frustration over regaining lost skills and learning new ones.
Loss of certainty	Pre-migratory, migratory, and post-migratory uncertainty generates ongoing questions, sometimes with no clear answer. For example, will one ever reach safety? Will the opportunity to reunite with family back home arise? Will information about abducted loved ones be forthcoming?

2017) may also be experienced by those who have lost their home country, cultural connections, and all that was familiar.

To better understand the presentation of such grief responses, overlapping and intersecting phenomena could collectively manifest as symptoms of post-traumatic stress (e.g., hypervigilance, sleep disturbances, confusion, or emotional dysregulation), continuous grief and loss characterized by uncertainty about what will happen next, disenfranchisement, ongoing helplessness and powerlessness, and/or physical numbness, burnout, or exhaustion (Harris & Gorman, 2011). Support and treatment options would need to be done by skilled professionals knowledgeable in these areas and with an understanding of the role of society and culture in informing the ways that people who are forcibly displaced may process loss and grief.

The importance of social context is central within contemporary loss frameworks such as meaning reconstruction, or meaning-making, which is a process whereby "grieving is the attempt to reaffirm or reconstruct a world of meaning that has been challenged by loss" (Neimeyer, 2016, p. 66) and which is influenced by societal norms (Neimeyer, 2001). Current grief theories such as meaning-making place emphasis on the sociocultural context in which individuals navigate grief experiences (Hibberd, 2013). Amidst the indescribable injustice and inhumane cruelty that is experienced by those who are forcibly displaced, it may not be possible to *make sense* of horrifying violence and cultural injustice; however, individuals may be able to *make meaning* of new opportunities or experiences through what Hibberd (2013) referred to as *life significance*. Hibberd (2013) explains the distinction between sense-making and life significance: An individual may be unable to make meaning of an inherently senseless experience (e.g., homicide, war, genocide) or may not feel the need to make sense of an event, yet still lead a fulfilling life. Similarly, an individual may be able to reconstruct a cohesive narrative, or rebuild a belief system, yet without life significance may feel that life is empty or meaningless. She highlighted that sense-making asks "Why?" and "Why me?" whereas life significance asks, "What now?" and "What matters?" Daily engagement with social and cultural resources could facilitate meaning-making and discovering life significance after such overwhelming loss. For displaced Muslims, ritual practices such as prayer, charity giving, or religious festivities may be helpful in this process, as well as having faith in Allah's will and a grand spiritual narrative to derive meaning out of life and death (Kristiansen, Younis, Hassani, & Sheikh, 2016).

Suggestions and Clinical Recommendations

The diversity of losses experienced by refugees at different stages in their forced displacement point to the need for interventions that address mental health due to traumas prior to and during migration, as well as the basic needs of refugees after resettlement (Ryan et al., 2008). Thus, primary interventions for forcibly displaced adults, children, and families have centered around both trauma-focused treatments and psychosocial supports (Alfadhli & Drury, 2016; Ontario Centre of Excellence for Child and Youth Mental Health, 2016). Participation in processes that facilitate grief associated with leaving one's home country and assist refugees in coming to terms with their losses ought to be encouraged by practitioners. Culturally sensitive approaches are often understood as those characterized by cultural competence or humility. "Culture gives people identity" (Bordere, 2016, p. 10); thus, humility involves the need to be self-reflective regarding our own identities and a willingness to honor another's.

Constructing a therapeutic alliance in which mutual understanding of individual client needs must be combined with an awareness of the policies that affect refugees and the environment in which they interact with host societies. These understandings are necessary to facilitate the unique processes of meaning-making that these individuals use to understand their suffering and adjust to their new reality (Mekki-Berrada et al., 2015). The experiences of refugees may hold similarities, but their adjustment processes may well vary considerably (Mekki-Berrada et al., 2015). Regarding Loubna and Karim, the familiarity of a local mosque provided them with a sense of comfort, and their religion was a means to explain and make meaning of both tangible and intangible losses. Many refugees often find this useful (Kristiansen et al., 2016; McLellan, 2015), although others may not (Mekki-Berrada et al., 2015).

One goal for practitioners working with refugees is to help reestablish the agency of people who had control over their lives taken away from them. Culturally humble practice is therefore instructive in such cases, where a diversity of beliefs and values may guide the adjustment processes of different people even if they come from a similar background or have experienced similar losses. The utility of the cultural humility framework lies in its merging of typical cultural competencies in counseling and social work with an accountability that seeks to address the prevailing social context in which clients experience profound, life-altering losses (Jisrawi & Arnold, 2018). This means avoiding a one-size-fits-all approach and instead developing a holistic understanding of client needs, be they spiritual, physical, or psychological in nature (Pacione et al., 2013). Ultimately, the realization that refugees are as diverse as their needs and that "being an open and respectful learner is often the ultimate cultural competence" (Rosenblatt, 2016, p. 69).

Conclusion

Forced displacement is not a new phenomenon, but as the scale of violent conflict around the world increases, so does the number of people migrating from their homes to seek safety. To provide adequate care for forcibly displaced people, practitioners require an accurate understanding of violent conflict, its impact on those affected and on host society perceptions, and the associated losses. A keen awareness of the culturally relevant tools that people use to make meaning out of their experiences and the diversity of coping strategies is also of critical importance.

Glossary

Cultural Humility: The understanding that cultural identity is unique to everyone; represents the practice of remaining respectful, humble, and supportive of people with differing ideas, principles, beliefs, and practices.

Forced Displacement: The coerced and involuntary migration of human beings. Forced displacement often connotes political, social, economic, or environmental dangers that are life-threatening. Displacement may be temporary or permanent.

Immigration: The action of choosing to move and settle permanently in another location.

Therapeutic Alliance: The unique relationship with a client that ensures that focus is solely on the needs of the client, whereby the client feels safe, supported, and understood.

Questions for Reflection

1. What did you find most surprising about this chapter? What non-death loss experience from this chapter would pose the greatest difficultly for you to find meaning?
2. What negative and/or mistaken perceptions exist in Western industrialized societies that pertain to individuals who have experienced or are experiencing forced displacement? Reflect upon how this chapter relates to Terror Management Theory (TMT), and how TMT may influence inaccurate perceptions of reality (see Chapter 5).
3. How can we, both individually and as a society, assist the millions of people who are residing in refugee camps and are grieving/struggling to survive? How can resiliency and healing be fostered towards the layers of non-death loss experiences that are occurring from forced displacement?
4. Explore why cultural humility is important for individuals who wish to work in the helping professions. Create five recommendations outlining culturally sensitive practices that individuals in the helping profession can utilize as to effectively support others with their grief and loss experiences in relation to forced displacement.

References

Alfadhli, K., & Drury, J. (2016). Psychosocial support among refugees of conflict in developing countries: A critical literature review. *Intervention, 14*(2), 128–141. https://doi.org/10.1097/WTF.0000000000000119

Attig, T. (2001). Relearning the world: Making and finding meaning. In R. A. Neimeyer (Ed.), *Meaning reconstruction and the experience of loss* (pp. 33–53). Washington, DC: American Psychological Association.

Bordere, T. C. (2016). Social justice conceptualizations in grief and loss. In D. L. Harris & T. C. Bordere (Eds.), *Handbook of social justice in loss and grief* (pp. 9–20). New York: Routledge.

Boss, P. (1999). *Ambiguous loss: Learning to live with unresolved grief.* Cambridge, MA: Harvard University Press.

Esses, V. M., Medianu, S., & Lawson, A. S. (2013). Uncertainty, threat, and the role of the media in promoting the dehumanization of immigrants and refugees. *Journal of Social Issues, 69*(3), 518–536. https://doi.org/10.1111/josi.12027

Harris, D. L., & Gorman, E. (2011). Grief from a broader perspective: Nonfinite loss, ambiguous loss, and chronic sorrow. In D. L. Harris (Ed.), *Counting our losses: Reflecting on change, loss, and transition in everyday life* (pp. 1–13). New York: Routledge.

Hibberd, R. (2013). Meaning reconstruction in bereavement: Sense and significance. *Death Studies, 37*, 670–692.

Janoff-Bulman, R. (1989). Assumptive worlds and the stress of traumatic events: Applications of the schema construct. *Social Cognition, 7*, 113–136.

Jisrawi, A. N., & Arnold, C. (2018). Cultural humility and mental health care in Canadian Muslim communities. *Canadian Journal of Counselling and Psychotherapy, 52*(1), 43–64. Retrieved from https://cjc-rcc.ucalgary.ca/cjc/index.php/rcc/article/view/2928

Kristiansen, M., Younis, T., Hassani, A., & Sheikh, A. (2016). Experiencing loss: A Muslim widow's bereavement narrative. *Journal of Religion and Health, 55*, 226–240. https://doi.org/10.1007/s10943-015-0058-x

McLellan, J. (2015). Religious responses to bereavement, grief, and loss among refugees. *Journal of Loss and Trauma, 20*, 131–138. https://doi.org/10.1080/15325024.2013.833807

Mekki-Berrada, A., Quosh, C., el Chammay, R., Deville-Stoetzel, B., Youssef, A., Jefee-Bahloul, H., . . . Song, S. (2015). *Culture, context and the mental health and psychosocial wellbeing of Syrians: A review for mental health and psychosocial support staff working with Syrians affected by armed conflict.* Retrieved from UNHCR website: www.unhcr.org/protection/health/55f6b90f9/culture-context-mental-health-psychosocial-wellbeing-syrians-review-mental.html

Neimeyer, R. A. (2001). Meaning reconstruction and loss. In R. Neimeyer (Ed.), *Meaning reconstruction and the experience of loss* (pp. 1–9). Washington, DC: American Psychological Association.

Neimeyer, R. A. (2016). Meaning reconstruction in the wake of loss: Evolution of a research program. *Behaviour Change, 33*(2), 65–79.

Olshansky, S. (1962). Chronic sorrow: A response to having a mentally defective child. *Social Casework, 43*(4), 190–193. https://doi.org/10.1177/104438946204300404

Ontario Centre of Excellence for Child and Youth Mental Health. (2016, March). *Evidence in-sight: Best practices for working with trauma-affected newcomers.* Retrieved from www.excellenceforchildandyouth.ca/resource-hub/best-practices-working-trauma-affected-newcomers

Pacione, L., Measham, T., & Rousseau, C. (2013). Refugee children: Mental health and effective interventions. *Current Psychiatry Reports, 15*(2), 341–349. https://doi.org/10.1007/s11920-012-0341-4

Roos, S. A. (2017). *Chronic sorrow: A living loss* (2nd ed.). New York: Routledge.

Rosenblatt, P. C. (2016). Cultural competence and humility. In D. L Harris & T. C. Bordere (Eds.), *Handbook of social justice in loss and grief* (pp. 67–74). New York: Routledge.

Ryan, D., Dooley, B., & Benson, C. (2008). Theoretical perspectives on post-migration adaptation and psychological well-being among refugees: Towards a resource-based model. *Journal of Refugee Studies, 21*(1), 1–18. https://doi.org/10.1093/jrs/fem047

United Nations, United Nations High Commissioner for Refugees. (2017, June 19). *Global trends: Forced displacement in 2016.* Retrieved from www.unhcr.org/5943e8a34

CHAPTER 21

Loss of Love: When the Relationship Is What Dies[1]

Darcy L. Harris

Introduction

When I began to explore the topic of the ending of intimate relationships, I found a plethora of literature and popular readings. Indeed, this loss is probably one of the most common and deeply distressing experiences that individuals in our society endure. In this chapter, I will discuss the layers of loss that occur when one loses an intimate partner through separation or divorce. I have also identified areas of social change that I believe give insight into this experience, which I hope might provide a framework for supporting individuals who experience a true loss where something has indeed died, but there is no funeral or wake.

In this experience, the very fact that both individuals continue to live, and may have ongoing contact through shared events that surround their children, family, friends, social gatherings, public outings, and even the workplace, creates a very difficult scenario for adaptation and accommodation. In essence, it is the relationship that dies, but the individuals continue living. This idea is in stark contrast with the continuing bonds theory of bereavement that describes the ongoing relationship between individuals that may continue even after death and is often summed up in the phrase *death may end a life, but not a relationship* (Klass & Steffan, 2017). Hence, the very crux of this loss immediately differs from the loss of an intimate partner through death. The fact that one partner usually chooses to leave the other or there has been a "leaving" by the partners of each other before there is a physical separation actually fits the criteria for our earlier discussion of an *ambiguous loss*, as the partners are still physically present but psychologically and emotionally absent to each other. That the relationship ends through some form of intentionality rather than an act of fate sets up significant secondary and intangible losses related to self-esteem, self-worth, and one's views of the world and others (Grych & Fincham, 1992; Yarnoz Yaben, 2009). Complicating these losses is the discomfort of many individuals with the "messy" process that may be involved with relationship dissolution, so loss of support or the diminished support that is available may cause further difficulty to both partners. Widowed individuals often find there are offers of support and assistance, whereas individuals whose relationship ends by separation or divorce may find a significant lack of support as they lose many of the friends and family members that were affiliated with their former partner, or who are uncomfortable with their situation or their perceived part in the dissolution of the relationship.

Current statistics on divorce in Western-oriented industrialized nations vary somewhat, but the general understanding is that approximately 40–50% of all marriages in these societies will end in divorce (Amato & Irving, 2006; Organisation for Economic Co-Operation and Development [OECD], 2018). This statistic is made problematic by its exclusion of individuals who cohabit and do not marry, and for individuals in same-sex partnerships whose relationship status is not recognized legally. I have intentionally not entitled this chapter to include only divorce after marriage. The grief of the loss of an intimate partner is not dependent upon the status of the relationship, but upon the attachment bond that is formed between the partners that exists whether or not the relationship is legally recognized (Hazan & Shaver, 1992; Weiss, 2006; Yarnoz Yaben, 2009). The issue of attachment in intimate dyadic relationships will be discussed later in this chapter. However, there is some difficulty in drawing upon the available literature for such an inclusionary approach, as most information pertaining to the dissolution of intimate relationships is written about married heterosexual couples. I will therefore attempt to navigate through this topic to provide a broader approach, while recognizing that there may be limited literature and research upon which to draw for some of this discussion.

The Influence of Social Changes

Even though divorce is now more accepted in industrialized societies, language that reflects blame, stigma, and shame is still frequently used to converse about those whose marriages end. In my clinical practice, dealing with the damage caused by negative social messages on top of the pain of the loss of one's relationship is often a very challenging task. The use of the term "failed marriage," or the need of others to assign blame to one of the partners, often causes a great deal of secondary pain to individuals who are already struggling with a great deal of personal angst and hurt (Grych & Fincham, 1992: Martin, 1989). It is common for the partner who initiated the separation process to experience considerable grief with the realization that the relationship could no longer continue as s/he had hoped from the beginning. It is important to keep in mind that partners who initiate the ending of the relationship often do so after a long and painful process of negotiation, attempts to reconcile difficult issues, and feelings of guilt for causing pain to the other person when they finally decide to leave (Emery & Dillon, 1994).

The influence of the media tends to magnify feelings of guilt, as public figures, popular media psychologists, and religious leaders talk about the need to return to family values; yet their call to do so carries the implication that it is possible to reverse the social changes that have led to the current practice and exploration of intimate relationships in this same society. I would like to propose that perhaps we are not in a "crisis" of moral values, nor is there something wrong with the rate at which intimate relationships dissolve; the current state of how intimate relationships form and are dissolved is a natural outgrowth of many social and demographic factors which would be impossible to change without unraveling the social fabric upon which our current lives are now woven.

There have been many significant changes in the social structure of Western industrialized societies that have had a profound impact upon how intimate relationships are viewed. Until the early part of the 20th century, marriages were formed mostly within the backdrop of rural farming communities. Families tended to stay close together, and the family unit was structured along the division of labor according to prescribed gender roles and practicality. Men were physically stronger and performed the heavy labor that was required. Women tended to the children and the maintenance of the household. Families often had strong ties to formal religious beliefs and practices, which reinforced the maintenance of the dyadic marital relationship. In addition, the average life expectancy in the early 20th century was between 40 and 50 years. Infant mortality rates were high, and it was not uncommon for women to die in childbirth. Life was difficult, and most of daily life was consumed by basic functioning to ensure safety, security, and maintaining the necessities of life (Amato & Irving, 2006; Toth & Kemmelmeier, 2009).

By the 1920s, the Industrial Revolution had begun. People moved away from their rural farms to find work in large urban areas where large companies established their manufacturing centers. The initiation of public health and sanitation measures, along with the discovery of how communicable diseases were spread, led to a better quality of life for many people and an increase in life expectancy. Women also had entered the workforce when men had gone to serve in the wars, and the early discussion of women's rights began with the women's suffrage movement in the 1920s in the United States. By the 1950s, the use of antibiotics to treat infections, along with the rise of allopathic medicine, led to greater possibilities for individuals to live longer and with a better quality of life than in the past (Amato & Irving, 2006; Toth & Kemmelmeier, 2009).

Currently, the average life expectancy for both genders in developed countries is well into the 80s, which is double that from just over a hundred years ago (World Health Organization [WHO], 2016). The ideas of leisure and self-discovery have become commonplace—ideas that were barely in conscious awareness for most individuals prior to this time. The 1960s brought a new wave of idealism and social awareness to the forefront. The universe and the physical world were explained in scientific terms rather than in religious ones, and an accompanying secular and humanistic view of society and social institutions followed. Sexual intimacy was no longer confined to marriage for the purpose of procreation. The introduction of the birth control pill and effective forms of contraception gave women choice in the planning of pregnancy and the timing of sexual intimacy (Fine & Harvey, 2006). By the end of the 20th century, the majority of women were working outside of the home and were economically independent (Statistics Canada, 2015).

Changing Relationships

In reviewing the social changes over the past 50 years, we can make the following statements regarding expectations and assumptions in industrialized societies:

- People live longer and with a higher quality of life than in the past; it is highly likely that one would outgrow a life partner instead of outliving one.
- The nuclear family is now the basic unit of a community rather than the extended family system.
- People generally have time to pursue leisure activities and personal fulfillment; however, people also spend less time at home due to work-related responsibilities.
- The focus is upon individual accomplishments and independence rather than upon the community and shared accomplishments.
- Sexual intimacy is no longer tied strictly to pregnancy and procreation.
- There has been an increased secularization of social norms, with an emphasis on individual rights and choices over the principles espoused by formal religious traditions.
- Women are able to live economically independent from men.
- Women no longer define themselves strictly by their marital status, as there are many more opportunities for social status that they are able to achieve through work and personal pursuits.

Thus, to expect that the way marriage is viewed would remain the same over this period of time in the face of these significant changes would be unrealistic.

In addition to these social changes is the undercurrent of individualism and achievement for both men and women in Western industrialized societies. It makes sense that living longer with a high standard of living and quality of life would lead to a greater ability to achieve self-actualization over that time. The purpose of marriage has changed accordingly, from one where marriage was accepted as a social and religious obligation designed mainly for security and procreation to the present expectation that marriage is a joint partnership, where the purpose is to advance the personal growth and fulfillment of each of the partners. This change is sometimes referred to as the *deinstitutionalization* of marriage (Amato & Irving, 2006; Walker, 2016). Marriage is no longer seen as an institution necessary for social definition and survival of the community, but as a support system for the self-actualization of each person in the relationship, which is often referred to as the *companionate* model of marriage (Burgess, Locke, & Thomes, 1963). In light of this view, staying in a marriage that interferes with the personal growth and achievement that are strongly valued in a highly individualistic and achievement-oriented culture would be very difficult. My wish in exploring these social changes is to move away from the tendency to look at the dissolution of intimate relationships in Western industrialized societies as a result of individual self-centeredness and narcissism to one that exposes the natural outcome of a society where the majority of individuals' basic needs for safety and security are met and where the push for personal and professional achievement for both men and women is highly prized and lauded.

If one in two marriages ends in divorce, and the trend in relationships is towards serial monogamy, the obvious question is whether marriage is relevant to current social trends (Amato & Irving, 2006; Toth & Kemmelmeier, 2009). Why would individuals choose to marry, or risk another partnership, even after a previous relationship ended or a marriage ended in divorce? Weiss (2006) offers an answer to this obvious question. Drawing from attachment theory, he posits that the dyadic partner relationship is one that carries significant value as an attachment relationship for adults. Since the attachment system in humans exists mostly outside of conscious awareness, the choices that are made to satisfy the attachment system may also stem from an unstated but known need for humans to identify feeling safe, secure, and more content when in a dyadic intimate relationship. In his descriptions of clients who were separated or divorced, Weiss noted difficulties in daily functioning, high levels of anxiety, irritability, and depression. He found an explanation for his clients' symptomatic manifestations while attending a lecture on attachment that was given by Dr. John Bowlby. Weiss applied Bowlby's theory of attachment to adult relationships, finding in his clients the very same types of behaviors that were initially described by Bowlby in children who were separated from their attachment figures.

Weiss (1975, 2006) later postulated that adults form dyadic relationships as part of their attachment system, satisfying a deep, unconscious need to feel safe and secure by partnering with and maintaining a proximal bond to another person. Based upon this work, it would appear that dyadic partnering and marriage will continue to be pursued in societies that are focused upon individual growth and achievement. Marriage as it was once understood as a social institution has been replaced by a consensual partnership. Unfortunately, the laws that hold marriage as a social and legal entity do not reflect the current state of social norms and understandings; therefore, the ending of a marriage or intimate relationship may be normative given the above social changes, but the legal and emotional ramifications of the ending are certainly anything but painless.

It seems that there is a split in how marriage and partnering are perceived from a social standpoint versus the legal and structural issues that surround these partnerships. Although socially, women and men may no longer need the institution of marriage in the way that individuals of 50 years ago may have for self-definition and stability, there are structural pressures that continue to favor marriage. For instance, it is often problematic to name a common-law or same-sex partner as the beneficiary of insurance, extended medical benefits, or a pension that may be supplied by a workplace. Laws that govern the distribution of property and support after the end of a marriage may not apply to common-law relationships, with the possibility that one of the partners may be more vulnerable in a non-marital relationship should it end. Decisions regarding health care, funeral choices, and the disposition of the body are left to a spouse, relatives, or next of kin unless stipulated in a legal document, and laws regarding common-law relationships are often inconsistent or nonexistent. Part of the controversy over the ability of same-sex partners to marry pertains to these issues, as the legal recognition of the union through marriage affords these benefits to the partners, which might be otherwise denied. It is also a painful reality that the dissolution of a relationship is not considered by many to be as significant if a couple was not married. *Since the response to loss is determined by the attachment bond that is formed between the partners and not the legal definition of the relationship, it is important to recognize the presence of profound grief when any intimate dyadic relationship ends for whatever reason.*

There is also a dichotomy in popular thinking regarding intimate relationships. Ideas of romance, idealized love, and unrealistic relational hopes and expectations continue to abound in popular movies, television shows, and fiction. One variation of this theme is the twist on the wounded person who is either cynical about relationships or considered a poor soul who is "reborn" when s/he meets the "right person." Popular culture sets up an idealized notion of the intimate partnership that is far removed from the realities of day-to-day existence. Whether the longing for this type of romantic love is a form of denial or hope, the loss of an intimate relationship when one's expectations have been shaped by popular culture towards idealized romantic love is a harsh reality.

Hagemeyer (1986) refers to the loss of the dreams associated with an intimate relationship as "the fall." Because of the flux in the social views of intimate relationships, there is a mixture of public opinion towards the dissolution of these same relationships. There can be judgment for leaving a relationship, and there can also be judgment for staying in a relationship. Individuals who leave a relationship may be judged for their lack of commitment or for being self-centered. Negative assumptions and attributions about the partner who initiates the ending of the relationship are often pointed and severe. These negative commentaries can place highly sensitive and private information about the person into a public forum of scrutiny and shame, especially with the widespread use of social media to disseminate personal information. However, the person who stays in a relationship may also be subject to criticism. Hagemeyer (1986) discusses the dilemma of individuals who remain in relationships in which they are unhappy or unhealthy. For example, an individual who stays in a relationship that is not meeting his or her needs may be viewed as dependent or stunted in some way, as there is an expectation that you are responsible for your own happiness and the master of your destiny. Thus, if you are unhappy in a relationship, the message is to stop whining and leave. There is also very little understanding of those whose sense of self and safety have been so undermined from living in an abusive relationship that they are afraid to leave. Social supports for these individuals are often burned out due to tendency of the victimized partner to return back to the relationship repeatedly, even after incidents involving threat and harm.

Divorce versus Death

Yarnoz Yaben (2009) compares and contrasts the dissolution of a marriage through divorce versus death. Unlike widowhood, divorce is a voluntary process, and although there are similarities in the grieving process between divorce and the death of a partner, this author's view is that the adjustment to divorce has the potential to be more difficult than adjustment to widowhood. Death is seen as a fact of life, and in death, there is often an idealized view of the deceased. However, divorce brings forth the ambivalent feelings that were present in the relationship, and there is often a longstanding pattern of conflict, attachment, hurt, humiliation, and shame that complicate the grieving process after the relationship ends. Emery and Dillon (1994) describe divorce as a process of change that can extend over long periods of time. Divorce is not a one-time event, but a culmination of many losses and pain typically over an extended period of time. Furthermore, death does not require a renegotiation of boundaries and relationships, as the deceased individual is gone and there is generally much sympathy extended to the widow or widower. However, after divorce, many boundaries must be renegotiated with family members and friends from both partners, as well as with children that were a part of the family system. There are also issues with loyalties that others may feel toward one partner and not another that are not present when a relationship ends through the death of one of the partners. Boundaries must be renegotiated in the midst of uncertain normative expectations, intense and painful emotions, incompatible desires, limited contact, and difficult communication. There is often a discrepancy between the partners, as the one who decides to formalize the end of the relationship may have already withdrawn emotional investment, while the partner who has not initiated the process will most likely be experiencing fresh and intense emotions in response to the news. The result is often a protracted period of intense interpersonal conflict and inner distress (Emery & Dillon, 1994; Sbarra, Law, & Portley, 2011). You will not run into your deceased spouse in a grocery store, but you may very well run into not only your former spouse but your spouse's new partner in the same venue, and the possibility of ongoing contact can be very difficult, triggering new feelings of pain, anxiety, and humiliation.

Layers of Loss

The losses associated with the dissolution of an intimate relationship can be very encompassing, consisting of both tangible and intangible losses. The intangible losses may include the loss of love, and the loss of the hopes and dreams for this relationship. One or both partners may experience loss of innocence and belief in the goodness of others, or the belief in a fair and just world. These associated losses are hugely significant, but not readily observable or frequently discussed with anyone other than very close confidantes. As mentioned previously, there is the feeling of "paradise lost" upon the realization that the relationship is perhaps not all that was hoped for. Cynicism about relationships, the legal system, religious beliefs, and ultimately about one's self are common in the aftermath of a lost intimate relationship. There is an assumption that the person who initiates the actual ending of the relationship fares better because s/he has had time to absorb the ensuing reality and may already be looking to a better future once the relationship has ended. This view may be inaccurate, however, as it does not take into account the existence of an anticipatory grief process that one may experience when letting go of the hopes and dreams regarding the relationship prior to any action taken to bring the relationship formally to an end (Hagemeyer, 1986). Martin (1989) describes a strong sense of painful ambivalence when choosing to exit a relationship, played out by a desire to leave the difficulties and pain in the relationship, while experiencing a great deal of anxiety and fear about the unknown and being alone. We can harken back to the concept of attachment; when attachment bonds are threatened, there is an instinctually mediated sense of unease, along with an intrinsic pull toward the attachment figure at a time when there is also a need to withdraw from the relationship.

Loss of self-esteem and identity are common after the dissolution of an intimate relationship as well. These losses carry a sense of shame and humiliation with them, as even though divorce is generally viewed as an unfortunate necessity and a more common occurrence in industrialized societies, there is still an assumption that one of the partners caused the "failure" of the relationship (Fine, Ganong, & Demo, 2005; Grych & Fincham, 1992). The implication is that there must be some flaw in one of the partners for the relationship to have ended. In my counseling office, a good deal of the work that occurs with clients who have lost an intimate relationship is the rebuilding of their sense of self without the partner as a key reference point for their identity and self-worth. Ironically, it is this deep sense of loss that often leads to a desire to re-partner quickly after the ending of a relationship. Weiss (2006) describes this behavior as the activation of the attachment system, which draws individuals to seek out relationships that will enable them to feel safe and secure. The need to feel safe again in another relationship may be a very strong part of this desire, even in the presence of the conflicting emotions about intimate relationships that were described earlier.

The more tangible losses may include the loss of home for at least one of the partners if they were living together, as well as removal of outward signs of the relationship (such as rings, if these were exchanged between the couple). One or both partners may show up at social functions with another person instead of the original partner, which is quickly noticed by those who knew the couple prior to the ending of the relationship. There are also financial losses that occur with the division of property and assets, payment of legal fees, name changes, credit cards, and joint account cancellations. Earlier in this chapter, it was discussed that women are no longer financially dependent upon men as they were in the past; however, they tend to fare worse financially after the ending of an intimate relationship in which they cohabited. Women are still paid less for their work than men, and many women have taken time off work to raise children or have fewer options for choosing work due to the need for flexibility related to child care issues. Ironically, it is women who now tend to initiate the ending of marriages more than men, even though they are more likely to lose financially in the process (Amato & Irving, 2006; Sayer, 2006).

Although the scope of this chapter does not include the experiences of children after their parents separate, conflicts that can occur through attempting to co-parent in a situation where even basic communication has become very difficult adds to the stress of this process. Children's general standard of living tends to decline after their parents separate (Sayer, 2006). There are often ongoing losses associated with raising children in an environment of mistrust and conflict, and for parents who are in high conflict long after the relationship has ended, the emotional and financial exhaustion can take a heavy toll on both the parents and children alike. The experiences of children in the justice system associated with divorce are discussed in more detail in Chapter 13.

Clinical Implications

Supporting individuals after the loss of an intimate relationship can pose many challenges for clinicians. This is an area where social change in the past 50 years has had a direct impact upon peoples' lives, and it is an area where individuals feel a great deal of ambivalence and vulnerability. It is important to find ways to assist individuals to piece together what happened in their relationship and to validate the many losses that occurred during the relationship and after it ended. Clinicians need to recognize the tendency for there to be ongoing grief after the loss of an intimate relationship, due to intentionality of the decision ultimately to end the relationship, and the possibility of ongoing contact with the former partner. Individuals may describe a sense of being lost as well as feelings of emptiness and abandonment. It is important to remember that these feelings are common manifestations of an attachment bond that has been broken, and not signs of weakness or over-dependence.

Individuals who leave the relationship may have had more time to plan for their departure and make new living arrangements, but they may need to sort through feelings of guilt and responsibility for their choice, and possible repercussions from friends and family members for being seen as the one who is causing pain to the remaining partner. Partners who are on the receiving end of the news of the dissolution of the relationship may be in shock and be disadvantaged in making decisions because they have not had time to absorb the news. As a result, clinicians may need to offer practical support in the form of referrals to resources as part of their therapeutic work with these individuals. Reviewing the social changes and how they have had an impact upon the experience of relational dissolution may help individuals to move away from feelings of shame and humiliation that cripple their ability to move forward after this loss. Clinicians who work with individuals who seek help due to intimate relational loss need to accept the "new normal" of the diversity in beliefs about marriage, divorce, and what constitutes a family system, and to be able to work within many different belief systems and frameworks in order to fully support their clients.

It is important for clinicians to be very familiar with resources that are available for individuals facing the ending of their intimate relationship. It may be helpful to become familiar with the family law practitioners in your area and some of the basic legal jargon and procedures that surround marriage, cohabitation, separation, and divorce. This is the world in which clients are now trying to navigate, and awareness of this aspect of their experience may allow clinicians to be very specific and understanding in supporting and working with them at this time. It is very difficult to grieve the loss of the relationship while embroiled in a legal system that can add an incredible amount of stress to the situation. Many individuals find their feelings of grief must be set aside until after there is a settlement or resolution of the outstanding material or child care issues, which carries implications for a "second wave" of assistance and support at a time when the social expectation might be to move forward because "it is over."

We run the risk of minimizing the experiences of individuals whose intimate relationships end because this loss is no longer uncommon. However, for the individual who faces the loss of a partner through separation or divorce, the pain is not diminished just because many others have shared the same experience. It is very possible, and even likely, that this loss can lead to a great deal of personal growth and depth once the individual has been able to reflect upon what has happened and allow the adaptive aspects of the grieving process to heal the wounds that have been opened. Our role as clinicians is to validate the complex and painful aspects of this experience and support the healing aspects of the grieving process for these individuals within the current social context and expectations where they reside.

Key Terms

Deinstitutionalization of Marriage: The societal shift seen in the purpose of marriage from a necessity and social obligation to the optional establishment of a partnership and no longer a societal obligation.

Industrial Revolution: A historical technological revolution that generated an ability to increase production of goods at an accelerated pace, and as a result changed the structure of societies.

Industrial Societies: Societies that utilize technology to implement mass production. These societies developed in the Western world after the Industrial Revolution.

Questions for Reflection

1. How does the loss experience of relationship dissolution differ from the death-related loss of a partner? Furthermore, choose one bereavement theoretical model (see Chapter 1) and explore how it may be applied to a relationship dissolution in contrast to death-related loss.
2. If, as the chapter states, we can "outgrow a life partner instead of outliving one," why do you think individuals struggle with the fact that partners may consistently experience personal transformation? If change is the most fundamental aspect of life, why is there so much shame, guilt, and blame surrounding divorce?
3. Have you ever experienced the dissolution of an intimate relationship or divorce? What loss experiences did you encounter as the initiator or as the person who did not initiate the process? How did you navigate this experience, and what helped you the most through your grief? What lessons would

you utilize from this experience as to support others who are grieving losses from relationship dissolution or divorce?
4. Create five suggestions for what one should not say to a grieving person experiencing relationship dissolution and provide justification for your propositions. Subsequently, share a few suggestions for ways of offering support that may be helpful in allowing one's grief to unfold naturally after the experience of relationship dissolution.

Note

1. This chapter is a revision of a chapter by the author entitled "Navigating Intimate Relationship Loss: When the Relationship Dies, but the Person Is Still Living," which was originally published in 2011 in *Counting Our Losses: Reflecting on Change, Loss, and Transition in Everyday Life* (pp. 65–74). New York: Routledge.

References

Amato, P. R., & Irving, S. (2006). Historical trends in divorce. In M. A. Fine & J. H. Harvey (Eds.), *Handbook of divorce and relationship dissolution* (pp. 41–57). Mahwah, NJ: Erlbaum.

Burgess, E. W., Locke, H. J., & Thomes, M. (1963). *The family: From institution to companionship*. New York: American Book.

Emery, R. E., & Dillon, P. (1994). Conceptualizing the divorce process: Renegotiating boundaries of intimacy and power in the divorced family system. *Family Relations*, 43, 374–379.

Fine, M. A., Ganong, L. H., & Demo, D. H. (2005). Divorce as a family stressor. In P. C. Henry & S. J. Price (Eds.), *Families & changes: Coping with stressful events and transitions* (pp. 227–252). Thousand Oaks, CA: Sage Publications.

Fine, M. A., & Harvey, J. H. (2006). Divorce and relationship dissolution in the 21st century. In M. A. Fine & J. H. Harvey (Eds.), *Handbook of divorce and relationship dissolution* (pp. 3–14). Mahwah, NJ: Erlbaum.

Grych, H. H., & Fincham, F. D. (1992). Marital dissolution and family adjustment: An attributional analysis. In T. L. Orbuch (Ed.), *Close relationship loss: Theoretical approaches* (pp. 157–173). New York: Springer.

Hagemeyer, S. (1986). Making sense of divorce grief. *Pastoral Psychology*, 34(4), 237–250.

Hazan, C., & Shaver, P. R. (1992). Broken attachments: Relationship loss from the perspective of attachment theory. In T. L. Orbuch (Ed.), *Close relationship loss: Theoretical approaches* (pp. 90–108). New York: Springer.

Klass, D., & Steffan, E. (2017). *Continuing bonds in bereavement: New directions for research and practice*. New York: Routledge.

Martin, T. L. (1989). Disenfranchised: Divorce and grief. In K. J. Doka (Ed.), *Disenfranchised grief: Recognizing hidden sorrow* (pp. 161–172). Lexington, MA: Lexington.

Organisation for Economic Co-operation and Development (OECD). (2018). *OECD Family Database: SF3.1: Marriage and divorce rates*. Retrieved August 6, 2018, from www.oecd.org/els/family/SF_3_1_Marriage_and_divorce_rates.pdf

Sayer, L. C. (2006). Economic aspects of divorce and relationship dissolution. In M. A. Fine & J. H. Harvey (Eds.), *Handbook of divorce and relationship dissolution* (pp. 385–408). Mahwah, NJ: Erlbaum.

Sbarra, D. A., Law, R. W., & Portley, R. M. (2011). Divorce and death: A meta-analysis and research agenda for clinical, social, and health psychology. *Perspectives on Psychological Science, 6*(5), 454–474.

Statistics Canada. (2015). *The surge of women in the workplace*. Retrieved August 6, 2018, from https://www150.statcan.gc.ca/n1/pub/11-630-x/11-630-x2015009-eng.htm

Toth, K., & Kemmelmeier, M. (2009). Divorce attitudes around the world: Distinguishing the impact of culture on evaluations and attitude structure. *Cross-Cultural Research, 43*(3), 280–297.

Walker, L. M. (2016). Deinstitutionalization of marriage. In *Encyclopedia of family studies* (pp. 1–3). Hoboken, NJ: Wiley. doi:10.1002/9781119085621

Weiss, R. S. (1975). *Marital separation*. New York: Basic Books.

Weiss, R. S. (2006). Trying to understand close relationships. In M. A. Fine & J. H. Harvey (Eds.), *Handbook of divorce and relationship dissolution* (pp. 605–611). Mahwah, NJ: Erlbaum.

World Health Organization (WHO). (2016). *Global Health Observatory (GHO) data: Life expectancy*. Retrieved August 6, 2018, from www.who.int/gho/mortality_burden_disease/life_tables/situation_trends/en/

Yarnoz Yaben, S. (2009). Forgiveness, attachment, and divorce. *Journal of Divorce & Remarriage, 50*, 282–294.

PART VI

Pulling It All Together—Change, Loss, and Transition

Darcy L. Harris

Importance of Language

In order to better understand the different types and descriptions of non-death losses, we have up to this point focused on each type of loss individually. In reality, most non-death loss experiences often have elements of several different types of losses jumbled all together. Thus, it's not a case of one type of loss or the other, but of seeing the areas of overlap and recognizing how the various aspects of grief in non-death losses are experienced. As stated in Doka's chapter in this volume, disenfranchised grief is a recurring theme in all types of living losses, as many are unrecognized, are unacknowledged, and have no rituals associated with them. The descriptors for different types of losses are important, as they offer language and words for these experiences and the feelings that may accompany them. When people can use language that accurately captures their experience, a sense of enfranchisement and empowerment can occur.

Overlapping Constructs and Shared Experiences

A single non-death loss may have elements of ambiguous loss, nonfinite loss, and chronic sorrow readily applicable to various aspects of the same experience. A living loss may also have a mixture of tangible and/or intangible aspects (Figure VI.1). For example, the primary focus of ambiguous loss is the loss of a relationship or an important aspect of a relationship with the discrepancy between the psychological and physical absence/presence of someone; the foundational experience in nonfinite loss and chronic sorrow relates to the loss of one's life as it once was, along with the hopes, dreams, and certainty that were present beforehand. The ambiguous loss construct emphasizes losses that are relational in nature (i.e., the psychological or physical absence/presence dichotomy of a loved one), while the emphasis in nonfinite loss may or may not be centered on another person (i.e., loss of another not due to death) or to one's self (i.e., loss of one's faith, hope, or sense of certainty). It is also apparent that situations of ambiguous loss may lead to chronic sorrow, as the lack of clarity about what has been lost or the uncertainty about the absence/presence dichotomy can lead to an ongoing, unrelenting cycle of disequilibrium

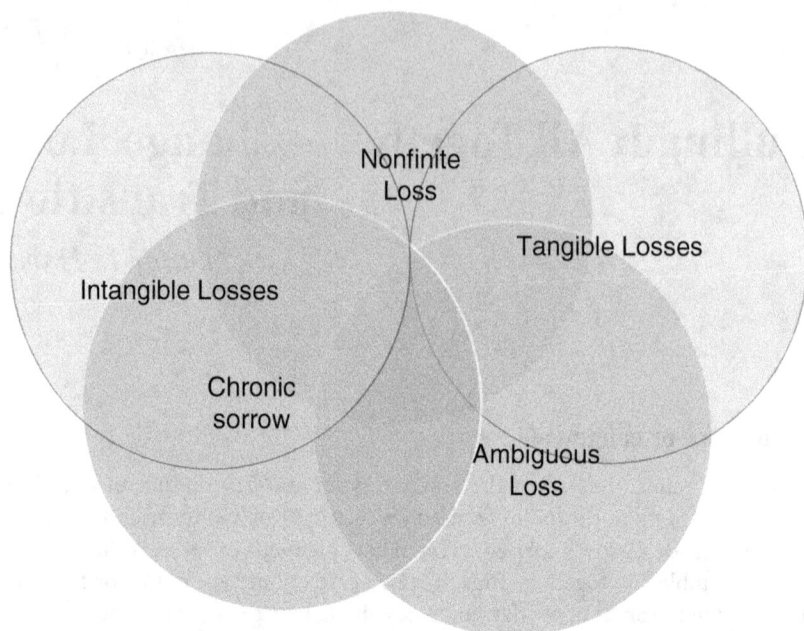

Figure VI.1 Overlaps of Different Types of Non-Death Losses

and despair, temporary adaptation, and re-entry into the uncertainty that is the hallmark of chronic sorrow.

An example of the overlap between the constructs may be seen in situations where a loved one has been diagnosed with progressive dementia. Family members may find that they gradually come to terms with some of the cognitive difficulties as they are confronted with the realities of their loved one's declining abilities (a time that is usually associated with difficult decision-making regarding care and living arrangements), only to find that these abilities fluctuate greatly from day to day. There is no ability to predict the course of the changes in cognition and functionality, no way of knowing what will happen next, or if their loved one will recognize them or even acknowledge their presence with time. This scenario fits the description of a psychological ambiguous loss (physically present/psychologically absent), and it is also an ongoing nonfinite loss, coupled with the uncertainty of chronic sorrow (Table VI.1).

As in Chapter 6 which covered the topic of birth mothers who choose adoption for their babies, overlaps can be seen (Table VI.2) with descriptions of ambiguous loss and chronic sorrow as many birth mothers struggle with the inability to know what happened to their children; likewise, as many of these children grow up, they realize that they do not know their birth parents, and many do not have access to their own genealogical heritage and genetic family history. For both the birth mothers and their babies who are adopted, there is the sense of psychological

Table VI.1 Example: Overlapping Losses Associated With a Diagnosis of Dementia

Presenting Loss	Diagnosis of dementia in loved one.
Ambiguous Loss	Loved one physically present but psychologically/emotionally absent due to disease process.
Nonfinite Loss	Diagnosis of dementia typically ongoing, usually progressive in nature.
Chronic Sorrow	Loss of loved one's ability to engage and participate in family life are ongoing with no foreseeable end.
Tangible Loss	Outward signs that loved one is compromised; incidents of not remembering names, confusion, inability to function outwardly noticeable.
Intangible Loss	Grief over lost relationship while loved one alive; changes in family dynamics, affinities, and interactions.
Disenfranchised Aspects	If loved one is physically present, grief not acknowledged socially; however, loved ones may be acutely grieving before death of the loved one with dementia. Compromises made by family members who provide care of loved one are often unrecognized but may have significant impact upon family system (i.e., financial, emotional).

Table VI.2 Example: Overlapping Losses for Birth Mothers Who Choose Adoption for Their Baby

Presenting Loss	Birth mother releases child for adoption.
Ambiguous Loss	Child psychologically present to birth mother, but physically absent to her.
Nonfinite Loss	Child's absence will remain with birth mother in an ongoing way.
Chronic Sorrow	Grief over loss of the relationship with the child or not knowing about the child is ongoing in nature.
Tangible Loss	Pregnancy was tangible, as it was physically evident.
Intangible Loss	Loss of the child not apparent; child never a part of family experiences; usually no photos of child to confirm presence.
Disenfranchised Aspects	Decision to relinquish seen as intention; mother made the decision and any resulting grief is viewed as related to her choice. Rationally evaluating the birth mother's living conditions, age, or situation often not a comfort in the absence of child's presence. Lack of recognition of prenatal attachment and impact of loss on both mother and child.

awareness of the other in the presence of their physical absence from one another (ambiguous loss), with ongoing grief and despair (chronic sorrow) associated with the knowledge that they may never be present in each other's lives.

In another example, many couples who experience infertility describe the loss of a child that they have hoped for, dreamt about, and sometimes saw briefly as an embryo under a microscope prior to its transfer into the mother's body, where it simply disappeared from existence afterwards. This loss is also ambiguous and may lead to chronic sorrow, especially if the realization of involuntary childlessness begins to replace the hopes of parenthood. Infertility is also a nonfinite loss, even if infertility is resolved by the successful delivery of a baby after treatment, adoption of a child, or the decision to discontinue treatment and remain childless. The awareness of infertility and the process of infertility treatment create permanent changes in the assumptive worlds of most of those involved in the experience (Harris, in press).

Another overlap might be seen in those with vanished loved ones whose fates are unknown, such as individuals who are missing in military action, kidnap victims, and those who have inexplicably disappeared without a trace. There are unavoidable reminders of the loss (or lost person), with no foreseeable end or sense of closure. In this type of ambiguous loss, and in the presence of chronic sorrow, the ability to adapt or attempts at finding some form of resolution are fraught with significant obstacles. Periodic resurgence of both predictable and unpredictable points of stress and renewed grief is inevitable.

While ambiguous losses are focused upon unclear or incomplete disturbing relational changes, the experiential core of nonfinite losses focuses on life taking an abrupt turn with no view for how things will turn out (go back to the broken glass image from the introduction); chronic sorrow results from a painful disparity between the thoughts and dreams about what should have been, might have been, and still may be hoped for—versus what actually is the present reality (Roos, 2017). All of these experiences are characterized by grief responses that are normal given the context, yet these same losses are frequently misunderstood or unrecognized. As the source of the loss continues, grief is continuing and resurgent, usually within the context of uncertainty, without a foreseeable end or resolution.

Summary

Although non-death loss experiences are frequently disenfranchised, the ongoing grief in response to these losses is normal and understandable. Recognition that life as it has been or was expected to be is forever lost and has been replaced by an initially unknown, unwanted, and often terrifying new reality can be traumatic, forcing a new appraisal of core aspects of one's assumptive world. Notions that life is predictable and fair, and any underlying sense of justice, are crushed in the new reality that now defines one's life. The self and the world must be relearned at profound levels that are central to the individual's ability to function and navigate in the world. This process is often all-encompassing; redefining aspects of the world, others, and one's self in ways that ripple across all aspects of daily life, including one's hopes and dreams.

Key Terms

All-Encompassing: Non-death loss and grief affects every aspect of an individual's life, and is a far-reaching phenomenon that generates a myriad of experiences for individuals.

Uncertainty: Non-death grief theories are founded upon the notion of uncertainty, defined as experiences without foreseeable ends or resolutions.

Questions for Reflection

1. Identify overlapping themes and shared experiences among ambiguous loss, nonfinite loss, living losses, and chronic sorrow.
2. What strategies would you utilize to integrate non-death loss and grief theory into practice? What possible barriers may prevent you from accomplishing this?
3. What do you view as the most significant issue in attempting to educate others about the theories discussed in this chapter? Additionally, create a working definition for each of the major theories in this chapter using only lay language that is non-clinical, understandable, and accessible in nature.
4. Why is it important to know the theoretical underpinnings and frameworks of grief surrounding non-death losses? How can the experiences of change and transition observed in non-death losses be differentiated from those observed in death-related losses?

References

Harris, D. L. (in press). Grief and loss in infertility. *Grief Matters*.
Roos, S. (2017). *Chronic sorrow: A living loss* (2nd ed.). New York: Routledge.

CHAPTER 22

Where's the Grief in Non-Death Loss Research?
Mae-Lynn Germany

Introduction

Loss is inherently part of living and experienced across the lifespan in expected life events such as in the death of a loved one, post-parental transition, loss of functionality related to aging, and loss of important relationships (Harris, 2011; Schultz & Harris, 2011). Loss is also present in unexpected life events such as emotional, sexual, or physical abuse, experiencing a crime, war, or natural disaster, or the diagnosis of a chronic illness (Bruce & Schultz, 2004; Harris, 2011). As Sewell and Williams (2001) describe, we navigate the world by seeking to accurately anticipate and predict our experiences; however, when we lose the ability to predict and anticipate events based on previously held assumptions, our losses can become "traumatic," especially for those losses that are "dramatic, extreme, and on constructs (dimensions of personal meaning) that are held dear" (p. 293). As mentioned in the first chapter of this book, significant loss holds the potential to challenge our basic, core world assumptions about the way others should operate, our view of self, and beliefs around how the world should work. For life events that do not involve the death of a loved one, grief is rarely considered or studied as a potential response, although many stressful, adverse, or traumatic life events require a relinquishing of "life as it was" or of letting go of highly anticipated dreams and expectations for the future. Little societal recognition or space for nondeath loss experiences and the grief that follows them, creating difficulty in processing and coping with these events as well as receiving adequate support during a highly vulnerable time. Individuals may personally perceive non-death loss events as producing grief-like reactions similar to or even greater than death-related losses. However, the lack of societal and/or familial acknowledgment and the perception that grief will not be validated is seen to influence the likelihood of seeking informal (e.g., friends, parents) or formal (e.g., counseling) support (Cohen, 1996). Bordere (2016, p. 14) writes:

> People who exist in the margins of society (e.g. youth in urban areas, death row inmates), have relationships with deceased individuals deemed as peripheral (e.g. friend, co-worker, dating partner) or stigmatized (e.g. interracial

unions), or who have losses not viewed as significant (e.g. pet loss, divorce, home foreclosure) often experience grief that is "disenfranchised" or unacknowledged and unsupported both within their sub-cultures and within their society at large.

(Doka, 1989, 2002)

When grief is disenfranchised, or losses are unrecognized/unacknowledged, it typically follows that these experiences are understudied (Bordere, 2016), subsequently leaving researchers and clinicians with scant information and limited ability to provide supportive resources. Further complications exist in the study of non-death losses, such as the ongoing nature of the loss, or grief waxing and waning as the loss event or catalyst changes over time.

Enfranchisement can occur when loss experiences are named, and the resulting grief is validated and normalized. Normalization is particularly important since these losses are often difficult to define and describe, and ongoing losses that result in chronic sorrow might be mislabeled in medical terms and inadvertently pathologized (Granek, 2016). This chapter will highlight how grief is examined in research related to non-death losses, including nonfinite loss, chronic sorrow, and ambiguous loss. The chapter will conclude with recommended measures for clinicians and researchers interested in examining grief related to non-death loss events.

Grieving Non-Death Losses: What Do We Know?

The occurrence of non-death loss experiences are nearly inevitable across the lifespan (Harris, 2011), with a majority of individuals experiencing at least one, if not multiple potentially traumatic events in their lifetime (Kilpatrick et al., 2013; Benjet et al., 2016). These losses may be tangible, such as relationship losses and resources, or intangible, such as identity and social roles. Not only do these events occur in various points across the lifespan, they are also influential in the shaping of one's life story. One example of research in this area occurred when researchers asked college students to identify the most significant loss in their life, and a majority of individuals selected a non-death loss event, such as dissolution of an intimate relationship, sexual assault, or being arrested (Cooley, Toray, & Roscoe, 2010). Similarly, in one of the first studies exploring complicated grief symptomatology in survivor reactions of those affected by Hurricane Katrina (Shear et al., 2011), over half of the participants reported their most severe hurricane-related losses were non-death related. Participants described these losses as tangible (i.e., 29.0%, such as: home, possessions), interpersonal (9.5%, such as: separation from friends and family or reduced quality of relationships), intangible (8.1%, such as: quality of life, control, security, sense of well-being), and financial (4.2%), with only 3.7% reporting the death of a loved one as the most severe loss. In a bereavement study that was meant to gauge complicated grief in university students (Varga, 2016), responses by participants suggested non-death loss events as more impactful than death-related losses. As one participant noted,

> My greatest loss came from my fiancé leaving me and not from a death. This was a more significant loss than any death in my family so far and affected my studies to the point of me having to take time away from my education.
>
> (Varga, 2016, p. 182)

Taken together, these findings suggest that many individuals may experience significant life events that are personally conceptualized as losses even though they may not involve the death of a loved one.

Although non-death loss experiences are likely occurrences across the lifespan and many are identified as significant by the individual, grief experiences are often muddied by use of measures that focus on depression, anxiety disorders, and/or post-traumatic symptomatology as the focal point of inquiry. One of the previous barriers in non-death loss research has revolved around the varying ways that grief is operationalized and predominantly viewed as a reaction to the death of an individual. Traditionally, death loss has been thought to be a unique loss due to the dissolution of a significant attachment relationship, which then triggers the grief reaction, characterized by intense yearning and separation distress. However, the loss of a relationship by means other than death also disrupts aspects of daily living, with the potential to have difficulties engaging meaningfully in one's environment afterward (Papa & Maitoza, 2013). A constructivist perspective encompasses the wide range of non-death loss experiences and resulting grief afterward, with the focus of the grieving process as the means whereby meaning is re-constructed after world assumptions have been damaged or destroyed by the experience (Neimeyer, Burke, Mackay, & van Dyke Stringer, 2010).

Grief has been suggested as a common phenomenology across loss types (Harvey & Miller, 1998; Papa, Lancaster, & Kahler, 2014), particularly when an event is perceived as negative and changes in one's social environment as well as schemas related to self-worth and/or worldview occur. Recent research has suggested that there are commonalities between grief responses among the bereaved and those who encounter nondeath losses. Specifically, Papa and colleagues (2014) found that a pattern of reaction (i.e., depression, anxiety, and grief) was similar across bereavement-related[1] loss and nondeath losses, including involuntary unemployment and divorce. Levels of grief, using a modified version of a measure examining prolonged grief (Prolonged Grief Scale-13 [PG-13]; Prigerson et al., 2009) across the three samples, were best predicted by time since the loss and how central the loss was with one's identity. This study suggests that grief may not be singularly related to the loss of an attachment figure but the process of accommodating the loss of a central role or aspect of identity (Papa et al., 2014). Similarly, Papa and Maitoza (2013) used a modified version of the PGS-13 scale to explore the relationship between loss-related disruption and an individual's sense of self in response to involuntary unemployment. Prolonged grief (PG) was related to the loss of a significant social role, if that role was deemed essential for the individual's primary relational self. However, assumptions about justice did have a direct impact on PG symptoms, independent of contextual factors (i.e., change in income, length of employment), suggesting that if the loss experience was seen as part of a larger system of justice, and assumptions about fairness and justice were intact after the loss, then the effects of job loss were buffered to some extent.

Perception of Loss

Past experiences and cultural norms shape how we respond to loss with various facets of our identity influencing our experience and perceptions of loss, such as age (Brown, 2017), gender identity, race, ethnicity, religion/spirituality, sexual orientation, and ability. How an individual perceives an event or experience as a loss will likely influence the severity of distress that is experienced as well as the support that is sought. For example, in a study of veterans who experienced a spinal cord injury, the perception of loss in physical functioning, conceptualized as resource loss, was inversely related to psychological well-being (deRoon-Cassini, Aubin, Valvano, Hastings, & Horn, 2009). For these individuals, it was not the severity of spinal cord injury that related to psychological well-being but the perception of physical resources loss. However, this relationship becomes nonsignificant when considering the mediating influence of global meaning-making, indicating that meaning and purpose in life can lead to an increased sense of well-being. Similarly, for mothers with a child diagnosed with Autism Spectrum Disorder, grief was positively associated with perceptions of loss and the diagnosis as being unjust. Interestingly, perceptions of loss were not associated with the amount of time since their child's diagnosis, suggesting an enduring nature of these perceptions, although the association between grief and time since diagnosis revealed that severity of grief is likely greater for mothers where the diagnosis was more recent. Upon closer examination, mothers' perceived losses centered around worries for their child's future, including difficulties in life related to the diagnosis and anticipated dreams and expectations for their child's life that might not be met (Wayment & Brookshire, 2018).

Nonfinite Loss

In situations when a loss is mishandled by others, defenses are overwhelmed, or negative learning has occurred, the indelible effect of loss may slide into nonfiniteness, the continuing presence of the loss in an ongoing way (Bruce & Schultz, 2004). These losses are typically characterized by shattered hopes and dreams, being launched into a significant search for meaning, a sense of the loss gathering significance over time, and the experience of the loss being ongoing in nature with no clearly marked conclusion (Schultz & Harris, 2011). As discussed throughout this book, nonfinite and ambiguous losses and the experience of chronic sorrow pose a challenge to grief researchers, as grief reactions may wax and wane depending on whether loss triggers are heightened or in a steady state during the time of research participation. Ott, Sanders, and Kelber (2007) examined grief and personal growth experiences of spouses and adult children caregivers to a loved one with Alzheimer's disease or related dementia. Results indicated that grief increased as the severity of the disease increased. When the spouse with a diagnosed disease lived at home, caregivers experienced greater sadness, longing, worry, isolation, and personal sacrifice burden than did adult child caregivers who cared for parents in their homes. Additionally, the majority of caregivers experienced personal growth, which is also an intermittent outcome amidst ongoing loss (Ott et al., 2007). Similarly, other studies have found that caregivers, in the early stages, who perceived levels of care as more manageable, grappled more with changes to identity and loss of independence. As needs increased, changes in relationships and loss of motivation or energy for other relationships were seen where a sense of self became more threatened when the caregiver's identity began to center primarily around the caregiving role (Ray & Street, 2007).

Although nonfinite loss has typically been examined in the context of adaptation to chronic or severe mental stress (Richardson, Cobham, McDermott, & Murray, 2013), physical illnesses (Ray & Street, 2007) or disabilities (Collings, 2008), nonfinite loss has been used as a framework in interpreting reactions to a variety of non-death loss experiences, such as foster and adopted children grieving their lost birthparents (Fineran, 2012; Mitchell, Chapter 11 in this volume), mothers of African American sons in the context of American racism and discrimination (Brown-Manning, 2013), and loss of self and related losses due to sexual assault (Bordere, 2016; 2017). The importance of examining reactions to stressful or potentially traumatic life events as non-death loss, particularly nonfinite loss, is that the shift in language takes into account the context in which the loss occurs and allows for the validation of subsequent chronic grief reactions as being a normative response in the face of an ongoing, fluctuating loss.

Chronic Sorrow

A related concept to nonfinite loss is chronic sorrow, which is a recurrent, periodic, and unpredictable sadness that is triggered by internal or external events reminding one of the loss (Lindgren, Burke, Hainsworth, & Eakes, 1992; Roos, 2017). This research emerged from studies by Olshansky (1962) that highlighted a unique form of grieving that never ended for some parents of children born with congenital disabilities. Despite the children continuing to live, the parents' hopes held for their children appeared repeatedly dashed across time. For many of those living with a chronic illness or disability, qualitative interviews revealed themes of tangible losses surrounding loss of physical functioning, relationships, and activities such as work, leisure, and driving (Ahlström, 2007). Numerous intangible losses also permeated the experience of chronic sorrow for these individuals, such as the loss of roles, an autonomous life, identity, a life imagined, and uplifting emotions (Ahlström, 2007). However, individuals may experience chronic sorrow on an intermittent basis and experience a sense of adaptive well-being between episodes (Kendall, 2005).

Much of the current research explores what are the lived experiences of individuals and caregivers grappling with chronic sorrow in the context of chronic disease, disabilities, and deterioration of physical and mental attributes, including the factors may trigger this re-emergence of pervasive sadness. The inability or delay to achieving expected developmental milestones, such as school entry, graduating high school, and transitioning into adolescence, was reported as a contributing and recurring factor in chronic sorrow, particularly among parents (Coughlin & Sethares, 2017). As children entered into adulthood, identifying adult health care providers and potential guardians for their adult child after their own death brings about a reemergence of sadness. Additionally, discussions of diagnosis or prognosis, medical procedures, and increasing caregiver responsibilities could lead to the reemergence of chronic sorrow. Internal triggers, such as fearing a future where the child would be missing out, parents also appeared to grieve an expected future that would no longer come to fruition. Changes in lifestyle impacted the experience of chronic sorrow with community reactions, such as having to explain limited time of social supports and having to decline social events due to the child's illness held to potential to catalyze chronic sorrow (Coughlin & Sethares, 2017). Similarly, in a study examining chronic sorrow and social support needs of HIV-positive men and women, a mixed-methods approach highlighted worsening depression after diagnosis with chronic levels of depression occurring around loss of employment, financial problems, and social isolation (Lichtenstein, Laska, & Clair, 2002).

The meanings tied to gender and particular social roles has been seen to influence the experience of chronic sorrow as well. In a review of the literature in parents with children who have a chronic illness, Coughlin and Sethares (2017) found distinct gender differences where mothers were seen to experience more intense sorrow due to illness or disability marked with feelings of emptiness, self-blame, guilt, fear, and depression. In contrast, fathers were seen to experience confusion and concern over future problems and stigma associated with physical disabilities, although they reported little to no depression. Mothers often reported periodic recurrences as well as persistence of sorrow, whereas fathers appeared to adjust to the diagnosis over time although the recurrence of sorrow emerged in response to mothers' health care concerns (Coughlin & Sethares, 2017). These findings suggest that chronic sorrow may be significantly influenced by how central the loss event is to one's identity and life narrative. Gender differences may arise due to cultural expectations regarding gender-based caretaking responsibilities as well as socially prescribed gender-based grieving styles.

Similarly, Lichtenstein and colleagues (2002) found experiences of chronic sorrow were marked with significant gender differences as well, where men in this study experienced sorrow surrounding untimely, frequent deaths of friends and uncertainty regarding their future although women experienced greater stigma and rejection, particularly those with children. In this study, the authors suggest that sexual orientation appeared a factor in receiving support, where men who identified as gay typically perceived support from a community of gay men contributing to a sense of "communal self," where women appeared bound by stigmatizing assumptions in the heterosexual community surrounding HIV resulting in greater social distance.

Much of the literature has also sought to understand the needs of individuals and families grappling with chronic sorrow. Caregivers' reactions revolve around a need for increased understanding from health care professionals around grief and hope (Collings, 2008), including needing a break from caregiving responsibilities (Coughlin & Sethares, 2017), health education, availability of informed counseling, culturally-oriented strategies for living with sorrow (Chang, Huang, Cheng, & Chien, 2018) and community sensitization (Olwit, Musisi, Leshabari, & Sanyu, 2015). Many individuals and families who experience nonfinite loss and chronic sorrow often report negative encounters, feeling that counselors may inadvertently undermine needed hope in the immediate aftermath of diagnosis (Collings, 2008).

Ambiguous Loss

As already discussed in previous chapters in more detail, ambiguous loss exists where there are both elements of presence and absence leading to complications in the grieving process. These losses are typically ongoing with little possibility of closure. In the past 12 years, ambiguous loss has been widely applied to a range of populations, such as: LGBT couples, lesbian couples with children, disappearances or missing persons in international contexts, immigration, refugee displacement, military deployment, chronically ill children, autism, and gender transition in families with a transgender loved one (see Boss, Bryant, & Mancini, 2016). Much attention has been given to the phenomenological experience of ambiguous loss, with quantitative analyses being dedicated to the study of boundary ambiguity, the perception of the event or situation about who is inside or outside of the family structure[2] (Boss, 2016). In terms of grief, little empirical work has the examined conditions that give rise to the grief responses in ambiguous loss, although it has been hypothesized that immobilizing ambiguity, particularly for mastery-oriented cultures, is a significant stressor (Boss, 2016). Boss (2016) suggests that the symptoms resulting from ambiguous loss are likely similar or the same as complicated grief; however, in ambiguous losses, it is not the grief that is complicated, but the context of the loss experience where there is lack of clarity and no likelihood of resolution or closure of the ambiguous situation.

A recent review of psychological symptoms in people confronted with the disappearance of a loved one suggests that levels of psychopathology did not differ between relatives of deceased loved ones and missing persons, particularly in terms of complicated grief (Lenferink, de Keijser, Wessel, de Vries, & Boelen, 2017). Similarly, in a study that examined prolonged grief (PG) reactions among Colombians displaced due to internal armed conflict, bereaved Colombians and those who had lost significant others through disappearance did not differ in terms of traumatic exposure, depression, PG, or PTSD symptom severity. However, there appeared to be a statistically higher prevalence of PG if those who had lost a loved one to disappearance had hope that the missing person was still alive. It was suggested that those who have continuing levels of hope may grapple with lack of closure, thereby prolonging or continuing the grief process (Heeke, Stammel, & Knaevelsrud, 2015). As Boss (2006) suggests, sustained hope for a loved one's return may be beneficial in the early stages of ambiguous loss; however, hope may become a hindrance across time as those affected begin to face a future without the possibility of closure. Self-compassion appeared to buffer against the rumination that was associated with PG, depression, and post-traumatic stress levels in a sample of Dutch participants who had a family member disappear (Lenferink, Eisma, Keijser, & Boelen, 2017). Specifically, grief rumination surrounding the meaning and consequences of the disappearance, reactions of others to the disappearance, and unfairness of the disappearance were found to be significant linking factors in the relationship between PG and post-traumatic stress levels (Lenferink et al., 2017). It is possible that self-compassion may aid in adjusting mastery orientation by fostering kindness to the self and recognition of suffering versus a need to control or simply "get over it." Hollander (2016) identified a range of external stressors that were linked to complicated grief, highlighting themes of social disenfranchisement, isolation, and stigmatization for parents and family members of persons who were missing in Uganda. Specifically, conflict (e.g., violence, displacement), poverty (e.g., livelihood support), and ambiguity (e.g., hope for return with resulting intense worry) were seen to naturally prolong and complicate the grief process for these relatives. Additionally, community support appeared to dwindle in the subsequent months following the disappearance, and open mourning was typically discouraged as there was no confirmation of the death. Families of those that disappeared often found themselves avoiding community members due to perceptions of stigma where prolonged disappearance of a loved one was related to the belief that relatives had willingly joined rebel groups.

Implications and Measurement

Language has the power to normalize and validate one's experience, which can be incredibly ameliorative, particularly when losses are marked with uncertainty, lack societal recognition, and have no rituals to validate or normalize them. As Carrington (2016) found in a qualitative study of counselors in training, many clinicians in training are either not aware of or feel inadequately trained to identify loss symptomatology or to assess for loss, particularly when clients do not present discussing loss or grief. Similarly, familial supports and community members may be unaware of the grief that follows in the aftermath of non-death losses, particularly those that are ongoing and where there is no verified death.

To examine grief related to non-death losses, some researchers have chosen to adopt measures commonly used in the bereavement literature, such as the Prolonged Grief Inventory-13 that measures symptomatology of Prolonged Grief Disorder (Prigerson & Maciejewski, 2006), or the Inventory for Complicated Grief (Prigerson et al., 1995), modifying bereavement references to more loss-specific language. Although using modified measures in this way may contribute to a recognition that reactions to non-death loss can include severe grief symptomatology, the criteria of symptom duration being six months or longer is not necessarily applicable for non-death losses, as many are ongoing in nature. Others have chosen to adopt measures of normative grief such as the Hogan Grief Reaction Checklist (Hogan, Greenfield, & Schmidt, 2001; Saban et al., 2016) or Texas Revised Inventory of Grief (Faschingbauer, 1981; Wayment & Brookshire, 2018). A main issue in non-death loss research is the recognition of the normative nature of grief as an outcome with an awareness that grief may abate and arise again across time. Examining a range of contextual factors and external stressors may contribute to this recognition.

Sewell and Williams (2001) state that in potentially traumatic or stressful life events, individuals will engage in an attempt to make sense or meaning of an event when assumptions of world and self are challenged. Consistent with Park's Meaning-Making Model (2010), the Integration of Stressful Life Experiences Scale (ISLES; Holland, Currier, Coleman, & Neimeyer, 2010) is a measure of meaning made of stress that assesses the discrepancy between situational meaning made of a particular event (i.e., appraisals of the event) and global meaning (i.e., overall beliefs, goals, and worldview). This measure has been used successfully in situations of both death and non-death losses (Holland, 2016), and can be used to explore the ways that an individual makes meaning in non-death loss events. As meaning is reconstructed in an intricate social environment, a recent measure that examines social validation and invalidation in life events is the Social Meaning in Life Events Scale (SMILES; Bellet, Holland, & Neimeyer, 2018), which holds promise for the study of different forms of disenfranchised grief.

As potentially traumatic events can disrupt the way we construe events (i.e., how the world is supposed to work) and social world (i.e., with whom and how I am socially related), these domains of construal are important for research related to non-death losses, as many of the themes in the research thus far have highlighted how non-death loss events challenge how one makes meaning of the world, the experience of disrupted identity, and uncertainty about how a significant other fits in the midst of change and transition. As researchers seek to elucidate the ways that grief may arise and persist in relation to non-death losses, exploring event centrality may prove useful due to the strong associations with psychological distress (Reiland & Clark, 2017), post-traumatic growth (Groleau, Calhoun, Cann, & Tedeschi, 2013), post-event psychopathology (Boelen, 2012), and bereavement symptomatology (Bellet, Neimeyer, & Berman, 2016). Specifically, the Centrality of Events Scale (CES; Berntsen & Rubin, 2006) has been used in a number of studies and correlates positively with a range of measures relating to trauma, PTSD, grief, and autobiographical memory (Gehrt, Berntsen, Hoyle, & Rubin, 2018). Personal relevance of the loss can also be examined by exploring role centrality, how a particular social role or aspect of identity is central to one's sense of self, as this can indicate how a loss may challenge aspects of social construal.

Grief or reactions to loss have also been studied in specific populations or type of non-death losses with several authors having created population-specific measures to capture grief and loss responses within a particular population, such as persons with spinal cord injury (Kalpakjian, Tulsky, Kisala, & Bombardier, 2015), general disability (Niemeier, Kennedy, McKinley, & Cifu, 2004), college students (Cooley, Toray, & Roscoe, 2014), and caregiver grief (Marwit & Meuser, 2005). Similarly, the Burke Nursing Consortium for Research in Chronic Sorrow (NCRCS) Chronic Sorrow Questionnaire is a 16-item interview protocol that aims to explore the experiences of chronic sorrow in caregivers surrounding the diagnosis and progression of severe mental health concerns (Eakes, 1995; Olwit et al.,

2015) and can be used for the exploration of developmental disabilities as well as suddenly acquired diseases or disabilities related to injury. In attempts to examine chronic sorrow with quantitative methodology, the revised Kendall Chronic Sorrow Instrument (KCSI-R; Kendall, 2005) is an 18-item self-report, single-factor instrument that measures the phenomenon of chronic sorrow with scores reflecting the degree that chronic sorrow is likely present.

Conclusion

This chapter highlighted that non-death loss events occur at a high rate across the lifespan and, for some, these experiences are highly significant life events that result in grief. As event and social domains of construal can be challenged by loss, reconstruction of meaning surrounding the loss event or identity is likely warranted, although more work is needed to understand the grief and meaning-making processes in non-death loss events. In addition, meaning-making occurs within a social context, and non-death losses are not typically recognized or supported. Thus, understanding social meanings associated with non-death losses may help to address the problematic disenfranchisement of the grief associated with these experiences. It is hoped that as the awareness of the significance of non-death losses increases, so too will researchers develop ways to study these experiences in greater depth, increasing our understandings of loss and grief in a broader and more inclusive way.

Key Terms

Complicated Grief: Involves prolonged acute grief symptoms, and situations in which the grieving person is unable to rebuild a meaningful life after the loss. There is currently a movement toward the development of a consensus of criteria dictating complicated grief. This is difficult due to the confusion regarding differing terminology across disciplines to refer to difficult grief, such as complicated grief, traumatic grief, complicated mourning, and prolonged grief disorder.

Normalization: Validating, acknowledging, and supporting the experience of conflicting thoughts and emotions that will naturally arise from non-death loss and grief experiences.

Questions for Reflection

1. Apply the major grief theories of nonfinite loss, chronic sorrow, and ambiguous loss in relation to non-death-related losses. Do you think these grief theories are portrayed accurately in common understandings of grief in your local community or media? Why or why not?
2. Has your thinking about research methodology in grief and non-death loss changed from what it was previously? Do you believe there are areas in which non-death loss and thanatological research is lacking? If so, in what ways?

3. What do you think are the ramifications for non-death loss being ignored or misdiagnosed across research disciplines? Why is there a need to promote interdisciplinary research? How can this be accomplished?

Notes

1. For the purposes of this review, bereavement refers to the response to death-related losses; grief is an all-inclusive term that refers to the response to both death and non-death losses.
2. For a review of research related to family boundary ambiguity, see Carroll, Olson, and Buckmiller (2007).

References

Ahlström, G. (2007). Experiences of loss and chronic sorrow in persons with severe chronic illness. *Journal of Clinical Nursing, 16*, 76–83.

Bellet, B. W., Holland, J. M., & Neimeyer, R. A. (2018). The Social Meaning in Life Events Scale (SMILES): A preliminary psychometric evaluation in a bereaved sample. *Death Studies*, 1–10.

Bellet, B. W., Neimeyer, R. A., & Berman, J. S. (2016). Event centrality and bereavement symptomatology: The moderating role of meaning made. *Omega: The Journal of Death and Dying, 7*, 56–65.

Benjet, C., Bromet, E., Karam, E. G., Kessler, R. C., McLaughlin, K. A., Ruscio, A. M., . . . Alonso, J. (2016). The epidemiology of traumatic event exposure worldwide: Results from the world mental health survey consortium. *Psychological Medicine, 46*, 327–343.

Berntsen, D., & Rubin, D. C. (2006). The centrality of event scale: A measure of integrating a trauma into one's identity and its relation to post-traumatic stress disorder symptoms. *Behaviour Research and Therapy, 44*, 219–231.

Boelen, P. A. (2012). A prospective examination of the association between the centrality of a loss and post-loss psychopathology. *Journal of Affective Disorders, 137*, 117–124.

Bordere, T. C. (2016). Social justice conceptualizations in grief and loss. In D. Harris & T. C. Bordere (Eds.), *Handbook of social justice in loss and grief: Exploring diversity, equity, and inclusion* (pp. 9–20). New York: Routledge.

Bordere, T. C. (2017). Disenfranchisement and ambiguity in the face of loss: The suffocated grief of sexual assault survivors. *Family Relations, 66*, 29–45.

Boss, P. (2006). *Loss, trauma, and resilience: Therapeutic work with ambiguous loss*. New York: W. W. Norton & Company.

Boss, P. (2016). The context and process of theory development: The story of ambiguous loss. *Journal of Family Theory & Review, 8*, 269–286.

Boss, P., Bryant, C. M., & Mancini, J. A. (2016). *Family stress management: A contextual approach* (3rd ed.). Thousand Oaks, CA: Sage.

Brown, K. (2017). *Changing perceptions of loss: The influence of generation effects and message framing*. Doctoral dissertation. Retrieved from ProQuest.

Brown-Manning, R. (2013). *We don't give birth to thugs: We give birth to children: The emotional journeys of African-American mothers raising sons under American racism*. Doctoral dissertation 2013. Retrieved from ProQuest. (3561574).

Bruce, E. J., & Schultz, C. L. (2004). *Through loss*. Melbourne: Australian Council for Educational Research Press.

Carrington, C. P. (2016). A counselor's first encounter with non-death loss: A phenomenological case study on new counselor preparation and experience in working with non-death loss. Doctor of Philosophy (PhD) dissertation, *Counseling and Human Services, Old Dominion University*. Retrieved from https://digitalcommons.odu.edu/chs_etds/6

Carroll, J. S., Olson, C. D., & Buckmiller, N. (2007). Family boundary ambiguity: A 30-year review of theory, research, and measurement. *Family Relations, 56*, 210–230.

Chang, K. J., Huang, X. Y., Cheng, J. F., & Chien, C. H. (2018). The chronic sorrow experiences of caregivers of clients with schizophrenia in Taiwan: A phenomenological study. *Perspectives in Psychiatric Care, 54*, 281–286.

Cohen, D. A. (1996). An empirical study of college students' grief responses: Death vs. non-death losses. *Dissertation Abstracts International, 58*, 94A. Retrieved from http://surface.syr.edu/chs_etd/35/

Collings, C. (2008). That's not my child anymore! Parental grief after acquired brain injury (ABI): Incidence, nature and longevity. *British Journal of Social Work, 38*, 1499–1517.

Cooley, E., Toray, T., & Roscoe, L. (2010). Reactions to loss scale: Assessing grief in college students. *Omega: The Journal of Death and Dying, 61*, 25–51.

Cooley, E., Toray, T., & Roscoe, L. (2014). Assessing effective coping with bereavement in college students: The reactions to loss scale. *Omega: The Journal of Death and Dying, 68*, 241–257.

Coughlin, M. B., & Sethares, K. A. (2017). Chronic sorrow in parents of children with a chronic illness or disability: An integrative literature review. *Journal of Pediatric Nursing, 37*, 108–116.

deRoon-Cassini, T. A., de St Aubin, E., Valvano, A., Hastings, J., & Horn, P. (2009). Psychological well-being after spinal cord injury: Perception of loss and meaning making. *Rehabilitation Psychology, 54*, 306–314.

Doka, K. J. (Ed.) (1989). *Disenfranchised grief: Recognizing hidden sorrow*. Lexington, MA: Lexington Books.

Doka, K. J. (Ed.) (2002). *Disenfranchised grief: New directions, challenges, and strategies for practice* (pp. 187–198). Champaign, IL: Research Press.

Eakes, G. G. (1995). Chronic sorrow: The lived experience of parents of chronically mentally ill individuals. *Archives of Psychiatric Nursing, 9*, 77–84.

Faschingbauer, T. R. (1981). *Texas revised inventory of grief*. Houston: Honeycomb Publishing.

Fineran, K. R. (2012). Helping foster and adopted children to grieve the loss of birthparents: A case study example. *The Family Journal, 20*, 369–375.

Gehrt, T. B., Berntsen, D., Hoyle, R. H., & Rubin, D. C. (2018). Psychological and clinical correlates of the centrality of event scale: A systematic review. *Clinical Psychology Review, 65*, 57–80.

Granek, L. G. (2016). Medicalizing grief. In D. Harris & T. C. Bordere (Eds.), *Handbook of social justice in loss and grief: Exploring diversity, equity, and inclusion* (pp. 111–124). New York: Routledge.

Groleau, J. M., Calhoun, L. G., Cann, A., & Tedeschi, R. G. (2013). The role of centrality of events in posttraumatic distress and posttraumatic growth. *Psychological Trauma: Theory, Research, Practice, and Policy, 5*, 477–483.

Harris, D. L. (Eds.). (2011). *Counting our losses: Reflecting on change, loss, and transition in everyday life*. New York: Routledge.

Harvey, J. H., & Miller, E. D. (1998). Toward a psychology of loss. *Psychological Science, 9*, 429–434. doi:10.1111/1467-9280.00081

Heeke, C., Stammel, N., & Knaevelsrud, C. (2015). When hope and grief intersect: Rates and risks of prolonged grief disorder among bereaved individuals and relatives of disappeared persons in Colombia. *Journal of Affective Disorders, 173*, 59–64.

Hogan, N., Greenfield, D., & Schmidt, N. (2001). Development and validation of the Hogan grief reaction checklist. *Death Studies, 25*, 1–32. doi:10.1080/07481180125831

Holland, J. M. (2016). Integration of stressful life experiences scale (ISLES). In R. A. Neimeyer (Ed.), *Series in death, dying, and bereavement. Techniques of grief therapy: Assessment and intervention* (pp. 46–50). New York, NY: Routledge/Taylor & Francis Group.

Holland, J. M., Currier, J. M., Coleman, R. A., & Neimeyer, R. A. (2010). The Integration of Stressful Life Experiences Scale (ISLES): Development and initial validation of a new measure. *International Journal of Stress Management, 17*, 325–352.

Hollander, T. (2016). Ambiguous loss and complicated grief: Understanding the grief of parents of the disappeared in northern Uganda. *Journal of Family Theory and Review, 8*(3), 294–307.

Kalpakjian, C. Z., Tulsky, D. S., Kisala, P. A., & Bombardier, C. H. (2015). Measuring grief and loss after spinal cord injury: Development, validation and psychometric characteristics of the SCI-QOL Grief and Loss item bank and short form. *The Journal of Spinal Cord Medicine, 38*, 347–355.

Kendall, L. C. (2005). *The experience of living with ongoing loss: Testing the Kendall chronic sorrow instrument.* Unpublished doctoral dissertation, Virginia Commonwealth University.

Kilpatrick, D. G., Resnick, H. S., Milanak, M. E., Miller, M. W., Keyes, K. M., & Friedman, M. J. (2013). National estimates of exposure to traumatic events and PTSD prevalence using DSM-IV and DSM-5 criteria. *Journal of Traumatic Stress, 26*, 537–547.

Lenferink, L. I., de Keijser, J., Wessel, I., de Vries, D., & Boelen, P. A. (2017). Toward a better understanding of psychological symptoms in people confronted with the disappearance of a loved one: A systematic review. *Trauma, Violence, & Abuse, 20*, 287–302.

Lenferink, L. I., Eisma, M. C., de Keijser, J., & Boelen, P. A. (2017). Grief rumination mediates the association between self-compassion and psychopathology in relatives of missing persons. *European Journal of Psychotraumatology, 8*, 1378052.

Lichtenstein, B., Laska, M. K., & Clair, J. M. (2002). Chronic sorrow in the HIV-positive patient: Issues of race, gender, and social support. *AIDS Patient Care and STDs, 16*, 27–38.

Lindgren, C. L., Burke, M. L., Hainsworth, M. A., & Eakes, G. G. (1992). Chronic sorrow: A lifespan concept. *Scholarly Inquiry for Nursing Practice, 6*, 27–40.

Marwit, S. J., & Meuser, T. M. (2005). Development of a short form inventory to assess grief in caregivers of dementia patients. *Death Studies, 29*, 191–205.

Neimeyer, R. A., Burke, L. A., Mackay, M. M., & van Dyke Stringer, J. G. (2010). Grief therapy and the reconstruction of meaning: From principles to practice. *Journal of Contemporary Psychotherapy, 40*, 73–83.

Niemeier, J. P., Kennedy, R. E., McKinley, W. O., & Cifu, D. X. (2004). The loss inventory: Preliminary reliability and validity data for a new measure of emotional and cognitive responses to disability. *Disability and Rehabilitation, 26*, 614–623.

Olshansky, S. (1962). Chronic sorrow: A response to having a mentally defective child. *Social Casework, 43*, 190–193.

Olwit, C., Musisi, S., Leshabari, S., & Sanyu, I. (2015). Chronic sorrow: Lived experiences of caregivers of patients diagnosed with schizophrenia in Butabika Mental Hospital, Kampala, Uganda. *Archives of Psychiatric Nursing, 29*, 43–48.

Ott, C. H., Sanders, S., & Kelber, S. T. (2007). Grief and personal growth experience of spouses and adult-child caregivers of individuals with Alzheimer's disease and related dementias. *The Gerontologist, 47*, 798–809.

Papa, A., Lancaster, N. G., & Kahler, J. (2014). Commonalities in grief responding across bereavement and non-bereavement losses. *Journal of Affective Disorders, 161*, 136–143. doi:10.1016/j.jad.2014.03.018

Papa, A., & Maitoza, R. (2013). The role of loss in the experience of grief: The case of job loss. *Journal of Loss and Trauma, 18*, 152–169.

Park, C. L. (2010). Making sense of the meaning literature: An integrative review of meaning making and its effects on adjustment to stressful life events. *Psychological Bulletin, 136*, 257–269. doi:10.1037/a0018301

Prigerson, H. G., Horowitz, M. J., Jacobs, S. C., Parkes, C. M., Aslan, M., Goodkin, K., . . . & Bonanno, G. (2009). Prolonged grief disorder: Psychometric validation of criteria proposed for DSM-V and ICD-11. *PLoS Medicine, 6*, e1000121.

Prigerson, H. G., Maciejewski, P. K., Reynolds III, C. F., Bierhals, A. J., Newsom, J. T., Fasiczka, A., . . . Miller, M. (1995). Inventory of complicated grief: A scale to measure maladaptive symptoms of loss. *Psychiatry Research, 59*, 65–79.

Ray, R. A., & Street, A. F. (2007). Non-finite loss and emotional labour: Family caregivers' experiences of living with motor neurone disease. *Journal of Clinical Nursing, 16*, 35–43.

Reiland, S. A., & Clark, C. B. (2017). Relationship between event type and mental health outcomes: Event centrality as mediator. *Personality and Individual Differences, 114*, 155–159.

Richardson, M., Cobham, V., McDermott, B., & Murray, J. (2013). Youth mental illness and the family: Parents' loss and grief. *Journal of Child and Family Studies, 22*, 719–736.

Roos, S. (2017). *Chronic sorrow: A living loss.* New York: Routledge.

Saban, K. L., Mathews, H. L., Collins, E. G., Hogan, N. S., Tell, D., Bryant, F. B., . . . Janusek, L. W. (2016). The man I once knew: Grief and inflammation in female partners of veterans with traumatic brain injury. *Biological Research for Nursing, 18*, 50–59.

Schultz, C. L., & Harris, D. L. (2011). Giving voice to nonfinite loss and grief in bereavement. In R. A. Neimeyer, D. L. Harris, H. R. Winokuer, & G. F. Thornton (Eds.), *Grief and bereavement in contemporary society: Bridging research and practice* (pp. 235–245). New York: Routledge.

Sewell, K., & Williams, A. (2001). Construing stress: A constructivist therapeutic approach to posttraumatic stress reactions. In R. A. Neimeyer (Ed.), *Meaning reconstruction and the experience of loss* (pp. 293–310). Washington, DC: American Psychological Association.

Shear, M. K., McLaughlin, K. A., Ghesquiere, A., Gruber, M. J., Sampson, N. A., & Kessler, R. C. (2011). Complicated grief associated with Hurricane Katrina. *Depression and Anxiety, 28*, 648–657.

Varga, M. A. (2016). A quantitative study of graduate student grief experiences. *Illness, Crisis & Loss, 24*, 170–186.

Wayment, H. A., & Brookshire, K. A. (2018). Mothers' reactions to their child's ASD diagnosis: Predictors that discriminate grief from distress. *Journal of Autism and Developmental Disorders, 48*, 1147–1158.

CHAPTER 23

Supporting People Through Living Losses
Darcy L. Harris

Living With Loss

An overarching theme of this book has been the dynamic experience of living with change, loss, and transition in everyday life. While grief is often difficult, painful, and exhausting, it is part of our shared human experience and not a malady to be treated. Our basic human nature is to quickly respond to people who are in distress; how we interpret that distress and the ways that we respond will be the result of an interplay of our values, beliefs, socialization, and past experiences. Helping professionals receive training in how to respond to different aspects of human experience, and their training will inform how they interpret the experiences of those who seek their assistance. It is important to remember that grief is one of the few experiences that we will all encounter at some point in our lives; therefore, we may be the professional who is bearing witness to the grief of a client, and we may also be the wounded healer, who deeply understands the arduous process of rebuilding our lives after being shattered by significant loss events.

Unique Aspects of Non-Death Loss Experiences

As discussed earlier, grief is the response to the loss or shattering of our assumptive world. While the main premise of this book is that grief occurs in response to both death and non-death losses, there are some notable differences between these two experiences. After the death of a loved one, the grieving process can be overwhelming. As the bereaved individual begins to rebuild a world without the loved one, there is gradual accommodation and adaptation to the loss that has occurred. There will be surges, triggers, and reminders of the lost person that occur in an ongoing way, and it is likely that the grief will be readily present during these times. With non-death, or living losses, the grief can continue as an undercurrent on a day-by-day basis if the loss itself remains present and is ongoing in nature. Rather than resulting from the griever's inability to resolve a finite loss, chronic sorrow related to living losses is triggered by an ongoing pattern of new and recurring losses that are often of increasing severity and intensity (Rossheim & McAdams, 2010). While the response to loss is certainly complex and may involve a myriad number of affective features, the most common emotional responses to the loss of a loved one tend to be sadness, guilt, and anger. In contrast, the uncertainty, ongoing and continual adjustment, and fluctuations that occur alongside non-death loss experiences often produce a prominent sense of being unsettled and anxious about how life will now unfold, in addition to sadness and anger over what has been lost (Mayer, 2001; Roos, 2018; Rossheim & McAdams, 2010).

The ongoing nature of non-death loss experiences means that those who experience these losses often endure a protracted, lifelong need to continually accommodate and adjust to the loss. The chronic sense of grief and anxiety that accompanies living loss experiences is certainly exhausting for the individual who is affected by the loss; in addition, it can be very difficult for the individual's support system to tolerate the intensity and chronic grief over a long period of time. Thus, it is common for those experiencing non-death losses to become isolated, as friends and family members tire of not seeing "progress" in the person's grief, or the loss is not one that they can see, comprehend, or even acknowledge. For example, a couple going through infertility treatment for many years may look fine on the surface, with their appearances betraying the potential devastation to their relationship, finances, plans, and hopes for their future (Harris, 2013).

As described earlier in Chapter 2 on disenfranchised grief, many non-death losses are not recognized or acknowledged, have no rituals to provide meaning or offer support for those affected, and their invisibility, ambiguity, and chronicity make fulfilling the social expectation to "get over it and move on" unrealistic. Self-reliance and independence are highly prized and idealized in Western-oriented societies. The messages to people who seem "stuck" in their situation may be overt or covert; typically, there is an underlying sentiment that "these people need to just pick themselves up and move on with life" or that they can conquer their circumstances by trying harder (Harris, 2016). These expectations are all social constructions that have been internalized from childhood (remember being told to stop crying when you were young, and to simply "grow up," which equates maturity with hiding feelings and denying vulnerability). The actual reality is that most individuals dealing with ongoing, living losses would do anything to be able to move on or to be free of their experience. We like our lives to be predictable (and we expect this predictability and routine in life); in many of our assumptions about the world, we believe that we have control over our lives and our choices, as long as we (insert here) eat well, get enough sleep, do well in our studies, pick the right friends, etc. However, despite all that we believe about determining our health, our happiness, and our future, living losses are painful reminders that life is messy, unpredictable, uncontrollable, and rarely what we expect it to be or hope it should be (Harris, 2011).

Many professionals also struggle with patients/clients who don't seem to respond to their interventions. Professional training programs tend to emphasize fixing, curing, and treatment with specific outcome objectives, most of which simply don't work for long-term, chronic loss experiences. Gradually, the sense of frustration and failure at not being able to effectively remedy the situation can lead to withdrawal, avoidance, and, at times, stigmatizing and labeling (i.e., becoming the "problem patient," professionals begin to question if the person is malingering, or "attention-seeking"). With the focus on what can or can't be done, the importance of presence, bearing witness, and intention are overlooked or devalued as essential aspects of therapeutic support (Boss, 2016; Boss, Roos, & Harris, 2011; Roos, 2018). Pivotal issues arise in living loss experiences:

1. *Lack of acknowledgment and validation*—losses that are not readily identified or understood tend to be disenfranchised, leaving those affected without validation of their experience by family, friends, and many professionals.
2. *Emotional intensity*—losses that are ongoing in nature are intensified by the anxiety and uncertainty that is intermingled with the grief. Thus, these individuals can present as intense, nervous, needing an inordinate amount of control, and even desperate, which can be overwhelming to the people around them, including professionals.
3. *Stress in the present; uncertainty about the future*—the stress of coping with what has already happened combines with uncertainty about the future, adding another layer to the exhaustion in the present. Both those who are living with loss and their loved ones have to adapt to erratically changing versions of self and of the world, often at a time when it is very difficult to access internal and external resources.
4. *Burnout of supports*—it is hard to find good support that doesn't burn out or tire from the ongoing intensity and lack of apparent resolution. People stop asking, "How are you?" or they don't listen to the answer because they don't want to know if you are still struggling. Watching someone struggle over a long period of time can create a sense of powerlessness and helplessness that in turn, leads to empathic overload and exhaustion in both professionals and friends/family members. Unrealistic expectations about recovery and closure can create a great deal of stress and pressure to try to fix what can't be changed.
5. *Financial impact*—there are usually limits on insurance coverage for services and equipment that are required in an ongoing way (i.e., psychological support, assistive devices, in-home care providers, etc.) Once limits are exceeded (or if there is no coverage), huge financial strain can occur. Adding to these concerns are the potential financial impact of cutting back work hours, retraining and changing careers (if the loss affects abilities that are required in the workplace), mounting expenses, or having to leave work completely.

Clinical Implications for Professionals

Living losses can present a big challenge due to the difficulties in balancing expectations regarding outcome with experiences that are not amenable to standard intervention strategies. This is not meant to say that professional support is unhelpful or unwarranted; however, in these situations, the focus of the professional needs to be redirected toward intention more than outcome. This stance may seem contrary to training that is outcome-oriented by nature; the focus on "doing" over "being" and the mandate to meet objectives and to demonstrate positive responses to interventions can become a burden that may hinder effective therapy with individuals who are living with ongoing loss experiences. Geller and

Greenberg (2012) make a point to discuss the importance of therapist presence as foundational to being effective in providing therapeutic support. Their point is well taken; with the strong focus placed on diagnosis, intervention, and solution-focused therapy (often driven by funding models for reimbursement of services), very little emphasis is placed upon the essential act of being fully present to someone, bearing witness to another's story and descriptions of struggle, and of holding the intention to make a difference, even in the absence of being able to make things better or to demonstrate a positive, measurable outcome.

At the outset, it is important to keep in mind that by the time many people struggling with living losses seek help from a clinician, they have most likely already experienced many of the very unhelpful attitudes and expectations about recovery and closure that were described in the previous section. They are most likely exhausted, anxious, and struggling with the isolation and mixed messages from those close to them who have been overwhelmed by their experience. Thus, the relationship that you form with the client is going to serve as a lifeline to provide invaluable human contact and support. Fundamental to this support is your ability to remain present, to stay clear with your intention, and to build a foundation for your work together on a fundamentally compassionate stance (Harris & Winokuer, 2016).

Presence

Our ability to offer our full attention and empathetic presence to another human being is one of the greatest gifts that we have to offer. Being present is described as something that is multilayered—that in addition to offering our physical presence, there are deeper forms of "being with" someone. For example, being psychologically and emotionally present and attentive with someone involves good listening, empathy, being nonjudgmental, and being fully open to someone and his or her experience. McDonough-Means, Kreitzer, and Bell (2004) describe a deeper form of connection that occurs when a person is centered, grounded, and intuitively open to another person. Geller and Greenberg (2012), describe therapeutic presence as

> The state of having one's whole self in the encounter with a client by being completely in the moment on a multiplicity of levels—physically, emotionally, cognitively, and spiritually. Therapeutic presence involves being in contact with one's integrated and healthy self, while being open and receptive to what is poignant in the moment and immersed in it, with a larger sense of spaciousness and expansion of awareness and perception. This grounded, immersed, and expanded awareness occurs with the intention of being with and for the client, in the service of his or her healing process.
>
> (p. 7)

One of the most important skills required of a clinician in situations of living losses is the ability to "be with" someone, and not focusing solely on what to "do to" someone or monitoring the "progress" of the client. Techniques and book knowledge are not going to be enough when you have someone sitting in front of you whose world has been shattered by loss and is experiencing ongoing pain, afraid that there is more loss and pain in the future.

A good amount of counseling research indicates that what clients experience as the most important aspect of therapy work is not the techniques that were used or the theoretical orientation of the clinician; rather, feeling heard, understood, and sensing genuine care from the clinician mattered far more (Geller & Greenberg, 2012; Harris, 2016; Yalom, 2009). In short, *the relationship that you form with your clients/patients and their sense of your attentive, engaged presence provides the foundation from which healing can begin to occur, even in the absence of a cure or remedy for the situation.*

Intention

In this context, your intention is the underlying reason for why you do what you do, and it deeply reflects who you are. Being aware of your intention, both in a broader, overarching view as well as in the context of the present, provides you with the opportunity to have a "home base" where you can return if you are unsure, stressed, or feeling overwhelmed. The focus on intention relieves you from getting caught up on the expectation of a specific outcome. For example, if you were working with someone with a health condition that causes ongoing, chronic physical pain, it would be easy to try different ways to address the pain and to look for relief of the pain as your goal. But what if all the interventions that were tried to relieve the pain were ineffective, and the pain continues unremittingly? Most likely, the person who is struggling with the chronic pain has also endured being shuffled from one care provider to another, looking for relief. In addition, chronic pain affects not just the individual experiencing it, but also those individuals who are close to this person as well. If the treatment goal is focused only on relieving the pain, then not being able to take away the pain is seen as failure, and the therapeutic relationship becomes centered around the clinician's sense of shame and avoidance. If your goal is to accompany this person in the pain and the angst that accompanies the pain, whether or not there is lessening of the pain in response to interventions, then at least you are not adding to the sense of isolation, shame, and failure that have probably become frequent companions for this individual. Thinking, "I cannot take this pain away from this person, but I can ensure that s/he will not have to go through this pain alone" may help to reframe some of the expectations around the role of the clinician in similar contexts (Vachon & Harris, 2016).

In joining with someone in their painful experience, your intention is to be fully present and connected with that person on a moment-to-moment basis. In this intention, you are not hindered in your relationship by a looming sense of failure or unmet expectations (Harris & Winokuer, 2016; Rossheim & McAdams, 2010). The acronym NATO can be very helpful:

Not
Attached
To
Outcome (All Acronyms, 2018).

Adopting this stance means letting go of expectations and not being drawn into trying to change what is not amenable to change. Letting go is not the same as giving up, is not abandonment of the person who is struggling, and it is not the same as resigning in failure. Learning how to remain present when you can't fix something, can't make it better, and can't change the outcome is hard work and requires a deep awareness of the realities of life and our human limitations. Focusing on the present moment and your choice to be where you are, without needing a client to be a certain way or to respond the way you would like, provides freedom to be fully present and open in a way that is quite rare in our social settings. So, for example, your intention with someone who is struggling with an ongoing, living loss could be to offer your full, compassionate presence in the time that you are together, instead of being frustrated and feeling powerless in the situation of a painful loss that can't be undone.

Compassion

Compassion is defined as the ability to demonstrate kindness, understanding, and nonjudgmental awareness towards human responses, especially those involving suffering, inadequacy, or perceived failure of some sort (Neff, Kirkpatrick, & Rude, 2007). Halifax defines compassion as a capacity that allows us to be attentive to the experience of others, to be able to wish the best for others, and to sense what will deeply serve others (Halifax, 2011). Compassionate responses take into account the awareness that we all share common human experiences and traits. Nobody is perfect; nobody is immune from painful life experiences, and nobody is spared from suffering at some point in time. People who are identified as compassionate are those who see the suffering of others and are moved to address this suffering in some way. Cultivating compassion involves a willingness to care for your own suffering while recognizing the pain of others, as self-compassion is a key to compassion that is directed toward others. With a compassionate intention, you allow yourself to be exposed to others' suffering, and you then choose to be an instrument of relief to that suffering in ways that are possible.

What is important to remember is that we cannot remove many of the causes of suffering, such as death and significant losses. So, our compassion must also contain insight and discernment so that we can recognize that while we desire to relieve suffering, we will not be able to relieve all the suffering that crosses our path. Far from being a passive process or a "soft and fluffy" superficial niceness, true compassion requires us to actively and decisively "be with" another individual when others may leave quickly or get frustrated because they cannot "fix" what has happened. Being compassionate requires a great deal of inner strength and awareness, and it takes time and practice to cultivate the ability to remain grounded, focused, and fully present in such an engaged and open way, especially in the face of suffering that is not amenable to relief (Vachon & Harris, 2016).

A key component of compassion is the ability to learn to tolerate distress without needing to remove yourself, avoid contact, or shut down emotionally. It is very important to be able to stay fully present without becoming engulfed by what is happening around you. Cultivating distress tolerance enables us to stay with the experience of suffering. "Being able to bear and cope with distress allows us to actively listen and work out what is helpful." (Gilbert & Choden, 2014, p. 112) Likewise, there needs to be an awareness of what it feels like to be grounded and fully present with ourselves so that we readily occupy this way of being when we are confronted with the pain and suffering of others. Halifax (2013) suggests that cultivating awareness and focus through contemplative practices allows for the deepening of attention and discernment, which then inform us when faced with unrelenting suffering and pain. Learning how to focus attention and awareness toward the "bigger picture" of life will serve us very well when we encounter situations that call into question our own assumptive world.

Contemplative practices cultivate an important first-person focus, sometimes with direct experience as the object, while at other times focusing on complex ideas or situations. Incorporated into daily life, they act as a conduit to connect us to what we find most meaningful; we learn how to regulate our own emotions and know what it is like to remain grounded and centered so that we can return to this way of being when we need to do so. The Contemplative Mind in Society has created a pictorial image entitled *The Tree of Contemplative Practices* (Figure 23.1) to illustrate

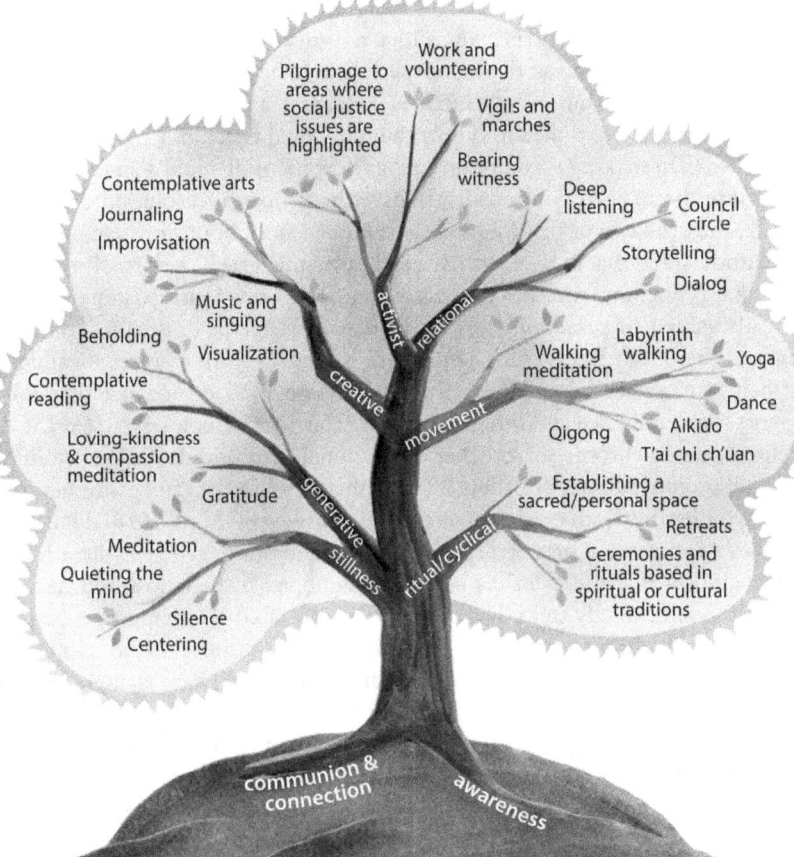

Figure 23.1 The Tree of Contemplative Practices

a wide variety of possible contemplative practices currently in use in secular organizational and academic settings (Bergman & Duerr, 2014). Reviewing this image may provide ideas for cultivating grounded awareness in a variety of different ways.

Practical Suggestions for Working With Living Losses

This chapter spends a great deal of time on the helper's intention and presence because these make up the foundation that will sustain you in working with people whose painful loss experiences may have ramifications for the rest of their lives. To be a support for the long haul, you need to be clear about what is and is not possible, and you need to be able to separate your desire to be a support from any expectations or outcomes that may never happen.

Validate the Loss and the Ongoing Nature of the Grief

As has been described in many of the chapters of this book, many non-death loss experiences and the grief that accompanies them are disenfranchised; they may not be recognized or acknowledged for their significance (Boss et al., 2011). Thus, in supporting someone who is living with a non-death loss experience, it is imperative to begin by validating the loss experience. In acknowledging the impact of these experiences as your client describes them, you are offering yourself as a safe, open support, willing to listen to how the individual is *actually experiencing* this loss rather than making assumptions about how the individual *should experience* it. Because the majority of non-death losses have no real resolution or sense of closure, the grief can persist for an indeterminate amount of time. Help your client to understand that in these scenarios, the ongoing grief is a normal reaction to a loss that is ongoing, whether the loss is related to a relationship, something that is greatly valued, or something less tangible, such as a hope or dream. Taking this stance at the outset frees your clients from having to work to receive validation for their experiences from you, allowing them to begin to engage in activities that support their resilience and innate strengths (Harris & Winokuer, 2016). The difference between chronic sorrow that is associated with non-death loss (nonfinite loss) and prolonged grief disorder (PGD) is that in PGD, the grief continues unremittingly after the death of a loved one (a finite loss event; Roos, 2018). Figure 23.2 provides a comparison between chronic sorrow and prolonged grief disorder.

Recognition that life as it has been or was hoped to be is lost and has been replaced by an initially unknown, unwanted, and often terrifying new reality is extremely difficult, forcing a re-appraisal of one's assumptive world. Go back to the assumptive world construct, and name how the loss(es) have shattered various aspects of the foundational beliefs that had formed this person's world before this experience. How do they now view people? What defines fairness and justice now? How has their sense of self been altered as a result of this experience? This process of naming is important; providing words to these experiences can be empowering for people, giving language and voice to what has most likely been minimized and misunderstood by many others.

Comparison of PGD with Chronic Sorrow

PGD	Chronic Sorrow
Protracted and incapacitating response to a single death loss event.	Ongoing grief in response to a loss that is also ongoing in nature.
Bereaved individuals struggle to re-enter life because of issues that interfere with coping and attachment.	Individuals are often prevented from engaging with life because the loss itself creates barriers and interference.
Viewed as disordered grief and responds to intervention.	Normal reaction to an ongoing loss and responds to supportive care.

Figure 23.2 Comparison of Prolonged Grief Disorder with Chronic Sorrow Associated With Nonfinite Loss

Consider Rituals

Rituals help us to attach meaning and significance to our experiences. They may also provide us with ways to enact feelings and more deeply understand experiences that defy words (Lewis & Hoy, 2011; Norton & Gino, 2014). Instead of dismissing or avoiding the pain of a loss, rituals give us time to bring the loss into full view and to bear witness to an experience that is difficult but also can be potentially transformative. Typically, meaningful rituals arise from the client's story and experience. Listen carefully to what the client shares and consider how metaphors, symbols, and/or depictions of their experience might be incorporated into some form of ritual. One of my clients came to talk about the grief she was experiencing after undergoing infertility treatment for several years. She had counted the number of fertilized eggs that had been retrieved with each IVF (in-vitro fertilization) procedure, but there had never been a successful pregnancy after the embryos were placed back into her body. She grieved the loss of her dream of being a mother. She also grieved the loss of her "children" that never grew in her body and that she would never hold in her arms. During one of our sessions together, she used modeling clay to form round balls that symbolized all the embryos that were created and lost. One by one, she said goodbye to each and then placed them into a clay bowl that she had shaped to resemble her uterus, and then she covered them with soft tissue. She then took the bowl and clay "embryos" home and buried them in her garden.

Remember the Problem Is With the Situation and Not the Person

In her recommendations for clinicians assisting people with ambiguous loss, Boss (2016) emphasizes the importance of recognizing that it is the situation that is problematic and not the individual(s) within the situation. It is easy to equate the problem with the person, which further disenfranchises the associated grief.

As has been stated many times in this book, many non-death losses lack a sense of closure and/or resolution, which creates many issues related to the chronicity, uncertainty, and exhaustion that are often present. Many of these losses are difficult to describe, lack clarity, and are not readily observable to others, and these factors combine to create a situation that can be the stuff of crazy-making. In scenarios of living losses, always re-frame negativity about the affected person(s) back to the real issue—a loss experience that defies boundaries, time, and, for many, meaning. Many people will express shame, guilt, or self-negativity because of the erosion to their sense of self that can occur alongside non-death loss experiences. If your client voices these feelings, normalize them and redirect the focus back to the pressure from unrealistic social expectations for closure, recovery, and moving on in life quickly—none of which are realistic or possible in these experiences.

Allow for the Possibility of Transformation and Resilience

Many people will share about the devastating consequences of their loss experiences—relationships, functionality, hopes, dreams, and life as they once knew it. However, they may also share their learnings, new perspectives, and appreciation for life. Validating the profound and often unrelenting grief associated with non-death losses doesn't close the door to the potential for growth, meaning, and transformation that can also occur in these same experiences. The clinician's goal is to strengthen and reinforce the client's innate resiliency to live with the ambiguity surrounding a loss, and the new reality that is created. In my practice, I have heard many clients talk about the ending of significant relationships through breakups or through choices to let go of the other person as being incredibly difficult and painful; these same clients often later talk about how they have re-framed their sense of self, and appreciate that they are stronger than they ever thought they could be, with greater clarity about what is important and matters the most to them. The grief over lost relationships will inevitably surface at various times, and the grief can be co-mingled with feelings of relief, along with increased awareness of inner strength that may not have been accessible prior to the ending of the relationship.

Be Aware of Available Resources

Helping clients with information about community resources and other supports is a high priority. Even in the absence of good community supports, there are now many helpful online resources that can be readily accessed at any time. A caution with suggesting online resources is to ensure that the information provided is accurate, and that any interactive aspects of the site (i.e., chat rooms, list serves, postings) are monitored regularly by someone who keeps the site focused appropriately. Many community and online resources work on the helper therapy principle, meaning that those who have an experience create an online community with others in similar situations to relieve the loneliness and isolation that can occur (Harris & Winokuer, 2016).

It is also important to be aware that even well-meaning professionals and community supports can make things worse by pushing for resolution or closure in situations where these are not possible. In this regard, clinicians need to understand that many individuals with living losses have had prior experiences with professionals or well-meaning but uninformed helpers that were shaming or unrealistic, causing them to hesitate to ask for assistance or support to avoid further stigma or judgment (Boss, Bryant, & Mancini, 2016; Harris, 2011).

Identifying resources may also include personal resources that are available to the client. For example, one of my clients whose husband had been diagnosed with dementia spent a session describing the intolerable situation she was in, being essentially homebound with a man whose declining mental capacity and functionality overwhelmed her strength and patience. Interestingly, the session turned into an opportunity to brainstorm how she might engage one of her husband's friends to organize all of his other friends and extended family members to regularly come for "shifts" to do something with him at the house so that she could plan to do the things she needed to do on her own or wanted to do with her own friends away from the home. In her sessions, she began to realize that she was initially trying to protect her husband from embarrassment about his condition by not inviting people to their home. However, she realized that the shame over his loss of functionality had essentially trapped them together in the home, causing more tension and stress for them both.

Conclusion

Many non-death losses will continue as an ongoing presence for the rest of an individual's life in some way, shape, or form. The chronic grief (chronic sorrow) associated with losses that are ongoing in nature is often misunderstood and can be debilitating for the person experiencing it. In addition, being able to support an individual over the long haul through the chronic, ongoing grief can be exhausting for those who care for and about that same person. The importance of cultivating therapeutic presence, letting go of expectations regarding outcome (i.e., closure), and clarifying the intention to journey alongside the individual whose life has been shattered by loss can offer a sense of healing, even in the presence of losses that may never end.

Key Terms

Compassion: Sensitivity to the suffering of one's self and others with the desire to relieve that suffering; the ability to demonstrate kindness, understanding, and nonjudgmental awareness toward human responses, especially those that involve suffering, inadequacy, or some form of perceived failure.

Intention: The psychological experience of connecting with who you are, and why you do what you do as a human being. This moves away from the attempt to create specific outcomes in other people's loss experiences.

Presence: The act and intention of "being with" another individual, providing them your full attention and engagement.

Questions for Reflection

1. The author states that "we cannot remove many of the causes of suffering." Why do we have such great difficulty with simply being present for others who have experienced chronic ongoing losses? How can one "be" for others instead of trying to "fix" others?
2. What issues can arise in living loss experiences for individuals grieving non-death losses? How can we cultivate compassion and intention towards ourselves and others when faced with these challenges in living losses?
3. Reflect upon a specific ongoing non-death loss that one could experience. Construct a case study that captures the nuances of this loss experience and realistically illustrates what issues one may struggle with given this unique loss experience. After creating your case study, identify at least three practical strategies that would assist in supporting the person's grief experience.

References

All Acronyms. (2018). *NATO—not attached to outcome*. Retrieved August 7, 2018, from www.allacronyms.com/NATO/Not_Attached_To_Outcome

Bergman, C., & Duerr, M. (2014). *The tree of contemplative practices*. Retrieved August 7, 2018, from www.contemplativemind.org/practices/tree

Boss, P. (2016). The context and process of theory development: The story of ambiguous loss. *Journal of Family Theory & Review, 8*(3), 269–286.

Boss, P., Bryant, C. M., & Mancini, J. A. (2016). *Family stress management: A contextual approach*. Thousand Oaks, CA: Sage Publications.

Boss, P., Roos, S., & Harris, D. L. (2011). Grief in the midst of ambiguity and uncertainty: An exploration of ambiguous loss and chronic sorrow. In R. Neimeyer, D. L. Harris, H. Winokuer, & G. Thornton (Eds.), *Grief and bereavement in contemporary society: Bridging research and practice* (pp. 163–176). New York: Routledge.

Geller, S. M., & Greenberg, L. S. (2012). *Therapeutic presence: A mindful approach to effective therapy*. Washington, DC: APA.

Gilbert, P., & Choden. (2014). *Mindful compassion*. Oakland, CA: New Harbinger Publications.

Halifax, J. (2011). The precious necessity of compassion. *Journal of Pain and Symptom Management, 41*(1), 146–153.

Halifax, J. (2013). GRACE for nurses: Cultivating compassion in nurse/patient interactions. *Journal of Nursing Education and practice, 4*(1), 121.

Harris, D. L. (2011). Concluding thoughts. In D. L. Harris (Ed.), *Counting our losses: Reflecting on change, loss, and transition in everyday life* (pp. 247–252). New York: Routledge.

Harris, D. L. (2013). Infertility and intimacy: Life's layered losses. In B. DeFord & R. Gilbert (Eds.), *Living, loving, and loss: The interplay of intimacy, sexuality and grief* (pp. 101–118). Amityville, NY: Baywood.

Harris, D. L. (2016). Social expectations of the bereaved. In D. L. Harris & T. C. Bordere (Eds.), *Handbook of social justice issues in loss and grief: Exploring diversity, equity, and inclusion* (pp. 165–176). New York: Routledge.

Harris, D. L., & Winokuer, H. R. (2016). *Principles and practice of grief counseling*. New York: Springer.

Lewis, L., & Hoy, W. G. (2011). Bereavement rituals and the creation of legacy. In R. A. Neimeyer, D. L. Harris, H. R. Winokuer, & G. F. Thornton (Eds.), *Grief and bereavement in contemporary society: Bridging research and practice* (pp. 315–323). New York: Routledge.

Mayer, M. (2001). Chronic sorrow in caregiving spouses of patients with Alzheimer's disease. *Journal of Aging and Identity, 6*, 49–60.

McDonough-Means, S. I., Kreitzer, M. J., & Bell, I. R. (2004). Fostering a healing presence and investigating its mediators. *The Journal of Alternative and Complementary Medicine 10*(Suppl. 1), 25–41.

Neff, K. D., Kirkpatrick, K. L., & Rude, S. S. (2007). Self-compassion and adaptive psychological functioning. *Journal of Research in Personality, 41*, 139–154.

Norton, M. I., & Gino, F. (2014). Rituals alleviate grieving for loved ones, lovers, and lotteries. *Journal of Experimental Psychology: General, 143*(1), 266.

Roos, S. R. (2018). *Chronic sorrow: A living loss* (2nd ed.). New York: Routledge.

Rossheim, B. N., & McAdams III, C. R. (2010). Addressing the chronic sorrow of long-term spousal caregivers: A primer for counselors. *Journal of Counseling & Development, 88*(4), 477–482.

Vachon, M. L., & Harris, D. L. (2016). The liberating capacity of compassion. In D. L. Harris & T. C. Bordere (Eds.), *Promoting social justice in loss and grief* (pp. 265–281). New York: Routledge.

Yalom, I. (2009). *The gift of therapy*. New York: HarperCollins.

CHAPTER 24

Meaning-Making After Non-Death Losses

Robert A. Neimeyer and Lara Krawchuk

Case 1: Loss of Career and the Collapse of Identity

At 67, Steve was a picture of mature vitality—trim, energetic, with a piercing gaze and single-mindedness of purpose that seamlessly matched his professional persona as a high-profile player in the field of corporate litigation, a career in which he had risen to the top and achieved national visibility. But now he found himself not in the familiar context of the courtroom or conference room, but instead in a therapist's office, as he struggled with complex emotions two weeks after release from a psychiatric hospital following a serious suicide attempt. Only the unexpected early arrival of his wife from a business trip saved him from the well-planned and deliberate overdose that otherwise would have proven lethal, as he sought to end the seemingly endless cascade of losses that had followed his retirement—of his leadership role in professional societies, his partnership in a prestigious law firm, the daily docket of challenging cases that structured his time, his relationships, and his sense of identity. Acutely aware of his pain but only vaguely conscious of its source, he was reluctantly and vulnerably approaching a therapist to understand the depth of his decimation, and to grapple with the question of whether a sustainable life could be built on the rubble of the one he had nearly ended.

Case 2: Cancer, Motherhood, and Unresolved Attachment Losses

Ali was a vivacious, 34-year-old woman, recently married after two years of dating and working as a physical therapist in a thriving practice, work she found both challenging and rewarding. She and her husband had been trying for a few months to get pregnant, and she had been very much looking forward to becoming a mother. She longed to offer a child the love and support she felt she never got from her parents who both struggled with alcohol addiction. After a routine mammography Ali learned that she had an aggressive and invasive cancer in both breasts. Suddenly Ali found herself thrust into the chaos of navigating a busy academic medical system, frantically searching for information on best treatment options on the Internet, absorbing sad looks from tongue-tied friends and colleagues, and struggling through the web of fear and anxiety plaguing her every night. Ali's doctors got her into surgery quickly and she opted for a double mastectomy due to the aggressive nature of her cancer. She wanted to have plastic surgery performed while she was getting the mastectomy, but her doctors advised against this. After surgery Ali received eight weeks of radiation therapy, and she struggled throughout with deep sadness, anger, anxiety, and hopelessness. She began to self-isolate and lash out towards her husband, Tom, who responded by working longer hours at his office. Ali refused to accept an anti-depressant quickly offered to her by her family doctor and explained to her nurses that she felt sure her distress could not be medicated away so easily. Concerned for his wife's well-being and feeling at a loss to adequately support her, Tom asked the hospital social worker for help. Ali was referred for counseling. Ali embraced the idea and sought to better understand her emotional pain and make sense of a life she felt had been shattered by cancer.

* * *

To live is to confront an unending sequence of life transitions, whether welcome or unwelcome. At birth we are delivered from the intimate and protected world of our intrauterine development into an expansive and unpredictable outer world into which our parents and eventually many others beckon us, fostering our growth but also our vulnerability to losses of all kinds. In the course of living, we naturally gravitate toward myriad people, places, projects, professions, and possessions that anchor our sense of self and confer a sense of connection and continuity as we construct a life story that is uniquely our own. But it is these very attachments that predispose us to grief, as we inevitably, at the point of the loss of the cherished person or thing, face the need to relinquish them and reorient to a changed life. Another way of saying this is that grieving entails reaffirming or reconstructing a world of meaning that has been challenged by loss (Neimeyer, 2019).

In this chapter we touch on the themes of ambiguous loss, non-death loss, and chronic sorrow that weave through this volume, drawing on the stories of two of the countless clients who have consulted us as they attempt to reckon with transitions both subtle and profound, and seek to find a way forward in a changed landscape of life. In doing so, we will situate our comments in the growing body of evidence that adaptation to unwelcome change is shaped by our struggle or success in making sense of such transitions, and of ourselves in their aftermath. We will therefore review some of the recent research on meaning reconstruction, and then consider its practical implications for grief therapy and support for clients striving to integrate losses that are as compelling as they are complicating, whatever their cause. We will then conclude by returning in greater detail to the case of Ali to convey the principles and practices of a meaning reconstruction approach to non-death loss as they inform the process of grief therapy.

Meaning Reconstruction in Non-Death Loss: Principles and Practices

Whether viewed through the wide-angle lens of history or the magnifying glass of the psychological study of a single life, human beings are revealed as inveterate makers of meaning. Across centuries and cultures, we as a species have formulated countless religious, philosophic, political, scientific, legal, and aesthetic systems for comprehending, engaging, and organizing our lives. Sometimes these collective efforts to find or impute significance and regularity to our experience are as concrete as a tenet of religious faith or a binding law or principle. At other times, they exist as a gist-like procedural knowledge of how to negotiate a particular social situation, or as an implicit assumption of how the world works or should work, in a way that conforms to our sense of predictability, control, justice, and a working knowledge of self or others. In this context, our personal quest to understand life and our participation in it draws on these cultural and communal themes, while refining and revising them in the course of our particular lives. And mostly, this quest for meaning proceeds "under the radar" of our conscious attention, as across the course of development we become better able to navigate the complexities of our world in a way that "makes sense" of life, of who we have been, and of who we are becoming. The resulting pursuit of meaning can be understood existentially or spiritually (Frankl, 1992), psychologically (Kelly, 1955), phenomenologically (Merleau-Ponty, 1962), or epistemologically (Polanyi, 1958), but in any case, it seems to be endemic to being human.

Unfortunately, however, significant losses of all kinds challenge and sometimes shatter our sense of security in our interpreted world. The death of a loved one, especially when it traumatically assaults our sense of fairness, predictability, or control, can trigger a profound struggle to reassert or reconstruct these world assumptions, both to make sense of what we have suffered and to grasp its implication for our changed future. Likewise, with the death of someone on whom we greatly rely for a sense of security and encouragement, or to whom we extend a similarly intimate caregiving, we may find ourselves bereft of the very bonds of attachment that give our lives meaning and that anchor our most central identity (Neimeyer & Thompson, 2014). In either case—and many forms of bereavement entail overwhelming challenges in both of these domains—the resulting grief and disorientation can be as profound as they are prolonged, launching mourners into an anguished quest for meaning that can become ruminative, circular, and seemingly without answers. However, when core meanings are retained or when they are successfully revised or replaced, grieving is marked by swifter or gradual accommodation to a changed world, and not infrequently leads to personal, relational, and spiritual growth.

Over the past 20 years, a great deal of evidence has accrued to support the key propositions of this meaning reconstruction model. Across dozens of studies of bereaved young adults, parents, and widowed persons in older age, an inability to find sense or significance in the experience of bereavement is associated with a range of poor health and mental health outcomes, whereas the ability to comprehend the death of the loved one and its ramifications or to learn valued life lessons is perhaps the leading marker of more favorable adaptation to the nonetheless deeply unwelcome changes it implies (Neimeyer, 2019). Meaning-making regarding a loved one's impending death in palliative care has been found to be the strongest predictor of anguished anticipatory grief in family members (Burke et al., 2015), as well as a powerful prospective predictor of complicated grief symptomatology months after the death occurs (Burke, Neimeyer, Bottomley, & Smigelsky, 2017). Likewise, meaning-making has been found to moderate the impact of highly "central" losses that otherwise portend poor adjustment (Bellet, Neimeyer, & Berman, 2017), as well as to mediate the impact of numerous known risk factors observable in the early months of loss (e.g., violent death, insecure attachment, loss of a partner, low social support) on complicated grief symptomatology an average of eight months later (Milman et al., 2018, 2019). Finally, the pivotal role of challenge to world assumptions as a function of the loss has been found to bridge between the network of symptoms of complicated grief on the one hand and the network of features that define post-traumatic growth on the other (Bellet, Jones, Neimeyer, & McNally, 2018). In sum, meaning-making or its absence has been found to carry sweeping significance for adaptation to bereavement, giving rise to a cornucopia of meaning-oriented procedures that enrich the practice of grief therapy (Neimeyer, 2012d, 2016; Thompson & Neimeyer, 2014).

Though the majority of research on meaning reconstruction has focused on the death of a loved one, it is highly likely that significant non-death losses pose at least as substantial a challenge to finding sense or significance in the experience, with similar implications for the survivor's adaptation. Because the losses of careers and purposeful work undermine our sources of worth, self-definition, and sustaining relationships with others, they can profoundly challenge our sense that life is worth living, as Steve discovered following his retirement from a high-profile career as a litigator. When loss of health assaults not only our presumption of wellness but also our sexuality and valued roles and hopes, as it did for Ali following her diagnosis of cancer, even our most basic sense of security in our bodies can be called into question. These and myriad other non-death losses—of relationships, country of origin, faith, dreams, statuses, and even cherished possessions—separate us from the once meaningful life we led, and usher us into another that erodes or explodes a self-narrative that now requires major rewriting. The resulting anxiety, threat, and grief can range from subtle to substantial and result in prolonged agitation, protest, and anger on the one hand, or depressive resignation, chronic sorrow, or suicide risk on the other. As detailed in previous chapters in this volume, non-death losses may in some respects be even more challenging than literal bereavement for those who suffer them, as they characteristically lack the level of social recognition and support accorded to the loss of a loved one, with corresponding roles and rituals to soften and validate such transitions (Boss, 2010).

In view of the unique challenges that non-death losses pose to our world of meaning, we offer here a few principles and associated practices to guide practitioners like ourselves who confront them commonly in their work. We make no claim to be exhaustive in doing so, and in fact are confident that a close reading of the other chapters in this volume would yield many more. But we find these to provide useful orientation to addressing losses of all kinds, especially when they are pervasive, perturbing, and deeply personal, but at risk of being unseen or unvalidated by others in the client's social world.

Principle 1: Don't Just Do Something, Stand There

Too often, clinicians feel pressured to diminish the client's distress by quickly proffering facile advice, simplistic positive reframing, demeaning interpretations of the client's coping, distancing diagnoses of their symptoms, or even the immediate prescription of medication that Ali was offered. While well intended, all such interventions risk discounting the existential gravity of the client's suffering by conveying that it is in some sense optional. Instead, we have found it essential to first simply stand respectfully in the reality of the client's pain, to witness it, to hold it in the space between us, and to honor its implications for their life. This does not imply passivity or resignation, however, as this same patient emphasis on being rather than doing commonly yields a deeper understanding of the significance of the loss, and what is needed and possible in the client's life to accommodate it. Stated in other words, therapist *presence* provides the grounding for a responsive reading of the therapeutic *process*, and with it, the selection or co-construction of specific *procedures* that help the client embrace the changes required, and move forward with integrity in spite or because of them (Neimeyer, 2012c). Mindful presence to the therapist's own process can also mitigate the cumulative stress that can attend witnessing the pain of others struggling with losses of all kinds (Krawchuk, 2012).

Principle 2: Be a Secure Base in a Foreign Land

By definition, deeply unwelcome transitions of all kinds usher in profound changes to our sense of self and world, requiring that we relearn both in their aftermath (Attig, 1996). To meet such challenges and re-weave the fabric of meaning that has been stretched or sundered by loss, we require the safe haven provided by others who will tend and befriend us, balancing the *caring* we crave with the *daring* we require to grieve what we have lost and embrace the life that now opens before us (van Wielink, Wilhelm, & van Geelen-Merks, 2019). This is to say that clinicians who work with non-death losses practice an attachment-informed grief therapy (Kosminsky & Jordan, 2016), even when the client's attachments are ruptured by processes other than death, to people, places, and possibilities that challenge their security in a previously known world.

Principle 3: Name It and Claim It

One of the most vexing features of non-death losses is that they are commonly unspoken, unsayable, and sometimes utterly unspeakable. They fall outside the conventional language of loss that is more generously available in the case of bereavement, where customary consolations may be conveyed in the sympathy cards available at the corner pharmacy, or in the flowers easily ordered through an online florist. Lacking an adequate language to even verbalize our distinctive losses to ourselves, we may feel only a wordless void of grief or other unvoiced emotions when and if we give attention to our sense of decimation or diminishment. A first step toward mourning and moving through our troubling transition is therefore to name and claim what we have lost—in Shakespeare's apt phrase, "to give sorrow words." Practices like the slowly repeated recursive question to a client, *What have you lost?* invite this naming, and with it the identification of both primary and secondary losses that range from the concrete to the abstract (Neimeyer, in press). When words are not enough, art therapy techniques can help us hold and honor our losses in a vocabulary of imagery, music, movement, and metaphor (Thompson & Neimeyer, 2014). Once recognized in the space of therapy, such nonfinite losses can then be followed by a further cycle of recursive questioning, *What do you feel ready to change?* which can help the client pivot from acceptance to agency (Neimeyer, in press).

Principle 4: Engage the Community of Self

Especially when losses are traumatic or poorly recognized by conventional social discourses, those who suffer them may find that their inner emotional landscape of loss is just as unvoiced as are these same experiences in the silent space that separates them from others. And yet, as recognized by many psychological theories (Mair, 2014; Schwartz, 1995), close attention to our inner processes may put us into contact with a "community of self" comprised of many voices, some frightened and vulnerable, some strident and judgmental, and others wise and compassionate, all of which require a witness if therapy is to attend to the multiple implicit needs of a client in distress, as well as the inner voices that compound their suffering. Listening between the lines of the speakable story that clients tell themselves and others about their suffering can grant these inner voices an outer audience, whether through encouraging use of metaphor and imagery to convey experiences that resist literal formulation (Mair, 2014), fostering encounters between distinct voices in the client using chair work (Neimeyer, 2012b), or perhaps constructing a symbolic landscape using small stones and other natural materials to depict multifaceted relations within the "dialogical self" in the wake of a troubling transition, in order to work toward "recomposing" them in a new way (Konopka, Hermans, & Goncalves, 2018). Whatever the tool or technique, the fundamental goal is to create a safe "holding environment" in which all aspects of the client's self, whether wounded or resourceful, can be heard and invited to play a role in a change that embraces them all.

Principle 5: Seek Sense and Significance

A key tenet of our approach is that *grieving entails an attempt to reaffirm or reconstruct a world of meaning that has been challenged by loss* (Neimeyer, 2019). This struggle to find sense in the loss and significance in our lives in its aftermath is nowhere clearer than when such losses are ambiguous, disenfranchised, pervasive, chronic, or abstract. It can therefore be helpful to map their impact explicitly, as through inviting clients to complete the Integration of Stressful Life Experiences Scale (ISLES) in its non-bereavement version (Holland, Currier, Coleman, &

Neimeyer, 2010; Holland, Currier, & Neimeyer, 2014) to assess struggles with the comprehensibility of the loss event (e.g., *I have difficult integrating this event into my understanding about the world*) and one's own sense of secure grounding or footing in the world (e.g., *I don't understand myself anymore since this event*). Alternatively, therapists can work to reveal the implicit meanings of the loss at the level of one's embodied felt sense of the grief, in a way that fosters its symbolization, articulation, and evolution (Neimeyer, 2012a). Complementing this "bottom up" quest for meaning, "top down" navigation of the loss experience in light of the client's higher-order spiritual or philosophic meaning system (Park & Halifax, 2011) or cherished personal goals (Holcomb, 2012) can provide a reorientation to or "re-visioning" of life in the aftermath of deeply unwelcome change.

Principle 6: Restore Relation

One of the pernicious effects of nonfinite losses is that they stress and often sunder the bonds of connection with relevant others in the family or community on whom we rely to negotiate the meaning of what has transpired, leaving us alone in the experience (Boss, 2010). Assessing the extent of the *social invalidation* of the client's attempts at meaning-making using the non-bereavement version of the Social Meaning In Life Events Scale (SMILES; Bellet, Holland, & Neimeyer, 2018) can therefore help identify points of rupture in the web of sustaining relations that help clients make sense of difficult transitions, just as assessing the extent of *social validation* of these same passages can suggest vital allies in the process. More broadly, therapy can move beyond the predominant focus on individual grievers to encourage couples and families to weigh the advantages and disadvantages of "talking and not talking" about mutual losses (Hooghe, 2012), as well to foster collective healing in group (Spence & Smale, 2016) and community contexts (Smigelsky & Neimeyer, 2018).

Principle 7: Reaffirm Growth

A focus on the potential complications of contending with nonfinite losses should not obscure the reality of resilience commonly reported by those who suffer great adversity (Bonanno, 2009) and their frequent experience of post-traumatic growth (PTG; Calhoun & Tedeschi, 2013). Just as those who are bereaved may be prompted by their grief toward growth in the form of greater personal strength, perspective, compassion, and investment in living (Currier, Holland, & Neimeyer, 2012), so too those whose losses are more intangible or less recognized can experience a gradual evolution in valued directions, even if they never would have chosen the suffering that ushered in this transformation. "Leading from one step behind," therapists can discern the seeds of such growth and cultivate them where they are found in the changed landscape of the client's world. This patient and attuned responsiveness to "innovative moments" in grief therapy (Piazza-Bonin, Neimeyer, Alves, Smigelsky, & Crunk, 2016; Piazza-Bonin, Neimeyer, Alves, & Smigelsky, 2016) contrasts with an "activist" stance in which a therapist pushes a client prematurely toward "positive reframing" of an anguishing experience, which can amount to a profound empathic failure and contribute to a therapeutic rupture.

Having considered some of the principles and practices that animate meaning reconstruction in the wake of ambiguous loss, we return to one of the case vignettes with which this chapter opened to offer a fuller case study of their implementation in the clinical context.

In the Shadow of Cancer

Ali came to me (LK) riddled with a myriad of losses, both old and new. The distress she experienced due to her cancer diagnosis was compounded by childhood attachment injuries and the perceived forfeiture of significant future hopes and dreams. Though Ali's life was marked by many seismic shifts, she had not previously identified a need to grieve. Each step of this year-and-a-half-long healing journey was deeply collaborative. Ali was the uncontested expert on her own life and as such set the agenda for the work. Blending principles from constructivist (Neimeyer, 2019), mindfulness (Cacciatore & Flint, 2012), and Internal Family Systems (Schwartz, 1995) theories, I acted as a kind of *Grief Sherpa*, who intimately knew the territory of loss, empathetically witnessed her great pain, assisted her in making sense of disparate inner voices clamoring to be heard, and gently guided Ali towards meaningful healing activities. Early to middle sessions were spent in meaning-making activity, identifying how her many living losses were connected to feelings of sadness, anger, anxiety, and hopelessness. We practiced the Dual Process Model of coping with bereavement (DPM; Stroebe & Schut, 2010) and taught Ali to honor each loss, then shift back to daily living. Creative tools, such as mindfulness meditation, directed journaling (Lichtenthal & Neimeyer, 2012), and musical playlists that traced the emotional storyline of her losses (Berger, 2012) were used to facilitate meaning-making. I took care not to rush Ali as she struggled to make sense of how illness and loss had altered the course of her life. Though much of our work was individual, we invited her husband Tom to join us several times to build a deeper understanding of how loss shaped the course of their marriage and to develop their skill for communicating about emotional pain. Later sessions were dedicated to deciding what now constituted a meaningful life for them both. The principle of chronicity was important to my work with Ali. We were aware that the cancer could recur and that the healing work would continue for a lifetime, ebbing and flowing with the current of post-treatment health maintenance, fertility, and identity concerns. At no point did I ask Ali to complete her loss work. Due to an increasingly busy work schedule, Ali chose to end regular sessions after a year and a half, but with the understanding that she could re-engage my services whenever needed. For me, this work was a deep honor, but it also carried an emotional toll. I kept an open and honest eye towards my own loss work throughout the process of helping Ali. Countertransference deserved my careful attention so that my own loss history and my concerns for Ali's health did not complicate or erode the work.

In the Beginning: Honoring Living Losses and Reconstructing a Meaningful Life

From the start, my work with Ali was a powerful collaboration between Ali, Tom, myself, and her medical team. Ali was referred to my private therapy practice from her cancer center social worker, who reported concerns about Ali's poor mood and stated hopelessness. Ali's first six sessions were generously paid for by the hospital's community-based wellness grant initiative. She chose to continue the work beyond that. Though Ali reported that she was not sure that therapy would be helpful, she came because the social worker urged her to give it a chance and her first sessions cost her nothing to try.

Ali came to the first session with her husband and allowed him to do much of the talking while she mostly cried and held her face in her hands. Tom shared the story of Ali's recent breast cancer diagnosis, surgery to remove both breasts, radiation treatments that left the skin on her chest blistered and burnt. He discussed the likelihood of chemotherapy and related fertility concerns that seemed to plague Ali's every waking moment. Tom shared his worry that Ali was giving up on herself and that he felt scared because he could not seem to cheer her up. Ali said little but sometimes shook her head in agreement and cried through the entire session. Towards the end of our time together I thanked Tom for sharing details of the situation and overtly shifted my attention towards Ali. Slowly, she lifted her head and looked into my eyes. We sat in silence for a brief moment, allowing our connection to form. I quietly told Ali I was sorry for all that she was going through, felt I could help her, and shared that it was my professional opinion that she had suffered from many important living losses and needed to deeply honor and grieve them. Suddenly, Ali stopped crying, sat a little straighter, wiped her eyes, and smiled. She shared that she felt totally robbed by cancer and that throughout her entire life she had been taught repeatedly to be grateful for all that she had and not cry about things she could not change. She reported that she had never been given permission to cry in her childhood, and she felt the messaging from much of the outside world was the same now. She was tired of pressure from family and friends to "Look on the bright side, fight, don't look back, move forward, keep pushing forward at all costs." She revealed that she felt she would implode if she were forced to pretend that everything was okay, because from where she sat, it felt like everything she had dreamed of for herself had been brutally snatched away. I offered to help Ali identify all of her important losses and start to explore what each one truly meant to her so that she could release some of the burden of carrying them all around while navigating the rigors of cancer treatment. I was careful not to promise meaning reconstruction or even emotional healing in this first session, but rather offered to patiently witness the depths of Ali's pain. Ali took a deep breath and agreed to come in the next week. She asked that Tom let her come by herself next time, and he readily agreed.

Over the course of the next month, as Ali healed from her surgery and radiation treatments, she came in weekly to talk about her experiences. Ali was curious about why her cancer diagnosis had reopened old pain from childhood. We explored how new losses opened up old wounds and how anxiety sometimes served to block Ali from exploring the deep grief underneath. She recognized that she had never been given an opportunity to make sense of the pain of her parents' alcoholism and that these disenfranchised parts of herself compounded her current emotional distress. I encouraged Ali to create a timeline of all her lifetime losses, concrete and abstract, death-related and non-death-related, big and small. Ali was surprised to see, on paper, how many things she perceived as losses from her turbulent childhood. She noted that it felt like a relief to frame her experience in this way because it normalized her intense distress. She marveled that no one had ever before helped her grieve. Ali began to use a mantra she encountered in her readings, "where there is great loss there is great grief." She would report that as she would say these words aloud, it felt as if a deep part of her breathed a great sigh of relief. She reported that she preferred to be viewed as someone who was grieving a lifetime of losses, rather than someone who was depressed and anxious. With Ali's permission, I shared with the medical team that Ali preferred to be asked "How's your grief?" when assessing her emotional state at the cancer center. The team embraced this change and shared that this reflected their view of Ali as a mentally healthy young woman overwhelmed by unexpected illness. We also held a joint session with Tom to share Ali's new mantra, help him see that she wanted to be given space to grieve her living losses and explore the ways in which he too may have losses to grieve. Tom was reluctant to admit that he needed to grieve and reported worry that Ali would become depressed and stop fighting her cancer if she spent too much time thinking about her losses. He expressed that he really wanted Ali to focus on getting better, not "all the bad stuff that had happened to her in her childhood." With my advocacy, Ali was able to gently help Tom see that creating some space to honor old hurts would in turn create new space for fighting her cancer. Tom agreed to trust Ali on her stated needs, instead of trying to cajole her back to good humor when she felt sad. Ali expressed deep gratitude to Tom for supporting her need to grieve and encouraged him to speak up if he felt she had become hijacked by sorrow. I reminded them that though their emotional needs may not match up on any given day, they could still hold space for one another's struggle. We discussed that being overt in their communication about emotional needs would be helpful in this process. The newlyweds readily agreed and left the session with arms wrapped around each other.

A month and a half into our work together Ali started chemotherapy treatments. By necessity, we slowed the frequency of our sessions to match cycles of treatment and the often-difficult side effects that accompanied them. With this new treatment came a predictable dip in Ali's mood. We explored a myriad of cancer-related losses, including her questions about what it meant to be a woman and her difficulty looking in the mirror due to her bald head, missing eyelashes, eyebrows, and breasts. We facilitated a brief healing ritual for Ali to say goodbye to her breasts and her cherished, long mane of blond hair. In time, Ali identified that the "worst part" for her was the belief that her cancer and chemo had shattered her dream of becoming a good mother. Though her medical team had helped her preserve eggs for future use, Ali feared that her illness would prevent her from being the kind of engaged and attuned mother she longed to be. She reported that she would rather never become a mother than be the kind of parent who allows her needs to eclipse those of the child. We honored the deep roots of these concerns and helped Ali explore the powerful meaning of motherhood, shaped by a childhood in which her own mother was consumed by the illness of addiction. We honored the deep sense of loss Ali felt as she recognized that she too would need to factor illness into her parenting should she and Tom choose now to have a child. We explored the ambivalence Ali now felt about motherhood. Ali could hear that one part of her still longed to get pregnant one day, and another part wanted her to give up this dream for good. Losses related to motherhood cut deep and became the focus of our work for several months. Ali learned to listen to all her conflicted inner voices, be mindfully present with her distress, and then purposefully choose to shift focus back to her daily life. Ali reported that this DPM-inspired shifting of her focus from loss to daily living initially was difficult but found that if she took time each day to notice her pain and then journal about it, she could then shift and engage in the many ways her life still contained love and joy.

When the end of Ali's chemotherapy treatments appeared on the horizon, she recognized a new loss she was initially fearful to explore. She realized that though she hated chemotherapy, she also viewed it as a powerful cancer safety net. Losing this treatment, and the regular connection to her medical team, left her feeling completely overwhelmed. Ali identified a significant loss of trust in her body and an anticipatory grief around a feared cancer recurrence. One part of her wanted to throw a party to celebrate the end of chemo, and another part of her wanted to wail and scream about it. Again, we normalized and validated each inner voice, explored the meaning of the felt loss, honored related fears, and supported Ali as she made sense of living a life shadowed by the possibility of cancer returning, or perhaps even ending her life prematurely. This grief was intense. Tom was unable to hold it with Ali, and she took refuge in the safe space we created to explore her fears and make sense of their impact. We moved slowly and took breaks, as this was likely to be a repeating theme in Ali's posttreatment life. As part of this work I encouraged Ali to utilize her love of music in facilitating healing, and she created two musical playlists: one that gave voice to her lifetime losses and later another that offered a glimpse into the beauty and possibility her life still held. She listened to these playlists often, sometimes journaling to their melodies, as yet another concrete way to honor the truth of her experiences. At this time Ali also decided to accept her doctor's offer of an anti-depressant to help her manage her high level of emotional distress. She felt this medication could lessen the intensity of her emotions so that she could continue to make sense of her intense grief related to living with cancer. I readily supported this decision. Ali felt the medication did in fact dial back the intensity of her emotions, and she felt glad she had come to this decision.

Through our work together, Ali learned to notice living losses and stay deeply present with her grief. She discovered that sorrow ebbed and flowed and that she could tolerate being both okay and not okay at the same time. She explored the many, often disparate, voices in her internal world and took time to honor the call of each one with tenderness and compassion. She understood that clear answers were neither always achievable nor required for healing. She discovered that she and Tom could continue to construct a meaningful life over time, anchored by their love and mutual commitment to one another. She deepened her gratitude for the richness of this connection and overtly shared her deep love for Tom with him on a regular basis. Ali's report to me showed clearly that she could shift freely between deep sorrow, love, and joy while she and Tom continued to build a life rich with meaning and possibility.

My work with Ali was powerful. I cherished my time with her and appreciated her great courage in doing complex inner work. Along with my great affection for her came significant concern for her well-being and the weight of worry about recurrence. My fear of recurrence for Ali was influenced by my own personal experience with a father's cancer, recurrence, and ultimate death to cancer. I recognized that to continue to serve Ali well, I needed to tend to my own losses in the past and in this work. I too practiced mindful presence, journaling, playlist creation, and sense-making with my grieving inner parts. I was awed by the ways in which her work pushed forward my own. Though Ali need not know the depth of our parallel healing, I have come to see it as an important aspect of this kind of work, and I am deeply grateful to her for allowing me to accompany her on this important journey.

Key Terms

Meaning Reconstruction: Reaffirming or rebuilding a sense of coherence and workable assumptions about the world after experiencing an event that challenges previous views of the world that fostered a sense of meaning and relevance prior to this event.

Secure Base: A term that originates in attachment-informed therapy, where the therapist functions as a source of security and safety in a time when clients may feel vulnerable and lost due to the shattering of their assumptive world and the foundations upon which the world previously felt predictable and meaningful.

Therapist Presence: The quality of "being with," and fully open to experience as it occurs on a moment-to-moment basis. Presence involves the full attention and intention of the therapist to be aware and open to both the client's experience as well as the therapist's experience in the time that is shared.

Questions for Reflection

1. Take a moment and bring to mind your memories from when you were younger. Start with your earliest memories, then proceed forward every five or ten years, recalling what you remember about that time, including what was most important to you at these times, what brought you joy, and what caused you pain. Complete this reflection for yourself now. Are you the same

person as you were during these younger times? How are you now different? What were the moments in life that shaped who you are now?
2. How do you think the process of meaning reconstruction is similar between non-death losses and death-related losses? How might this process be different between these types of loss experiences?
3. Non-death loss experiences are often socially invalidated or not recognized. Why do you think this is true? Can you think of times in your own life when you experienced a significant non-death loss that others around you failed to affirm for its significance to you?

References

Attig, T. (1996). *How we grieve: Relearning the world*. New York: Oxford University Press.
Bellet, B. W., Holland, J. M., & Neimeyer, R. A. (2018). The Social Meaning in Life Events Scale (SMILES): A preliminary psychometric evaluation in a bereaved sample. *Death Studies*. doi:10.1080/07481187.2018.1456008
Bellet, B. W., Jones, P. J., Neimeyer, R. A., & McNally, R. J. (2018). Bereavement outcomes as causal systems: A network analysis of the co-occurrence of complicated grief and posttraumatic growth. *Clinical Psychological Science, 6*, 797–809. doi:10.1177/2167702/18777/454
Bellet, B. W., Neimeyer, R. A., & Berman, J. S. (2017). Event centrality and bereavement symptomatology: The moderating role of meaning made. *Omega: The Journal of Death and Dying*. doi:10.1177/0030222816679659
Berger, J. (2012). Playing with playlists. In R. A. Neimeyer (Ed.), *Techniques of grief therapy: Creative practices for counseling the bereaved* (pp. 211–213). New York: Routledge.
Bonanno, G. A. (2009). *The other side of sadness*. New York: Basic.
Boss, P. (2010). The trauma and complicated grief of ambiguous loss. *Pastoral Psychology, 59*, 137–145.
Burke, L., Neimeyer, R. A., Bottomley, J. S., & Smigelsky, M. A. (2017). Prospective risk factors for intense grief in family members of veterans who died of terminal illness. *Illness, Crisis & Loss*. doi:10.1177/1054137317699580
Burke, L. A., Clark, K. A., Ali, K. S., Gibson, B. W., Smigelsky, M. A., & Neimeyer, R. A. (2015). Risk factors for anticipatory grief in family members of terminally ill veterans receiving palliative care services. *Journal of Social Work in End-of-Life and Palliative Care, 11*, 244–266. doi:10.1080/15524256.2015.1110071
Cacciatore, J., & Flint, M. (2012). ATTEND: Toward a mindfulness-based bereavement care model. *Death Studies, 36*, 61–82. doi:10.1080/07481187.2011.591275
Calhoun, L. G., & Tedeschi, R. G. (2013). *Posttraumatic growth in clinical practice*. New York: Routledge.
Currier, J. M., Holland, J. M., & Neimeyer, R. A. (2012). Prolonged grief symptoms and growth in the first two years of bereavement: Evidence for a non-linear association. *Traumatology, 18*, 65–71.
Frankl, V. E. (1992). *Man's search for meaning: An introduction to logotherapy* (4th ed.). Boston, MA: Beacon Press.
Holcomb, L. E. (2012). Goal setting for self-care during the grieving process. In R. A. Neimeyer (Ed.), *Techniques of grief therapy* (pp. 289-291). New York: Routledge.
Holland, J. M., Currier, J. M., Coleman, R. A., & Neimeyer, R. A. (2010). The Integration of Stressful Life Experiences Scale (ISLES): Development and initial validation of a new measure. *International Journal of Stress Management, 17*, 325–352.

Holland, J. M., Currier, J. M., & Neimeyer, R. A. (2014). Validation of the integration of stressful life experiences scale—Short Form in a bereaved sample. *Death Studies, 38*, 234–238. doi:10.1080/07481187.2013.829369

Hooghe, A. (2012). Talking about talking with couples and families. In R. A. Neimeyer (Ed.), *Techniques of grief therapy: Creative practices for counseling the bereaved* (pp. 323–325). New York: Routledge.

Kelly, G. A. (1955). *The psychology of personal constructs*. New York: W. W. Norton & Company.

Konopka, A., Hermans, H. J. M., & Goncalves, M. M. (Eds.). (2018). *Handbook of dialogical self theory and psychotherapy: Bridging psychotherapeutic and cultural traditions*. London: Routledge.

Kosminsky, P., & Jordan, J. R. (2016). *Attachment informed grief therapy*. New York: Routledge.

Krawchuk, L. (2012). Wisdom circles for when helping hurts. In R. A. Neimeyer (Ed.), *Techniques of grief therapy: Creative practices for counseling the bereaved* (pp. 359–361). New York: Routledge.

Lichtenthal, W. G., & Neimeyer, R. A. (2012). Directed journaling to facilitate meaning making. In R. A. Neimeyer (Ed.), *Techniques of grief therapy* (pp. 161–164). New York: Routledge.

Mair, M. (2014). *Another way of knowing: The poetry of psychological inquiry*. London, UK: Raven Books.

Merleau-Ponty, M. (1962). *Phenomenology of perception*. London: Routledge & Kegan Paul.

Milman, E., Neimeyer, R. A., Fitzpatrick, M., MacKinnon, C. J., Muis, K. R., & Cohen, S. R. (2018). Prolonged grief symptomatology following violent loss: The mediating role of meaning. *European Journal of Psychotraumatology*. doi:10.1080/20008198.2018.1503522

Milman, E., Neimeyer, R. A., Fitzpatrick, M., MacKinnon, C. J., Muis, K. R., & Cohen, S. R. (2019). Rumination moderates the role of meaning in the development of prolonged grief symptomatology. *Journal of Clinical Psychology*. doi:10.1002/jcp.22751

Neimeyer, R. A. (2012a). Analogical listening. In R. A. Neimeyer (Ed.), *Techniques of grief therapy: Creative practices for counseling the bereaved* (pp. 55–58). New York: Routledge.

Neimeyer, R. A. (2012b). Chair work. In R. A. Neimeyer (Ed.), *Techniques of grief therapy* (pp. 266–273). New York: Routledge.

Neimeyer, R. A. (2012c). Presence, process and procedure: A relational frame for technical proficiency in grief therapy. In R. A. Neimeyer (Ed.), *Techniques of grief therapy* (pp. 3–11). New York: Routledge.

Neimeyer, R. A. (Ed.). (2012d). *Techniques of grief therapy: Creative practices for counseling the bereaved*. New York: Routledge.

Neimeyer, R. A. (2019). Meaning reconstruction in bereavement: Development of a research program. *Death Studies, 43*(2), 79–91. doi:org/10.1080/07481187.2018.1456620

Neimeyer, R. A. (in press). What have you lost? In R. A. Neimeyer (Ed.), *New techniques of grief therapy: Bereavement and beyond*. New York: Routledge.

Neimeyer, R. A. (Ed.). (2016). *Techniques of grief therapy: Assessment and intervention*. New York: Routledge.

Neimeyer, R. A., & Thompson, B. E. (2014). Meaning making and the art of grief therapy. In B. E. Thompson & R. A. Neimeyer (Eds.), *Grief and the expressive arts: Practices for creating meaning* (pp. 3–13). New York: Routledge.

Park, C. L., & Halifax, J. (2011). Religion and spirituality in adjusting to bereavement. In R. A. Neimeyer, D. L. Harris, H. R. Winokuer & G. F. Thornton (Eds.), *Grief and bereavement in contemporary society: Bridging research and practice* (pp. 355–364). New York: Routledge.

Piazza-Bonin, E., Neimeyer, R. A., Alves, D., & Smigelsky, M. A. (2016). Innovative moments in humanistic therapy II: Analysis of change across the course of three cases of grief therapy. *Journal of Constructivist Psychology*, 1–20. doi:10.1080/10720537.2015.1118713

Piazza-Bonin, E., Neimeyer, R. A., Alves, D., Smigelsky, M. A., & Crunk, E. (2016). Innovative moments in humanistic therapy I: Process and outcome of eminent psychotherapists working with bereaved clients. *Journal of Constructivist Psychology*, 1–29. doi:10.1080/10720537.2015.1118712

Polanyi, M. (1958). *Personal knowledge*. Chicago, IL: University of Chicago Press.

Schwartz, R. C. (1995). *Internal family systems therapy*. New York: Guilford Press.

Smigelsky, M. A., & Neimeyer, R. A. (2018). Performative retelling: Healing community stories of loss through Playback Theatre. *Death Studies*. doi:10.1080/07481187.2017.1370414

Spence, S., & Smale, U. (2016). Facilitating safety in group work. In R. A. Neimeyer (Ed.), *Techniques of grief therapy: Assessment and intervention* (pp. 299–302). New York: Routledge.

Stroebe, M., & Schut, H. (2010). The Dual Process Model of coping with bereavement: A decade on. *Omega: The Journal of Death and Dying, 61,* 273–289.

Thompson, B. E., & Neimeyer, R. A. (Eds.). (2014). *Grief and the expressive arts: Practices for creating meaning*. New York: Routledge.

van Wielink, J., Wilhelm, L., & van Geelen-Merks, D. (2019). *Loss, grief and attachment in life transitions: A clinician's guide to secure base counseling*. New York: Routledge.

Conclusion: Impermanence, Change, and the Dynamic Experience of Living

Darcy L. Harris

In the process of editing this volume, I had many wonderful conversations with the contributors, my colleagues, and personal friends about the role of loss in shaping our lives. I continue to be reminded of the ubiquitous nature of loss and grief, and how much the language of loss permeates life. This realization is in contrast to our natural tendency to resist significant change, and our unrealistic desire for stability, which Janoff-Bulman (1992) describes as *cognitive conservatism*. An underlying theme in this book is the profound ways that change, loss, and transition (and the accompanying grief) are a part of everyday life. There is an adage that if you are a hammer, then everything will look like a nail. While I am a grief professional, and most of the contributors in this volume are engaged in work that focuses on grief and loss in various ways, the desire to bring these experiences into awareness, with the hope of providing readers with a deeper awareness of the human experience unites the contributed writings in the book.

In reading through these chapters, it is apparent that loss is a frequent companion in life. We lose those whom we love through normal milestones, transitions, relational change and dissolution, distance, and death. We lose the objects that we value and bestow with meaning. We can lose a sense of connection to our community, our country, and our beliefs. We can even lose ourselves, a little piece at a time or all at once. Life is not static; it can be messy, unpredictable, and rarely what we expect or assume that it should be. Thus, letting go is something that we must learn, even as we instinctively attempt to hold on tighter to what we know, value, and love. The language of loss, expressed in these stories, the associated feelings, and potential for growth from these experiences, makes up a large part of our human experience, albeit often unacknowledged as such.

Dr. Robert A. Neimeyer has astutely pointed out the dichotomous nature of human existence, stating that we are beings who are wired for attachment, but we exist in a world that is defined by impermanence, change, and loss (personal communication, October 19, 2018). Navigating life in this world means that we love while knowing we will lose; we appreciate our surroundings with the recognition that all that is around us can change in a moment through a tragic event; and finally, while we can be filled with wonder as we experience the depth and beauty in life, we can also become disillusioned by the injustice and cruelty that may present themselves to us.

The defining statement of the Thanatology program where I teach is that *Life is precious; every moment matters*. Certainly, a big emphasis in the death awareness movement has been upon recognizing that life is a limited resource that shouldn't be squandered. Likewise, if we truly live in awareness that all aspects of life are infused with change and impermanence, we realize that *every moment is precious*. Even the moments of uncertainty, pain, loss, and disenfranchisement can shape us in ways that open us to cultivate greater sensitivity to others, allow for an appreciation for what might be possible, and even surprise us by bringing forth our own resilience and strength. Grief accompanies losses of all types, and we tend to view grief as problematic because it is often a painful process. However, it is also a process that deepens us and helps us to rebuild our world in ways we could never have imagined before.

With the contributors to this book, I share a sense of hope that as we acknowledge and understand the ways that change, loss, and transition shape us, we also develop a greater appreciation for life, and those who share this life with us during our time here.

References

Janoff-Bulman, R. (1992). *Shattered assumptions: Towards a new psychology of trauma*. New York: Free Press.

Index

Note: Page numbers in *italics* indicate figures; page numbers in **bold** indicate tables; page numbers that include n indicate notes.

2014 National Survey on Drug Use and Health, data on 109–110

aboriginal peoples, treatment of 53–54
addict grief: as ambiguous loss 105–106; treatment 109–110
addiction 101–111; and ambiguous loss 103–104; clinical implications for 106–110; impact of grief on substance abuser 101
addiction grief 101
adopted children, laws around rights of 86
adoption: changes in 83; emphasis on new family versus birth mother's reciprocal loss 83–84; mediated-contact and ongoing grief 83; open 86; seen as birth mothers' choice 85–86; *see also* birth mothers; open adoption; relinquishing child
adoption registries 85; changes in laws on 83
adoption triad: explained 82; and losses 81–90
affected family and loved ones, and addiction grief 106–107
aging out of foster care 148; as threat to assumptive world 152; *see also* foster care

aging parents: and caregiver burden 182–183; informal care for 185; social context of caring for 184–187; social norms and 186
alienation, as process operating at personal, cultural, and structural levels 57
Aloi, J. A.: birth mothers' suppressed grief 85–86; health care professionals as not recognizing birth mother's grief 87–88
Alzheimer's Disease 29, 38, *74*; and anticipatory grief 42; early-onset 244; grief of caregivers 93; neuropsychiatric symptoms of (NPS) 96; and nonfinite loss 300; and overlapping losses **293**; and psychological absence 103; and social death 44; social stigma around 95; *see also* dementia-related family caregivers; *Somebody I Used To Know* (book) [Mitchell]
ambiguity: increasing tolerance for 75; normalizing 121; *see also* ambiguous loss
ambiguous loss 76–77, 84; and addiction 103–106; Alzheimer's Disease 94; and coming out as trans* 112–113, 116–119; defined 73; identity-related losses as 57; living with mental illness as 232;

341

342   Index

loss of relationship as 279; and myth of closure 132; pathology from external situation versus individual psyche 73; phenomenological experience of 303; physical absence with psychological presence 74; psychological absence with physical presence 74; research on 298; social death as 103; Types of Loss Versus Types of Grief 76; and unresolved grief 85; *see also* ambiguity

American Association of Retired Persons (AARP) 185

ancestor worship, social death and 37

anticipatory grief 30–31, 55–56, 326; and Alzheimer's Disease 42; and social death 42; and Trump election 61; *see also* mourning, anticipatory

Arlow, J., role of fantasy in chronic sorrow 195

assumptive world 10; categories of 9; and grief 144; and nonfinite loss 142; and parenting child with disability 205; significant loss as challenge to 8

asylum-seekers *see* forced displacement

attachment: and benevolence 9; of birth mother to relinquished child 87; and ethological (biological) origins 8; grief response as extension of system 8; rupture of 87; styles 233; system 8; *see also* Bowlby, J.

attachment disorder, addiction as 105

attachment figure, loss of 7

attachment issues, unresolved 324

Attig, T., relearning worled 245, 249

Barnard, M., family and addiction 103, 104

Becker, E., terror management 62–63

bereavement 326–328; companioning model of counseling for 196; death versus nonfinite losses 143–144; as disenfranchised grief 31–32; and Dual Process Model *11*, 233, 331; equating loss with 21; research on 298; symptomology 304; theory 5

birth mothers: and absence/presence 84; attachment to relinquished child 87; and contact with relinquished child 85; ongoing uncertainty of 85; and overlapping losses **293**; pregnancies as "out of time" 83; prenatal attachment and 83; and relinquishing child 82; and suppressed grief 85; therapeutic activities for 87; and unresolved grief 85

birth mothers and adoption triad, clinical implications for 87

Blackfish (film) 221

"Blue Mind Rx, The: Wild Waters Can Be Lifelong Medicine for All People" (article) [Nichols] 218–219

Boelen, P., & Prigerson, H., prolonged grief disorder (PGD) 144

Bordere, T. C. 297–298; sexual assault and suffocated grief 259

Boss, P. 107–108, 303; ambiguous loss 103–104; frozen grief 75

boundary ambiguity: quantitative analysis of 303; and trans*itioning 115, 117, 120

Bowlby, J. 7, 12, 105, 109, 282; attachment for safety and survival of children 87; "working models" of self and world 8

Bruce, E., and Schultz, C., nonfinite losses 140–144

Burke, Tarana, and creation of #MeToo campaign 264

Burke Nursing Consortium for Research in Chronic Sorrow (NCRCS) Chronic Sorrow Questionnaire, grief measurement instruments 305

Burnes, T. R., & Chen, M., performance of gender identity 120

Canter, D., social death 36

Card, C., erasure of memory of ethnic or racial group 43

career, loss of 324

caregiver(s): burden 182; and chronic sorrow 196; dementia-related family caregivers 96, 187; family as 91; and other-loss 200; primary 95; and stress 183; *see also* aging parents

Casado, B. L., Hong, M., & Harrington, D., immigrants and grief 241

Catalpa, J. M., & McGuire, J. K., interplay of personal and family identities 120

cathexis and grief 55–56

Center for Victims of Torture (CVT) 248

Center for Whale Research 216–218

Centrality of Events Scale 306

chameleon effect 106; and family addiction grief 103–104

charismatic populist leaders 63–65

Chavis, G., bibliotherapy 250

children: relinquishing 82; voices of in custody and access disputes 170, 175–176; *see also* birth mother(s); children in foster care; parenting child with disability

children in foster care: aging out of 148, 152; effect of divorce on 173; multiple placements and multiple losses 150; and

relational losses 151; support for 153; tangible and intangible losses 149
children's voices *see* family justice system
children with disabilities *see* parenting child with disability
chronic sorrow *11*, 194, 222, 232, 298, 301–303, 329, 333–335; Comparison of PGD with Chronic Sorrow *319*; and existential issues 199–200; family identity disrupted by 196; and forced displacement 273–275; as influenced by meanings tied to gender and social roles 302; and living losses 311; and overlapping losses 291–294; and parenting child with disability 205–206, 208–210; and people living with mental illness 228; research on 297, 298
client diversity, and loneliness 164–166
clinical implications 4–5, 287; for birth mothers and adoption triad 87; of caregiving for aging parents 187; and children with disabilities 212–213; and dementia-related family caregivers 97; of disenfranchised loss 21; for environmental grief 222–224; of forced displacement 275–276; for grief and mental illness 232–233; for living losses 313–317; for loss of relationship 287–288; and non-death losses 330–332; and strategies around addiction 106–110; and transitioning 113, 121–124
Clinton, H. and political grief 61
closure, as myth 132
Cohen, F., Ogilvie, D. M., Solomon, S., Greenberg, J., & Pyszczynski, T., mortality salience 65
Cohen, F., Solomon, S., Maxfield, M., Pyszczynski, T., & Greenberg, J., mortality salience 65
collaborative approach, to treating people living with mental illness 233
coming out as trans*: and ambiguous loss 116–119; and perceptions of loss 114; tangible and intangible losses 112–113; *see also* transitioning
Community Environmental Legal Defense Fund (CELDF) 223–224
"community of self," inner processes as 329
companioning model, for bereavement counseling 196, 202
Constand, Andrea, and Bill Cosby sexual assault 260–261
constructivist psychology: grief and rebuilding assumptive world and life narrative 144; meaning-making 13; and non-death losses 299
context: of dementia-related caregiving 94; for forced displacement 271; of loneliness 158–160; of loss 12; for trans* and GNC identity 113
Contextual Model of Family Stress 75
continuing bond, intangible relationship with deceased 8; and social death 37
Cosby, Bill, and sexual assault 256, 260–261, 264; *see also* sexual assault
Coughlin, M. B., & Sethares, K. A., child with disability 302
counseling: disenfranchised grievers 32; loneliness and 164–166; *see also* clinical implications
Counting our Losses: Reflecting on Change, Loss, and Transition in Everyday Life (book) [Harris] 142
cumulative loss 147–156; and foster care 148–149
custody and access trials: and children's voices 170, 175–176; and family justice system 170; high conflict disputes 171–172; *see also* family justice system

Dean, Amy F., *Night Light* (book), Alzheimer's Disease 97
death and dying, as social processes 39; *see also* bereavement
death education 32
dementia-related family caregivers 93–95; and Alzheimer's Disease 173; caregiver burden on 96; clinical implications for 97; and self-care 97
Demo, D. H., & Fine, M. A., children and justice system 173
demographics, changes in of birth mothers 83
Denny, G. M., & Lee, L. J., addiction 106
depression, and dementia-related family caregivers 96
de Vries, K. M., transitioning and relation to racial/ethnic identities 119
"dialogic self" 329
disability 205–215; and social justice 198–199; *see also* parenting child with disabiity
discrimination 50–52, 58
disenfranchised grief 3, 13, 21–22, 28; chronic sorrow as 194–195; as conceptual framework 33; and counseling 32; and living with mental illness 232; and loneliness 159–160; normalizing 298; overlap of with nonfinite loss 144; and transitioning 113; typologies of 29–31; as understudied 297

Disenfranchised Grief: New Directions, Challenges, and Strategies for Practice (book) [Doka] 3
disenfranchised grievers *see* disenfranchised grief
disenfranchised loss, *see* disenfranchised grief
displaced people *see* forced displacement
Dittberner-Jax, N., shattered family dreams 244
diversity, of clients 164
divorce: effect of on children 170, 173; *see also* family justice system; loss of relationship
Doe, Emily, and Brock Turner assault 264
Doka, K. J. 21–22, 32, 245; disenfranchised grief 75; *Disenfranchised Grief: New Directions, Challenges, and Strategies for Practice* (book) 3
Doka, K. J., & Aber, R., other-loss 200
dreams: historical or collective 247; *see also* shattered dreams
Drentea, P., Clay, O. J., Roth, D. L., & Mittelman, M. S., Alzeheimer's Disease 95
drug attachment: as attachment disorder 105; *see also* addiction
drug-effected behaviors 108; *see also* addiction
dual dying: caregiver grieves loss before and at care recipient's actual death 97; *see also* anticipatory grief
Dual Process Model *11*, 331; and bereavement 233; and grief of parents of child with disability 207–208; and nonfinite loss 143; and people living with mental illness 233
Durkheim, E., social expectations and grief 27–28

economic migrants *see* forced displacement
elderly, and social death 42–43
Elliott, C., *Ghost in My Brain* (book), self-loss 200
emerging adult(s): expectations and loneliness of 160; psychosocial development of 158–159
Emery, R. E., children and family justice system 172–173
Emery, R. E., & Dillon, P., divorce 285
empathic failure 28; and counseling disenfranchised grievers 32
environmental grief: clinical implications for 222–224; and disenfranchised grief 221; Southern Resident Orcas 216–218; and vicarious trauma 221

erasure of memory of ethnic or racial group, as central evil of genocide 43
Erikson, E., identity development 158
Esses, V. M., Medianu, S., & Lawson, A. S., migration and grief 272
euthanasia, as hastening physical death to avoid social death 44
Examples of Losses That Might Be Experienced by a Person with a Family Member or Friend with Mental Illness **231**
Examples of Losses That Might Be Experienced by a Person with Mental Illness **230**
existential anxiety 64

family addiction grief 103–104; treatment of 106–110
family as primary unit of social organization, kin ties acknowledged in social norms 27
family justice system, children's voices in 170, 175–177
Fassinger, R. E., & Arseneau, J. R.. trans*itioning 119–120
Feinberg, L., Reinhard, S. C., Houser, A., & Choula, R., adult children and caregiving 185
forced displacement: clinical implications for 275; context for 271; life significance of 275; and prolonged grief 303; and PTSD 274; tangible and intangible losses from 273, *274*
forced migration *see* forced displacement
"For the Butterflies I Never Chased, I Grieve: Incorporating Grief and Loss Issues in Treatment with Survivors of Childhood Sexual Abuse" (article) [Sofka] 2
foster care: and identity as foster child 148–150; system 147–148, 153; *see also* aging out of foster care
foster care timeline *see* aging out of foster care
Frankl, Victor, *Man's Search for Meaning* (book) 108
Franzen, J., Alzheimer's Disease 251
Fravel, D. L., McRoy, R. G., & Grotevant, H. D., adopted children and birth mothers 84
Freud, S.: grief and cathexis 55–56; *Mourning and Melancholia* (book) 25

Gabler, N., political grief 65–66
Geller, S. M., & Greenberg, L. S., psychotherapists 314

gender non-conforming (GNC) 112–113; *see also* coming out as trans*; transitioning
gender transitioning *see* trans*itioning
Gervai, J., addiction and grief 105
Ghost in My Brain (book) [Elliott] 200
Glaser, B., and Strauss, A., "awareness contexts" 39
Goffman, E. 40, 195; "mortification of the self" 41; *Stigma: Notes on the Management of Spoiled Identity* (book) 228
Goldberg, M., addiction and grief 109
Goody, J., social death 37
Greenberg, J., Pyszczynski, T., Solomon, S., & Rosenblatt, A., political grief 53
grief 75; and addiction 101, 105; and assumptive world 10, 144; and cathexis 55–56; and coming out as trans* 112; danger of overlooking social and cultural differences in 18–19; of dementia-related family caregivers 93; ongoing 140; and personal growth 300–301; as process of healing 56; research on 298; response as separation distress 8; sibling(s) 104–105; suppressed 85; types of 76; *see also* bereavement; grieving; loss(es)
grief measurement instruments 304–305
grieving: and coming out as trans* 114; constructing/reconstructing world of meaning 325; framing norms for 26–27; rules and rituals of 27

Hagemeyer, S., divorce 284
Halifax, J., compassion 316
Hansen, T., & Slagsvold, B.. caregiver stress 183
Hardy, K., disenfranchised grief 245
Harlow, H. F. influence on Bowlby 7
Harris, D. L. 31, 163–164; ambiguous loss 75; *Counting our Losses: Reflecting on Change, Loss, and Transition in Everyday Life* (book) 142
Harris, Meena, on Clarence Thomas 261–262
Havemann, J., *A Life Shaken: My Encounter with Parkinson's Disease* (book) 251–252
Hertz, R., death in non-Western societies 37
Hibberd, R., life significance 275
high conflict parents: and custody and access trials 171–172; *see also* family justice system
Hill, Anita, and sexual assault 261
Hochschild, A. R., social norms 26

Hoffer, E.: charismatic populist leaders 64; economic and/or psychological insecurity as impetus for populist movements 63; *The True Believer: Thoughts on the Nature of Mass Movements* (book) 63
Hollander, T. complicated grief 303
Holocaust denial 54–55
hospice care, as delaying social death until physical death 44
Hyde, J., & Kammerer, N., children in foster care 150–151

identity: collapse of 324; as psychosocial phenomenon 53; reconstructing 121
identity-related losses 52–53, 324; as ambiguous losses 57; *see also* coming out as trans*
immigrants *see* forced displacement
Independent Living Program (ILP), and children leaving foster care 154
intangible loss(es) 140–141, 143–144, 159, 210, 279, 318, 330; as disenfranchised 13; as invisible loss 239; *see also* tangible and intangible loss(es)
Integration of Stressful Life Experiences Scale, meaning-making and stress 306
Integration of Stressful Life Experiences Scale (ISLES), non-bereavement version of 329–330
internally displaced persons *see* forced displacement
intersectionality 51
Invasion of the Body-Snatchers, The (film), as metaphor for other-loss 200
Inventory for Complicated Grief 304
It Can't Happen Here (book) [Lewis] 61

Jamison, K. R., illness and grief 250
Janoff-Bulman, R. 12, 248–249; assumptive world 8–10; cognitive conservatism 339; shattered assumptions 232
Jennings, P. S., addiction 109
Jones, S. J., & Beck, E., nonfinite loss 141

Kamerman, J., organizational burden of extending grieving leave 27
Kauffman, J., intrapsychic dimension to disenfranchised grief 28
Keen, S., fathers and grief 253
Kendall Chronic Sorrow Instrument 306
Khan, S. R., Hirsch, J. S., Wamboldt, A., & Mellins, C. A., sexual assault 262

Klass, D., Silverman, P., & Nickman, C., continuing bonds theory 143
Králová, Jana, use of term "social death" 39
Králová, J., and Walter, T., social death 36

language suppression 53–54
Last Child in the Woods: Saving Our Children from Nature-Deficit Disorder (book) [Louv], "nature deficit disorder" 218
Lewis, S., *It Can't Happen Here* (book), facism 61
Lichtenstein, B., Laska, M. K., & Clair, J. M., HIV diagnoses and depression 302
Life Imprint 123
life narrative(s), construction of 13; grief as springboard to rebuild 144; re-authoring 49; use of narrative re-framing after loss 13; *see also* assumptive world; Neimeyer, R. A.
Life Shaken, A: My Encounter with Parkinson's Disease (book) [Havemann] 251–252
Lifestyle Changes: a Clinician's Guide to Common Events, Challenges, and Options (Book) [Maas] 2
life transitions, and loss 325
living losses 140, 145, 195, 232–233, 239, 291, 331–334; clinical implications for 313; pivotal issues in 313
loneliness 159; contextualizing 158; of dementia-related caregiving 95; and disenfranchised grief 159–160; and Dual Process Model 163–164; and intimacy versus isolation 158; themes of 160–162
loss(es) 140; cathected and non-cathected 55–56; cumulative 149; hidden 244–245; identity-related 52–53; of intimate partner; overlapping 291–294, **293**; perception of 300; of relationship with sibling(s) 105; self- and other- 200–201; types of 76; *see also* grief; ambiguous loss; disenfranchised grief; living losses; intangible loss(es); loss of relationship; nonfinite loss; tangible and intangible loss(es)
Loss History Checklist 3, 5
loss of relationship: as ambiguous loss 279; changes in relationships 282–284; and changes in social structures and demographics 281–282; divorce versus death 280, 284–285; tangible and intangible losses 285–287
loss orientation and restoration orientation 143, 207; individuals' oscillation 12

"loss pileup" 149
Loss Timeline 121
loss versus grief, types of 76
Louv, R., *Last Child in the Woods: Saving Our Children from Nature-Deficit Disorder* (book) 218
love, loss of *see* loss of relationship
Loya, R. M., sexual assault 263

Maas, V. S., *Lifestyle Changes: a Clinician's Guide to Common Events, Challenges, and Options (Book)* 2
Man's Search for Meaning (book) [Frankl] 108
marginalization 3
marriage, changes in 282–283
Martin, T., and Doka, K., styles of grieving 31
Martin, T. L., divorce 286
master narrative *see* assumptive world
McCullough, D., Trump as unfit to hold office 61–62
McDonough-Means, S. I., Kreitzer, M. J., & Bell, I. R., presence 314
McKibben, B. 218; *see also* environmental grief
meaning-making 13–14; and adaptation to bereavement 326; and forced displacement 274; versus sense-making 275; *see also* meaning reconstruction
meaning reconstruction: and "dialogic self" 329; and engaging "community of self" 329; principles of in non-death losses 326–331; research on 325–327; *see also* meaning-making
mediated-contact adoption 86; *see also* adoption; birth mothers
mental illness: clinical implications in addressing grief 232–233; as chronic sorrow 227–228; examples of losses 300
Messenger, The (film) 221
midlife children *see* aging parents
migrants *see* forced displacement
migration: as forced displacement and immigration 272; language around 272; *see also* forced displacement
Miller, J. R. 105; addiction as attachment disorder 105
misgendering, and feelings of loss 114–115; *see also* transitioning
missing people 128–138; ambiguous loss of 128; and prolonged grief 303–304; rituals 131–135; therapeutic approaches for families of 135–137

Mitchell, W., *Somebody I Used to Know* (book), Alzheimer's Disease 244
mortality salience hypothesis 63, 65
mourning 65, 68, 98, 329; and addiction 101, 106; anticipatory 30; complicated 306; cultural norms for 251; and disenfranchised grief 32; as inter-psychic process 27–29; and political grief 61; research on 304; Victorian conventions of 43
Mourning and Melancholia (book) [Freud] 25
Moynihan, D. P., African American families 67
Murphy, S., stillbirths 241
Muslims; views of 273; *see also* forced displacement
myth of closure 132

Nakashima-Brock, R., moral injury 248
narrative therapy, and addressing loneliness 162–163
National Alliance for Caregiving (NAC) 185
National Institute on Drug Abuse, effect of drugs on brain 107; *see also* addiction
Necessary Losses (book) [Viorst] 2
Need for a Multidisciplinary Family Justice Approach 176
Neimeyer, R. A. 123, 339; master narrative 13; meaning-making 232; use of narrative re-framing after loss 13
Neimeyer, R. A., Laurie, A., Mehta, T., Hardison, H., & Currier, J. M., coherence of life narrative disrupted 9
Neimeyer, R., and Jordan, J., emphatic failure 28, 32
Nichols, W., "The Blue Mind Rx: Wild Waters Can Be Lifelong Medicine for All People," 218–219
Night Light (book) [Dean] 98
non-death loss(es): as disenfranchised 13; and Dual Process Model 11; failure to recognize as losses 52; of future plans 140; and grief 11; living with mental illness as 232; principles of meaning reconstruction 326–331; research on 298; unique aspects of 311–313
nonfinite loss 140–144, 148–149, 158–159; and Alzheimer's Disease 300; and chronic sorrow 145; as framework for interpreting reactions to 301; research on 298; validating loneliness as 162–163

Norwood, K., how family members make meaning of gender transition 116
Nussbaum, M., people with disabilities 199

Ober, A. M., Haag Grenello, D., & Wheaton, J. E., grief training 148
Olshansky. E. 301; and chronic sorrow 193–194
open adoption 86; *see also* birth mothers
Oreo, A., & Ozgul, S., families and substance abuse 103, 107
O'Rourke, M., and grief over Trump's election 61
overlapping losses **293**
Overlaps of Different Types of Non-Death Losses 292

Papa, A., & Maitoza, R., engaging environment after non-death loss 299
Papa, A., Lancaster, N. G., & Kahler, J., phenomenology of grief 299
parenting child with disability 212–213; and ambiguous loss 211; and chronic sorrow 210; shattering assumptive world 205; disenfranchised grief of 207; and marginalization 209; traumatic stress symptoms and grief 208; and nonfinite loss 210; *see also* Dual Process Model
Park, C. L., Meaning-Making Model 305
Parkes, C. M. 248, 249; assumptive world 8; significant loss as threatening assumptive world 8
Patterson, O., "natal alienation" of slavery as social death 43
PCS 20–21, 57; analysis 51
Penrod, J., & Hupcey, J., chronic sorrow 194
Peppers, L., & Knapp, R., prenatal attachment 84
permanence: as goal of foster care system 153; versus losses in foster care experiences 153; *see also* foster care system
personal, cultural and structural (PCS); *see* PCS
personhood and rights, loss of and social death 46
Phillips, L., addiction and recovery 109
Pine, V., critical role of rituals in enfranchising grief 28
Pinquart, M., & Sörensen, S. 184; dementia-related family caregivers and stress 91
political grief 3, 62–72

Pope, N. D., Kolomer, S., & Glass, A. P., women as parents' caregivers 185
post-traumatic growth 2
Price, Reynolds, serious illness and grief 249
Prigerson, H., et al., prolonged grief disorder (PGD) 144
prolonged grief disorder (PGD) 299–300; Comparison of PGD with Chronic Sorrow 319; following death of significant other 144
PTSD: and chronic sorrow 196; and displaced people 274

Quinlan, A., and rape kits 262–263; *see also* sexual assault

Racing Extinction (film) 221
racism 3
racist practices, in education and employment 53
Rando, T. A. 250; anticipatory grief 31; anticipatory mourning 30
Rankin, C., race and stereotypes 247
re-authoring stories, to address shattered dreams 249; *see also* life narratives; shattered dreams
reductionism 18–20
refugees: demonization of 272; helping to reestablish agency of 276; *see also* forced displacement
relational losses: for children in foster care 151
relationship(s): changes in 282–284; loss of contact and meaningful connection 3; *see also* loss of relationship
relearning, reality and assumptions about the world 10
relinquishing child: and adoption 82; attachment to 87; birth mothers 82; and later contact 85; prenatal attachment of birth mother 83; *see also* adoption; birth mother(s)
research: on ambiguous grief 73; on anticipatory grief 31; on grief 298; on meaning reconstruction 325–327; on non-death loss(es) 298; *see also* birth mother; tangible and intangible loss(es)
resilience 2; and ambiguous loss 76–77
Ritter, N., and rape kits 262
rituals 27–28, 128, 198, 312, 327; creation of 123, 132–133, 319, 333; for displaced Muslims 275; exclusion from 30–32; lack of 73, 86, 115, 141, 291, 304
Robson, P., & Walter, T., hierarchy of grief 241
Roles, P. E., therapeutic activities for birth mothers 87
Rolland, J., psychological topology of illness 196
Roseby, V., & Johnston, J. R., children and family justice system 173
Rosenblatt, A., Greenberg, J., Solomon, S., Pyszczynski, T., & Lyon, D., mortality salience 63
Rosenblatt, P. C., cultural competence 250
Rosenhan, D., mental institutions 228
Rossheim, B. N., & McAdams III, C. R., spousal caregivers 93
Rubin, R., shared prenatal experience during gestation 84
Ryan, D., Dooley, B., & Benson, C., "resource pool" 273

Sanders, S., & Corley, C. S., Alzheimer's Disease 94
Schneider, grief versus depression 56
Seale, C., end of social self versus material end of body 36
self- and other-loss 200–201
separation *see* loss of relationship
Sewell, K., & Williams, A., meaning-making 297, 305
sexual assault: African American women's grief around 261; barriers to healing and enfranchisement 258–259; Bill Cosby and 256, 260–261, 264; Brock Turner and 261, 264; dominant discourse about 258–259; enfranchisement of women in 259; need for participatory research on 265; non-death loss and grief 257; rape kits 262–263; and stigmatization 262; suffocated grief and 257; survivors' loss and grief 260–264; survivors' resistance 264; Tarana Burke and creation of #MeToo campaign 264; victim-survivors 257; "Weinstein Effect: Sexual Misconduct Claims Led to Losses for These Men" 263
shattered dreams 244, 248, 250, 252; components of 244; loss of future story 243; and moral injury 248; narrative/bibliotherapeutic approaches to 249–250; and torture 248–249; variations of 246

Shear, M. K., McLaughlin, K. A., Ghesquiere, A., Gruber, M. J., Sampson, N. A., & Kessler, R. C., Hurricane Katrina 241
sibling(s): effect of chronic sorrow on 197–198; effect of substance abuse sibling on 104; loss of for children in foster care 151; loss of relationships 105; *see also* family addiction grief; foster care system
Silko, L., historical trauma 248
Silverstein, M., & Giarrusso, R., ambivalence in family relationships 183–184
social death 36–37, 200; and Alzheimer's Disease 42; and anticipatory grief 42; continuing bonds theory 37; continuum of 46; countering 44; and extended longevity 38; anthropological study in non-Western societies in 37; physical absence with psychological presence 74; psychological absence with physical presence 74; as social isolation, exclusion, and abandonment of individuals by society 36; steps to minimize 44–45; versus socially alive while biologically dead 37; steps to minimize 44–45; *see also* ambiguous loss
social divisions, and candidacy for social death 41–42
social injustice 50
social isolation, of dementia-related caregiving 95
social justice 3; and disability 198–199
socially alive while biologically dead: ancestor worship 37; deceased granted social presence through social practices 37; *see also* social death
Social Meaning in Life Events Scale, and disenfranchised grief 306; and meaning reconstruction 330
social media: implications of for loneliness 165–166; use of to ameliorate loneliness 159
social norms: and aging parents 186; changes in around single mothers, adoption process 86; experience of loss as outside of 13; as frames for grieving 27; *see also* bereavement; rituals
social relationships, ambiguous loss and trans*itioning 115
social support, and positive outcomes for children in foster care 148

"social viability," and moral entitlement to care 41–42
Sofka, C. 3; Loss History Checklist 3
Somebody I Used to Know (book) [Mitchell] 244
Song, H., Zmyslinksi-Seelig, A., Kim, J., Drent, A., Victor, A., Omori, K., & Allen, M., social media 159
sorrow: and cathexis 55; and disenfranchisement 245; hidden 245; and nonfinite loss 141, 300; overlaps of different types of 292
Southern Resident Orcas *see* environmental grief
Steele, C., identity contingencies 247
Stigma: Notes on the Management of Spoiled Identity (book) [Goffman], "passing" and stigma 228
stress, and dementia-related family caregivers 91
stress-based model, and ambiguous loss 77
Stroebe, M., Schut, H., & Stroebe, W.: Dual Process Model 10–12; individuals' oscillation between loss orientation and restoration orientation 12
structural changes, needed to counter social divisions leading to social death 45
substance abuse *see* addiction
Substance Abuse and Mental Health Service Administration Texas Revised Inventory of Grief
substance abuser, impact of grief on 101
Sudnow, D., social death 39
suffocated grief and sexual assault 257
support for children in and leaving foster care 153–154
supporting families of missing people 133–135
suppressed grief, of birth mothers who relinquish children 85
survivors of sexual assault *see* sexual assault

tangible and intangible loss(es): ambiguous losses 76; children and 149; and displacement 273; intangible relationship with deceased 8; loss of relationship 285–287; non-death losses 298; and transitioning 112–113
tangible loss(es) *see* tangible and intangible loss(es)
Tasks of Grief (book) [Worden] 109
Terror Management Theory (TMT) 62–63

thanatologists 29, 153
Thanatology; defining statement of school of 340
therapeutic approaches, for families of missing people 135–137
Thom, K. 249
Thomas, Clarence, and sexual assault 261
threshold times or places 243
timeline, of foster care 148; *see also* aging out of foster care
training, to support children in and leaving foster care 153–154
trans* 112; coming out as 113; identity 113; *see also* coming out as trans*; trans*itioning
transgender *see* trans*; transitioning
trans*itioning: ambiguous loss as framework for experiences of loss and 113, 115–116; and clinical implications 121–124; coming out as trans* 113; and disenfranchised grief 113; naming and validating losses 121; self as both present and absent 114; tangible and intangible losses and 112–113; *see also* coming out as trans*; trans*
trauma: as distinct from grief and loss 153; Trump election as 61
treatment, for family addiction grief 106–109
Tree of Contemplative Practices, *317*
Trump, D., grief over election of 61
Turner, Brock, and sexual assault 261, 264; *see also* sexual assault
Types of Loss Versus Types of Grief 76
typologies of disenfranchised grief 29–31

United Nations High Commissioner for Refugees (UNHCR) 271
unresolved grief: and ambiguous loss 85; underlying assumptions about living with 75–76

Van Dernoot Lipsky. L., "trauma stewardship" 221
victim-survivors of sexual assault *see* sexual assault
Viorst, J.: loss as normal part of life 142; *Necessary Losses* (book) 2

Wallerstein, J. S, overburdened child 170
Wallerstein, J. S., & Blakeslee, S. 171
Walsh, N., *When Everything Changes, Change Everything* (book) 2–3
Wang, K. T., Heppner, P. P., Fu, C. C., Zhao, R., Li, F., & Chuang, C. C. 240
Weber, M., charisma 63
Weiss, R. S. 286; marriage as attachment relationship 282
When Everything Changes, Change Everything (book) [Walsh] 2–3
Whiston, S. K., assault as non-death loss 259
White, M., re-authoring stories 249
Wolfelt, A., "companioning" model for bereavement counseling relationship 196
Worden, J. W., *Tasks of Grief* (book) 109

Yaben, Yarnoz, divorce versus death 284–285

For Product Safety Concerns and Information please contact our EU
representative GPSR@taylorandfrancis.com
Taylor & Francis Verlag GmbH, Kaufingerstraße 24, 80331 München, Germany

www.ingramcontent.com/pod-product-compliance
Lightning Source LLC
Chambersburg PA
CBHW071148300426
44113CB00009B/1131